P9-CQE-314

Information Telecommunications

Networks, Products, & Services

Robert K. Heldman

McGraw-Hill, Inc.

New York San Francisco Washington, D.C. Auckland Bogotá
Caracas Lisbon London Madrid Mexico City Milan
Montreal New Delhi San Juan Singapore
Sydney Tokyo Toronto

Library of Congress Cataloging-in-Publication Data

Heldman, Robert K.
    Information telecommunications : networks, products, and services
/ by Robert K. Heldman.
        p.   cm.
    Includes index.
    ISBN 0-07-028040-1
    1. Telecommunications—Social aspects. 2. Information networks—
Social aspects. 3. Information science—Social aspects.
    I. Title.
    HE7631.H453 1993
    384—dc20   93-8259
                                                                        CIP

     3 4 5 6 7 8 9 0 DOC/DOC 9 8 7 6 5 4

ISBN 0-07-028040-1

The sponsoring editor for this book was Steve Chapman. Sally Glover was the manuscript editor, production supervisor was Katherine G. Brown. This book was set in ITC Century Light. It was composed by TAB Books.

Printed and bound by R. R. Donnelley & Sons Company.

In order to receive additional information on these or any other McGraw-Hill titles, in the United States please call 1-800-822-8158. In other countries, contact your local McGraw-Hill representative.   **MH93**

To my many colleagues.
Once a man was asked why he had taken time
to build a bridge
over a treacherous creek that he had already
successfully crossed.
He answered, "Why, to help those who come
after me to safely cross,
not tire, and reach greater destinations!"
Hence, this book is for those who care to take
the time to pause to think,
to learn perhaps a better way, an easier way,
to achieve their destiny.

I hope this analysis will serve as a stepping
stone in our human quest
for a better quality of life in the forthcoming
Information Era.

I wish you a safe voyage!

Contents

Part I
The information society

Part II
The information era

Foreword

Peter W. Huber
Senior Fellow
Manhattan Institute of Counsel
Kellogg & Huber

Broadly defined, the "information" sector of the economy now accounts for 34 percent of GNP and 41.23 percent of the work force. By all indications, these fractions will continue to grow rapidly. Any analysis of telecommunications must, therefore, clearly recognize that creating, processing, and distributing information will be the dominant activities of the U.S. economy in the twenty-first century.

Even companies outside the information arena are allocating a steadily increasing fraction of their budgets to telecommunications. In 1993, for example, telecommunications expenditures constitute approximately 10 percent of the Fortune 1000 companies' budgets. Because most unit costs of telecommunications are dropping rapidly, even a slowly growing telecommunications budget represents a much more rapid growth in telecommunications use.

To remain competitive in manufacturing, virtually all analysts agree that U.S. firms must be able to accommodate dispersed production facilities, just-in-time delivery of supplies, rigorous inventory control, customized production, stringent quality control, and rapid feedback from the consumer. Dispersion, fragmentation, and flexibility of this order are only possible with a communications system to match. Major manufacturers like General Motors are even defining their own electronic communications protocols (such as the "manufacturing automation protocol," or MAP) to smooth and accelerate information transfers.

Telecommunications is more crucial still to financial and commodities markets, in which information processing and transfer represent virtually the entire business. Indeed, all financial markets—and currency itself—use or manipulate commodities whose value depends almost entirely on their informational content. The point need not be belabored—every aspect of banking, credit processing, and stock and commodities exchange is now being transformed by telecommunications. Many of the larger institutional players have become major telecommunications companies as well. It's more than coincidence that the most ambitious, competitive metropolitan area fiber network in the country, New York Teleport, was launched by Merrill Lynch, a financial service company. Banks and other financial institutions have already developed specialized communications services such as the Society for Worldwide Interband Financial Telecommunications (SWIFT). As the telecommunications infrastructure evolves and regulatory constraints are relaxed, you can expect the electronic bank, checkbook, and credit card to reach out all the way to the consumer. The telephone network is already the backbone of the now ubiquitous automatic teller machine. Predictions of a paperless office have proved to be very premature, but a paperless financial world is a much closer prospect.

The transition promises great new efficiency in retailing and other transactional services, as well as greatly enhanced consumer convenience. Telecommunications allows the small retailer to create a national presence by listing a single 800 number. Even such seemingly modest advances as automatic number identification, which supplies the called party with the calling party's phone number, can considerably streamline credit verification, as well as retail sales and virtually all other forms of online customer service.

Telecommunications is fundamentally transforming the transportation sector as well. For national and international airlines, much of their corporate value, and even a larger part of their competitive edge, depends on seamless operation of a highly dispersed reservation system. Vehicle locators, for everything from interstate trucks to downtown taxis, promise important new efficiencies (and thus lower demand for energy and less pollution) in getting the right vehicles to the right place at just the right time. (Somewhat similar technology is being developed for the related function of tracking down stolen vehicles.) Nationwide paging systems already operate as efficient "people locators," and the rapid rise of cellular telephony promises more of the same. Just as in manufacturing, telecommunications is crucial to efficient control of the flow of materials and parts; so too in transportation, advanced telecommunications promises great new efficiencies in the movement of vehicles and people.

As Michael Kellogg, John Thorne, and I wrote in *Federal Telecommunications Law* (Little, Brown, 1992), there's much dispute about what the "right" regulatory policies really are in this arena. There's much less dispute, however, about how the technology of telecommunications is propelling these networks into the twenty-first century, largely oblivious to the endless debates engaged in by the lawyers and lobbyists that congregate around these markets. In this book, Robert K. Heldman offers a perceptive description of where the converging technology of the computer and the telephone is leading us. Nobody who seeks to understand the end of the twentieth century, and the dawn of the twenty-first, can do so without coming to grips with the extraordinary technological revolution that this book describes.

Acknowledgments

This book concludes many years of marketing and technology research, from which I gained knowledge and understanding from: 465-L data networks, Minuteman II, 490-L Autovon, advanced public data networks research, advanced digital switching design projects, and international studies and planning workshops concerning ISDN users, networks, and services.

I'm deeply indebted to those who expressed their views and opinions in the many thousand articles that were researched to determine "what's happening" and "where we are going;" special thanks to Dr. Peter W. Huber for providing the Foreword, and to Tom Bystrzycki, Dr. John Mayo, Richard McGee, and Dr. Koji Kobayashi for their visions of the future, as well as to the thinkers and planners whose views are expressed in this book directly or indirectly; to editors of industry journals, particularly Bob Stoffles of *TE&M* and Carol Wilson of *Telephony*, and to those who have shared their thoughts with me as they played the information game of planning, designing, and providing information networks, products, and services in this complex, changing arena.

I especially want to thank Tom Madison and Tom Bystrzycki and my many colleagues within both the computer and communications industries, with whom I have participated in the exciting and challenging formation and transition phases of the information era: Larry Hager, Neil Levine, Steve Chapman, and Sally Glover, my editors at McGraw-Hill, without whose understanding and support this analysis couldn't have been accomplished, as well as the visionaries whose views are explicitly expressed in the case studies and workshops.

Finally, I want to thank my son Peter, whose valuable assistance in assessing and researching the forthcoming information marketplace was essential for the timely completion of this final book of the series.

Introduction

This analysis on telecommunications information networking is intended to translate the networks, products, and services theories (identified in my books *Telecommunications Management Planning, Global Telecommunications,* and *Future Telecommunications*) into private and public networking strategies for "the information marketplace." In the first two chapters, this book specifically attempts to provide knowledgeable "visions of the future," as well as an understanding of "what's happening" and "where we're going." Once this is accomplished, chapters 3 and 4 address "where we want to go," from both a marketing and technical perspective. Next, chapter 5 covers "how we can get there," while chapter 6 reviews "what we've achieved!" These analyses are supported by detailed reviews of a particular technical, marketing, or regulatory aspect of the information marketplace in corresponding case studies and workshops in chapters 7 and 8, followed by final thoughts and "the last word" in chapter 9. (See FIG. I-1.)

This book is for both marketing and technical planners and thinkers. Any endeavor of this nature is somewhat difficult because people from different disciplines have different backgrounds, needs, and interests. For example, if you were describing an automobile to a technical person, you'd need to describe many of the aerodynamics of the car, as well as its drive train and engine capabilities. On the other hand, if you were describing the new vehicle to a marketing person, you might ignore many of the technical details and simply discuss the car's lines, shape, and interior from a human needs and comfort point of view. A sociological description could note the what, where, when, and how aspects of the vehicle's impact on society, both from the industrial revolution point of view of the manufacturer, and in terms of how automobiles have transformed society into what it is today, and how dependent we've become on them and their fuel. Finally, you could analyze the automobile in terms of stark financial numbers, indicating the cost to build, the cost to support, sales per year, and total bottom-line profit. However, you must keep in mind that this "mechanical vehicle" can be more easily described today, now that we have many versions of it, than it could have been described before Henry Ford began his mass production lines.

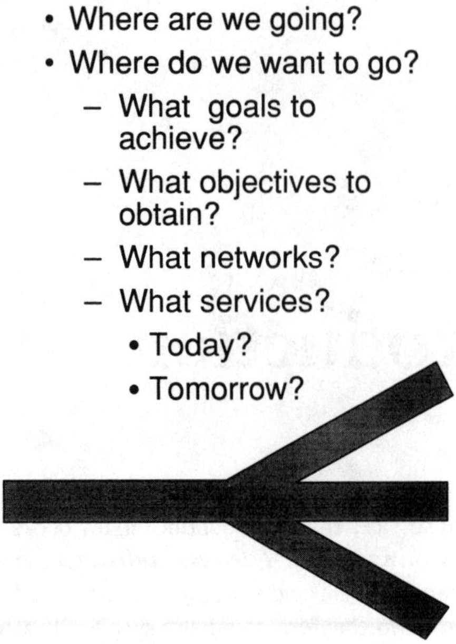

- Where are we going?
- Where do we want to go?
  - What goals to achieve?
  - What objectives to obtain?
  - What networks?
  - What services?
    - Today?
    - Tomorrow?

Fig. I-1. Visions.

So it is with the "information marketplace." A marketplace can be described from many points of view, taking into account technical, marketing, environmental, financial, and social aspects. To understand the "world of information telecommunications," we need to step back and attempt to put our arms around its complex issues in order to totally appreciate its potential features and services, based on its expanding networks and interfaces.

Recently, many trade articles have observed that some in marketing don't really want to know the technical details of these information networks. Others prefer to talk about the network as a nebulous "cloud" that exists to meet user needs, once these needs are understood and defined. When asked what type of technical analyses are performed, their response is, "We push clouds around all day." Unfortunately, this type of approach doesn't provide concrete results, especially where success depends on fine-tuning where and how selected features are packaged around specific network architectures and structures. Users are becoming very sophisticated these days, and some know a great deal more than the marketing representatives of many of the suppliers, who must bring along technical support teams to help them discuss even the simplest solutions with the client. There's also the marketing person who wants to distance himself or herself from tomorrow's technical possibilities and focus only on today's opportunities. However, with technology moving so quickly to achieve greater and greater capabilities, tomorrow's technologies quickly become today's. Conversely, there are the technical planners who have not challenged their designs to determine if they truly meet the needs of specific user types in the various market segments, thereby missing the opportunity to obtain a better fit, a more desirable version, or a new feature that would have made their product successful. (See FIG. I-2.)

- How can we get there?
- When will we get there?
  - What paths to take?
  - What steps to make?
  - What tasks to perform?
    - In anticipation?
    - In preparation?
    - In sequence?
    - In parallel?

Fig. I-2. Plans.

Hence, this book doesn't try to separate the technical aspects from the marketing. The analysis integrates these two worlds. This will require the technical person to read and understand what forces and factors other than technology will influence future networks and products. The book will also provide a solid technical base for marketing people to identify new features and services in terms of specific phases of information technology for the "new users" of the Information Era. With this in mind, you can enhance your thinking by considering the scope and range of future technical possibilities and market opportunities noted in the visions of the future by Tom Bystrzycki, Senior Executive Vice President, U S West Communications, Dr. John Mayo, President of AT&T Bell Laboratories, Richard McGee, IBM's Information Network Architect, and Dr. Koji Kobayaski, the father of computers and communications (C&C) and Chairman Emeritus, NEC.

In conclusion, the topics discussed in the text are further expanded and extended by numerous case studies, workshops, and references. Each chapter refers to particular studies in chapters 7 and 8 that help advance and illustrate particular ideas, concepts, issues, or observations. I encourage you to diligently pursue these endeavors in order to acquire a full understanding and appreciation of the sublime aspects and complexities of telecommunications. I then conclude my analysis with an interesting review of the forthcoming information society. (See FIG. I-3.)

"Some see the world as it is and
ask why? . . . I see the world
as it could be and ask why not? . . ."

J. F. Kennedy

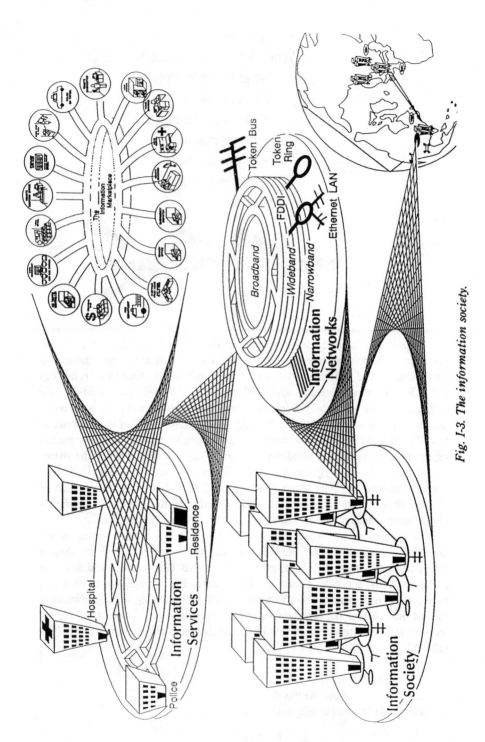

Fig. I-3. The information society.

Part I

The information society

*"Where are we going?
I don't know, but we'd better decide,
as we won't know we've gotten there,
when we've arrived!"*

Dr. Doolittle

1

Visions of the future

Several leading executives of the future information networks, products, and services have provided the following visions of the future.

Information Telecommunications:
A Vision of the Future

Tom Bystrzycki
Executive Vice President
Mass Markets & Operations
U S WEST Communications

Over the years, society's issues have become more and more complex, and the resulting problems have become so severe that we need more extensive, real-time solutions to address and resolve these highly volatile, real-time situations. As huge, supersonic airplanes traverse the continents of the globe, making hundreds of trips each day with thousands and thousands of passengers, the world becomes a little smaller as countries become more interrelated and their businesses become more integrated and interdependent. Just as in the past, train travel gave way to air travel to provide faster physical transport, today there's a need for a more economical use of our resources, both human and environmental, to achieve timely transport of the full range of voice, data, text, image, and video communications to better facilitate the sharing of thoughts, exchanging of ideas, formation of agreements, establishment of partnerships, and forging of friendships. As we look at the complexity of life, it's quite evident that we must have the necessary telecommunications infrastructure to appropriately support the layers and layers of new, exciting, highly sophisticated information services that will make life a little better, a little easier, a little less threatening. These new high-speed, high-quality communication facilities will first augment and then surpass past transportation endeavors to provide instantaneous exchanges of information over new high-definition, high-resolution audio and visual media.

In so doing, information telecommunications will play a major role, a necessary role, in enabling new technical possibilities to better address new market opportunities across many diverse industries. Instantaneous communications is simply the next step. It's the logical continuum of evolving transport, substituting a new medium for enabling human dialogue and achieving better understanding. This will allow those living in remote rural towns and villages to comfortably, efficiently, and effectively interface with their urban counterparts, thereby removing the need for highly centralized and populated megatropolises. In fostering a return to more dispersed populations in less compact and concentrated habitats, this use of future information telecommunications will reduce the pressures of everyday living and improve our quality of life in our ever-changing global society.

As the telecommunications industry looks forward to its 125-year anniversary (some time in the early phases of the Information Millennium) it's both interesting and essential to occasionally pause and assess not only where we're going, but also where we've been and how we achieved our present position. For in reviewing our somewhat evolutionary path, noting its twists and turns, we can assess our strengths and weaknesses and establish realistic goals for our new endeavors.

Today, the telecommunications marketplace has awakened to a full range of information-handling service opportunities—from conception to transfer, to storage, to access, to processing, to manipulation, to presentation . . . Traditionally, the common carriers, both local exchange (LEC) and interexchange (IXC), had been preoccupied with establishing a switched network that was extensively automated to handle voice calls—many to many, any to any . . . With this mission, the core business was made universally and ubiquitously available and affordable via its highly efficient and effective operation. Over the years, the black phone has been replaced by numerous varieties of differing shapes and colors; similarly, former manual "operator-please" services are now established directly by customer dialing, direct-dial access has become global, services are customized, and data transport bandwidth has become greater, shared, and less expensive.

By the mid '90s, competition has entered every segment and sector of the marketplace, vying for every form of customer communication: voice, data, image, text, graphic, and video over both the wire-line and wireless media. Unfortunately, or fortunately, depending on your perspective, data user needs and expectations were mainly ignored in the '60s, '70s, and '80s, and these customers turned to private networks to address their data transfer requirements. Local area networks (LANs) were established on customers' premises to extend the internal backplane bus of computer mainframes throughout the external local user environment, in order to send and receive information at somewhat respectable speeds over existing copper and coaxial facilities. Then, the new computer-on-a-chip microelectronic technologies enabled smaller, highly versatile computers to participate in every facet of operation of every major industry, from health care to education, thereby helping to automate many, if not all, internal tasks. These local internal networks were deployed to enable numerous new families of peripheral systems to exchange information with sophisticated, large mainframes and achieve access to huge central databases. (See FIGS 1-1A, 1-1B, and 1-1C.)

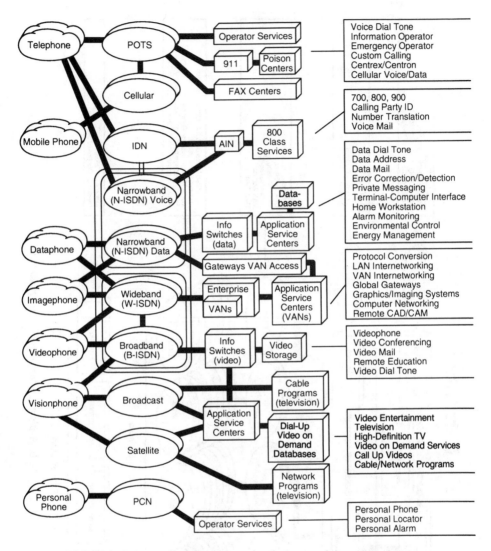

Fig. 1-1A. Information telecommunications — a vision of the future.

Through this, the many-to-one, one-to-many data networks were developed, allowing remote stations to exchange information with more and more powerful supercomputers, establishing the need and paving the way for wide area networks (WANs) and metropolitan area networks (MANs) to extend the reach of these supersystems to more and more disparate terminals located in any industry throughout the community.

As evolution would show, the next step in computer networking was to enable different terminals to talk to different mainframes. Protocol converters enabled disparate systems of any size, shape, and form to interrelate. Some believed this

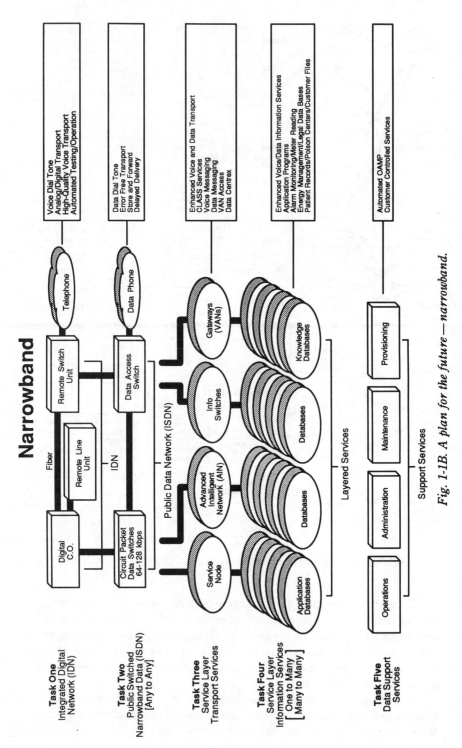

Narrowband

Task One
Integrated Digital Network (IDN)

Voice Dial Tone
Analog/Digital Transport
High-Quality Voice Transport
Automated Testing/Operation

Task Two
Public Switched Narrowband Data (ISDN) [Any to Any]

Data Dial Tone
Error Free Transport
Store and Forward
Delayed Delivery

Task Three
Service Layer Transport Services

Enhanced Voice and Data Transport
CLASS Services
Voice Messaging
Data Messaging
VAN Access
Data Centrex

Task Four
Service Layer Information Services [One to Many Many to Many]

Enhanced Voice/Data Information Services
Application Programs
Alarm Monitoring/Meter Reading
Energy Management/Legal Data Bases
Patient Records/Poison Centers/Customer Files

Task Five
Data Support Services

Automated OAMP
Customer Controlled Services

Telephone
Data Phone

Remote Switch Unit
Data Access Switch
Remote Line Unit
Digital C.O.
Circuit Packet Data Switches 64-128 kbps

Fiber
IDN
Public Data Network (ISDN)

Gateways (VANs)
Info Switches
Advanced Intelligent Network (AIN)
Service Node

Knowledge Databases
Databases
Databases
Application Databases

Layered Services

Provisioning
Maintenance
Administration
Operations

Support Services

Fig. 1-1B. A plan for the future — narrowband.

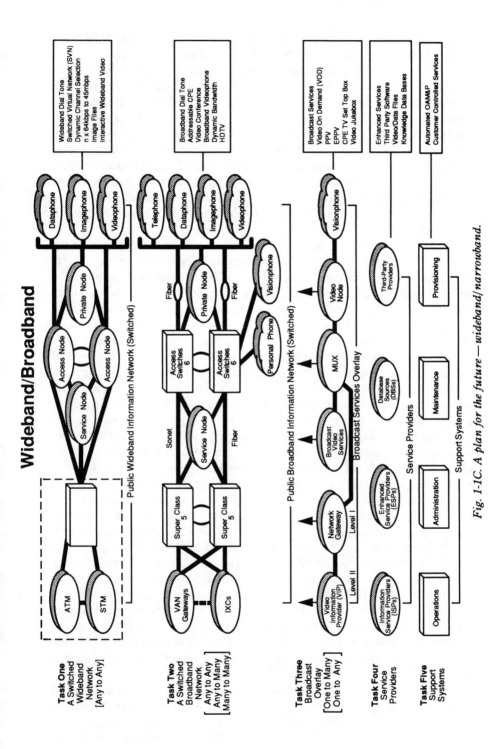

Fig. 1-1C. A plan for the future — wideband/narrowband.

would be the destiny of computers, as processing power and versatility doubled and doubled again approximately every two years or so throughout the '80s.

By the early '90s, it was quite apparent that other forces were at work, as integrated circuit manufacturers developed workstations having only a few chips but achieving the power and capabilities of earlier mainframes. Data creation, manipulation, and processing could now take place at these remote satellite workstations, requiring less and less communication with single mainframes, but more and more communication with numerous, multiple distributed data storage and processing systems — located locally, nationally, and internationally. These personal computers (PCs) and knowledge workstations (WSs) will advance during the '90s to become quite sophisticated in operation, enabling multimedia communication — but no longer between many-to-one or one-to-many applications, but for many-to-many or any-to-any!

Hence, the need is now established for public data networks that traverse the spectrum of narrowband, wideband, and broadband offerings, where data handling in the narrowband world becomes more and more information handling, as its breadth and scope is advanced in the wideband and broadband domain. There, the customers are provided switched bandwidth facilities that enable them to dynamically, as needed, transfer *n* number of channels of information to any location. As initial, bursty variable-bit-rate (VBR) dataphone and imagephone traffic gives way to more and more continuous-bit-rate (CBR) videophone and viewphone use, it's essential that packet switching facilities are augmented with circuit switching capabilities, enabling the availability of expanding bandwidth provided by photonic switching systems to meet increasing market demands. Hence, not only must fiber transport capabilities expand with expanding video use, but switching capabilities must also expand and adapt with changing information traffic attributes as users shift from voice to data, to image, to video, to view . . . For to deploy a few fibers to handle all voice traffic needs will not address the facility loads generated by high-definition videophone calls. Similarly, to deploy a broadcast facility to offer a few conventional television channels doesn't address the possibilities of providing hundreds of full, high-definition, high-resolution offerings in the twenty-first century. Thus, switched fiber facilities arise to the challenge, especially as radio spectrum becomes scarce.

However, fiscal balance is needed. High expectations require high expenditures to achieve ubiquitous fiber-based offerings. To be achievable and realistic, fiber deployment plans must be phased in over an extended program. We can maximize the use of existing copper plant during the transition phases by offering narrowband switched data services. Thus, as FIGS. 1-1A, B, and C note, as we view and plan for the future, there's a shift from the traditional telephone-handling POTS (plain old telephone services) network, to integrated digital networks (IDN) to form the basis for shared voice and data movement in the digital mode over copper facilities using the ISDN (Integrated Services Digital Network) format.

Here, new public data-handling highways are available in both circuit- and packet-switching form at speeds of 64,000 and 128,000 bits per second. These fully addressable dataphone offerings can be expanded to provide image-handling capabilities, which are then augmented by more bandwidth capabilities as switched wideband systems become available at speeds up to 45 million bits per second in the early stages of fiber deployment. First selectively and finally ubiquitously, full videophone/viewphone switched SONET-based broadband facilities can be overlaid and integrated with broadcast capabilities, providing not only eye-to-eye, person-to-person, high-quality communication, but also television and selective high-definition, high-resolution educational and entertainment programs. Supplementing this array of wireline offerings are the wireless cellular and the personal phone capabilities that enable anyone to be reached anywhere, anyplace, anytime . . .

The plans for the future extend the vision of the future, showing the network-of-networks picture of potential telecommunication technical possibilities. Once these information highways are established to the information marketplace, their information services will flourish as new singular and shared, integrated and autonomous service centers are equipped to offer the full spectrum of many different varieties of information services, enabling the customer to pick and choose one flavor over another, or with another. Indeed, by the turn of the century, 125 years after the invention of the telephone, 100 years after the formation (and subsequent break up) of the Bell system, we've come a long way, but we're only at the beginning of a new path, a new highway, an information highway. Hopefully, it will lead us to more and more exciting possibilities and opportunities that will help us address our changing, complex society's needs in a new century, the Information Century, in a new millennium, the Information Millennium . . .

Moving Beyond Today's ISDN

John S. Mayo
President
AT&T Bell Laboratories

The service capabilities of Integrated Services Digital Network (ISDN) are at the heart of the telecommunications revolution of the 1990s, and the key, underlying information technologies of microelectronics, photonics, computing and software will drive the telecommunications revolution through the 1990s and beyond. Just as microelectronics has propelled telecommunications for the last 20 years and will continue to do so for at least 10 more years, photonics—supported by high-speed electronics—will increasingly become the dominant driving force for the future and will be a major factor underlying the evolution of today's ISDN into tomorrow's Broadband ISDN (B-ISDN).

The goal of the revolution is to have access to voice, data, and images, in any combination, anywhere, at any time—and with convenience and economy. The goal is clearly set by the marketplace need for greatly enhanced information productivity, by the human desire for telepresence (a substitute for travel), and by our insatiable craving for entertainment.

These needs can be met by using information efficiently and effectively through such services as multimedia teleconferencing, distributed computing, remote interactive education programs, high-definition TV, and two-way switched video on demand. The need for information productivity, the desire for telepresence, and the appetite for entertainment are powerful marketplace incentives for the evolution of a fiber network.

Framework for tomorrow's network

The network of the future must evolve gracefully from the network of today. The key next step is to establish a framework for tomorrow's information network, and it's taking shape today—based on the use of digital technology in the public network, on the Integrated Services Digital Network (ISDN), and on the photonic transmission standard called Synchronous Optical Network, or SONET. At AT&T, we call that framework Service Net-2000.

For the future network, digital technology enables more cost-effective switching and transmission of information than analog systems. ISDN offers an increase in access bandwidth (along with a signaling channel separate from the call-carrying channels) for precise routing and call-handling instructions. Also, the SONET standard will enable products from different vendors to work together.

Service Net-2000 will help today's network evolve to that of tomorrow by offering higher-capacity networking; highly reliable, self-healing networks; advanced intelligence; and service on demand.

Higher-capacity networking is being made possible mostly by photonics and SONET. Fiber backbones carry information throughout the network at billions of bits per second. Also, fiber is being brought ever closer to end-users, making high-speed services possible. However, the rate of capacity growth and fiber deployment must be matched to marketplace demands and economics. Thus, we must consider the prudent use of existing copper plant in the network. ISDN is an important example of a technology for achieving increased capabilities from twisted-pair copper wire—and can be viewed as an evolutionary step on the way to fiber-based Broadband ISDN (B-ISDN).

Because of the high cost of replacing copper wire with fiber, ISDN is an important step preceding widespread deployment of fiber to the home. ISDN employs the same twisted-pair copper wire that's in place today, and would enable widespread availability of voice, fax, data, image, video and multimedia applications in a relatively short time frame, at reasonable infrastructure cost, and at an affordable price for most users.

There are two forms of ISDN: Basic Rate ISDN, which offers speeds of more than a hundred kilobits per second over existing residential copper access wire, and Primary Rate ISDN, which offers speeds of more than a megabit per second using specialized copper access plant. With new enabling technologies, however, Primary Rate ISDN can potentially be provided over existing residential copper wire as well. Basic Rate ISDN can bring conference-quality video, data transport with graphics displays, high-speed facsimile, and multimedia communications to a home, office or school. Primary Rate ISDN can go a step further and support several simultaneous users, or support large-screen video. With consensus among service providers and equipment vendors, today's hundreds of thousands of ISDN users can potentially be expanded to many millions within three years.

In addition to higher capacity, networks will be more reliable and self-healing, due to the emergence of fiber rings that readily recover from service interruptions. SONET standards have helped foster this as well.

Service Net-2000 will also permit the spread of network intelligence to virtually all elements of the network — intelligence that was formerly concentrated in switching systems. In cooperation with the global intelligent network, as defined by Bellcore and the CCITT, network intelligence is now shared among elements of Service Net-2000 and the intelligent network products of various vendors — e.g., AT&T's A-I-Net™ Product Family. The SONET overhead channel — separate from other information pathways — will allow individual network elements to talk to one another to provide enhanced network services, as well as to improve the operations, administration, maintenance, and provisioning (OAM&P) that will support these new services. With this OAM&P intelligence, and that which is built into switching and transmission systems, the network will become self-aware, self-adapting and self-provisioning. Network elements will be able to know the nature and quality of services they're providing, to predict a network failure and recover from it automatically, and to handle all provisioning almost automatically when initiated.

Also, Service Net-2000 will offer service on demand via flexible access configurations and networking, using an integrated family of access products. End users will have easy access to a variety of services ranging from ISDN and video to data, special services, and the ability to dial up 1.5 megabits per second (Mbps) and 45 Mbps services — and do so as easily as making ordinary calls today.

The basic architecture of Service Net-2000 unifies today's switching, transmission, operations systems and cable systems into two entities — the access node and the service node. The access node is the network point where residential and business customers gain access to network services. From there customers' calls move via optical fiber to the service node, the network point where most service and control functions take place. This node is similar to today's central office and contains the intelligence to process customers' calls.

One type of access node is designed for large businesses, and the other for small businesses and residences. The node for large businesses will accommodate broadband ISDN, enhanced video, and metropolitan area networks. The node for small businesses and residences will handle future broadband and video services, and will be able to distribute cable-TV signals. In addition, both access nodes will enable service providers to offer service on demand and to allocate bandwidth when and where it's needed.

At the heart of the service node is the 5ESS^R switch, with an enhanced switch module that's able to handle at least ten times as many lines as today's counterpart. Another unit in the service node will allow control of switching and cross-connect functions for narrowband, wideband, and broadband transmission. A packet switch in the node will enable service providers to offer end-to-end broadband data networking services over the public network.

One packet technology that's especially worth mentioning is Asynchronous Transfer Mode (ATM). A high-speed broadband transmission and switching technology, ATM will permit customers to receive numerous multimedia applications over a single fiber-optic cable. Standard ATM will do this by converting signals into small 53-byte fixed-length cells, or packets, and transmitting them over the public network at rates up to 2.4 gigabits per second.

Replacing copper with fiber

Photonics has had a tremendous impact through the progressive replacement of copper with fiber that began during the 1980s. During that decade and beyond, transmission made the transition to photonics. Photonics pervades virtually every aspect of transmission, from long-distance links to undersea cables to the local loops linking the customer with the central switching office. Also, optical fibers are replacing or complementing copper conductors under streets and oceans. Virtually all long-distance routes in the U.S. now contain optical fiber systems operating at rates of 1.7 gigabits per second and higher. However, microwave technology will continue to complement fiber in applications involving mobility and geographic constraints.

For transmission among business locations, we're seeing a network evolution toward fiber-based local area networks (LANs) interconnecting computers and databases. There's also an evolution toward fiber-based metropolitan area networks (MANs) to interconnect the various LANs. Even cable TV companies are replacing backbone cables with optical fibers.

Fiber advantages

Fiber has clearly emerged as the medium of choice for high-capacity transmission. To achieve the same information-carrying capacity as one fiber lightguide cable, we would need at least 155 twisted-wire copper cables.

The lightguide cable is 23 times lighter than the copper cable, and its cross-sectional area is 36 times smaller. These two advantages—light weight and small size—make it easier to handle fiber cable in the field, and especially in crowded cable ducts. Fiber cable can also carry signals 28 miles before they need regeneration or amplification, compared to just over one mile for copper. Moreover, each 28-mile segment of fiber cable needs only about 100 two-way repeaters, while a copper system of equivalent information capacity would need about 20,000 two-way repeaters.

Lasers for transmission and logic

In addition to low-loss fiber, viable semiconductor lasers were needed to launch photonics as the transmission technology of the 1980s. The first such lasers that operated at room temperature were fabricated in the 1970s. They were the size of grains of ordinary table salt, and they could be easily coupled to the large multimode optical fibers of that day.

Today's most advanced semiconductor lasers are even smaller. Two million of them fit on a chip the size of a fingernail. These lasers emit light from their surfaces, instead of from their edges, as do most lasers. After fabrication, that characteristic enables the surface-emitting lasers to be tested while they're still on a wafer. The surface-emitting property also allows them to be coupled in free-space architectures with other photonic components.

Eventually, a single chip will be able to emit millions of parallel beams of light. This light will be transmitted onto logic chips that, in turn, parallel-process the millions of beams and pass onto other stages of logic.

Capacity versus distance

The overall capability of lightwave communications systems is measured by the product of two variables: the transmission data rate in megabits per second, and the distance in kilometers that signals can travel before they need amplification.

That product or capability continues to double every year—driven by increasing data rates and decreasing fiber losses. This amazing pace will most likely continue for another two decades before we reach known physical limits. That means we can expect a thousand-fold improvement over the capabilities of today's most advanced research lightwave systems.

Improvements in capability

Recent improvements in lightwave capability have come from using coherent technology and optical amplifiers. Coherent systems offer the advantages of greater receiver sensitivity and longer fiber spans between amplifiers. (They also offer greater receiver selectivity and ease of adding or dropping channels—in much the same way as radio stations are tuned in.)

The optical amplifier uses light to control light, and therefore eliminates the need for high-speed electronics to regenerate signals. This amplifier is independent of bit rate. Also, just one amplifier will boost signals carried by many different wavelengths or "colors" of light. This is especially important for systems using the capacity-building technique of wavelength division multiplexing—in which different "colors" of light are sent down the same fiber, each carrying different information. Optical amplifiers will lead to fiber links across oceans—without the need for conventional regenerators.

Toward this end, in May, 1992, AT&T and Kokusai Denshin Denwa (KDD), the international telecommunications services provider of Japan, successfully tested the world's longest optically amplified fiber-optic system in the laboratory. The companies linked two independently produced 4500-kilometer test beds at AT&T Bell Laboratories. The resulting 9000-kilometer system test bed was equivalent to the world's longest transoceanic cable route, and it operated error-free at a transmission rate of five gigabits per second, nearly 10 times faster than TAT-9, the transatlantic fiber-optic system that began service in March, 1992. At five gigabits per second, a system could transmit the text from the entire 30-volume *Encyclopedia Britannica* in less than one second. In a complementary approach to ultra-long-distance optical transmission systems, Bell Laboratories researchers are employing optical amplifiers in combination with *solitons*—light pulses that retain their shape over long distances.

Meanwhile, undersea photonic cable systems are being installed in increasing numbers. Before the end of the decade, the equivalent of more than one million voice circuits will be placed under the oceans. About a dozen such major systems are either in service or planned.

Taking fiber home

The next step toward all-fiber transport is to extend fiber to businesses and selected homes. This next move, extending fiber to the end user, has been stimulated in large part by the desire to provide video services to end users, and by the introduction of the new digital format called Broadband Integrated Services Digital Network, or B-ISDN.

B-ISDN is an international standard that supports multiple services such as voice, data, and new video services over fiber-optic transmission facilities. B-ISDN is based on fast-packet technology—called Asynchronous Transfer Mode, or ATM. It could introduce an exciting new era in global telecommunications networking as computer and LAN vendors as well as service providers adopt compatible standards to provide sophisticated high-bandwidth services. B-ISDN is currently defined at interface rates of 155 megabits per second and 622 megabits per second. It's expected, however, that with the inherent flexibility of ATM technology, operation at 45 megabits per second is likely for some data applications as well.

Copper wire pairs can't carry these higher bit-rate signals more than a few hundred feet. Fiber has the appropriate transmission characteristics to carry very high bandwidth signals over extended distances—and to accommodate all video, data, telephony, and interactive database services.

Fiber to the curb

As previously noted, marketplace and economic considerations make ISDN an important step preceding the long-range deployment of fiber to the home. During this time, fiber can selectively be deployed for businesses and for a small set of consumers who want to use broadband services such as broadband ISDN, and who in turn are willing to pay their share of the costs associated with deployment of fiber access.

For the longer term, fiber should be extended to concentration points close to the residence, with fiber links generally terminating at the curb, a few hundred feet from the residence, rather than at the residence itself. Sharing a fiber and its associated optoelectronic circuits among several residences will enable the costs of fiber access to be less than copper wire for new housing developments.

Once the fiber is deployed to the curb, the link from the curb to the residence can be made with either copper wire, copper coaxial cable, or fiber. The choice will depend on the kinds of services the customer selects. Higher-speed services can be made available to any customer by simply upgrading the link between the curb and the residence.

Photonic switching

Today, we're seeing the dynamic transition from electronics to photonics in other segments of telecommunications besides transmission. Photonics will probably never totally displace electronics, but will perform functions now thought to be beyond the capability of electronics.

More specifically, during the 1990s, we'll see the transition to switching by photonics. Photonic switching research now underway offers the promise of optical switching machines with terabit capacity — one trillion bits per second. That capacity might be needed in the future if we have massive amounts of high-quality, full-motion video and three-dimensional images. Moreover, arrays of lasers can beam their signals into optical media or even into free space to reach other photonic arrays. So photonics will enable connections without wires, freeing us from the constraints of physical wiring, and allowing us to reconfigure systems rapidly and at will.

The switch in switching

Switching has undergone successive transitions over the years. During the 1960s, we saw the transition of switching to software control of electromechanical switch elements. In the 1970s, we saw the introduction of software control of electronic switch elements, in the form of all-digital toll switches. In the 1980s, we saw digital switching extended to local offices. Also, during the 1990s, we'll see the transition to broadband switching — first in cross-connects and then in electronically controlled packet-switching subsystems.

This packet switch — for bursty types of data — will provide broadband ISDN, initially at data rates of 150 megabits per second. Broadband ISDN switching modules will be added to AT&T's 5ESS[R] network switch, and perhaps to other switches as well. Software control of photonic switching fabrics in the latter part of the 1990s will use advanced electronic computers, at least until the beginning of the twenty-first century.

Creating photonic devices

One of the most important device technologies to emerge to date for photonic switching and processing is Self-Electro-optic Effect Device or SEED technology. This technology allows both detection and modulation of light by devices fabricated with multiple *quantum wells* — which are multilayer structures of different crystals. Arrays of Symmetric SEEDs have been fabricated with as many as 32,000 individually addressable elements. They've also been demonstrated to switch in times of 33 picoseconds or trillionths of a second, although in system demonstrations they've been shown to operate at megahertz rates.

Continued engineering of devices and photonic systems should result in systems that operate at hundreds of megahertz. To achieve high speeds and to add functionality, so-called "smart pixels" have been designed, built, and demonstrated. These are elements of an array that contain electronics for processing and optics for input and output. The smart pixels have the ability to receive data from an optical beam, process the data locally, and modulate an output beam. Smart pixels are advancing photonic switching and computing one step closer to reality.

The Symmetric SEED or S-SEED was crucial to the fabrication of the world's first photonic switch at Bell Labs in 1990. In 1991, a more advanced photonic switch was fabricated using S-SEEDs and free-space interconnections. This system, demonstrated at Telecom '91, consisted of an arrangement of lasers, lenses, and S-SEED arrays on a custom optical mount. The system featured more than 4000 individual connections between each pair of six S-SEED devices tailored to this application. As a result of customized packaging, the volume of the system has diminished in size from about 110 cubic inches for the 1990 switch to less than 17 cubic inches for the 1991 switch. Improvements in optics, in the optical mounting system, and in S-SEED devices have increased system capacity 16-fold while decreasing size by a factor of almost seven. Continued advances of this technology should result in ever-more highly complex and capable systems.

Building photonic computers

In January of 1990, Bell Labs scientists used SEED devices to demonstrate the world's first digital photonic processor — which uses light instead of electricity to process information. This experimental processor demonstrated the simple logic functions of counting and decoding. The processor consists of 4 arrays of 32 optical logic gates — formed from symmetric SEEDS. Each array occupies one corner of a square assemblage of lasers, lenses, and mirrors. The output of one array becomes the input for another array, and so on. Information carried on the laser beams moves in and out of this four-stage cascade of logic gates, where it's processed.

The next stage in the evolution of photonic processors is to use VLSI technology to miniaturize and integrate optical components — to fabricate a compact system with fewer parts, requiring far less crucial alignment of components. The processor the Bell Labs scientists demonstrated is primitive. However, the wireless interconnections of photonics should ultimately provide nearly instantaneous computing. Also, because light beams don't interact with one another, massive parallel computing architectures should be possible. So photonic processing offers the promise of computers with 1,000 — even 10,000 — times the processing power of their electronic counterparts.

Putting it all together

Thus, we have a vision for the future and a framework for getting there. As the vision comes together during the next decade, photonics will move to center stage: photonic transmission, photonic switching, and photonic computing. The first two of these technical forces will have a tremendous impact on the telecommunications revolution of the 1990s, moving us ever closer to the ultimate goal, universal information services, the ability to provide voice, data, and images in any combination, anywhere, at any time, with convenience and economy. The third force, photonic computing, will continue the pace well into the twenty-first century. (See FIG. 1-2.)

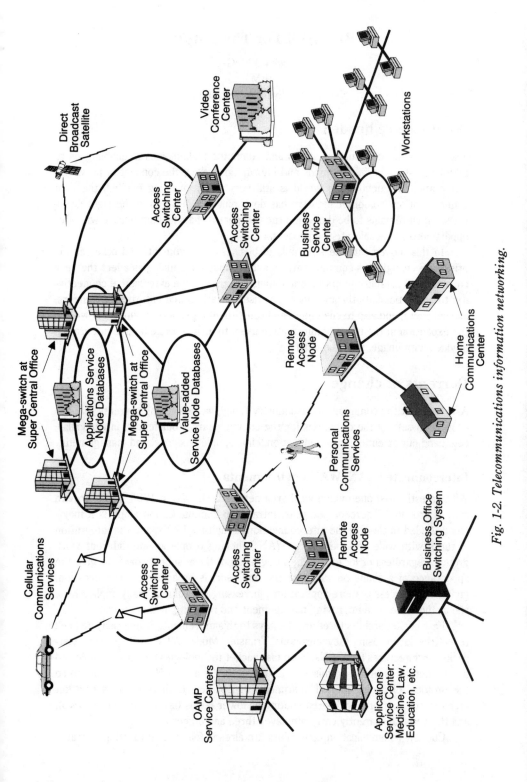

Fig. 1-2. Telecommunications information networking.

Blueprint For The Future

E. Richard McGee
IBM
Networking Systems Architecture

Where we're headed

The integration of communications and computer technologies is enabling us to take large steps in linking minds and information. While the concept of pervasive cooperation throughout the world is still very far from being fulfilled, the joint communications/computer industry has done much to move us in the right directions. Much remains to be done, and the prospect is that the next decade will offer opportunities to accelerate the process.

In this movement, the key tools of business, government, and other enterprises are changing as communications and computer technologies affect the very core of these establishments. In one dimension, we see the extension of connectivity: to all participants throughout enterprises; to associated enterprises, vendors, and suppliers; and also to customers and constituents. In another dimension we see the expansion in the types of information used, to include the effective integration of video with image, voice, and data.

Currents of change

As we look at the communications industry today, we see strong currents that are decisive in setting the directions for the coming years. Four forces, in particular, command our attention: interconnection, choice, independence, and management.

Interconnected LAN/WAN environments

With an estimated one-million local area networks (LANs) in 1990, and a growth rate of around 40 percent per year, intragroup communication alone is a major trend. Added to this are the interconnection of multiple LANs, and the integration of these with wide area networks (WANs), linking people among different work groups, regardless of location. The integration of these subnetworks, to give the appearance of a single network for the end user, is broadening communication, giving users access to more applications, increasing the value of many applications, and at the same time improving management and reducing overall costs.

Fast-packet architectures are the keys to this movement. Frame relay and cell relay (the latter using Asynchronous Transfer Mode, ATM) will provide fast-packet architectures for WANs. Both fast-packet technologies will grace public and private networks. ATM promises wider use in WANs and LANs, and appears to be the protocol of choice for full multimedia capabilities. Both types of fast-packet architectures perform wide-area routing at lower levels (layer one or layer two), and this can transparently carry any layer-three and higher protocols.

Current communication controllers are already featured to function as frame relay providers. Early replacement controllers can be expected to be optimized for fast packet operation. We thus have the opportunity to transform the current single-protocol networks (that use TCP/IP, SNA, or OSI for routine in WANs) into fast-packet networks. Single protocol networks gradually are becoming fast-packet networks that easily handle multiple network protocols and are capable of full multimedia transport.

In the meantime, we've created a medley of highly effective worldwide packet data networks. With the widespread use of X.25 packet switching networks (particularly in Europe), the very rapid spread of the TCP/IP internet, plus more than 70,000 SNA-oriented networks and thousands of WANs using other protocols, a tremendous work load is now being very effectively carried around the globe. All this diversity must be effectively integrated into the evolving future networks, as we advance by adding newer technologies. The evolution must preserve full communications ability and a return on prior investments.

The networking blueprint

Looking to the future of networking, therefore, we need a framework that embraces diversity, incorporating standards and multivendor agreements, fostering protocol and technology consolidation where appropriate, remaining open to dramatic new technologies and services, and at the same time preserving continuity with the older networks and a return on investments already made. Thus, the focus of the networking industry for the rest of this decade will predominantly be the integration and evolution of today's multiple, specialized technologies into a fewer number of higher-speed, multidimensional technologies.

The classic approach to system design in such environments is the careful partitioning of the total system along natural functional boundaries, and the interconnection of functional blocks with well-defined and controlled interfaces. To the system designer, this approach is natural and necessary. Its application to the heterogeneous networking world therefore comes as no surprise. (See FIG. 1-3.)

A particular result of this process has been under development within IBM for several years, incorporating the realities of heterogeneous systems with multiple protocols, multivendor offerings, and multimedia. Because it provides a framework for evaluating options and then building towards the future, this document has been called the Networking Blueprint. Though evolved within IBM, it's a view of the networking industry as a whole. It amounts to an IBM-generated reflection of the computer and communications industry solutions. Its purpose is to help clarify requirements, define the technological relationships among multiple protocols, and guide the selection of paths to the future.

Many of the interfaces and protocols of the Networking Blueprint are drawn from international and industry standards. They also are drawn from X/Open, the OSF Distributed Computing Environment (OSF/DCE), and the OSF Distributed Management Environment (OSF/DME). The Networking Blueprint features inclusiveness and optionality, so that it can be used in each circumstance to develop a tailored networking strategy. A particular value of the Networking Blueprint is that

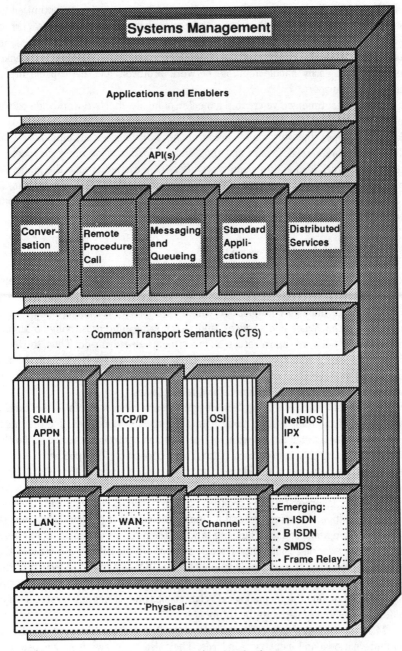

Fig. 1-3. Blueprint for the future.

it prescribes technically sound relationships among its diverse architectures and standards; it's not simply a wish list of protocol relationships.

Choice

The Networking Blueprint is structured to increase the ability to freely choose applications and the use of networking components in new combinations. To achieve its modularity, the Blueprint breaks apart the traditional ties between applications (and application-services) and particular network protocols like SNA, TCP/IP, IPX, OSI, etc. The Blueprint is functionally divided into four large layers with three key boundaries among them. The Blueprint layers are: applications and enablers, application-support, transport/network, and subnetwork. A given layer contains components drawn from different protocols and allows the addition of new technology components. The boundaries between layers promote independence of underlying protocols and the ability to split protocol stacks. The blueprint projects the use of mixed stacks using parts from different protocols. In general, different components above a boundary can be used with different components below a boundary. Some of the options thus envisioned include the following:

- Operation of applications across transports other than those for which they were designed—for example, sockets (TCP/IP) applications over SNA, SNA applications over TCP/IP, and other split-stack operations.
- Access to applications via multiple network protocols (for example, accessing a database service via TCP/IP, SNA, NetBIOS and OSI).
- Consolidation of network protocols to move towards a strategic set of protocols and so reduce training and operational expenses.
- A wide variety of subnetworks, such as different types of LANs, FDDI, X.25 PSDNs, ISDN, frame relay, and different cell-relay facilities, each available for use with multiple network protocols (such as TCP/IP, OSI, and SNA).
- Multiprotocol routers that join different multiprotocol subnetworks.

Network independence for applications

Maximizing the value of investments in applications is a top priority for many enterprises. An important part of this is the freedom to select applications and to allow wide access to applications, unhindered by communication protocol limitations. That freedom is improved when the applications are made independent of the underlying communication facilities. That independence is obtained in several stages in the Networking Blueprint.

The upper boundary of the Blueprint currently provides application programming interfaces (APIs) for the three common communication modes: conversational mode, remote procedure call (RPC), and queued messaging. Each has corresponding support for end-to-end data exchange. The three modes are complementary, and multiple modes can be used by a given application. The conversational API (CPI-C)[1] is the same whether one prefers OSI-TP[2] or SNA-APPC[3] conversational support. Additional interfaces can be added when required.

The middle boundary of the Networking Blueprint extends earlier concepts of using mixed stacks. In the TCP/IP environment, RFC 1006 enables the use of OSI upper stacks across TCP/IP. The X/Open Transport Interface (XTI) likewise facilitates having an application run on either TCP/IP or OSI transports. The middle boundary of the Blueprint, called the Common Transport Semantics (CTS), extends and generalizes this concept to enable virtually any upper stack to operate on any lower stack. (See FIG. 1-4.)

All three APIs and their data-exchange support (APPC, OSI-TP, RPC runtime support, and MQI[4] support) become multiprotocol services with the aid of the Common Transport Semantics (CTS). The CTS serves as a switch point so as to allow any of the data exchange facilities to be used with any of the network protocols, TCP/IP, OSI, SNA, NetBIOS . . .

The lower boundary then further allows the use of any subnetwork such as LANs, frame-relay, or ISDN. Again, the framework allows for the addition of new subnetwork technologies such as cell-relay and ATM. Any subnetwork is available for use by any network entity such as OSI, TCP/IP, or SNA.

For example, applications and application-services using the CPI-C conversational interface can use either OSI-TP or SNA-APPC data exchange support, and either TCP/IP, SNA, OSI, or other network services, and any of the subnetworks such as LANs, frame-relay, or ISDN. (See FIG. 1-5.) A given product could be built to use only one module in each layer of the Networking Blueprint; another product could be built able to choose among multiple options in a given layer.

Through this independence at the boundary layers, many distributed application services such as distributed database, file, print, and messaging (e.g. X.400) services can become independent of the network and subnetwork protocols. System-oriented distributed services like directories (e.g. X.500), security, and resource-recovery services also can become network independent. This contributes to the prospect of a distributed network operating system that's communications independent.

Also, with the Common Transport Semantics, a valuable application in an

---

[1]The acronym CPI-C stands for Common Programming Interface for Communications, as defined by X/Open and IBM. CPI-C is supported by a large number of software vendors. Applications using CPI-C also communicate with systems from a large number of vendors that provide APPC conversational support.

[2]The acronym OSI-TP stands for Open Systems Interconnection-Transaction Processing. It provides conversational support comparable to that of APPC.

[3]The acronym APPC stands for Advanced Program-to-Program Communication, which provides conversational support. APPC can be accessed by the CPI-C conversational interface. More than one million computers in the U.S. and nearly two million computers worldwide are already running APPC on IBM and other machines.

[4]The acronym MQI stands for Message Queue Interface. It is the API for the messaging and queuing service.

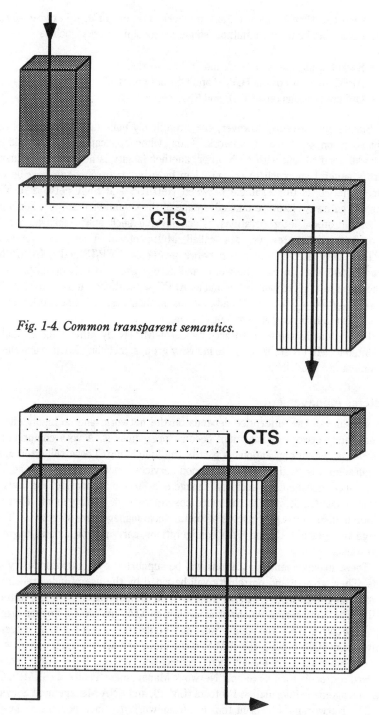

Fig. 1-4. Common transparent semantics.

Fig. 1-5. Transport gateway.

end-system can then be used on any network. For example, otherwise "foreign applications" can be used on multiple single-protocol networks, such as:

- Socket applications on SNA and OSI networks.
- APPC applications on TCP/IP and OSI networks.
- OSI applications on TCP/IP and SNA networks.

Simple end-systems, however, are often firmly built as single protocol units, usable only on one type of network. Then, when applications on two different networks need to talk with each other, another facility is needed. The Blueprint offers a general approach to this problem by using *transport-gateways* between adjacent networks (for example between NetBIOS and SNA networks). These transport gateways likewise take advantage of the Common Transport Semantics.

Multiprotocol interoperations, which involve such split-stacks at the CTS and/or transport gateways, are called Multiprotocol Transport Networking (MPTN). The case of only two network protocols, TCP/IP and SNA/APPN, is shown in FIG. 1-6. In each network, and across the two networks, all sockets applications can talk to each other and all APPC applications can talk to each other. Native TCP/IP and SNA/APPN end-systems on their respective networks could, of course, also fully participate without change.

IBM is encouraging broad acceptance of MPTN by other vendors and has presented its MPTN architecture to industry groups, including X/Open and the OSI Implementor's Workshop.

Systems management

The very life of the enterprise depends on the network, and so highly effective systems and network management become prerequisites. A very comprehensive set of management applications is part of the foundation. These will often include configuration, installation, and distribution services, backup and archive services, performance management, security management, usage accounting, and inventory or asset controls, as well as the more customary fault management. These will function in distributed-peer as well as hierarchical management structures. They'll manage all types of LAN and WAN configurations, carrying voice, data, image, and video traffic.

These management applications will be supported by multiple industry standards. Their growth and portability will be aided by the use of industry-standard programming interfaces such as the X/Open Management Protocol Interface (XMP). The Networking Blueprint incorporates XMP and draws further management structures from the Open Software Foundation Distributed Management Environment (OSF/DME), the IBM System View, and other industry frameworks. The communication of management information will be by multiple industry-standard protocols such as Simple Network Management Protocol (SNMP), Common Management Information Protocol (CMIP), and SNA Management Services.

The Networking Blueprint thus is a framework that incorporates comprehensive end-to-end management while it allows a staged evolution in the use of new

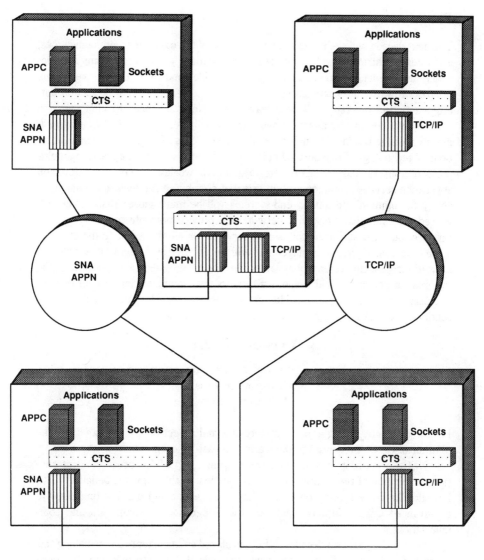

Fig. 1-6. MPTN.

technologies, standard services, and protocols. The Blueprint includes powerful tools to make possible interoperation among current and future end-systems, whether they be on LANs, fast-packet WANs, or single-protocol WANs. These tools include common programming interfaces, split stack operations via the Common Transport Semantics, multiprotocol routers, and multiprotocol transport-gateways. Together, they allow a paced evolution to the future high-speed multimedia networks while creating application freedom, ensuring continued interoperability across old and new segments, and preserving return on investments, particularly in applications and workstations.

Prognosis

The next decade will see increased intersections of the computer, communications, and video industries. A wide range of new applications will emerge, many incorporating multimedia and taking advantage of available bandwidth. Despite very good progress towards international standards and vendor consortia agreements, heterogeneity and diversity will be a way of life. New, advanced technologies and services will continually augment and only partially replace the installed base. A major challenge will involve multigenerational networks made up of several generations of technology. Transport subnetworks will, however, be integrated by multiprotocol routers and transport-gateways into a worldwide network. Common application services, common system-oriented distributed services, and a universal ability to communicate among end-systems will be much closer than today. Advanced pieces of that worldwide network will provide not only conventional data services, but also advanced cell/packet services for all classes of traffic at up to gigabit speeds. Systems management will be far better integrated across the network/processing-system boundaries. In short, progress will be substantial towards our goal of a world online, with any-to-any communication, instant responsiveness not limited by bandwidth or proprietary considerations, and all with continuous availability, high reliability, and largely automatic management.

A vision of C&C

Dr. Koji Kobayashi
Chairman Emeritus
NEC Corporation

Let's conclude by taking a moment to review and reflect on the message that the "Father of C&C" presented to the world at a past Telecom:

NEC Corporation is proud to be once again a part of this prestigious international exhibition of the frontiers of communications technology. On behalf of NEC, I would like to welcome you to this important event and our exciting displays of advanced C&C solutions, based on the integration of computers and communications.

During the past two decades, NEC has played an important role in making this a forum for developing farsighted goals to guide the growth of communications technology. It has been personally rewarding to see how the concept of C&C, which I first advocated a decade ago, has taken root and is producing fascinating new solutions in every phase of our industry.

Our theme of "One World through C&C" illustrates the fundamental purpose of C&C technology: to serve people through the increased capabilities, access, and simplicity of ISDN systems. Through this concept we demonstrate our latest advances in public, business, and personal systems, along with significant new breakthroughs in basic technology.

Communications today promises to connect the world in new ways, pioneer new levels of interdependence, and bring our world closer together. Major cities around the globe are being linked not only by voice communications, but also with data and other sophisticated service networks. The next great step is to expand the availability of these and other real-time communications through Integrated Services Digital Networks, or ISDN.

The promise of ISDN is that, based on digital technology, it will be possible to provide all types of information communication services, including voice, data, image, and video, over high-capacity integrated networks. Achieving this requires the total integration of computers and communications, the vision of C&C, which was pioneered by NEC.

C&C technology provides ISDN services through systems that are important steps in building a global network across the entire spectrum of public, business, and personal communications systems. Thus, C&C improves human communications for greater world harmony, productivity, and the advancement of the human race. I hope these thoughts will stimulate your imagination and turn your dreams into reality . . . (See FIG. 1-7.)

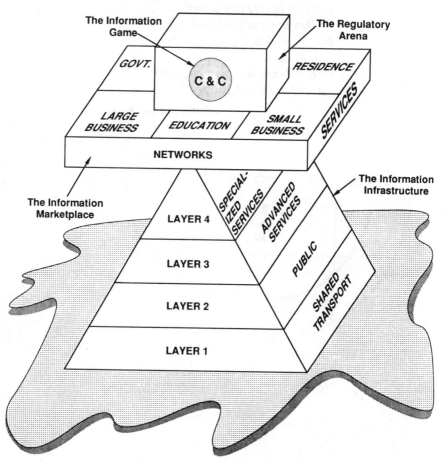

Fig. 1-7. The information society.

The remaining chapters of this analysis will help us better appreciate these visions of the future. For like the blind men in the child's fable, there's much more to be done to more fully grasp these visions, to better understand where we are going, where we wish to go and how we can get there.

> *"It was six men of Indostan,*
> *who went to see the elephant,*
> *though all of them were blind.*
> *The first fell against his side,*
> *and bawled "Is nothing but a wall!"*
> *The second feeling the tusk,*
> *cried clearly 'Is very like a spear!'*
> *The third taking the squirming trunk,*
> *I see 'Is very like a snake!'*
> *The fourth felt the knee,*
> *plainly 'Is very like a tree!' . . .*
> *So they dispute loud and long,*
> *though each was partly in the right,*
> *and all were in the wrong,*
> *as they prate about an elephant,*
> *not one of them has seen!"*
>
> **John Godfrey Saxe**

2

The information arena

> "It was a time of change,
> a time of uncertainty and risk,
> a time to tear down, a time to build anew.
> As was once said in a tale long ago, . . . 'for some it
> was the best of times, for others the worst' . . ."
>
> **Charles Dickens**

Section one: the formation period

The winds of change are swirling around us, changing formerly prosperous lands into stark, desolate, barren places, shifting here and turning there to provide warmth and comfort to new areas, encouraging growth and prosperity, forming new lands and places.

As we attempt to look at the grand scheme of things and consider the forces and shifts that are taking place around us, we need to attain a higher vantage point to take in a larger perspective. This will enable us to better assess and understand the impact of change, more comfortably embrace it, and successfully channel it to establish our own particular destiny.

Once change reaches hurricane force, resisting it is a fruitless, time-consuming, painful gesture. Technological advances of gigabit fibers, megabit memory chips, powerful, physically distributed processors, photonic switches, superconductive devices, intelligent terminals, high-level languages, and expert systems are enabling the formation of new families of sophisticated, flexible networks, products, and services.

This has caused the previously stable worlds of computers and communications (C&C) to collide. Depending on your vantage point, this can be viewed as the collision of the industrial revolution and the information revolution, the integration of technology and marketing, the demarcation of the regulated and nonregulated arenas, the formation of national and international information networks, the merging of private and public domains, the separation of skilled and unskilled labor forces, the shift from fixed to usage price offerings, and the increased interdependence between suppliers and providers.

One observation is quite clear from any perspective: this is indeed the time of the integration of computers and communication. As noted in FIG. 2-1, as the C&C integration becomes more and more extensive, it will eventually become unclear whether the computer industry overlaid and absorbed the communications industry, or vice versa.

In viewing the various phases of the forthcoming information society shown in TABLE 2-1, we see change in every endeavor. It's like a coil wrapped around itself, forming a tightly woven spring that applies pressure on its outer bounds, constantly pushing and expanding its containment in a never-ending struggle to release its potential energy. A great deal of effort has been expended by governmental bodies to capture these forces within artificial boundaries, as computers and communications constantly expand their interfacing capabilities to meet the real needs of the "new users" of the Information Age.

What's happening?

Many people today are asking questions about ISDN: "What is it? What will it cost? What services will it provide? When will it be available? Who needs it? Who will pay for it? Why do anything now? Why not wait and see what happens?" These questions and attitudes are quite similar to those expressed when digital networks and services were first introduced in the 1975–76 time frame. There were those who resisted the change and hung on to the analog technology into the mid '80s and early '90s. Many today have been left behind, no longer considered a leader or participant in the competitive arena. Others have embraced change, learned from each new transition, and built a knowledgeable base to play the game. Remember the expression "leapfrogging" technology? Several large, major firms didn't participate in the initial development, only to find that when they did enter the new technology and services, they couldn't perceive or appreciate the subtleties and

Communications &
Computer

Computer &
Communications

Fig. 2-1. Computers and communications.

Table 2-1. The Information Society

Preparation Phase (Pre 1984)
Formation Phase (1984 – 1988)
Transition Phase (1988 – 1994)
Application Phase (1994 – 2010)
The Information Era (2010+)

shifts of emphasis that the more seasoned players had developed; this made playing the game that much harder and more risky. However, even if we have been "playing the game," to survive in this intense arena, we need to pause and reflect on what's happening, where we're going, where we want to go, and how we can get there. It's time to think and reflect. It's time to learn how to successfully survive the transition to the Information Era . . . providing, supplying, and using the right services for the right products via the right network at the right time . . .

To appreciate and assess what's taking place, we need to look at the progression of events in terms of several phases of movement. Some have said that ISDN, the concept for providing and integrating new services on new digital networks (Integrated Services Digital Networks), is dead. There's a classic statement that "ISDN" means "I still don't know what ISDN means." In many cases, this might appear to be true. Change is often least apparent when it's doing its greatest work. Just before it actually erupts, a volcano causes a deadly silence, as animals sense that something is coming.

Other times the hype and festivity are quite apparent. However, as many have experienced, change usually takes place silently and subtly, many times quite without our knowledge. Others, perhaps more observant, have said that the "Information Era" is not coming; it's here now! Are the preparation and formulation phases over? Are we in the midst of the transition phase of the Information Society? TABLE 2-2 indicates that "the time is now," but is it? . . .

Table 2-2. The Time Is Now

To Reassess
  How are We Doing?
To Evaluate
  Where are We Going?
To Analyze
  Who is Providing/Supplying/Using What
  Networks, Products, and Services?
To Determine
  Where do We want to Go . . .
To Plan
  What Features and Services Should
  We Provide (When) to What New
  Users . . . ?
For Commitment
For Agreements
To Take Risks

As we attempt to determine where we're going, let's step back and see what's happening. It's time to see who is providing/supplying/using what information network/products services, and where and how.

In this evolving, competitive C&C marketplace, now is the time to determine:

- What future services and features can be successfully provided?
- For what price and cost?
- Under what regulated or nonregulated environment?
- By what organizational structures? (Partnerships?)
- Using what form of monitoring, control, and separation?

In considering FIG. 2-2, the spring of tightly coiled events and issues during the past years can be viewed in terms of an ever-increasing band of interdependent topics that are tightly interwoven to form the whole. No aspect can be changed

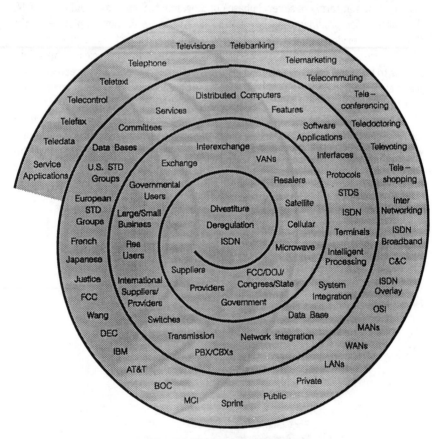

Fig. 2-2. What's happening?

without affecting the equilibrium of the spring. As time progresses and more and more "happenings" occur, the spring grows and expands to require larger and different containments. If the containment doesn't change, then pressure is exerted downward on the spring to the internal forces and factors, causing them to tighten more and more, which in turn causes further pressure to be exerted on the outer bounds.

The spring's outer regions consist of an interesting array of new services that are provided to different regions of the world in separate time slots and cycles, which aren't necessarily in sync with each other. Each region's springs has different containments and internal forces. The tension on the springs is constantly changing, as it's affected and controlled by "the human element." This is the resistive and sometimes explosive component of the equation. However, it's an essential key to the success and survival of the suppliers and providers, whose people must first overcome their own internal resistive factors in order to be able to provide new features and services to the other human element — the customers, the new users.

For change to be embraced, it must be understood; you can't comfortably participate in something that's not under control, or at least reasonably understood. This is the purpose of the comparison to the tightly interwoven dependencies of multiple aspects of the picture. As noted earlier, when they've been looked at from several points of view, they'll provide a true insight into what's happening. Then we'll better understand the risks and rewards, and perhaps feel a little bit more knowledgeable and comfortable, thus enabling us to participate and play the game . . . perhaps a little more wisely . . . a little more successfully.

Events and issues

As we consider the formation and transition phases of this new era, let's visualize them in terms of forces/factors, trends/shifts, functional areas, players' strategies, computer partitions, network phases, and new services that ring and circle each other, as noted in FIG. 2-3. They can be reviewed in terms of the events and issues of the late 1980s to mid 1990s.

In moving through the periods of the Information Era from preparation to use, we'll find that we need to play today's game today, as well as prepare for tomorrow's game. We'll progress through several phases of ISDN as it changes from an IDN (Integrated Digital Network) for voice to a broadband ISDN for voice, data, video, and image. The structures containing the spring will change and expand as the tension is released into ever-widening rings of new services and endeavors.

Forces and factors

The winds of change have been created by major technological breakthroughs and driven by the desire to translate these technical possibilities into marketplace opportunities. The major driving "killer/engine" technologies are fiber optics/optical switches, VLSI computer chips/megabit memories/optical discs, high-level

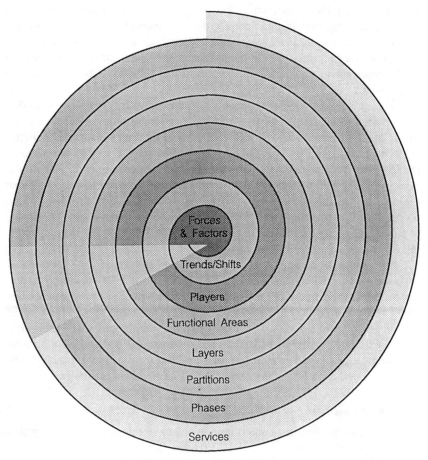

Fig. 2-3. The spiral of change.

languages/database management structures, and artificial intelligence/voice recognition/expert systems. These have focused attention on ISDN "information-handling" networks employing internetworking distributed processing systems. Many applications for these endeavors have surfaced in the competitive arena due to back-to-back divestiture and deregulation decisions. This has provided new freedoms and created new energies for the ultimate users to indicate new desires, cultivate new tastes, and exercise choice and selection.

Competition has now become a major driving force. It's a crucial factor that can't be ignored. Different forms of privatization have caused the United States, England, and Japan to promote different forms of competition. In the United States, the government has shifted from the position of specifically monitoring where technology is applied to reviewing how the competitive marketplace is achieved. Conflicts between customer provided equipment (CPE) and network terminating equipment (NTE) pushed the network channel terminating equipment (NCTE) boundaries closer to the end use from the original Inquiry II and Modified Final Judgment (MFJ) ruling to the more open Inquiry III, and on to Judge Greene's

Videotex Gateway[1] and Comparatively Efficient Interface (COI)/Colocation decisions, and the Appeals Court Information Services ruling.

England has partially privatized its network operation while retaining 49 percent ownership shares. It has fostered competition by enabling firms such as Mercury to establish parallel VANs (value-added networks) and to look for American RBOC partnerships. Similarly, Japan has privatized Nippon Telephone and Telegraph (NTT) and allowed specialized and general-purpose VANs to be established, allowing such partnerships as IBM and NTT, as well as Hughes and others to participate with Japanese firms to provide competitive VANS.

Some Europeans have called ISDN a new form of monopoly, in that the Germans have pushed for a new, fully integrated network based on ubiquitously moving gigabits of information efficiently, reliably, and cheaply. However, their Witte Commission recommended retaining the monopoly on the basic network and telephone service but having competition for value-added services, mobile radio, and satellite telecommunications without official guidelines. At the same time, four of the twelve members of the commission noted that the proposals didn't go far enough, and they prepared a minority report urging competition at all levels.

Alternatively, Broadband ISDN (B-ISDN) can be visualized as a backbone network, or infrastructure, upon which to integrate private networks to the world community via ISDN gateways and overlay networks. Others have become lost in the technology of IDN and have not applied the "S" (services for applications) to ISDN.[2] They've not fully understood that ISDN is the interfacing and interlacing of new and old services based on meeting the needs of the providers (who purchase the suppliers' products) and the customers of the providers, who purchase services from the provider's products. This has resulted in a new interest in understanding the users and their new information needs. Thus, the users have become a key, controlling force in the marketplace, but few can actually indicate what they really want until they see it.

Trends and shifts

The users have never been so suddenly and extensively observed and as deeply analyzed as they are today. Once the hype and hoopla have subsided for the initial fanfare of the entrance of ISDN 2B + D (Basic Rate Interface) and 23B + D (Primary Rate Interface)[3], these basic (BRI) and primary (PRI) interface offerings will become the new telecommunication vehicles that enable the transport

---

[1]Judge Harold H. Green, U.S. District Judge in the District of Columbia, is presiding over the United States of America vs. Western Electric Company et. al., Defendants Civil Action No. 82-0192.

[2]See Heldman, "ISDN Services," *Future Telecommunications,* McGraw-Hill, 1992.

[3]See the ISDN standards case study where the terminal's ISDN voice and data basic rate interface to the network (called the T interface) is 2B + D (where B = 64 Kbps and D = 16 Kbps). The primary interface typically for concentrators, multiplexors, and PBXs has the interface of 23B + D, where there are 23B (64 Kbps) channels and a signalling channel D at the 64 Kbps rate. The basic rate has a four-wire T interface rate of 192 Kbps from the terminal into an NTI/network terminating device, where it leaves on a two-wire U interface at a 160 Kbps rate to the network's central office.

movement of multiple channels of 64-kilobit voice and data information. As time passes, technological changes lead to positioning changes, as regulatory and financial restraints are constantly superimposed on the picture. Similarly, the usual "human element" resistance eventually changes from one of indifference to one of wanting "new toys," and then to requesting new features to make the toys into more practical tools.

This initial lack of ISDN demand caused many to say that ISDN was akin to the tulip mania of Holland. At the turn of the century, the Dutch had convinced themselves that the whole world wanted a particular tulip at outlandish prices. However, when the bulbs came to market, they found no external demand. This type of disillusionment has caused many of today's players to relate the "information rush" to the "gold rush," as they returned home to the more traditional "Centrex" voice world.

Others decided to stay and venture into new arenas such as "private networking." Here, the new information movement gained momentum as interest moved from public networks to private networks and then to publicly interconnecting private networks. As the arena shifted its focus onto large corporate fiefdoms, it also centered on the government marketplace, where contracts such as FTS-2000 for several billion or so dollars were considered by some as the sale of the century, but even this offering was considered by many government agencies and departments as too inadequate for their data-handling needs.

Reviewing the past, we see how California quickly grew to several hundred thousand people as the gold prospectors stayed to become farmers and business-people. California soon went on to become the 31st state of the union. Similarly, many of the initial information players have changed from technology planners to market planners, as they begin the long, tedious process of truly understanding "user needs," lest they too quickly develop an "Edsel network." They've recognized that we're not only moving to the "Information Age," but also to the "Knowledge Age," in which there will be intelligent use of the information as it's moved about the networks.

In analyzing user needs, it's apparent that information must be moved quickly, priced economically, and be ubiquitously[4] available in order to encourage growth.

---

[4]Ubiquitous has been a common term used throughout the telecommunications industry. In the past, every offering has been required to be available everywhere at the same time. With the new, competitive marketplace has come a questioning of the availability of new offerings. A workshop for providing the Congressional Office of Technology Assessment (OTA) with a view of the future of information network services has noted that the past emphasis on the ubiquitousness of new services will be challenged. Just as airplane deregulation has seriously affected airplane services in Helena, Montana, there's concern that the fully competitive information marketplace will question the need for providing ISDN data capabilities to the rural communities. Similarly, commonality of offerings will be needed across the Bell Operating Companies (BOCs) within each of the seven Regional Bell Operating Companies (RBOCs) in the Local Access and Transport Area (LATA) inside the local monopoly. These will be complex issues as new features are no longer available every place at the same time in the same manner. As you shall see throughout this analysis, ubiquitous—that single word—has come to mean the very reason for the existence of the future public information services network. It's a key strategy for deploying ISDN. Without a ubiquitous ISDN by the turn of the century, many believe that we'll have lost a strategic asset for America.

On the contrary, if it's fragile, expensive, inflexible, and unavailable, this can only encourage customers to use technology such as optical disks/CD ROM (compact disk read only memory) to store massive amounts of information more cheaply off the public network on private personal computer networks, where an optical disk can store 100,000 one-page letters or up to 200 million characters of information. Hence, there's the need to transfer and process information quickly, reliably, cheaply, and securely, especially with more and more industry contraction and fragmentation, as corporations reshape, resize, refocus, and relocate their operations using downsizing, right sizing, mergers, and partnerships. Their newly created private corporate networks require compatibility and standards to interconnect, interface, integrate, and internetwork through ISDN narrowband, wideband, and broadband public networks. Hence, the need for translation, transparency, and transfer of all forms of private information, in a secured, survivable manner, has become another new driving force.

This, then, requires a new look at what's happening in the regulatory arena to determine if "streamline regulation" steps should be enacted to eliminate the slow approval process for the BOCs to play the game. Similarly, how should the arena be opened to allow the BOCs, ISPs, and ESPs to provide information services and manufacture their own products? (Note the conflicting interest expressed in Congress by the Brooks Bill for inhibiting RBOC Information Services versus the Burns Bill for establishing Broadband Services.) Furthermore, how should the BOCs be allowed to interconnect cities within a state for inter-LATA intrastate interexchange traffic? This requires a more specific look at the "local monopoly" to readdress the bottleneck, comparably efficient interfaces, and open network architecture issues, as well as the methodology for obtaining tariff approvals. Finally, we need to resolve the state and federal concerns for universal service rate protection for the poor and for voice, data, and video services. We also need to ensure that cross-subsidies of service don't occur to inhibit competition.

In the 1980s and 1990s, suppliers and providers provided 5 Plus 5, 3 Plus 3, one-time career change, executive handshake, golden parachute offerings to encourage early retirement. Many companies had massive layoffs and unit closings to downsize (for example, as AT&T reduced its work force from 500,000 to 290,000). Today, it has not only become a question of how to become lean, trim, and aggressive, but how to prepare for tomorrow's future with new products. This is where the complexity of the picture changes dramatically. Understanding the future networks requires understanding future service needs and obtaining agreements to new standards, enabling the new products to be developed to provide these new services. Because "long-look" planning has not been a "long-term" tradition of many of the top Fortune 500 firms — especially for future Information Age products — numerous forums and cross-industry committees are needed to help facilitate agreements between users, suppliers, and providers. (See "Standard bodies" in chapter 7.)

Some of those formed to augment the International Telegraph and Telephone Consultative Committee (CCITT) were the U.S. ISDN Standards Committee (T1), Open System Interconnections, Bell Communications Research (BELLCORE) Technical Requirements Industry Forums (TRIFs), General Motors Manufacturing

Automation Protocol/Technical Office Protocol (MAP/TOP) committees, and North American ISDN user groups.

On the computer side, Digital Equipment Company (DEC), International Business Machines (IBM), and other computer suppliers recognized that not only must the networks exchange information successfully, but their users must also be able to see, manipulate, and process information from each others' computers so that any terminal/computer could communicate efficiently with another computer/terminal. This, then, brought about the need for layers of C&C programs to achieve the integration of their systems and their software products. Similarly, the Department of Defense (DOD) established standards for common word processor information interexchange; CCITT promoted high-level languages such as Common High Level Language (CHILL), and the military fostered contractor information-encryption specifications and common-systems database management structures, as well as information exchange protocol conversions in which the TCP/IP protocol must interface with the CCITT's OSI seven-layer hierarchy.

Thus, as we look at the spiral of change, we see many shifts and trends causing new forces and factors to motivate the players to reposition themselves in terms of meeting new user needs with new types of networks, products and services, formulating new markets and marketplaces.

The players and their strategies

In reviewing individual strategies, we can't help but note that two games are being played: one of evolution, the other of revolution. This is apparent in the continual extension of today's products and services for today's game, and the simultaneous planning and creation of new entities for tomorrow's game. Proposals have ranged from A to Z. Some have been insincere, unformulatable, and impractical, but they never lacked imagination and appeal. Similarly, despite rhetorical support for revolution, radical changes, and reforms, many of the suppliers, RBOCs, and users have been very traditional in accepting change, only gradually and slowly. (See FIG. 2-4.)

The governmental arena

As we review the players and their strategies, it's interesting to try to note the underlying "strategy of their strategies" upon which their overall direction and efforts are based. Let's begin by first reviewing the ever-changing governmental playing field. We're seeing a true test of democracy as we replace a totalitarian dictator, Ma Bell, (or a benevolent dictator, depending on your point of view) with a group of governmental bodies representing all interested and affected parties.

Justice

A brief review of past events and the now-exposed facets of the information iceberg sets the stage for determining the U.S. Department of Justice's future strategies and role. (See FIG. 2-5.) We can readily observe that throughout the early years after divestiture, the Baby Bells were severely limited by the Federal Communica-

Fig. 2-4. Planning is the key to the information game.

tions Commissions (FCC) Inquiry II/III and Department of Justice (DOJ) Modified Final Judgment rulings, which established the boundaries of today's playing field. High up above the press box, Judge Greene became the deciding umpire who was constantly requested by the various teams on the field to restructure the field's terrain, rules, and boundaries as the game was being played. Hence, as noted earlier, it became increasingly important for the players, who consisted of the various traditional and value-added providers, as well as the providers' suppliers, to not only play the current game very well, but also to identify and anticipate new rules and conditions in order to position themselves for tomorrow's game.

The initial boundaries were established to inhibit the RBOCs from suppressing new competition by sheer size, by having access to new providers' plans, by controlling prices, by inhibiting use of their network to connect users to new

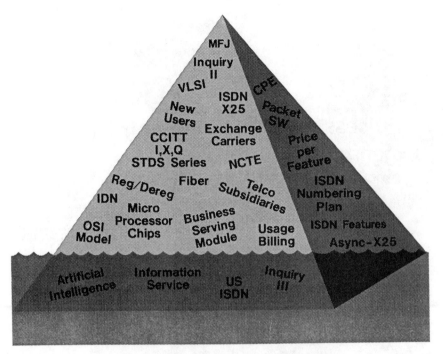

Fig. 2-5. Facets of the information iceberg.

providers, by having delays in enabling competing providers to offer new services, by obtaining cross-subsidization of their new service offerings from embedded plants, or by controlling the manufacturing and purchases of all major new products for the network.

This then leads to the MFJ, which stipulated "that no BOC shall directly or through any affiliated enterprise: provide interexchange telecommunications services or information services; manufacture or provide telecommunications products or customer premises equipment (except for provision of customer premises equipment for emergency services); or provide any other product or service, except exchange telecommunications and exchange access service, that is not a natural monopoly service actually regulated by tariff."

Similarly, Inquiry II, which was later modified by Inquiry III, established the initial FCC boundaries of the playing field by limiting the BOCs from providing information services and owning network terminating equipment on customer premises—thus establishîng Network Channel Terminating Equipment (NCTE) boundaries and Information Services Limits as follows:

The MFJ defines "information service" to mean "the offering of a capability for generating, acquiring, storing, transforming, processing, retrieving, using, or making available information which may be conveyed via telecommunications, except that such service doesn't include any use of any such capability for the management, control, or operation of a telecommunications system or the management of a telecommunications service."

The Huber report[5] noted that:

"The MFJ's lines roughly track the FCC's Computer 11 lines between 'basic' and 'enhanced' services. A 'basic' service involves pure transmission capability over a communications path that is virtually transparent in terms of its interaction with customer supplied information. In the provision of a basic transmission service, memory or storage within the network is used only to facilitate the transmission of the information from the origination to its destination, and the carrier's basic transmission network is not used as an information storage system. 'Enhanced' services are defined as services, offered over common carrier transmission facilities used in interstate communication, which (1) employ computer processing applications that act on the format, content, code, protocol or similar aspects of the subscriber's transmitted information; (2) provide the subscriber additional, different or restructured information; or (3) involve subscriber interaction with stored information.

Network Channel Terminating Equipment (NCTE). NCTE is equipment through which a customer connects phones, modems or computers to the Local Exchange Carriers (LEC) network. With the introduction of ISDN network technology, the NCTE market could come to rival the market for handsets; NCTE will certainly play an especially important role in the implementation of ISDN. NCTE stands at the interface between the network and terminal equipment and serves as a termination point for a digital channel. This is not a particularly well-defined product market; NCTE may provide a variety of functions such as multiplexing, signal regeneration and conditioning, error detection, error correction, testing, and equalization. Many of these functions may alternatively be supplied by other customer equipment, such as: modems, multiplexers and nodal point gateways.

In June 1983, the FCC ruled that NCTE is 'customer premises' (not 'network') equipment, which customers may obtain through third party vendors and which RBOCs may provide only through separate subsidiaries. The Commission subsequently granted waivers to three of the Regional Holding Companies (RHCs) to provide NCTE under certain circumstances on an unbundled, detariffed, but also unseparated basis pending final resolution of Computer 111. The decision that NCTE is CPE was reaffirmed in the Third Computer Inquiry, but may be relaxed somewhat. In its Supplemental Notice, the FCC suggested that some functions provided by NCTE, such as circuit termination, signal conditioning, testing, and multiplexing, may alternatively be supplied by carriers as a part of their networks. In response, carriers have nominated virtually all functions of NCTE for inclusion in the network.

This resulted in requiring organizational structural subsidiary market offerings consistent with new network architectural boundaries in an attempt to limit the BOCs from providing numerous new information services. It also resulted in a well-calculated effort to encourage and enable new providers to begin offering new

[5]The Geodesic Network, 1987 Report on Competition in the Telephone Industry. Prepared by Peter W. Huber as a consultant to the Department of Justice in accordance with the court's decision in the matter of U.S. v. Western Electric Company, 552 F. Supp. 131, 194-5 (D.D.C. 1982). Funded by the Antitrust Division, U.S. Department of Justice.

services and grow to a position in which they could formally challenge the BOCs. As a result, prior to Inquiry III, the BOCs could only offer limited new services from separate subsidiaries.

However, as ISDN technology integrated more and more transport services, a reassessment of the network architectural boundaries was required. The post-Inquiry II position of the FCC was to distance themselves from the technical arena and concentrate on the feasibility of the opening of the marketplace. This led to a series of questions and actions to ensure a nondominance or bottleneck BOC position that didn't prevent new services by any new provider. As a result, the BOCs were to provide a more open network architecture that ensured comparably efficient interconnection collocation or virtual collocation for the new providers to reach or be reached by their new information users.

As time progressed, congressional concern for the lack of a national public information network developed, as many new services were not being offered in the public arena due to emphasis on providing these offerings in the private or enhanced marketplace. This encouraged the FCC to give more freedom to the BOCs to provide new services such as the 800 and 900 information services. Similarly, concern arose to restore power (or at least the review and recommendation control) back to the FCC to enable them to have an increased role in the "control of the game, or at least the arena," because many believed that the waiver process for restructuring the game had shifted too much of the day-to-day decisions from the FCC to Judge Greene.

Justice, aware of the deteriorating situation, and required by law to have a review of the arena three years after divestiture, contracted Peter W. Huber to provide a report on the competitive status of the telephone industry. His views and visions of the future marketplace in terms of his distributed nodal point "Geodesic Network" caused a reevaluation of the playing field, as noted by the following analysis of excerpts from his report and the subsequent responses to it by the various players. Of the 130 responses, only 30 percent were in favor of letting the BOCs play in the complete arena, leaving a difficult decision to Judge Greene, who, before reaffirming his inhibiting decisions, requested the players to respond to his specific questions on "how to play the game."

Regulatory rulings — information services

Later, on July 25, 1992, Judge Harold Greene reluctantly relented by revising a key part of the historic 1982 agreement that broke up Ma Bell. In 1987, Greene ruled that the "Baby Bells" can only transmit information, not generate or own it. In April, 1990, the Appeals Panel told Greene to reconsider the information services restrictions on the RBOCs. On July 25, 1991, he lifted the ban, but took the unusual step of staying his order until higher courts could review his decision and protesters could file appeals.

Many experts noted that this decision would ultimately open a new era of the Information Age, an era that would enable the United States to maintain its reputation of having the world's most advanced telecommunications network well into the twenty-first century. Ray Smith, chairman and CEO of Bell Atlantic Corp., noted, "This is a very important day for American business. This will improve the competitiveness of U.S. business for years to come."

Many RBOCs saw immediate advantages of this ruling, enabling them to upgrade gateway services to provide more user-friendly access to databases, as well as to more adequately provide complete data-handling solutions to a wide range of customer multimedia applications.

Yet to be resolved is a 1990 ruling concerning Single Point of Interconnection (SPOI). As a result of this ruling, RBOCs are required to have a Signal Transfer Point (STP) in any LATA where inter-LATA call setup is being provided. Unfortunately, STPs are quite expensive. Some of the smaller LATAs fail economic deployment analyses. This might eventually cause a dearth of advance services platforms in the more rural LATAs. (The independent telephone companies have gone to overlay platforms that provide services for large areas, some as large as the entire state, such as in Iowa.) Though it's very difficult to predict how legal and regulatory decisions will evolve in the future, partial relief, at least for many new database access services, should be forthcoming during the mid '90s. Subsequent reviews and decisions on RBOCs equipment manufacturing might remove the bulk of these restrictions on the RBOCs, with the exception of providing inter-LATA networks. Now that the appeal process is complete and the RBOCs are allowed to provide information services independent of the manufacturing and inter-LATA services regulatory decisions, the RBOCs are able to establish a fuller spectrum of user-friendly offerings to better achieve some success in the information marketplace. In so doing, they'll need to better understand and address the needs of the human element . . . (See FIG. 2-6.)

The geodesic network

"Vertical Integration is the future of the telecommunications market, just as it is the past. However, the network architecture has changed, and that will change the market structure. The Geodesic Network can permit horizontal competition among vertical corporations, whereas the pyramid could not."

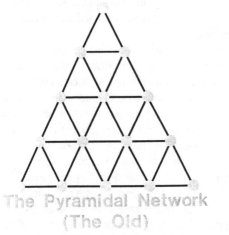 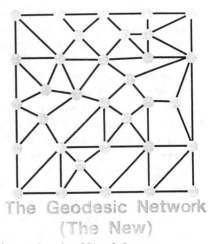

The Pyramidal Network
(The Old)

The Geodesic Network
(The New)

Fig. 2-6. Proliferation of interconnecting nodes: the old and the new.

Mr. Huber's noted *Geodesic Network* (1987) and subsequent *Geodesic Network II* (1992) analyses provided the industry with an excellent review of the networks, products, and services of the providers and their suppliers. He supported this with a technical assessment of switching and transmission technology and noted its impact on both the manufacturing and network arena. From these findings, he drew several conclusions regarding the direction of the future network in terms of his geodesic structure of distributed intelligent nodes connected together to provide a dynamic array of evolving information services. Because this network is horizontally distributed at all levels of the future telecommunications hierarchy, it offers numerous alternatives to bypass nodes, whose providers are exercising singular control.

He concluded that this structure can therefore support the virtual integration of providers, who can cluster together to provide various competitive offerings. Hence, a proliferation of future nodes was envisioned, as they attach or bypass various nodes of the public network. Mr. Huber and Judge Greene also saw the potential for packet switching to become a vehicle for the RBOCs to provide data transport to connect users through value added networks (VANs) to information service providers (ISPs) as a future alternative to the dial-up voice network, if priced competitively. With regards to manufacturing, Huber initially concluded that the high cost of R&D and the sophistication of the players translated into the unlikelihood of any single RBOC achieving a dominant role that could suppress future competitive offerings from the other players in this arena. (Note that the judge disagreed with this conclusion.)

On several of these various considerations, many planners have made similar observations and conclusions, especially as numerous private networks grow to meet the growing information needs of both large and small businesses and the more information-oriented residential users.

Subsequent to the initial Huber analysis, the DOJ concurred with many of his findings in their B2-0192 (report and recommendations of the United States concerning the line of business restrictions imposed on the Bell Operating Companies by the modification of final judgment). The DOJ observed that a key technical conclusion of Huber was that "technology innovation has changed the switching/transmission cost ratios in telecommunication."

However, this aspect could be challenged; indeed, switching component costs have greatly decreased, but R&D costs (as also noted by Huber with regard to manufacturing) have exploded due to increased software costs, since features and services are being provided by highly complex, integrated programs. In considering the potential for inexpensive, superhigh-capacity transmission facilities (where the cost per channel has decreased as dramatically as switching component costs), new networks would be established in which both switching and transmission costs would continue to drop considerably. However, software routing, control, and feature costs will greatly increase as they provide greater flexibility and versatility to interface and interconnect nodes. Also, the time frame and costs for nodal point deliverance are somewhat reduced in the private network arena, since there's somewhat better control in resolving internal interface standards and complexities. (Note: ISDN planning meetings have projected costs of adding to the network narrowband ISDN (with full data switching capabilities) at 1.5 times the traditional voice telephone line today, or, in other words, at about $100–$150 per line. Using copper facilities for n-ISDN, total switching system costs are in the low billions or so, rather than the several hundred billions needed for fully ubiquitous fiber broadband ISDN transport.)

Future inexpensive gigabit transport could combine with reduced switching components and limited feature software to achieve a new form of "gigabit" bypass. This would be attractive due to the many governmental limits of the Public Information Transport Network, as well as the delay and high tariffs of new feature offerings. These were not in sync with the expanding capability to move gigabits of information. Local Exchange Carriers (LECs) would provide the fiber, and other providers could then use the fiber's capability, or insert their own fiber to transport gigabits of information past the local network to networks above the local one. The future new "gigabit" bypass design architecture could use centralized service platforms, accessed via these gigabit bypass facilities, having local remote switch nodes/access switches that can directly interact with the users. Many believe that as we enter the age of gigabit information, this approach might become a private fiefdom's realistic alternative to using the Public Information Transport Network; these customers could use alternative carriers' transport, except to reach areas via public offerings, which are economically unattractive to privately owned switch nodes. On the other hand, LECs are now offering digital cross-connects (DCs) and high-speed frame relay, or SMDS transport, on a usage basis. These systems will, in time, evolve to a fully switched and integrated narrowband/wideband/broadband offering.

This then leads us to the following questions, as we enter the world of the "Geodesic Network." Who will be the "keepers of the network?" What will be the "Public Information Transport Network," upon which other networks enter and exit during their formation and growth to maturity, as the Geodesic Network blossoms? Who will pay the costs of interconnecting and interfacing layers of private-to-public-to-private networks? Who will ensure data information is ubiquitously available to all potential users? Who will provide and pay for the burden of routing, billing, and controlling the movement of information to all geographical sections of the public rural and urban communities? How will "public data packet information" flow economically within a state, across LATAs?[6]

In summary, note the following Huber conclusions:

"The first and most important regulatory object must be to promote competition entry at all levels of the network. This means encouraging the formation of new network nodes and new links between them."

"The networking challenge is altogether new. An altogether new network will certainly be required."

"The geodesic dome of vertical structures connected horizontally is truly effectively competitive."

---

[6]See Heldman, *Global Telecommunications: Layered Networks' Layered Services*, McGraw-Hill, 1992.

Dr. Huber provided an excellent assessment of the postdivestiture situation and emphasized the need for encouraging growth in the marketplace by both vertical and horizontal integration of providers' offerings, as new intelligent nodes are added to draw the network closer and closer to the user. As many pointed out, these nodes might not necessarily by geodesic, but they can be distributed enough to foster vertical integration by providing numerous alternative paths for many new providers' new services, thus rendering past restrictions and bottlenecks no longer applicable. (See FIG. 2-7.)

However, to achieve these objectives, potential technical possibilities must be realistically tied to true marketplace needs to ensure that necessary financial incentives exist to universally establish the new "Public Information Transport Network" with its "information services" offerings. It's essential to achieve this base as soon as possible because private networks can formulate their new nodes on this base. In its absence, the alternative might be numerous private nodes loosely connected in disjointed clusters . . . holding in the balance the life or

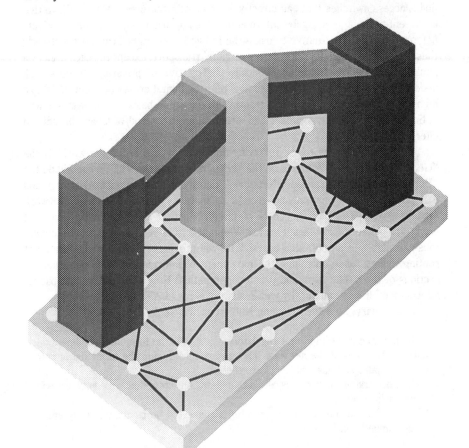

Fig. 2-7. Vertical integration.

death of The Public Information Transport Network.[7] (In the early 1920s, there were 29 separate communications companies in downtown New York City, none of which were interconnected.)

FCC

As we review the Fowler, Patrick, and Sikes years, we see more FCC focus on how to obtain the competitive marketplace, as the FCC concentrates on the economic factors with new streamline regulations. There have been many recommendations and positions provided to the FCC, Justice, and Congress to help them better assess what their role should be and how the RBOCs, AT&T, IBM, etc. should be allowed to play the game. During the formation period, we saw the Huber Report to Justice, the Office of Technology Assessment (OTA) Report to Congress, along with numerous other reports provided by Harvard and the Brookings Institute, to name a few.

The hard questions remain, such as: "How should we handle geographical pockets, where competition doesn't exist for a particular service? Can service point of interconnection (SPOI) restrictions be removed to enable access to service across LATAs? Should local packet transport across LATAs be inhibited or promoted differently? Should the burden of proving the lawfulness of a tariff be shifted from the carrier to those opposing the tariff? Should the FCC review-time for tariffs be cut substantially from 90 days to, say, 30? What services with what restrictions can be provided in basic transport operations and what should be provided without restrictions in enhanced services? When can the enhanced services be moved to and from the basic transport arena? How can we really achieve and monitor cross services between the regulated and unregulated arena? If the service is considered enhanced, will it remain unregulated; if basic, how should it be streamlined? What should be the role of Justice versus FCC versus State Regulators?"

As noted in Senator Dole's earlier Communication Bill, how should we attempt to move "the border patrol" function back to the FCC from Justice? In terms of ISDN and the contradiction it brings to bear between the FCC and technology, what should be the supporting role of the government, such as the Burns Bill or White House involvement, to ensure the achievement of a fully universal, capable wideband/broadband, capable network in the public domain? Should the network be allowed to terminate on customer premises? How should the public network providers enable ONA access to their public transport so that private networks and information services providers can offer the full range of forthcoming voice, data, video, and image information services? How can the FCC ensure that small businesses, rural businesses, and residential communities have access to a public information network that cheaply and effectively provides full information services? Everywhere?

---

[7]See Heldman, *Telecommunications Management Planning: ISDN Networks, Products, & Services*, TAB Books, 1989.

Has equal access become a commodity? Is it a term that can only be distinguished in the marketplace by service, image, and perhaps international access as it enters the look-alike realm of airlines and laundry detergents. As we see the growing conformity and equality of equal access voice services arrangements for MCI and Sprint, especially with 800 number portability, have we indeed successfully achieved nondiscriminating access, which was one of the key goals for a post-divestiture marketplace?

What's needed in equal access for public data and video networks? In reviewing the role of the FCC with AT&T, the FCC has attempted to equivocate pricing flexibility, but not provide total deregulation, creating an era of uncertainty. Even some other interexchange carriers (IXCs) recommended that AT&T's long-distance revenues be deregulated to ensure that true market forces will determine pricing strategies, not unrealistic governmental directives that could drop prices so far as to drive their companies out of business. Hence, we've had a new FCC pricing strategy to cap service prices and allow competitive pricing under this limit. Similarly, state regulators have provided new revenue incentives in the local arena, allowing RBOCs increased revenues that are more than the typical 12 percent rate of return, as high as 18 percent or so if the local plant is upgraded to digital throughout the state.

Restraints tied to divestiture in the '80s gave the illusion of regulation as "betwixt and between." This then left suppliers to attempt to determine how much intelligence should/could be located in a terminal such as the smart phone, which could have the ability to call, route, and provide answer supervision and not be dependent on the call processing of the central office. The FCC's term is "instrument implemented." How can the FCC balance the "free the BOC" movement to offer local telephone service, sell equipment, and provide enhanced data processing services all from one shop? How will the FCC resolve the dilemma that the public data networks were not designed for the computer industry? (The public network was neither data user friendly nor data reliable, and its tariffs on data services were too high.) How does the FCC ensure that the resulting telecommunication information structure will aid economic growth and social and educational progress?

Resolving Open Network Architecture issues remains the task of the '90s. For example, by allowing collocation of competitor equipment in the central office as the ultimate solution, the BOCs, who might not like the solution, will have to come up with an arrangement that's functionally and economically equal to collocation, such as "virtual collocation." Functional equivalence is technically feasible, but economic equivalence will require eliminating or mitigating separate interface costs as well as the cost of distance from the central office (CO). In so doing, this has been a very bold step that has set up a series of repercussions within and beyond the local exchange. Removing or mitigating the distance component alone has drawn the companies into other ONA-controversial areas such as equal access to intelligent networking interfaces by information service providers (ISP) and enhanced service providers (ESPs). Usage bit and byte, ckt and pkt, low- and high-speed, switched and nonswitched tariffs have been discussed for many years, especially as n-ISDN and B-ISDN services are being deployed. Nippon Telephone and Telegraph (NTT) has investigated the private services databases interfaces concept for its Information Network System. All of these issues will become more and more important as we move from voice-only services (see *Future Telecommunications* appendix on ONA services) to data- and video-based communications services.[8]

However, most of the industry has ignored the multimedia transport and service pricing subject except for rate averaging, and that indeed does mitigate the distance component of price. Whether or not the BOCs want to open Pandora's box for the industry, they might not be able to break the bottleneck theory without not only moving in this direction of "virtual collocation," but also in the direction of new service-based pricing rather than bandwidth-based pricing; for example, videophone at 45 Mbps can't be offered based upon its equivalent T3 bandwidth prices. In addition, a shared transport ring to enable access to anyone's switched network service throughout the local monopoly could be a plausible ONA solution.

Congress

As noted, some congressional leaders approved, while others challenged the appeals court decision in favor of letting RBOCs offer unrestricted information services. Some urged reconsideration of the elimination of RBOC barriers to providing information services, as well as other nonregulated activities. The Brooks Bill attempted to restore 1983 MFJ divestiture restrictions, while the Burns Bill attempted to establish 2015 as the mandatory goal for a universally available broadband network. Therefore, Open Network Architecture, collocation, compatibly efficient interface, international network ownership of the RBOCs, service point of interface (SPOI) location of service nodes serving several LATAs, inter-LATA transport for local public data network/RBOC software programs for enhanced services, mobile services, (software manufacturing), etc. are the congressional issues of the '90s. So it goes . . .

These issues and events have forced the communications industry to readdress the issue of the "local monopoly" in the mid '90s. Past opinions have noted unfair advantages should the BOCs continue to control the local arena. Thus, many continue to recommend not allowing long-distance interexchange transport capabilities for the BOCs, until they no longer have a local monopoly. However, at the same time some argue that BOCs need, at a minimum, local inter-LATA interstate networking capabilities in order to provide an economically attractive alternative public data network that connects local cities within a state together to compete against the proliferation of private bypass networks.

Hence, the real issue of the '90s will indeed continue to be "the local monopoly." It's necessary to meet the voice networking needs of the poor. However, it's also equally important to formulate a public information network as a "strategic asset" that encourages growth of the nation into the Information Age. However,

---

[8]This and all other observations were taken from numerous articles by the leading planners and thinkers noted in the acknowledgments.

some RBOCs are considering an effective Divestiture II, where they divorce themselves from the basic telephone company, either by outright sale or share splits, in order to participate more competitively in the information revolution without the restrictions that they believe will inhibit successful services, especially as they turn to the more lucrative cable television offerings . . . Therefore, the future of the local monopoly will be determined by governmental policy decisions. These will be translated into entrances and exits across the Geodesic plane in terms of providing for comparably efficient interconnections that use an open network architecture to access the public information network and interface with numerous parallel private information networks . . .

Section two: the positioning period

Visions[9] are important, as the Virginia Exchange Carriers Association noted when they decided to quit reflecting on events, hearings, rules, and actions that only just discuss access charge tariffs. They decided to move on to more optimistic "opportunity through technology" endeavors. We've seen numerous visions boldly set forth, such as AT&T's Universal Information Services Digital Network and Service Network 2000 plan, Northern Telecom's Dynamic Network and Fiber World plans, Bellcore's Intelligent Network, NEC's C&C vision, Siemens' Vision O·N·E, NTT's VIP, etc. These visions are vital for anticipating the potential of the network and providing direction, as they encourage planners to create the ideal network or even re-create a new form of monopoly. Ultimately, the network providers and the host of influential decision makers must say yes or no to these visions and determine a plausible solution to the local monopoly issue to enable the players to get on with the game . . . Alternatively, as noted, some players will "sell the store" and move on to other more soluble solutions. This is the "information networking" challenge to the democratic process . . .

The players' sand box

Today, the Bell Operating Companies (BOCs) under Regional Holding Companies (RHCs) form seven Regional Bell Operating Companies (RBOCs). They, together with the Independent Telephone Operating Companies (IOCs) such as General Telephone (Electronics) Operating Companies (GTE/Centel), have approximately ten thousand and nine thousand local exchanges, respectively. These local exchange carriers (LECs) have integrated switching systems with transmission systems to have the potential to provide numerous new voice and data transport services. They use direct access to short-haul and long-distance carriers for movement of information outside their geographical, monopolistic market boundaries (called local access and transport areas (LATAs)). As interexchange traffic from local central offices crosses the LEC's LATA office boundary, the information is handed over to interexchange carriers (IECs) to provide inter-LATA services.

---

[9]See chapter 1 for visions of the future by Tom Bystrzycki, Executive Vice President, U S West Communications, Dr. John Mayo, President of Bell Labs, AT&T, Dr. Koji Kobayashi, COB/CEO Emeritus NEC, and E. M. Hancock, President of IBM Communication's Product Group.

Here, AT&T, with a billion circuit miles, is the dominant carrier. Other common carriers (OCCs) such as MCI, US Sprint, Wiltel, etc., have a total of six-hundred million interexchange circuit miles in place. They all compete with microwave carriers (MCCs), radio carriers (RCCs), and satellite carriers (SCCs), sometimes using a carrier's carrier (CC) to reach areas that don't have their own circuits.

By the early '90s, 125 million lines were served by central offices in the United States. The installed world market appears to be around 600 million lines. Four hundred million will use the European 32 channel E1 digital format, and 200 million lines will use the American 24 channel T1 format (such as, U.S., Canada, Taiwan, Korea, Egypt). The life of switching machines is dropping from 20 to 10 to 5 years as the world converts from analog to digital. As part of the integrated digital network (IDN) formation program, some 10 million lines of digital switching capability has been installed each year over the late '80s to the mid '90s.

Similarly, 30 to 40 million lines for numerous businesses, hospitals, universities, and factories are served by digital private branch exchanges (PBXs). Most PBXs are integrating with local area networks (LANs) to provide gateways from private networks to the world. Similarly, the public networks' CENTREX offerings have been enhanced to work with LANs and provide ISDN interfaces for ISDN CENTREX services. PBX voice services have become more integrated, with data services under computer control to become new computerized branch exchanges (CBXs). They can be used as nodal point systems that provide shared tenant services (STS) for apartment and business complexes. Meanwhile, the regulatory control of the local arena is under the watchful eye of the Public Utility Commissions (PUCs), working together with the Federal Communications Commission (FCC). They remain concerned with such things as resolving usage-sensitive costs attributed to access charges, which the IECs pay to the LECs, as well as tariffs for numerous service offerings to the users. Looking back over the formation phase of the Information Era, there has been considerable local jurisdictional interplay battles between the role of the FCC and the PUC for resolving local issues such as shared tenant services. This then leads to a direct confrontation in the '90s over resolving the future fate of the "local monopoly."

Inquiry III decisions and subsequent judicial rulings in the late '80s and early '90s have enabled the BOCs to market all forms of customer premises equipment (CPE), including computers. Large switching systems today require one-half to $2 billion R&D expenditures. This has caused consolidations and partnerships, as the players exit or join forces to produce the next generation of product offerings. We've seen the exit of IT&T and the entrance of international players as the market shifts to embrace Ericsson, Alcatel, Siemens-Stromberg Carlson, Northern Telecom, Fujitsu, NEC, with AT&T in the large switching systems arena, together with Mitel, Intercom, and Harris in the PBX market, as well as in the hybrid PBX-key systems arena with players such as TIE. By the mid '90s, many multiplexer bridge/router suppliers were turning to ATM switching. This rigorous competition requires expensive R&D.

Much of the foreign competitors suppliers' research is subsidized by their country's Postal Telephone and Telegraph Company (PTT), where many have favored-supplier status as well. Hence, some need only capture 5 percent of the U.S. market to maintain a presence. Others, with several hundred million dollar R&D commitments, having no favorite supplier status, need to capture 10 to 15 percent of the world market to remain competitive. This then leads to new partnerships between these suppliers and the RBOCs, as RHCs construct their own 1,000-person product research and planning laboratories to identify and define new products and services. During the next twenty years, the next-generation products might require as much as $10 billion to develop, $30 billion to support, and $40 billion per RBOC to provide. Hence, RBOCs will be hard pressed to both supply and provide the new family of broadband ISDN systems.

In entering the era of integration of computers and communications, there's similar partnering as terminal and PC manufacturers align themselves with PBX and network providers and suppliers. Further movement is occurring toward information services in which the evolving role of information service providers (ISPs) becomes one of assembling a full array of services in a format accessible to both private and public users. New, enhanced information services will occur as the FCC and DOJ come to terms with new "integrated service" offerings by the RBOCs in the new competitive marketplace. (We've seen that "information" (MFJ) or "enhanced" (FCC) services have been defined in a slightly different manner, as noted earlier by Huber.) As time progresses, database source (DBS) companies will interface and merge with online service companies and gateway intermediary companies. Their users access them through value added networks (VANs), interexchange carriers networks, and dial-up telco networks. Judge Greene once unsuccessfully encouraged the RBOC formation of new circuit and packet switching data networks to interface to this growing group of private and public information network users, who wish to access the growing number of databases. Of the 3,000+ databases in the early '90s, there were 1,500+ producers with 500 or so online services. You need only to look at the initial success of the French Minitel Transpac Network to see growth and creativity in information access to information databases. This can only occur once relatively inexpensive "friendly" terminals are in place and transport access costs are inexpensively priced. Here, voice recognition and windowing technologies will increasingly play a key role.

In the early '90s, both the computer and communication system suppliers focused their attention on meeting the "internetworking" needs of their users, using the CCITT Open Systems Interconnection OSI model. (See the ISDN standards study in chapter 7.) Its higher-levels standards are being incorporated into the next generation of personal computers, which have numerous interactive programs to enable different terminals to talk to each other and exchange information from different systems' different types of databases. In this arena we've seen DEC establish internetworking capability to access both the large-frame (IBM) and mini computer systems. Similarly, IBM has put forth an SNA-PC-Token Ring network to internetwork other manufacturer's terminals and systems with their IBM product line. Second-generation Apple terminals can now interface to PC networks and run IBM-compatible programs. AT&T, who was able to maintain 70 percent of its interexchange IC market, also recognized the need to follow the DEC lead in becoming a full computer-network-CPE integrator, as they purchased NCR. From their Net 1000, ISDN, Unix, PCs, #1PSS, and hospital turnkey systems, they've learned the need to enter the world of national and international data networks that provide "computer networking" and "data networking" services, now called "information networking."

In terms of bypassing the LECs, many new alternative transport carriers (ATPs) have opted to establish a point of presence (POP) within the local monopoly to enable corporate users to achieve various forms and degrees of facility services and economic bypass to reach IXCs or to establish totally separate networks. Even the U.S. Congress and White House have become involved concerning free competition, especially in the international arenas for parallel transcontinental marine and satellite networks. This all brings us back to the Huber view that dispersal of network intelligence is occurring due to intensive advances in technology, forcing at the same time consolidation on the suppliers' side and consolidation on the service side due to the high cost of high technology. These factors and forces cause shifts and trends that will enable the players to create a geodesic network sphere that not only supports the vertical integration of numerous suppliers and providers, but also prevents any RBOC or consortium from halting the movement to a fully competitive, distributed information marketplace. (See FIG. 2-8.)

Who makes what?

"Some of the RBOCs might perhaps become their own suppliers in some niche areas, such as applications processors, fiber-optic cable, or feature software . . . However, there's no chance whatsoever that the seven RBOCs, start-

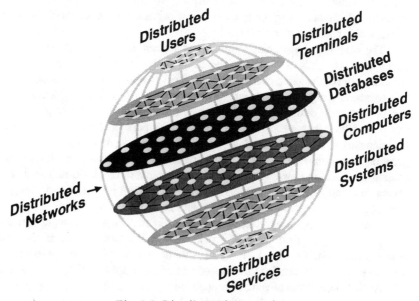

Fig. 2-8. Distributed information.

ing from scratch, could recreate seven Western Electrics and the closed buyer/ seller arrangements that used to prevail. The U.S. will consider itself lucky if it emerges from divestiture with just one company possessing a Western Electric's concentration of engineering design talent and production skill . . . Certainly, no RBOC's manufacturing efforts are going to knock out the NECs, Siemens-Stromberg Carsons, and Northern Telecoms of this world" . . .

"The center of the electronic information services market lies well beyond the edges of the traditional telephone network. With only comparatively minor exceptions, it's still entirely outside it. Electronic processing, reformation, storage, retrieval and all the other elements of an electronic service are available in a robustly competitive marketplace. Sophisticated capabilities for networking these machines on the other hand are still very limited. The information services markets are thus being built from the outside in" . . .

As we look at these two observations by Huber and consider what has happened in the information product arena during the past twenty years, one can't help but note the drastic changes in the manufacturing arena. In 1960, the first electronic switching systems were used in the military. They were essentially wired-logic, table-driven machines at costs of 24 million R&D dollars and 7 years to develop. This then moved to stored program design as Bell Labs completed their first field tests in Morris, Illinois in 1965. During this period, North and Automatic Electric went to the Ericsson half-hardware, half-software design approach for their 1967-72 new product offerings at R&D costs of $50–70 million. This then led to No. 2 EAX and No. 2 ESS type analog voice switching systems in the 1974 time frame, using full stored program control, having taken 5–7 years to develop at costs of $20 million to $40 million dollars per year. These systems required totally different manufacturing facilities than earlier crossbar or step-by-step switching systems (which had been built on the raw-materials-in, mechanical switching-systems-out type of production lines).

The next age of switching systems was a quantum jump as machines became digital and physically distributed, requiring an integration of transmission and switching. Here, the game changed in complexity, with a new emphasis on planning how to interface digital systems into an existing analog environment. Hence, a great deal of work moved to the planning and requirement definition of new products. At this time, high inflation took place, causing higher personnel costs. Designers and programmers in the new technology were in high demand, and program complexity grew until gruesome. As a result, software programs doubled and efforts tripled, causing the costs of new switching systems to move to the $700 million mark as several hundred experienced, sophisticated programmers and VLSI logic designers were required to construct these new families of switching systems.

Today, the IDN (Integrated Digital Network) switching systems, designed for voice, are being overlaid with data-packeting-handling capabilities, as the world moves toward ISDN facilities. Hence, the life of these systems will be extended a few more years until the fully integrated wideband/broadband networks are available. At that time, features will be "capped" for systems that already have grown to five to ten million lines of code in the mid '90s.

Hence, to build the next generation of systems will take in the order of five to seven years, requiring investments (depending on the product line) from $500 million to $2 billion per system. As noted earlier, the complete new family of broadband ISDN systems will most likely cost around $10 billion to develop and $30 billion to support, requiring a small army of sophisticated programmers and VLSI logic designers, as we move into the world of more integrated voice, data, and video multifeature offerings. (See FIG. 2-9.)

A new game

This is not a small feat for those who have been in the manufacturing arena for many years, and it's a Herculean task for those just entering, as noted by Mr. Huber. Hence, we're entering a new ball game . . . the information game.

The players

Watching the players position themselves to determine their strategies has always been an interesting and essential aspect of any sporting event for both the coaches and the spectators. Similarly, the information game in its formation and transition phases requires watching and analyzing the players as they attempt to achieve strategic advantages based upon their particular, unique arrays of new offerings. Hence, let's take a moment to briefly assess "what's happening" in terms of "who will be providing what" networks, products, and services by the mid '90s. This will be a useful reference checkpoint for future analyses to determine progress, direction, or lack of movement. This challenging international arena requires more than a single look at one nation, country, or state. It must be a more global view of the

A New Game . . .
New Ball . . .
New Playing Field . . .
New Players . . .
New Plays . . .
New Process . . .
New Rules . . .
New Referees . . .
New Services . . .

Fig. 2-9. Time to play a little "G" ball.

many corners of the world, encompassing: RBOCs, AT&T, Interdependents, Interconnects, Germany, France, Britain, and Japan.

We also need to assess the direction of private networks — as unfortunately, or fortunately, as noted in chapter 1, the computer manufacturers and user groups have been forced to develop nonswitched solutions to moving and exchanging data between terminals and host, between hosts, and between terminals. This has been due to the absence of a narrowband public data network, which has been unavailable for the last thirty years, in spite of substantial computer growth and universal data usage.

During this period, the internal computer bus structure architecture was applied externally among its peripherals, enabling LANs to be developed using proprietary address-and-message framing schemes. Over the years, there has been a proliferation of different types of LANs that needed to be bridged together to route information to more remote addresses. As this need expanded, wide area networks were developed using public circuit switched facilities. This was augmented by metropolitan area networks that provided high-speed transport connectivity throughout a limited geographical area. Nationally, from the initial data-handling military 465-L type networks, came the ARPA-net type of switched networks, sponsored by the Department of Defense (DOD) to allow scientific communities to inexpensively access and share remote databases. Subsequent data networks such as Tymnet and Telenet provided the packetized exchange of information on a value-added basis. From these networks came Internet, with its particular TCP/IP Internetworking Protocol and global addresses.

The RBOCs

During the '80s and early '90s, we've seen the RBOCs structure and restructure as they went through their divestiture and diversification process. They established numerous special-purpose subsidiaries only to collapse them back within a central unit with consolidation moves to provide more "total-solution," "market-focused" offerings, depending on regulatory/nonregulatory governmental decisions. Then, fully separated entities or new alliances were formed with cable companies and program producers.

A backward glance

As the telecommunications industry completes ten years of postdivestiture activity and we look to the future, the new frontier with its new mountains of opportunity, it's important to pause to determine how we arrived at this point in time, where we've been, and what we've learned along the way (as Tom Bystrzycki noted in his vision for the future.) It's been a somewhat turbulent and complex period — a period of positioning and politics as the new "baby Bells" entered the marketplace with all the high expectations and excitement of the young as they gained their new freedoms and independence. So, what has been accomplished over these past ten years, and how are these new players and their industry positioned to address the next ten years?

Let's review past activities and accomplishments in terms of the broad view of what actually, realistically, has been achieved and learned . . . It's quite evident that very little substantive progress has been made in constructing a totally new "information-handling" infrastructure. The telephone company today is still "the telephone company." Yes, there are some new services, but, for the most part, the RBOCs' businesses consist mainly of providing basic twisted-pair voice offerings. In the early '90s, capital expenditures and revenue pressures refocused the RBOCs' attention on the "telephone." After an explosion of acquisitions and mergers into every sector of business, from real estate to financial services, the majority of telephone industry leaders remained knowledgeable in only voice-based services. Hence there was a flood of intelligent network offerings concentrating on 800 services, 900 services, the second voice line, and number portability features of ISDN, Centrex, and Voice Mail.

Explorations into the data world generally stopped at facsimile platforms, which were based on using dial-up data modems over the analog voice switched network. A few did venture into data packet switching, but services remained unsold due to a lack of incentive for the telco's sales force, who, for the most part, lacked even general knowledge of data users' needs. Though ISDN was devised for integrating data and voice, it was simply sold, "where available," as an expensive interface for additional voice services. Few "marketers" ever requested that the ISDN networks be deployed. For them, the network was a cloud, where data networking capabilities were ignored as data transport interoperability issues were left to the "technoids" to eventually resolve.

Many new toys were acquired along the way and then discarded once their initial sparkle diminished, just as a child picks and chooses its favorite toy for the moment. Judge Greene attempted to put limits and boundaries on the new "babies," believing that they would completely smother anyone who attempted to join them in their newfound playbox. Unfortunately, history has shown that, in truth, the RBOCs really were little threat to new competition, and indeed their response to his restrictions simply shifted their attention to other worlds, other opportunities across the sea, resulting in little data/video switching upgrade of the American communication infrastructure, which was so badly needed to support the forthcoming information marketplace. Other competitive players, such as the information service providers, found that they needed a field in which to play, and, like it or not, it was the local operating companies who could most effectively, efficiently, and economically establish the ubiquitous "any-to-any" arena upon which all could play the information game. However, the RBOCs demanded relief from the MFJ restrictions before they would seriously play the game.

Without this arena, private local area networks for "one-to-many" or "many-to-one" flourished over the '80s. As they proliferated, their interconnect needs became more and more evident. As computers and communications merged, their interdependence became quite demonstrative, showing the need for internetworking, interprocessing, and interservices. By the early '90s, this opportunity was quite apparent, and it caused the communications industry to focus primarily on LAN-to-LAN interconnect issues, offering various forms of shared "pay-as-you-use" transport, causing a shift away from leased-line special services. This shift didn't go unnoticed, as alternative transport providers (ATPs) began offering parallel transport to encourage private-to-private networking over their privately "shared" facilities. Hence, a new emphasis developed on providing various forms of bandwidth to the customer for the dynamically changing transport capacity needs and the dynamically changing destinations.

As the '90s developed, there was a mad scramble to capture the larger customers, first by dedicated and then switched facilities. However, as time progressed, a realization set in that smaller firms needed to access larger firms' databases, and that residential services should include PC networking, database access, and video offerings. This then led to a reevaluation when video dial-tone restraints were removed, as not only the FCC but also Congress encouraged more competition and lower rates for video services to the home. Other bills, such as the Burn's Bill to refiber America, gave a further push, while some negative, inhibiting legislation was enacted to reestablish information services restrictions in attempts to pull the telephone companies back to earlier boundaries. Though highly critical of the existing infrastructure, Wall Street analysts continued to require increasing short-term growth gains without providing relief for long-term infrastructure expenditures. The net result was to force some of the RBOCs to consider more and more international partnerships and expenditures as they essentially became two firms, one a local telephone company, and the other a multinational partner in numerous international communications consortiums throughout the world . . .

Once removal of video dial-tone restrictions was accomplished, a new emphasis on CATV partnerships was promoted in an effort to quickly enter the video market using existing analog cable facilities. Later, for some RBOCs, it then became a financial choice to separate holding firms with international and CATV partnerships from the basic telephone companies, thereby creating "Divestiture II," where the market again waited for the newborn telcos to begin structuring the missing fiber- based local information-handling communication infrastructure.

ISDN narrowband arrived in full force in '92 and '93 with national ISDN-1,2,3, TRIP '92, and economical ISDN interface chips for CPE. This provided the impetus for medium-speed data networks to interconnect every aspect of every community of interest of the marketplace. New technologies, as well as new market opportunities, challenged the industry as wireless services vied for wire-line dollars. Once cellular possibilities had finally reached the acceptable price level of the $200 per phone and $30 per month rate, this network attracted not only the aggressive, overachiever executive in the BMW, but also the small-business construction worker/owner in a pickup truck. New opportunities in personal communication services arrived when the potential of the "Dick Tracy watch" captured everyone's interest. These possibilities chased scarce capital destined for upgrading existing plant. Similarly, satellite and microwave data networks rose to the forefront to offer wireless data transport. All these alternatives, as well as the newfound ability to upgrade existing copper plant to handle high-speed data, challenged new fiber deployment expenditures. However, in the long run, the full spectrum of interactive fiber offerings remained awesome and couldn't be ignored whenever fiber in the loop (FITL), fiber to the pedestal (FTTP), fiber to the curb (FTTC), fiber to the home (FTTH), fiber to the office (FTTO), and fiber to the desk (FTTD) deployments could be successfully achieved.

Therefore, there remains the need for taking the necessary steps to establish the right telecommunication infrastructure that will truly support a growing, blossoming, ubiquitous information marketplace. As we enter the next ten years after Divestiture I, the mid '90s and beyond, it's indeed a "crossroad in time" for both the computer and communications industries, but it's also a "crossroad in time" for society. We have the ability to enable work at home and interconnected satellite work centers in remote cities, where commuter traffic is less, homes are cheaper, children are nearer, and the quality of life is better. We're at the gate of a new frontier. It beckons us, but it offers many hazards and paths of no return. Those who stop to pause and consider the necessary steps needed to successfully achieve the new information-handling infrastructure will be better prepared to cross the new terrain and scale new heights.

Success in the global arena can only be achieved by the select few who are able to internationally hop here and there. However, this is a dangerous game, as past history has adequately demonstrated. Many will venture; there will be a continuum of new partnerships and alliances as communications become more global, but "to be global is to be local." There's a need for financial incentives by Congress to encourage communication leaders to locally spend their billions to make new billions. To achieve the needed local information infrastructures is a $200–$300 billion investment by each major country. For the United States, this translates into a billion-dollar-per-year investment during the next 20 years by each of the ten or so major players. Then, and only then, can the future destiny of the telecommunications industry, as it merges with the computer industry, be truly achieved . . . (See FIG. 2-10.)

The independents

As the forces of change provide new opportunities, many of the independents have captured the spirit and expanded their lines of business to include provision of cable television services, unregulated customer premise equipment and wiring, consulting services, interexchange services, resale services and billing, as well as "data handling."

As one observer noted:

"Perhaps the most profound effect of divestiture on independents will be the expansion and redirection of the competitive market for interexchange service. This change in basic telecommunication policy was driven by the desire of interexchange competitors to compete for traffic between the major cities, which are largely served by the RBOCs. Independents are in a somewhat different position than the RBOCs because of the cap on nontraffic sensitive costs inherent in the universal service fund. Independents should be looking at traffic sensitive access charges in light of any imminent or potential bypass threats.

A potentially dramatic disaveraging step is that of disaveraging access cost

Fig. 2-10. Market transfer to networks, products, and services.

within a company on a route by route basis. In access charge and bypass investigations, several state regulators suggested that special rate categories, contracts or flexible price ranges for services should be available to large users, who are in danger of being lost to competitors due to unrealistic average pricing; for example, if the transport segment of exchange access for an independent includes a very dense route between a small city served by an independent and an access tandem in the neighboring BOC, it may become necessary to disaverage transport charges to avoid bypass of the more densely trafficked routes by either AT&T Communications or by a small number of large users, who could group their traffic together and then run it directly on a satellite communication link or via microwave to an interexchange carrier's point of presence (POP)."

The interconnects

As suppliers and providers look at markets, they should remember that Willie Sutton claimed that he "robbed banks only because that's where the money is." Large business users are where the money is in the late '80s market. The large users are generally concentrated within limited geographical areas and the major interconnects are converging on these commercial centers to supply PBXs, Key

Systems, etc. However, the '90s market demonstrated the need for nodal point switches to first provide wideband T1 and T3 networking and then frame relay/ SMDS, as well as eventually ATM broadband switching for privately networking all business users within their community of interest.

In the early '90s, user telecommunication equipment budgets, using the 20/80 rule (20 percent of the market accounts for 80 percent of the dollars), yielded a total market in the 20+ billion dollar range. According to various groupings, 50 percent was for voice equipment, 30 percent for data equipment, and 20 percent for administration equipment. Users were concentrating and switching data through their PBXs so that 15 to 20 percent of their lines were handling data.

Both local area networks (LANs) and PBXs provided data-handling solutions using existing coaxial cable and twisted pairs. LANs were a favorite solution for computer-to-computer communications, while PBXs handled dial-up applications. Successful interconnection in today's market is in selling network planning capabilities, not just hardware, and in establishing strategic links with major PBX manufacturers, as well as understanding the demographics of the marketplace. For example, interconnects have noted the following:

"Twelve states ranging from New York to California are the mother lode of the interconnect. New York, Pennsylvania, Illinois, Texas and California count for 40 percent of the business phones in the continental United States, including the northeast corridor and the midwest hub . . . The five-state midwest area, for example, has more phones than any country except Japan and it has more computers than any other region by having 19 percent of the total U.S. . . . If California where an independent nation, its economy would rank 8th in the world, just behind Italy and ahead of Canada, where one in ten households in California already has a home computer . . . In Colorado 16 percent of the business customers account for 87 percent of the business long distance revenues and just 3 percent of the business customers bring in 47 percent of the total revenue."

Hence, as interconnects go about doing their business, they're developing a new world of satellite private networks hanging here and there onto the public information network. (See FIG. 2-11.)

AT&T

The '80s was a time of transition for AT&T. New strategies consolidated sales forces of AT&T Communications and AT&T Information Systems into a single customer-selling unit, which was subdivided into basically four business groups.

Their charter was to integrate operations into a "one-stop shopping" sales force for computers, PBXs, local area networks, enhanced services, long-distance telephone services, etc. We've seen, their "Reach Out" for residential usage, joined by "PRO America" for small business, and "Megacom and Software Defined Network" systems packages for large users.

In the late '80s and early '90s, AT&T (per FCC prodding) cut its long-distance rates, causing the classic cost-price squeeze on its competition. Users' access costs went up and AT&T's depreciated costs dropped, while its rates were being cut.

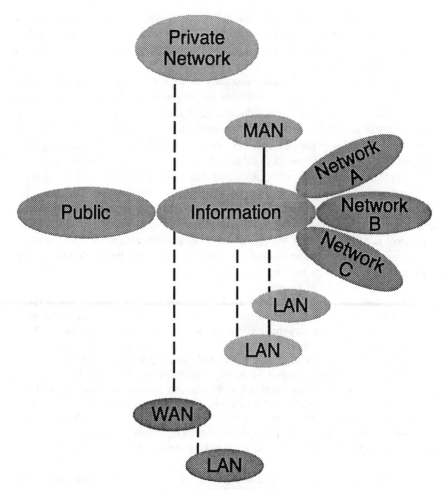

Fig. 2-11. Internetworking.

These price changes and strategies resulted in putting pressure on the traditional WATS service to encourage movement to new families of switched services. These covered the full range in the voice arena, from 0 to 1,000 hours of usage per month, with services such as Ready Line 800, MTS, WATS, Acunet, Teleconferencing, Pro America 1, AT&T 800 Service, Pro America 2, Pro America 3, Software Defined Data networks, along with new services such as Skynet and new releases for products such as Unix System 5 release 3 and System 3.3. These enabled AT&T to be a player in the "systems integrator business," providing new networking capabilities for itself, for value added resellers, and for customers.

However, as AT&T announced more than 200 new products, it was clear that putting new products out didn't necessarily achieve marketplace success in all instances. AT&T did successfully move into the transmission arena to provide SLC Series 5 to improve operating capabilities of SLC 96, Fiber Series G, a one to two gigabit-per-second system for long-distance metropolitan interoffice applications, and ADR, a digital microwave radio system to extend digital connectivity into remote areas where fiber was not yet justified. In addition, AT&T concentrated on data packet switching and various forms and shapes of data communications. It centralized its product development, initially using Olivetti and then NCR, as it continued its push to provide data packet switching in its hierarchy.

After divestiture, AT&T originally estimated the company's computer business to grow to 30 percent and reach 10 billion+ dollars in revenue by the '90s. Positioning moves in the late '80s and early '90s targeted data communications and computer networking, which they called "data networking." Their strategy was to address not only large customers, but mid-size and small business as well. To AT&T, networking meant to construct total data offerings, from terminals to networks, to provide an integrated solution for the customer and to carry that solution to their national and international networks to move the information in the data form to any place. Under the "data networking" charter was the need to integrate different families of computers with local and long-distance network capabilities, as well as to provide new types of customer-premise data communication equipment and computer-based network controllers involving workstations, PC computers, wide area networks, and other subsystems.

To help achieve their goal of universal services, AT&T fostered their Software Defined Data Network (SDDN) as a service overlay approach to the local ISDN framework. For example, this service will let users of several different data network protocols interface together using virtual private network controllers that can be configured by the customer and billed according to usage.

Other AT&T system strategies include the Dynamic Nonhierarchical Routing System (DNHR), which enables calls to be automatically routed over the best available path. DNHR will replace the hierarchical routing system that AT&T has used for years to route calls through layers of calling regions. This system requires calls to be routed from one specific call configuration to the next, using ISDN. In addition, AT&T has encouraged the integration of voice, data, and video by sharing a digital pipe using new SMDS transport and ATM switching techniques to handle them together. Finally, pricing strategies have been reassessed to encourage customers to use switched facilities rather than leased point to point. This is based on a migration strategy to integrate switching and transmission to provide a more attractive offering to customers and to formulate a network upon which customers can obtain shared switched services. This plan to achieve a migration to the switched AT&T Universal Information Services network will be especially effective as price stagnation occurs among long lines competition. By rapidly deploying a very effective "Integrated Data Networking Switched Service Migration Strategy," AT&T will attempt to retain as well as capture many new information customers.

After structuring and restructuring, as the '90s advance, AT&T appears to have settled in on the following strategies to:

1. Establish a renewed international thrust based on deploying their No. 5 ESS Digital Switching System worldwide with narrowband ISDN data-handling capabilities, followed by overlaid broadband fabric offerings.

2. Expand their digital base by their BNS Service Net 2000 20 Gbps vision of adding broadband transport SMDS frame relay techniques and virtual path/virtual circuit provision service. This will continue up to 80 Gbps and beyond by increasing ATM cross-connect and MUXs capabilities to their existing product line. They're also proceeding with adding access to intelligent network interfaces and service node platforms, as well as providing digital cross-connects to service T1, etc., transport networking.
3. Enter the computer arena with the purchase of NCR in a continuation of their ongoing data-handling effort to achieve C&C product line integration with new families of CPE equipment for retail point of sale, medical imagery/health care applications, etc.
4. Design new products. International Japanese and European ventures are driving the broadband activities, while the United States thrust uses the narrowband/wideband entities such as initial 64K picturephone. In time, as new broadband switching fabrics are developed, they'll be added to enhance and evolve existing product lines. In the interim, SMDS/Datakit type offerings will handle bursty LAN interconnect, file sharing, medical imagery, compressed video, CAD/CAM, and multimedia traffic.
5. Evolve the following products for the 5ESS-2000 base to BNS-2000, BNS-2000 20G, and BNS-2000 80G. These will include IDN, ISDN, ATM cell switching, frame relay adaptions, X.25-X.75 networking, SMDS terminal adaptors, DS3 trunk interfacing, VP/VC provisioning, ATM switching units (ASU-2000), ATM service management platforms (ASMP-2000), ATM remote units (ARO-2000), DACS III-2000/DACS IV-2000 digital access and cross-connect systems, SLC™-2000 access system subscriber loop carrier, DDM-2000 multiplexors, and FT-2000 lightwave systems.

Europe

The Europeans have established several organizations to work with OSI and CCITT to achieve international European standards for common network interfaces. These organizations include The European Commission (EC). It has the charter to help establish cooperation for European standards for new networks and services by supporting the CEPT Conform of European Postal and Telecommunication Administration, which is instrumental in ensuring telecommunications interconnections at the international level. Similarly, the ETCO-European Telecommunications Consulting Organization involves many PTTs in their attempt to achieve a transnational broadband backbone network. The European Commission will hopefully be able to ensure that this network can be used as a future switched wideband network across Europe.

The European data processing market is expected by the late '90s to be valued at $50+ billion. Europe has established several research telecommunications corporations such as RACE-Research and Development in Advance Communications and ESPRIT-European Strategic Program Research in Information Technology, where RACE is designed to integrate services that are currently provided by separate networks. It will not integrate providers, but it will combine technical links in networks for PTTs, cable broadcasters and TV, etc. Hence, several vehicles are now in place to encourage and foster the European players' cooperation to achieve international networks that can easily interface with national networks across Europe.

France

When we in the telecommunications industry think of France, we think of their earlier leadership role in digital switching, their Transpac Network, their Minitel Videotex System, and their buy out of ITT. Briefly reviewing their achievements, we see how they moved from Teletext, a one-way system to display text and graphics on existing TVs, to a more interactive system called videotex, which other European Countries (such as the British with PRESTEL) were exploring. The American Videotex Industry Association has defined Videotex as a generic term meaning "Interactive Electronics Services that are easy to use." The "Gallic" version of videotex was named TELETEL, derived from the Teletext technique called ANTOPE in France. The French, along with the Macintosh designers in America, realized that the ergonomic design of the terminal and dialogue with its user should be accomplished in the friendliest manner possible. This lead to their Minitel terminal.

In the beginning of the '80s, many European countries began a videotex operation or trial. The German post office had two videotex test centers one in Dusseldorf, the other in Berlin; the Dutch had their videotel and Spain their Ibertex. The French experimented with a central databased-type system at Velizy. Much was learned from these trials in terms of the similar habits and desires of all types of people across Europe. They found it economically unsatisfactory to simply try to compete with basic TV usage. Their studies clearly demonstrated the need for providing interactive access to multiple (not singularly controlled) databases, but it also showed the need to foster and encourage user acceptance to such things as home banking, etc.

The French made four aggressive decisions to establish their leadership role. The first was to achieve a solid backbone structural packet network called TRANSPAC and then overlay videotex on it, through videotex access points (VAPs). The second key strategy was to provide Minitel terminals to telco customers at a reasonable, long-term payback rate through a usage strategy that enabled users to access an electronic directory service and numerous other independent service providers. The third essential strategy was to use a billing system in which users pay the Postal Telephone and Telegraph (PTT) for both the communication cost and the service, but only when used, with low up-front costs for new service providers (SPs). The final strategy being implemented in the '92 – '93 time frame is "global information networking" with gateways established in each major country. These four strategies were based on the belief that users don't want to pay for a high-priced terminal because they really don't initially know how much use or good will come from it. This has been proven time and time again with the camera, CVR, computer, fax, and cellular industries. The users' recognition of their own needs is as essential as the suppliers and providers understanding of the users' needs.

What should be learned from the French, with their 5–10 million or so user-friendly terminals in operation in the later portion of the '90s, is that their key to success is their willingness to structure a ubiquitous, robust network (first locally, then globally), provide inexpensive versatile terminals, and attract service providers without an immediate, high, short-term profit. They realized that users will be attracted to the data network only by reducing their risk to zero in order for them to really begin using and accepting this new form of media; for there's much resistance to change, especially to a substantial change in life-style. (See "The human element" in chapter 8.) Hence, pricing strategies (as always) became an integral cornerstone to the deployment of other strategies.

This belief extended into service provisionary pricing strategies as well. Network access costs were, figuratively, a 10-cent-per-minute or $5-per-hour user fee translated into a 7-cent-per-minute or $4-per-hour service provider revenue, with terminals priced at a $150, or $10 per month rental and, in some cases, free two-year trial usage. Again, the secret was to make only a little bit of money on each transaction in order to encourage growth in transactions. Henry Ford was once asked if he wanted to make a lot of money from selling a few cars to a few wealthy people. "No," he replied, "I wish to make a lot of money from a lot of people by only making a little money from each one individually — so all can afford to own one of my cars."

Germany

Germany, with more than 30 million (western side) telephones, has a network strategy extending through the 1990s and beyond. In their telephone network, the existing analog system is rapidly being digitalized. ISDN rollout began in the '80s and continues in the early '90s. Broadband ISDN (B-ISDN) is also appearing, establishing their Integrated Broadband Fiber Network (IBFN). In parallel with the telephone network is their IDN, Integrated Data Network (different from the Integrated Digital Network — IDN). The Integrated Data Network is an overlay that provides a variety of circuit and packet services, as well as a fiber-optic network overlay for video conferencing. Even though the fiber-based broadband ISDN was not scheduled to begin until the mid '90s, fiber was installed in new homes prior to that date.

"Because of the high density of Germany's population and the comparative equal distribution of demand for communication services, both the local networks and trunk networks are so finely interlaced that the network has in fact the characteristics of a natural monopoly. Therefore, German's plan is to integrate all narrow and broadband communication services into just one ISDN network. This coupled with their tariff system to lease connections will make it increasingly difficult to resell fixed connections, thus initially ruling out competition in their basic transport arena."

However, as noted, the Wiite commission favored an overlay, competitive value added network in which the Bunderpost's existing exclusive right to provide the first telephone instrument would also disappear. As the Germans develop their wideband network strategies, they're recognizing the need for understanding cost incentives for moving different rates of information on different types of networks where costs differ, depending on the type of network selected for the amount of information moved, such as: 1 megabit to 100 megabits per day at different ISDN rates of multiples of 64k versus using 2400 bit-per-second modems. The challenge for the '90s is to continue the progress in western Germany while completely rebuilding eastern Germany's communication network, as they use both the new N-ISDN and B-ISDN product lines of Siemens and other suppliers . . .

England

England has long been involved in user service research with trials such as their Prestel videotex offering. Similarly, they've played a prominent role in CCITT standard working groups. Their Public Switched Telephone Network (PSTN) has been used for IT (information telecommunications) applications since it became widely available, providing V series interfaces to a variety of terminal equipment. Pre-ISDN configurations for customer access initially consisted of a 64-kilobit channel, an 8-kilobit-per-second channel, and an 8-kilobit signaling channel, which can be used for digitalized speech, visual communications, or data. Hence, England has entered the integrated services phase of network offerings. Next, the access system was enhanced to provide several 64-kilobit channels plus a 16-kilobit signaling channel. The term *integrated digital access* (IDA) is used in the United Kingdom to describe digital local access to the customer, whereas ISDN describes the whole networking, including trunk circuits. A 2-megabit interface called *Multiline IDA* is offered to large customers, but only in the metro communities. The key to British success appears to be their in-depth understanding of the services market, as noted by these excerpts from observations once made by Mr. Clark, Deputy Director Research British Telecom:

"In England, Cable TV Systems, otherwise known as wideband cable systems, have received considerable publicity in recent years. They come in two varieties; the tree and branch and the switched star. The latter offers fully switched service channels up to 2 megabits for residential or business premise. These types are considered good candidates for the local communication network of the future, since they're most suitable to exploit optical fibers. Services today must be considered in terms of the most effective and efficient network that can economically deliver them. For example, Switched Star Systems are not the least expensive media for distributing TV, so that switched wideband penetration is likely to take somewhat longer than initially anticipated. In taking a look at new services in England, we see that many video types have opened up, such as: Slow Scan TV, which transmits frames that change every five seconds from one location to another.

These can be used for security tracking and surveillance as well as distance teaching, collaborator research and medical research. Although the provisions of high-quality moving TV requires very high data rates, there have been new developments which offer commercially useful moving pictures within the 64 kilobit per second single ISDN channel. However, they're limited by the inability to cope with sudden movements affecting large parts of the picture, that can occur in a teleconference or view phone meeting. They do transmit the 'talking head' satisfactorily, unless the speaker suddenly enters or leaves the field of vision, causing the picture to break up.

In the late '80s there were between 300 to 400 private videotex systems operating in the United Kingdom. Today, there are many applications where very rapid access to videotex's frames and enhancement of high-quality pictures or images would be valuable. These include state departments, travel agencies, picture libraries, advertising, personal identification, police and other security applications and signature verification. These facilities can be readily provided in ISDN. An additional bonus for the use of ISDN video techniques would be the very low data entry cost for information providers. A foreseen advantage of 64 kilobit transmission is that pages of text are displayed in a fraction of a second, so when a customer is searching, data pages can be changed very quickly. This is similar to flicking the pages of a book; it greatly speeds access to textual information, particularly when they're arranged in alphabetical order.

Conventional computing wisdom on the need for keyboard access may need reexamination once the communication bottleneck is removed. Telewriting will be one of the substitutes with the customer using an electronic pen on a digitalized pad and the line form is reproduced both locally and at a distance. Many applications include distance teaching and signature verification.

In the '90s, there will be a new growth of personal computer business use in the home by 'home based knowledge workers.' Hence, rapid error free transmission of data packet programs will be essential to move such items as Telesoftware in the sale and distribution of software to personal computers at home, business, and retail outlets. As these better communication, error free systems are developed, it's interesting to note that, at 64 kilobit transmission, the quality of speech is much better. This may itself be saleable to those requiring a premium quality business service. Similarly, 64 kilobit (7 kHz) stereo music opens up possibilities for high-quality sound listening services comparable to the pay per view concept, which was much discussed in the context of cable TV. There's already in England a lively market for popular record music, using dial-up public voice network, and there may be a much larger market for a high-quality product. The ability to transmit high-quality digitalized speech also benefits centralized speech recognition, paving the way for a variety of voice-based information services.

There will be other new user applications, such as Closed User Groups (CUGs), which limit intercommunication and data access to certain categories of customers. This could be important to security surveillance and intracompany applications. Similarly, the American family of CLASS services based upon calling line identification have high interest in England to facilitate the identification in billing customers and identifying independent VANs to handle specific customers. The alternative in the absence of calling line identification is to go through the time-consuming, expensive process of registering each individual terminal with each VAN that it might wish to use. Calling/Call Line identification is also likely to be part of the security response against the growing threat of computer freaks and hackers.

Finally, services such as opinion polls and home environmental system controls can be handled by the voice systems today, but they'll eventually require the higher data rate systems currently visualized for England."

England has experienced more and more competition from their cable networks as U.S. RBOCs such as U S WEST established a presence. Similarly, British Telecom (BT) is expanding its influence as it establishes global networking data-handling gateways throughout the world.

Japan

Japan's Information Network System (INS) will be available in the early '90s, as Japan moves forward into the Information Age. The INS network combines a 64-kilobit signaling channel with a 45-megahertz broadband channel. The challenge is to ensure that INS conforms to CCITT standards. NEC is leading the way with new product concepts and offerings based on their integrated C&C computer and communications network vision. Japan has made a formal decision to deploy N-ISDN throughout Japan. In so doing, their ISDN market blossomed overnight from 10,000 to 200,000 lines in 1992. NTT is leading the way as they pursue their vision of VI&P . . .

VI&P

Hiroyuki Kasai and Jun Yamagata (in the *NTT Review*) described the comprehensive experiments related to VI&P (Visual, Intelligent and Personal Services), NTT's service vision for the twenty-first century. These experiments are currently underway at the company's Musashino and Yokosuka R&D centers. The two centers, about 100 kilometers apart, are connected with a fiber-optic transmission system (2.4 Gbps) and satellite communication links to build the experimental network. The purpose of the experiments is to verify and evaluate VI&P services as well as the structure and performance of networks that will form the infrastructure for VI&P prior to their provision to customers.

In March, 1990, NTT announced "VI&P service vision," NTT's vision for telecommunications services as they might be in the early twenty-first century. With the view of realizing VI&P, NTT laboratories are doing research and development ranging from revolutionary technologies such as ATM, IN (intelligent network), fiber-optic subscriber system, personal communication system, AI (artificial intelligence), automatic audio/video recognition, and various new telecommunication services that take full advantage of those new technologies.

Based on the results of recent successful experiments of basic ATM technologies and fiber-optic subscriber systems, the laboratories are now busy developing commercial versions of the systems with the view of commencing B-ISDN (Broadband ISDN) construction in Japan in 1995. Concepts of B-ISDN based on ATM and optic fiber systems such as FTTH (fiber to the home) have been launched in various countries as the next-generation network. Intending to start broadband network services around 1995, various organizations in Europe and North America are planning to perform trial operation of B-ISDN services such as high-speed data transmission and video information transmission.

VI&P service vision

As stated earlier, VI&P stands for visual, intelligent, and personal. The service vision was conceived taking into account society's demands and the predicted technological trends in the twenty-first century. The services will be "visual" because they'll use various types of video terminals for user interfaces. They'll be "intelligent" because they'll allow people to communicate with anyone in any media wherever they are, and customers will be able people to customize the services. Also, the services will be "personal" because they'll allow people to make phone calls from handy terminals using personal ID numbers assigned to each individual. These personal ID numbers replace telephone numbers.

The VI&P services are divided in two categories: basic and advanced. The former consists of "telephone," "text mail," and "visual telephone." The latter consists of versatile advanced services such as teleshopping, HDTV conference, and translation telephone, which take full advantages of high-speed, broadband, intelligent ISDN.

In order to assure the spread of already-operating N-ISDN services, the introduction of B-ISDN in 1995 and the realization of VI&P service vision in the early twenty-first century, comprehensive experiments related to VI&P were performed during 1991–1994. The purpose of the experiments was to verify and evaluate various VI&P services as well as the structure and performance of networks that will form the infrastructure for VI&P.

NTT carried out a similar experiment for N-ISDN, called "INS model system," in the Mitaka area of Tokyo from 1984 to 1987. In the model system, most of the INS services could be provided using the existing well-proven network facilities such as copper cables and digital switching systems. Therefore, the new services could be offered to customers with minimal risk, and the evaluation was mainly done efficiently by the customers.

On the other hand, B-ISDN services can be offered on the network, based on still-developing technologies. Therefore, in the VI&P experiments, the importance was placed on the evaluation within the laboratories, where the feedback to R&D activities can be easily made before the services are offered to customers.

The experiments were divided into two phases. Phase I was to verify ATM-based corporate network systems, fiber-optic subscriber systems, and narrow bandwidth (64 Kbps) services. Phase II generally aimed at evaluating broadband (156 Mbps) ISDN features. Typical experiment items for each phase are briefly explained in the following.

Phase I (1991–1992)

- Infrastructure-related items:
    a. Transmission system and local area network (LAN) both based on ATM technology, which is capable of handling broadband and narrowband

information, and thus is expected to play an important role in the twenty-first century communication network.

  b. Fiber-optic subscriber systems, which enable the simultaneous transmission of voice and visual information.
- Service-related items:
  a. Intelligent mail, which enables a customer to receive mail in any preferred media, e.g., text, fax, or voice.
  c. Image processing TELE-EYE, which enables the reception of video image from a dialed, distant camera through N-ISDN. The video information can be processed for further applications such as automatic recognition of movement of objects in the image.

Phase II (1993–1994)

- Infrastructure-related items:
  a. ATM node system, which is one of the key technologies for the construction of B-ISDN.
  b. Intelligent network system (IN), which brings about more flexibility and convenience to the telephone services.
  c. Personal radio interface system, which provides the radio access links for personal communications.
- Service-related Items:
  a. Visual telephone, which is listed as a main and basic VI&P service, enables face-to-face communications with image quality equivalent to that of today's television.
  b. HDTV TELE-EYE, which enables the reception of HDTV images from dialed, distant cameras.
  c. Personal multimedia workstation, which enables a customer to have a multimedia and multipoint teleconference through the desktop workstation while using the workstation for other purposes.
  d. Personal communications, which, employing personal ID numbers, enables call termination to individuals wherever they are and limited call termination from callers selected beforehand by the receiver.

Hence, we see the various players during the formation phase wandering around here and there, trying this or that as they attempt to establish direction and leadership roles in their quest to obtain successful goods for the information marketplace.

Technology phases

Many of the following key observations have been thoughtfully provided by network providers and equipment suppliers' technical and marketing planners, developers, and implementers.

R&D

Vice President Allen Chynoweth of Bell Communication Research wisely observed that "perhaps every major technological breakthrough carries with it the seeds of destruction of the environment that made it possible." This is an appropriate comment made at a point when the industry is most malleable, when the new regime of competition has not developed its own rigid organizational and intellectual patterns that can only be changed with considerable effort. As pressures grow to foster quick innovation of numerous new offerings, as suppliers compete to anticipate the market's next direction, research and development work will increasingly be undertaken to learn what the market requires and not just necessarily where the technology could go. However, severe competition will reduce the financial incentives necessary for long-term, fundamental R&D work. It might well ensure that there will be a lively marketplace but threaten to strangle creativity in the laboratory.

Technology

However, fortunately, we still have a few bastions of advanced research where leaders explore and assess the future potential of new technologies. They're projecting astonishing possibilities for continued increases in future capabilities in microelectronics, photonics, and software. These engines of the last twenty-five years of the twentieth century have shown spectacular growth, as Ian Ross, President Emeritus of Bell Labs once noted in the mid '80s and in his 1992 parting assessment of future technology. Here are just a few excerpts of his earlier vision and assessments:

"Over the last twenty years, we've doubled the density of components on a chip of silicon — every year during the first decade and about every eighteen months for the last decade. This is a very, very startling progress curve. In the mid '80s, we were already at nearly one million components on a chip of silicon. Although it's getting more and more challenging, I don't see any reasons why we shouldn't continue doubling the density approximately every eighteen months for ten to twenty more years; so we have another factor of 100 to 1,000 to go. That says we are about halfway there, about twenty years worth; that is the driving factor in our technology. Anything that is doubling every eighteen months is hard for anything else to keep up with . . .

In terms of photonics, the reason that photonics is so interesting is that it is a very nimble particle. Which means that you can turn things on and off quickly, and that is suitable to broadband information transfer, namely transmission. If you look at its measure of effectiveness — the simplest being bit rate times repeater spacing — this is doubling every year. And if you look at where its fundamental limits are, they are way off. So we see light transmission moving rapidly with lots of headroom . . . That is to say that this is the technology of choice. It is technology that will dominate the bulk of new transmission applications in the future . . .

There will be a place for satellites and a place for microwave radio, but the real drive is photonics. You can contemplate, and we are working on, integrated photonic systems that can perform complete functions with light, without the need to transfer back to electronics, but a word of caution — in order to make a photonic device, it has to be at least the size of a wavelength of light, and it has to be several wavelengths of light. A silicon integrated circuit today has a minimum line width that is comparable to the wavelength of light; it is going to be below that. When you go to a hundred million components on a chip, you are talking about a minimum line width of one-tenth of a wavelength of light. So silicon technology is going to be inherently smaller than light wave technology . . .

Secondly, one of the characteristics of the photon is that it is hard to interact with it; you don't get electrical interference; you don't get cross-talk because the photon doesn't have a charge on it. This is very nice. However, it also makes it hard to move. Therefore, interacting with the photon (input/output) takes more energy than does the electron. So fundamentally it takes more power to drive the photonic devices. Now you have devices that are inherently bigger and inherently more power consuming. These are not good characteristics for logic. So photonics will drive transmission and may have a major impact on switching. However, I question whether it will be the engine for logic and processing. This doesn't mean you do not work at it, but in the mid '80s, it looked like the two would complement one another. You have this perfect duo—with performance improving by a factor of two every twelve to eighteen months, one of which is good for logic and the other which is good for moving information from one place to another. My guess is we will end up with hybrid systems, which time has yet to see . . .

The third technology of the trio is software. Microelectronic systems are expensive to develop. To implement new CMOS (complementary metal oxide semiconductor) technology, it costs several $100 million in capital; it is an expensive, complex business. You need to make maximum use of it. That's why the trend is towards using standard hardware and customizing it in software. That is what is going on across the Bell laboratories. Whether it's switching, transmission, or computers, we use microelectronics hardware and customize it in software. Software itself is moving quite rapidly. Clearly, its progress is related to that of memory: the cheaper the memory, the more software you can have in it.

The software programs are becoming bigger. At the same time, through improved algorithms, a piece of software is much more effective than a few years ago. As a result of this combination, the capability of software, and the number of "somethings," you can calculate per-second is going up astronomically. There are other important activities, such as speech processing, that are very necessary if you're going to live with the complex machines that we're contemplating. It too feeds off the increased processing power; it feeds off improved algorithms and feeds off basic research on the fundamental properties of speech. In terms of material, the main contenders, of course, are the three/five compounds, the leader being gallium arsenide, a very attractive material. It has a higher energy gap so you can operate it at high temperatures. In gallium arsenide, electrons are more mobile than they are in silicon, so that the devices made with it are faster and use lower power. It also gives off light in a very useful range, which is good for photonics.

The negative side is that it is a two-element material rather than one. Also, when you're trying to put ten million of something on a chip, it is easier to do it with an element, than it is with a compound. What we are comparing is the simplicity of silicon moving 'very quickly' compared to the elegance of the more complex material, gallium arsenide. Today, gallium arsenide does those things that silicon cannot do—such as light generators for light wave systems. The industry today is building gallium arsenide integrated circuits to take advantage of light emission and intelligence on the same chip and to take advantage of the high speed and low power for very special applications. We were seeing the number of components on a chip of gallium arsenide increase rapidly, but (throughout the '80s) it was still behind silicon.

In looking at structures of new networks in terms of the relationship between switching and transmission using broadband capabilities, and messages being broadcast over networks rather than switched, we can see that as far as switching capabilities are concerned, customers will want more and more special features. This says you need machines with stored program control with more memory and more processing capabilities. Depending upon regulation, I think you will see intelligence distributed from end to end in the network. I don't believe it is going to remove the need for switching machines. What you might see is a simplification of the hierarchy. It is tending in effect to become a two-level hierarchy, but you must add processor or controlled PBXs, key systems, and even smart telephones; so maybe it is two of the traditional levels plus three new ones . . .

Therefore, when we are talking about ultimate limits, we are considering production devices whose structures might be smaller than 10^{-1} microns. We are visualizing working devices that would be 10^{-1} microns on a side with switching speeds of 10^{-12} seconds. That is 1,000 times smaller and faster than 1985 production devices. For example, we saw the realization of the cleaved-coupled-cavity (C^3) laser. This is an electronically tunable laser that gives off ultrapure light in the region in which fibers have maximum transparency. It can produce over a billion ($10^9>$) pulses of light per second and still operate as a single-frequency laser.

Experimentally, we had already in the mid '80s used the laser to send unboosted signals at a rate of 420 million times per second over a distance of 119 kilometers, error free. That's equivalent to transmitting the entire text of a 30-volume encyclopedia in one second . . ."

Now, in the '90s, we're entering the world of gigabit information movement and management (IM&M). In his parting comments to congressional and international forums, Ross noted, "the need to further use and challenge the advancement of microelectronics, photonics, and software." However, first let's review how we got here . . .

Computer processor power evolution/revolution

Joe Coursolle provides an interesting review of computer growth as distilled from numerous PC magazine articles, noting that in the future, we may indeed simply raise our voices a bit like Scotty in *Star Trek IV*, saying "com-pu-ter" when we want something done. (See TABLE 2-3.)

Data services/data communications

Over the years, a variety of methods have developed for "communicating" data information. Transmitting data over a transmission medium to a distant receiver is achieving "data communications." The data is generally encoded in the binary form of "ones" and "zeros," usually represented by the presence or absence (on-off) of a signal or voltage condition. The data terminal equipment (DTE) is the terminal, printer, or computer that transmits or receives the information, while the data

Table 2–3. Comparison of Intel Processors

Intel proc	Intro date	Base speed	# of transistors	Int'l bits	Ext'l bits	MIPS	Notes
8080	04/74	2 MHz	6,000	8	8	0.64	
8086	06/78	5 MHz	29,000	16	16	0.33	
8088	06/79	5 MHz	29,000	16	8	0.33	Note 1
80286	02/82	8 MHz	134,000	16	8/16	1.20	Note 2
80386DX	10/85	16 MHz	275,000	32	16/32	6.00	
80386SX	06/88	16 MHz	275,000	32	16	2.50	Note 3
486DX	04/89	25 MHz	1,200,000	32	16/32	20.00	
486SX	04/91	20 MHz	1,185,000	32	16	16.50	Note 3
486DX2	03/92	50 MHz	1,200,000	32	16/32	20.00	
Pentium	05/93	66 MHz	3,100,000	64	32	112.00	
P6	1994	100 MHz	10,000,000	?	64	?	
P7	1995	? MHz	?	?	?	?	

NOTES

The base speeds are those at which the chips were originally designed to run. Higher speeds were introduced later, resulting in better performance, higher operating temperatures, and reduced chip life.

# of transistors is the number of equivalent transistors required to duplicate the processor chip at a macro level. Int'l bits is the width of the CPU internal bus. Ext'l bits is the width of the external bus connection for expansion cards. Common buses used:

> 8 bit = PC bus
> 16 bit = PC/AT or ISA bus
> 32 bit = EISA or MCA bus
> 64 bit = not yet existent

MIPS means millions of instructions per second. This is a good benchmark for comparing processors. It ignores bus architectures, pipelines, and clock speed, and represents how many instructions a processor can execute regardless of how it does it.

Note 1: 8088 was used in the original IBM PC, and the Sperry HT.

Note 2: 80286 was used in the IBM PC/AT, and the Sperry IT.

Note 3: The 80386SX and the 486SX had their floating point numeric processors disabled. In the 80386, these were chips where the main processor was okay but the co-processor was defective, and they were sold at a lower price. This turned to be so popular that the 486SX was designed without a numeric processor.

communications equipment (DCE) multiplexes, *mo*dulates or *de*modulates (modem), or concentrates the information over the medium. Information is transmitted from point to point or multipoint (where several DTE's share the same medium). There are several protocols by which terminals talk to each other to ensure that they exchange the information, as well as several interface standards, such as RS-232-C, by which physical and logical connections are achieved. Information can be sent over two-wire or four-wire systems in the *simplex* (data flows in one direction), *half duplex* (both directions over the same path), or *full duplex* (separate each way over four wires or split channels) forms.

In considering previous data-handling methods for transporting bits and bytes, here are some interesting tidbits . . . Large *central processing units* (CPUs), sometimes called *mainframes* or *host computers*, have become more and more useful as their DTES have become more interactive or conversational. Usually, these terminals send information over low-speed modems in the asynchronous mode, using frequency shift keying techniques that send individual characters with a header and a tail. Some terminals are polled for information; others (such as smart terminals having limited processing capabilities, or intelligent terminals that process programs) send information in high-speed blocks synchronously to and from the mainframe. Personal computers have now proliferated, where they buffer (store) their results locally and interexchange results, processed data, or programs. PCs have become stand-alones or nice front-end processors for supercomputers. Thus, the more these devices (DTEs, CPEs, and PCs) are networked together, the more efficient and effective they are in providing solutions for today's distributed applications.

These distributed networks send information in analog form at 300, 1200, 2400, 4800, 9600, 14,400 and 19,200 bit rates. In earlier terminology, bit rates and baud rates were both referenced. Since they're the same at 300 bps (300 baud), the terms are interchangeable. However, baud rate cannot exceed the bandwidth of the line—for example, 2400 for the phone line, where, through coding techniques, more and more bits can be sent when, for instance, 9600 bps phase shift modulators are operating at 2400 baud (4 bits per baud). Hence, it has become less confusing to simply state bit rates. Similarly, coding standards have progressed from Baudot operating at a 5-level code; capable of generating 58 different characters, to ASCII, a 7-bit code, to EBCDIC (extended binary coded decimal interexchange code), an 8-bit code developed by IBM, capable of 256 characters. This latter code sets the stage for the 8-bit byte, where multiples of it achieve the 8-, 16- and 32-bit computer instruction or database data-bank memory.

For error correction and detection techniques, bits and bytes were added respectively in order to form vertical or horizontal parity, enabling errors to be detected using cyclic redundancy checks (CPC), where vertical parity checks the character and the horizontal parity checks the block in terms of even or odd counts. As errors are checked and detected, the protocol of ACKs (acknowledgements) or NAKs (negative acknowledgements) ensure retransmission until the proper delivery is achieved.

In the early analog frequency baud transmission world, narrowband was subvoice, or less than 300 Hertz (Hz), voice-grade baud was 300–3000 Hz, while wideband or broadband required bandwidth considerably more than 2500 Hz, enabling rates up to 64,000 bps or better. Local area networks were established using metallic leased lines or private coaxial cables. Here, baseband facilities carried information to a distance of a mile or two, while broadband could accommodate many channels for greater distances of approximately 10 miles or so.

Analog modulation techniques used by modems included frequency modulation, noted earlier as frequency shift key modulation (FSK), where the frequency is varied while the height or amplitude of the waves is kept constant. While FSK is limited to low speed, as it sends only one bit per baud, amplitude modulation is similarly limited, as it varies the height or amplitude at rates between 300 and 2400 bps. Phase modulation uses phase shifts of 180 degrees and can transmit up to 3 bits per baud. Quadrature amplitude modulation (QAM) combines both amplitude changes and phase shifts to achieve 4800 and 9600 bps. Phase quadrature modulation (PQM) can achieve four or more bits/baud to obtain 9600 or higher. Multiplexing techniques mix and match the various sources to achieve simultaneous transmission; here, frequency division multiplexing, statistical multiplexing, and time division multiplexing move from frequency mixing to bit and byte interleaving in time, to dynamically interleaving transmissions that contain only the information that's present without idle periods. This, along with various compression techniques, leads to pulse code modulation (PCM) and time space time (TST) switching, as conversations are sampled, quantized, and changed to digital bit streams, thus paving the way for the digital revolution and the end of the analog era.

Hence, over time, digital capability has come to replace analog in the interoffice circuits, long-distance switch centers, and now local offices. With ISDN, digital is extended to the customer premises, replacing the need for analog modems and changing the scope and range of narrowband, wideband, and broadband to what it is today . . . Hence, the technology is changing, the applications are changing, and the services, especially the data services, are changing and expanding as the world becomes more and more digital . . .

Digital services/digital communications

With the separation of voice services from data services during the '60s and '70s, the voice network progressed to achieve a fully automated, publicly switched offering with global addresses, while data proceeded to become privately multiplexed within local area networks with local addressing, wide area bridging, metropolitan area routing, and long-distance interfacing over leased lines or satellite/ microwave facilities. As time passed and LANs began to proliferate, it became essential to reconsider more integrated services and facilities in order to achieve simultaneous voice and data offerings.

In the late '70s, it became economical to digitize voice into bit streams, where 8,000 samples of the voice conversation were translated into representative 8-bit codes and multiplexed with samples of other conversations over shared facilities. In this manner, a single voice conversation requires $8 \times 8,000$, or 64,000 bits per second of transport facility. Twenty-four conversations are then interlaced (with appropriate network synchronization information) into a 1.544 million bits per second T1 digital communication facility. These T1s can then be multiplexed together to form T2s at 6.3 million bits per second, or T3s at 45 million bits per second. In this manner, networks were developed during the '80s to transport voice in the form of bits of ones and zeros. Transmission error rates were decreased from earlier analog achievements, as one error in 10^7 became the norm, while many digital facilities achieved one error in 10^{11} or better. This greatly improved the quality of voice transport and paved the way for its integration with data, which was also nicely represented by codes of ones and zeros . . .

Beginning in the late '70s and throughout the '80s, the International Telegraph and Telephone Consulate Committee (CCITT) took up the digital services challenge. CCITT is a worldwide group of national Public Telephone and Telegraph companies (PTTs) and private telecommunication companies. CCITT helps set norms for input for the International Organization for Standardization (ISO) (Geneva), a worldwide association of the national standards-setting groups with primary responsibility to create Open Systems Interconnection (OSI) standards. Their task was to add the services to digital communications, which was proceeding nicely as Integrated Digital Networks (IDN) were being established throughout the world. This then became Integrated Services Digital Networks (ISDN), where both voice and data services were made readily accessible to the user. ISDN used several models to accomplish this; one is the User Network Interface Model (UNI), the other is the seven-layer OSI model for denoting the stacking of communications and computer interfaces and protocols.

ISDN

ISDN (Integrated Services Digital Network) is different things to different people; it is standards, architectures, and signaling networks; it is a data network, a video network, and it is new user services and new pricing. As we look at "who is doing what" with ISDN, there have been several pre-ISDN networks, such as Britain's 80-kilobit version. So, the issue becomes, "How will universal ISDN or user ISDN become a reality, especially with so many uninformed users?" By 1992, some ten years after conception, polls still indicate that few, if any, potential users actually understand ISDN's potential data-handling capability. It's been said that "an informed customer makes the best customer." This implies that ISDN suppliers still face a big challenge.

This brings us to the question of: What will ISDN really be as it's bundled and unbundled by the RBOCs? How will it exist in private networks? In islands on the public network? In ubiquitous citywide, regionwide, nationwide offerings? At nodal access points? Spurred by competition, local exchange companies are looking longingly at ISDN as a solution now, or at least in time, to halt the customer exodus to alternative networks. A fundamental assumption is that the business market will be the major revenue source for ISDN, but to succeed, it must be ubiquitous. Data communications is being driven by the penetration of personnel computer (PCs) into the office. Some workstations need communications of the megabit-per-second range via local area networks (LANs), while basic terminals need data switching PBXs. One solution proposed is the integrated LAN-PBX. PCs will access the LAN and the PBX by way of the ISDN primary rate interface. Others recognize the potential of switched narrowband ISDN basic rate data.

According to Dorros (BCR), "ISDN is an evolutionary step to investment in the future, where the U.S. can learn a lesson from the Japanese. Their INS (Information Network Systems) is being promoted as an Information Age service. The man on the street sees function — not how it's achieved. In spite of the fragmentation, regulation, legislation, and antitrust concerns, we must find a structure in which CPE, ISDN transport and databases form a synergy to act in synchronism in the marketplace."

n-ISDN

Narrowband ISDN (n-ISDN) provides a fully digital interface that enables a single voice conversation, in digital form, at 64,000 bits per second. It also provides a data-handling capability at 64,000 bits per second, with another data path at 16,000 bits per second containing signaling/control information and a 9600 bits/sec packet-handling protocol called *X.25*. This basic rate interface (BRI) is defined as 2B + D, where the B channel operates at 64 Kbps and the D at 16 Kbps. In application, both B channels can contain a voice call or a data call. In this manner, a second voice line is available, or data can be handled at the rate of 128 Kbps (2 × 64 Kbps) by reverse multiplexing. In addition, eight terminals can be connected off a terminal adaptor (TA) using a collision detector algorithm and selective terminal address encoding.

In the United States, regulatory rulings don't enable the network provider (such as the regional Bell operating company) to own the network terminating unit on customer premises. As a result, there's a NT2 on customer premises and a NT1 on the network. While NT2 provides a four-wire 192 Kbps interface to the terminals, special encoding enables delivery of 2B + D channels in a two-way path from the NTI to the central office at 160 Kbps. Selective terminal adaptors provide for non–ISDN-to-ISDN interfaces for existing analog terminals based on previous RS-232, etc., type interfaces.

ISDN uses a seven-layer OSI model where the first three layers—physical, data link, and network—pertain to communication needs, and the higher layers (session, presentation, and application) pertain to the computer, with the fourth layer, transport, functioning as the transition layer between the two entities.

Unfortunately, ISDN was initially marketed simply as an interface, without providing access to public data networks across the country. In application, Basic Rate Interface, BRI-ISDN or n-ISDN does provide a B channel circuit switching data network at 64 Kbps, 128 Kbps, or a B channel packet switching data network at 64 Kbps and 128 Kbps, as well as the D channel packet switching network at 9.6 Kbps. Primary Rate Interfaces (PRI-ISDN or P-ISDN) provides a 23B + D interface, where B is 64 Kbps and D is 64 Kbps. These trunk-type interfaces are provided at 1.544 Mbps, which is equivalent to T1 rates. Fractional ISDN provides N number of 64 Kbps channels up to the 1.544 Mbps. Frame Relay ISDN will provide for handling LAN interfaces up to 1.544 bits per second. With proper addressing and networking features, these networks would provide a powerful universal data-handling backbone infrastructure for not only each country, but the entire world . . .

Broadband ISDN

B-ISDN will provide UNI interfaces of 155 million bits per second, as well as 622 Mbps. Its transport will be based on enveloping this information on the SONET/Synchronous Digital Network (SDN) hierarchy, where SONET provides multiples of Optical Carrier (OC) rates beginning at OC-1 (50 Mbps), OC-3 (155 Mbps), and OC-12 (600 Mbps). Broadband ISDN will use Asynchronous Transfer Mode (ATM) switching capabilities, where ATM breaks incoming information into groups of 53 bytes (8-bit cells containing headers), as it handles bursty variable-bit-rate (VBR) information. Continuous-bit-rate (CBR) information might be more efficiently handled by Synchronous Transfer Mode (STM) circuit switching techniques. It's believed that compressed HDTV will be in the form of 155 megabits or less, where videophone will be less than 50 Mbps. Here, homes will be able to have up to four different video channels with the ability to mix and match voice, data, and video to meet customer needs.

As the fiber is deployed more ubiquitously, as more and more frequency wavelengths are handled, the computer-to-desktop, or home-of-the-future usage can do nothing but expand, enabling more and more services that are yet to be visualized in the Information Millennium . . .

Issues and observations

In many cases, 64,000-bit digital data streams are simply moving digitized analog data encoded at the slow speed of 2400 to 9600 bits per second, with corresponding parity checks for short blocks of information transfer requiring slow speed checks and receiving acknowledgements for each block. We need to achieve an orderly transition from the dial-up world of analog modems and multiplexors operating at low speed with slow protocols to the advanced world of high-speed digital, where we actually take advantage of the full range of high-speed transport capabilities.

As digital replaces analog, as the public data network replaces dial-up analog voice grade data networks, we need to establish the deployment time frames for achieving partial and fully available, ubiquitous narrowband data services! For broadband fiber to the office! For fiber to the home! What about standards, standards, standards? We need to determine when national ISDN will be fully available for not only narrowband, but also for wideband and broadband interfaces! . . . For wideband private to public data handling networking! . . . For videophone networking! . . . For fully addressable service offerings! . . . So what about ISDN? . . .

ISDN standards

So, we must begin with standards. The CCITT I-200 series recommendation provides a classification and a method of description of the telecommunication services supported by ISDN. (See the standards arena case study in chapter 7.) They also form the bases for defining the network abilities required by ISDN. ISDN defines telecommunication services in two divided, broad categories: bearer services and tele services. While bearer services involve transport of information throughout the ISDN (OSI layers 2–3), tele services involve both transport and processing (OSI layers 2–7). Where supplementary services modify or supplement a basic service, they're similar to add-on user services of closed user groups (X series) and can't be considered stand-alone services. Stand-alone services include those such as CLASS's selected call waiting and call transfer, as well as "D" channel's alarm monitoring, energy management sensing, and control service functions. This approach was taken by CCITT in order to cope with the different domestic situations in various countries around the world.

However, it will take time to succeed using the new standard interfaces of the

I series of the OSI model. These ISDN standards must be defined and implemented as soon as possible to meet current needs. Delay could lead to just having a proliferation of private networks such as IBM's Netview Network Management software controlling private computer networks, or AT&T's software for virtual private networks, etc. This is especially true as RBOCs turn to LAN interconnect using frame relay and SMDS as their only public data network offering, rather than also establishing a universally deployed public data network based on n-ISDN.

Some strategies for using ISDN have been based on providing vertical network services as a way to lock in large accounts by offering low-level interconnectability at high-level proprietary functionality. Here, ISDN means different things to different people.

It's also interesting to analyze what the 'D' means in ISDN. The D is a means of achieving integration of separate voice and data networks by enabling protocol transparency, flexible bandwidth, and reduced private network interface costs to move information down a facility, like a pipeline that can deliver varying types of information to any point. ISDN will enable call redirection, calling party identification, etc., but it's more than that . . . It's more than an architecture; it's more than a set of standards. It will provide an avenue for new services, changing the world forever. In reviewing the various views on the "rewiring of America," it's often stated that the charter of ISDN is to give its users access to public data communications that are faster, more efficient, reliable, and a lot cheaper than analog alternatives, and at the same time enable providers to make more and more money with the high growth of new services that ISDN will provide.

Walt Disney's World of Tomorrow model contains a vision of the home of the future, which is, as yet, to be achieved. It could be, if based on ISDN. However, without end-to-end ISDN compatibility, many of the future data/video-handling advantages of a public network are lost. While its narrowband ISDN functions can be achieved today, massive investment will take another twenty years or so to actually achieve its potential broadband vision. To do so, existing equipment write-offs are needed at greater depreciation rates; customer needs for the new services must be carefully understood; standards must be established before products can be built; and facilities employing ISDN multiplexing or integrated voice data video services must be aggressively pursued in order for the single wall plug of the future to enable any type of terminal to connect anywhere to any type of terminal.

In reviewing the relationship between the FCC and CCITT, traditionally the FCC had almost no rule in the technical side of CCITT. However, as CCITT moved to politically establish CHILL, a common high-level language for the PTT's switching systems, the FCC, due to its concern for ensuring a competitive arena, moved to technically restrict where and how the traditional carriers had network interfaces and protocol offerings.

The commission stated several principles that it believed were important to consider in the design of ISDN for the United States environment:

1. The ISDN numbering plan must be sufficiently flexible to allow customers

to specify carrier of choice in those countries that choose to implement such an option.

2. ISDN recommendations shouldn't limit the number of satellite hubs allowed on an international connection but should provide for customer choice as a national opinion.

3. Customer provision of the network terminating interface device (NTI) must be a national option so that the United States can view this as competitively supplied customer premise equipment. In order to do this, a U interface is a connection between the customers premise and the network. CCITT recommendations must be sufficiently flexible to accommodate the U.S. basic enhanced dichotomy.

4. The commission further emphasized the need for detailed U.S. planning to proceed in an open manner in which all parties could readily participate where the issues and standards were generally available prior to approval for discussion. It was hoped that this flexibility could be achieved by proposing specific national options and recommendations that do not provide unrealistic burdens on those countries with a monopoly structure.

Thus, the stage has been set for ISDN. Many believe that it will progress through three distinct phases that will overlay on each other as they're implemented domestically and internationally around the world. As one supplier noted, "Where should the first stage of the ISDN concept be positioned: From the standpoint of human social activities regarding the trend in moving toward the information society or particularly from the standpoint of human communication activities or information-handling activities which include the former? In which direction will the second and third stages of the ISDN concept be expanded or fulfilled? Let's start from the place where a trend in the modern human society toward the information society is determined as a steady expansion in the fields of the integrated technology of computers and communicators (C&C).

Similarly, another supplier said that: "Telecommunications networks in different countries have developed different structures in response to particular needs and seeds for potential future growth. However, generally speaking, all these communications networks can be seen to comprise multilayered structures. From the various possible ways of defining the scope of "layer" in multilayered structures, this three-layer model reflects the present structures in advanced countries:

- Public communications network layer.
- Business communications network layer.
- Broadcasting distribution networks."

Another supplier noted that, "ISDN can be introduced in a variety of network situations. There are three natural phases of ISDN evolution; the first phase will be to provide customers with integrated network transport solutions to enable them to reduce their physical transmission requirements and to realize savings in maintenance and operation. The second phase of ISDN will involve providing value added services and features. In this phase, ISDN multifunctional terminals and work stations will maximize the utility of ISDN. The third phase of ISDN will involve providing a wide-based capability to accommodate the customers' growing needs for digital transport, video, and digital services."

As we look at the second wave of the Information Era, the promise of the Information Age, as one visionary once noted, "is to see what can be done to make the world healthier, richer, and wiser." He also observed "the need for a universal transport system that will enable users to mix and match and integrate machine intelligence in almost an unlimited variety of new ways. This will be a shift from previous years, where users centralized computer intelligence on premises and used the networks as a communication pipe to the world, moving information to the processor most equipped to perform the task. This expansion will place heavy reliance on common-user, robust networks, enabling reconfiguration with access to special provisioning and using internationally agreed standards to move billions of packets around. However, the market forces must create incentives for the technological innovation of new services, and government rulings must enable all the competitors to play on a level playing field, enabling the industry to extend its current pace of advancement based on the happy marriage of user needs met by new technology capabilities, leading to a major new era of social and economic progress."

Others have suggested "that how well we do as a nation would depend upon our regulatory policies and business leadership, as well as how wisely society deals with change created by the worldwide competition and rapidly advancing technology . . ."

The ISDN platform

Those and other views are summarized in FIG. 2-12. It depicts the various market segments supported by a platform of networks and service offerings, reminding us that as we enter the world of ISDN, we can't ignore the "S" services nor the "DN" digital networks. However, as we analyze the market in terms of its specific segments and user needs within each segment, we're brought quickly back to "I." The "integrated" aspect of ISDN allows us "I"s to communicate more and more to any place, with any system's service.

Hence, the "future ISDN" must enable "integrated services" as well as "integrated networks." Therefore, the real key for unlocking the door to the information society will be to provide numerous offerings of various degrees of "integrated networks' integrated services" (INIS). However, to achieve these possibilities, we must develop a progressive family of infrastructures that support the platform, enabling it to grow and expand to realize its full potential. These structural pillars must support ISDN as it moves through both its evolutionary and its revolutionary phases, from narrowband and wideband to broadband offerings. Essential to the deployment and development of ISDN is the central, pivotal pillar — the integration of computers and communication (C&C).

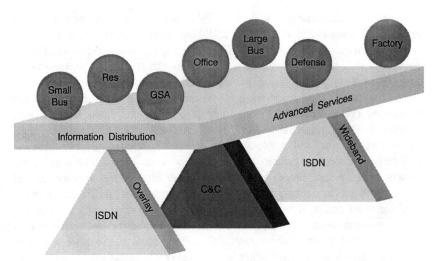

Fig. 2-12. C&C . . . the pivotal point.

Computer layers

Layered interface communications and application service programs is the name of the game for the '90s for the computer manufacturers, as they enter the world of "networking" their systems together and providing targeted software to resolve multiple user system/terminal interconnect needs. *Computer Week* each year now asks its users the following questions:

- Which of the following operating systems/environments do you use?
  Computer Operating Systems: Unix/Xenix, DOS, Windows 3, Windows NT, Apple, OS/2, Presentation Manager, MVS, VMS, VM . . .
  Network Operating Systems: Novell Netware, Microsoft LAN/Manager, Banyan VINES, IBMs LAN Server, DEC Pathworks, 3COM/3+ Open, ARTISOFT LANtastic, Sitka/TOPs . . .
- Which of the following LAN topologies do you currently have in use?
  Ethernet, Ethertalk, Localtalk (Appletalk), 10 Base T, FDDI, 16 Mbps Token Ring, 4 Mbps Token Ring, Arcnet, StarLAN . . .
- Which of the following network protocols do you currently use?
  X.25, Frame Relay, TCP/IP, Novell SPX/IPX, DECnet, APPC/LU6.2, netBIOS, SNA, OSI, DECLAT, Appletalk (Localtalk), ARCnet, GOSIP, NFS . . .
- What products and services do you consider?
  Internetworking Devices: Bridges (Local or Remote), Routers, Gateways, Intelligent Hubs, Bridge-Router . . .
  Local Area Networks: Adapters, LANS, LAN Software (e.g., network operating system), Cabling Products/Connectors, LAN Testing Equipment, Wireless LANs . . .
  Application Software: CASE, Database Management, EDI, E-Mail, Spread-

sheet, Word Processing, Call Accounting, Voice Processing, 4-GL, Groupware . . .

Computer Connectivity: Modems (9.6 Kbps and over), Modems (under 9.6 Kbps), Multiplexers, Micro to Mainframe Links, Communications Software, Front-End Processors, Cluster Controllers, Protocol Converters, Matrix Switches . . .

Servers: File Servers, Print Servers, Terminal Servers, Application Servers, Communication Servers, SuperServers, Database Servers, FAX Servers . . .

Computers: PCs/Microcomputers, Minicomputers, Mainframes, Workstations, Laptops, Terminals, X-Terminals . . .

Peripherals: Storage Devices, Tape Back-up, Optical Back-up, Uninterruptible Power Supplies, Laser Printers, Other Printers, Disk Drives . . .

Network Management/Maintenance: Network Management Systems, Network Management Software, Diagnostic Test Equipment, Network Security Systems . . .

Private Network Products: T-1 Multiplexers, T-3 Multiplexers, Fractional T-1 Multiplexers, Integrated Access Devices, PBXs, Packet Switching Equipment, Microwave, VSAT, CSU/DSU, Fiber Optic . . .

Wide Area Network: Packet Switching, E-Mail, ISDN, On-Line Information Services, Automatic Call Distributors, Video Conferencing/Teleconferencing, Local Service, WATS/MTS, Virtual Networks (SDN, VPN), Dedicated Leased Line, Centrex, Central Office LAN, Satellite, International Service, Network Test Equipment . . .

Public Network Equipment: Central Office Equipment, Transmission Equipment, Cellular and Mobile Equipment, Outside Plant Equipment, Customer Premise Equipment, Monitoring and Test Equipment, Network Management Support Systems, Fiber Optics/Wire and Cable.

- What type of business activity are you in?
  Government/Public Administration/Military; Finance/Banking/Accounting; Manufacturing other than computer/communications; Insurance/Real Estate/Legal; Entertainment/Recreation/Hospitality/Food Services; Construction/Engineering/Architecture; Media/Marketing/Advertising; Wholesaler/Distributor/Retailer; Agriculture/Forestry/Mining/Petroleum/Chemicals; Transportation/Travel; Aerospace; Utilities; Education; Consulting; Resellers of Computers/Communications products (VARs, VADs, distributors); Systems Integrators/Network Integrators; Computer/Data Processing Services; NonProfit; Health/Medical Services/Pharmaceuticals; Manufacturing/Design: communications equipment; Bell Operating or Regional Holding Company; Independent Telephone Company or Independent Holding Company; Other Carriers (including interexchange carriers, Long Distance, Cellular); R&D Labs.

As you can see, the arena is getting bigger and bigger, and the game more and more complex.

Here's a brief look at Apple, IBM, DEC, and the database suppliers' strategies as they enter the new "internetworking-interprocessing-interservices" game.

Apple

Apple's product lines have expanded its network connectivity options. This has been promoted by marketing surveys that showed that 80 percent of the 4 to 5 million PC desktop workstations sold in the United States in 1990 were interconnected. This amounts to a $13+ billion industry. With the new Apple "shared software" approach, Apple indicated that its LAN supported the OSI seven-layer model. Specifically, the network supports the coaxial cable, twisted-wire-pair, and fiber-optic media on the physical layer; data delivery protocols on the network layer; the Apple "Zip" transport protocols for the transport layer; Apple "data streamline" protocol of the session layer; Apple Filling and Postscript protocol on the presentation layer; and application-specific protocols on the application layer. ISDN basic rate chip sets are now available for connecting to the public data network.

DEC

DEC's top management, led by Jack Olson before he retired in 1992, had long ago established a network architecture to tie other computers together. They were a major sponsor of the newer, more powerful wideband Ethernet, having their own version, DECNet. Over the years they've attempted to make their systems a gateway between personal computers, smaller computers, and large mainframes. DEC, as others, intended to be a major player in the LANs and WANs of the future, providing DEC with access to IBM's largest accounts.

IBM

With 1990 income of $100 billion and more than $160 billion by 1994, IBM has now recognized the need for integrating multivendor computers and communications. Many years ago they entered the PBX game in Europe and subsequently formed an IBM-Rolm merger, which some believe was most effective when IBM used the Rolm communication capabilities to resolve the internetworking problem between private networks, rather than just specializing in PBXs/CBXs. Similarly, they later sold their Satellite Business Systems (SBS) to MCI, obtaining 16 percent shares in MCI—thus enabling them, for a period, to become a strategic partner with a major interexchange carrier (IC) for both national and international networks, as well as a partner within Japan on a VAN network with NTT.

Later, these and other relationships were revisited as they expanded their data networking influence around the world from their London base of operations. (See McGee's vision of the future in chapter 1.)

IBM's communication architectures have become structured around SNA/Token Ring/PC networks, designed to enable PCs and small computers to communicate with each other and with large mainframes. IBM provides modems, multiplexers, protocol convertors, cluster controllers, and front-end processors to link together their 3270 terminals, systems 36 and 38, 370s, etc.

We've seen Logical Unit 6.2 for peer-to-peer communications among computers implemented on IBM mainframes. Similarly, midrange systems are now able to have their own SNA network on their own, without mainframe control. This has been achieved by (APPN) advanced peer-to-peer networking and distributed data management (DDM) programs that allow systems to share a common database. SNA was enhanced with nondestructible route switching to improve network availability and enable reconfiguration in the event of nodal point component failures. In addition, strategies such as open communications architectures (OCA) allow third parties to develop programs based on SNA documentation, published by IBM, to encourage use of IBM systems for phone mail, text message programs, professional office systems (PROFS) and voice text messaging systems (VTMS) to tie small business users to their network. IBM Document Interexchange Architecture (DIA) and Document Content Architecture (DCA) (subsets of SNA) are becoming office systems standards.

IBM has encouraged applications interoperability between multivendor systems by promoting an element in its Systems Application Architecture (SAA) known as its Common Programming Interface/Communications (CPI/C) applicator programming interface, based on LU6.2 protocol in IBM Systems Network Architecture (SNA) networks. IBM also added Simple Network Management Protocol (SNMP) to its APPN Network Node Routing protocol. It has also worked with the X/Open Co. Ltd. Consortium of users and vendors who are defining standards for application portability in distributed environments by proposing the Common Transport Semantics (CTS) applications programming interface suite that enables developers to create applications that run over any type of transport network, including TCP/IP, Open Systems Interconnection, and IBM's Systems Network Architecture (SNA).

Similarly, other firms have systems that collect and distribute data as they transform terminal-to-host networks to client-server networks using IBM RISC System/6000 (RS/6000) workstations running on IBM's A1X version of UNIX operating systems. These communicate to mainframes via IBM's LU6.2 protocol, thereby improving transaction rates from, in one case, 250 transactions per second to 650 by dividing databases to separate data that changes constantly. This achieves the security and redundancy that comes with mainframes and uses open systems such as UNIX rather than proprietary products. Thus, perhaps IBM and Cray have found a way to continue to sell their mainframes and supercomputers, even through data manipulation and processing are being distributed to more powerful remote processors. Thus, with diverse systems interconnectability comes more, not less, mainframes sales . . .

All this is reflected in IBM's enterprise marketing program, which is a "you need it, we've got it" computer communications integration sales strategy, targeted initially at large users. It will eventually be targeted for every user as IBM makes plans to interconnect any user to their systems.

Networking firms

Infotran System Corporation has been described by one analyst as having an extremely comprehensive T1 Network Management System. Their Integrated Network Exchange (INE) network management system pulls together multiplexers, data switches, and workstation software to allow the communications manager to perform diagnostics from the global network level all the way down to the single channel.

T1's 1.54-megabit information stream has moved to the private network providers as their key workhorse after divestiture. The next step was to switch T1, using digital cross connect switches (DCS), once T1 bit streams were in the form of "clear channels" handling zero bit streams of data without loss of synchronization. This has now been followed by DS3 systems of 45-megabit voice, data, and video information that can be switched on 45-megabit STM (synchronous transfer rate) switches that have become augmented by ATM (asynchronous transfer rate) 155-megabit packet systems, based on SYNTRAN (45 Mbps)/SONET (multiples of 50+ Mbps) transmission systems.

Other firms, such as Bridge Communications provide protocol compatibility on broadband networks with communications services that will host computers to terminals, printers, and modems over 5 Mbps transmission systems. They deploy carrier sense, multiple access with collision detectors CSMA/CD mechanisms that allow Ethernet's products to access each other, interfacing and interconnecting across the bridge. Firms such as Bridge have subsequently embraced the OSI model, providing an all-layer interconnect strategy.

Databases

Online databases are growing at the rate of 20 new ones per month. By the early 1990s, there were more than 2,500 electronic databases serving their "end users." Many databased firms' strategies were to move out of just raw data and add intelligence or processing such as discount brokerage and stock exchange information to their systems.

Numerous server/client systems were established as database providers shifted from host/remote operations. Specialized application program interfaces (APIs) were established to facilitate access to various types of universally accessible offerings. Indeed, "Life will be different when we're all online."

IBM/Sears Prodigy

IBM/Sears Prodigy Services, Lockheed, Mead, Dow Jones, Readers Digest, H&R Block and the SEC are among those trying to change the world using their online databases. Customers for databases have also been changing. Many years ago, virtually all database users were research librarians. Today, a significant number of the searchers are busy executives who are actually going to use the information. In general, the industry prefers to sell to end users, who tend to run charges anywhere from $5 to $75 dollars an hour. Many interesting databases are becoming available, such as: Legislate, a database owned by a Washington D.C. company. Legislate can be used to check the current status of any bill or pending regulation or check the voting record of any member of Congress since 1979. WeatherScan International offers a weather data update every minute from any of 10,000 worldwide reporting stations.

NEWIS offers the largest sample of media databases, enabling users to view, search out, and retrieve the full text of news stories and articles from the major wire services. Dialog Information Services, a subsidiary of Lockheed, is in some measures the largest database empire of all. It offers subscribers access to more than 200 databases, and the company plans to add 30 a year during the '90s. Their "90" collection contains more than 100 million records, with citations of articles from 10,000 different journals. You might suppose that the continuing proliferation of databases means it's easy to enter the business. However, the economies of scale are huge in the business, which is why companies like Mead and Dialog have found it expensive but necessary to keep adding more and more data to their collections.

According to *Communications Week*, early '90s revenues for Mead were estimated at more than 150 million dollars versus a bit more than 70 million for Dialog, with an overall estimate of several hundred million dollars. Having achieved this scale, traditional businesses have tremendous advantages over newcomers; the less financially strapped traditional businesses are pricing for growth rather than emphasizing fancy profit margins.

However, business costs aren't cheap. One company noted the following:

"Offshore keyboarding was relatively expensive, costing the company around 70 cents per 1,000 characters. Electric scanning was entering the scene; unfortunately, scanners work only with sharply defined characters. An interesting alternative to online databases is the laser scan optical disk, whose data storage capabilities are clearly enormous. It is already possible to put 12,000 pages on one disk.

   Some people will prefer having their own electronic libraries. The Library of Congress has taken possession of the famous 'juke box,' the machine that can hold 100 of those amazing optical disks and can randomly access any piece of data on them."

(See FIG. 2-13.)

As we look at the overall direction of the mergers of computers with computers, we can't help but see the complete cycle of integration. No matter what task we're attempting to achieve using the computer—from initial generation to storage to retrieval to manipulation to final presentation—we can't achieve it without an information transfer of one form or another. As more and more machines desire to communicate with each other to provide their particular form of intelligence, we see more and more layering of programs, as computers and terminals talk (communicate) more and more with each other. Some might call this "an integration of computers and communications (C&C)." (See FIG. 2-14.)

- Information Generation
  - Information Transfer
    - Information Storage
      - Information Transfer
        - Information Retrieval
          - Information Transfer
            - Information Manipulation
              - Information Transfer
                - Information Presentation

Fig. 2-13. Information flow.

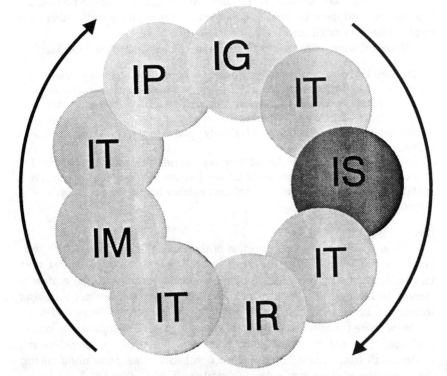

Fig. 2-14. C&C information integration.

Functional areas

The following analysis provides insights into the evolving, complex information arena and shows "what's happening."

Mobile

In the International Telecommunication Union (ITU) radio regulations, the definition of a mobile service is very broad: A radio communication service can be between mobile and land stations or between mobile stations.

Today, the demand for mobile communication continues unabated. Pagers can now provide a total alphanumeric display or full alpha display, which can receive and store complex messages. Pagers were originally used locally, such as within a hospital. These pagers where often expensive, given the small number of users in the local environment; now wide area and national systems are in use or are being developed.

Global sales of all forms of mobile communication, including paging, will be in the billions of dollars; however, growth will cost spectrum shortages. A lack of standardization has hampered and continues to hamper the growth of mobile communications. Worldwide, and notably in Europe, there's an alphabet soup of the different cellular systems, ranging from AMPS, Advanced Mobile Phone Service, developed by AT&T, to Total Access Communication System (TACS) used in the United Kingdom.

The International Maritime Satellite Organization (INMARSAT) provides satellite communications to ships and offshore oil rigs, which can use the service for telex, telephone, and data communications up to 1.5 megabits per second, enough for compressed video transmissions. In the next 10 years or so, there might be other mobile satellite systems.

Land mobile telephones were introduced decades ago, but their high cost and limited capabilities have kept them from becoming a popular consumer item. By contrast, the number of cellular phones is growing at a very rapid rate. Because they're controlled by electronic exchanges, cellular services can offer other services such as repeat call out, scratch memory, barred access, automatic call transfers and conference calls. They can offer value added services such as automatic telephone answering and electronic mail box services. Cellular systems can also be used for the transmission of facsimile and text data. Personal Communication Networks (PCNS) now offer Personal Communication Services (PCS) to mobile urban communities, as low-power, personal "Dick Tracy" phones enable people to call from anywhere using their own Personal Identification Number (PIN).

Cellular systems

As the technological problems of TDMA and CDMA are overcome, cellular will continue to provide more capabilities with current facilities. The satellite launching business is still an expensive, high-risk venture. With more than several million paging subscribers in the United States, the market is said to be growing at a rate of 25 percent to 30 percent a year, with a potential demand of 10 million to 20 million subscribers. Next, pagers will be extended to the personal phone, as the overlaid switched personal phone network becomes available.

Cellular handling networks are 80 percent mobile, 20 percent land, in both the 60 and 900 MHTZ. As local cellular radio networks of the 500 meter range are implemented, they move data at 60K, 64K and 80 kilobit rates. We've seen equipment costs for cellular phones drop from $3,000 to $1,500 to less than $200. Cellular service monthly rental prices are dropping to less than $20 a month, with usage charges between 20 and 47 cents a minute. There are other technical obstacles that need to be overcome to encourage growth. Current air-to-ground technology has not achieved the relay system that hands off calls from one cell to another as the terrestrial systems and cellular systems interact. Frequency switching from cell to cell might not be fast enough to capture information transmitted by a computer, although some say that data transmission and digital information will be included in cellular systems in the near future.

Microwave

Terrestrial point-to-multipoint (P-MP) microwave radio communication has been emerging with economical solutions for services that must be provided to multiple termination sites. Microwave is the bypass of choice, holding 49 – 50 percent of the market. By going directly to the point of presence or POP, a large user, usually one with 5 or more T1 links, can avoid paying line access charges that ordinarily would be paid to the local exchange company. Hence, microwave is still providing an excellent choice as an alternative access to long-distance networks, where the right of way for an underground fiber link is unavailable or too expensive. The pressure for shore haul digital microwave transmission equipment, typically operating at 18 and 23 gigahertz comes from many sides. A growing number of fiber-optic installations in the local loop will create more competition, plus keep prices down and margins thin, since fiber-optic bypass can exist at extremely attractive rates.

In the early '90s, microwave has a 49 percent share of the bypass transmission media, compared to fiber's 9 percent and satellite's 42 percent. However, there's a disproportionate amount of vendors in the business. BOCs are devising transport services to help keep large users from abandoning their networks; for instance, "microlink and megalink" offer of a wide range of tailor-made services, from DDS-type connection to 45 megabit per second trunking. In the mid '90s, frame relay and SMDS will be more ubiquitously available, encouraging public, competitive prices at SMDS rates initially to 45 Mbps and then to 100 Mbps. The yearly revenue forecast for short-haul digital microwave is somewhere near the $100 million revenue during the 1990 to 1996 time frame.

Satellites

The development in marketing of point-to-multipoint satellite networks for data and video distribution has triggered one of the most overworked acronyms of the year — VSAT for very small aperture terminals. *Telephony* noted the following:

"In the joint venture of RCA and Home Box Office to launch their KU Band Satellite, HBO took a major share of the risk associated with the development, launch, and management of the satellite. Soaring satellite costs have forced many companies that planned to enter the industry in the early '80s to reevaluate. Ford AeroSpace spent considerable time determining whether to gamble 600 million dollars to build the largest, ever, communication satellite equipped with 24C and 24KU Band transponders."

C Band capacity will handle common carrier traffic on AT&T's Telestar 301 and 302 satellites, which will come to the end of their design life during the 1993–1995 period. KU Band capacity will be used for broadcast distribution, satellite news gathering, corporate video, data networks, and remote printing.

VSAT revenue had risen to $765 million by 1990, with one-way data providing $90 million, two-way data — $550 million, and one-way video — $125 million. Due to the uncertainty on rocket launches and the expense of insurance on satellites, etc., Ford dropped out, but AT&T built and launched two Ford-designed space craft in the 1992-1993 time frame.

One trend is a move away from network services to concentrate instead on developing network business or building network capabilities and downplaying the transmission method as fiber, satellite, T1, whatever. Most people are interested in buying a private network. They aren't terribly interested in the technology associated with it. What they want to hear is how to tie terminals to data. According to *Telephony*, "The moral of the story is that satellites are no longer perceived as a stand-alone jewel in the sky; they're now simply to be used to meet the utilitarian networking needs of users."

After the shuttle disaster, some companies moved to fiber. On the other hand, in the more remote portions of the world, and in the new eastern Soviet block of nations, satellites continue to play a key role. The future will see satellite-to-satellite switching of data packets, as information is moved further around the world quickly and efficiently.

The competitive information arena is expanding, as the president once determined that deployment of new U.S.-based international satellite systems was required for the "national interest." Until recently, with the expansion of MCI and U.S. Sprint, a single carrier, AT&T enjoyed virtually a *de facto* monopoly over the international public switched voice communications. Message traffic was originally allocated by the FCC between submarine cable facilities and telecommunication satellite facilities. INTELSAT held a monopoly over the international space segment, and U.S. Signatory to INTELSAT, the Communications Satellite Corporation (COMSAT), enjoyed the exclusive franchise to market INTELSAT circuits in the United States. AT&T, until the mid '80s, was barred from providing alternative voice-data service. COMSAT was regulated as a matter of regulatory policy to serve as a carrier's carrier and thus was prohibited from marketing satellite circuits directly to the users. Not unexpectedly, therefore, international communication prices typically were much higher than comparable U.S. domestic charges.

Under the 1963 Communication Satellite Act, the president is obliged to make a national interest determination prior to FCC licensing of international satellite systems separate from INTERSAT. The issues raised by these applications there-fore were addressed by the Senior Interagency Group (SIG) on International Communication and Information Policy, co-chaired by the National Telecommuni-cations and Information Administration (NTIA) and the State Department. First there was consensus that the United States should have a strong, continuing interest in the economic strength and vitality of the global INTELSAT system. However, all agreed that this commitment to INTELSAT and our national policy favoring private sector competition could be accommodated. The executive agen-cies concluded that limiting the new entrants to providing services "not intercon-nected with public-switched networks" would safeguard INTELSAT from adverse economic effects while, at the same time, give users, particularly video transmis-sion and intracorporate network customers, new and potentially valuable interna-tional communications service options. Finally, the executive agencies determined that the terms and conditions of subsequent competition should be considered along with the issue of new entry. The FCC issues an opinion generally in accord with the administration recommendations. New international satellite systems should be allowed to compete for carefully presubscribed classes of service, thus extending the competitive marketplace into the satellite arena.

Fiber optics

Fiber optics provides high-capacity, high-quality, low-cost transport communica-tions while meeting price, quality, availability, security, and flexibility objectives. In 1992, there were 50,000+ miles of fiber in the United States, with the regional Bell companies having 25,000 or so miles at less than $1 to $2 per-mile cost, with target costs of less than $1,000 per-line to compete with coax. As previously noted, fiber will be the key component in the future of broadband ISDN. However, in the interim, some RBOCs have turned to combined fiber in the feeder and coax in the distribution plant to offer analog video in partnership with CATV firms. This technique is less effective than fiber-to-the-curb/coax-to-the-house in that the number of repeaters become a factor and the system is really analog and not designed to take advantage of the tremendous potential of a fully digital multiwave guide system. The tough decision for RBOCs is to bite the bullet and refiber America in a 15- to 20- year phased program, especially to deliver interactive video services, HDTV, and videophone.

Local area networks

Local area networks have sprung up everywhere to connect terminals to com-puters within office complexes or across town to satellite work locations. However, key LAN market players believe that, although there's a proliferation of LAN solutions, their real business growth will remain stalled until internetworking standards are established, applications are developed, and application-oriented marketing and distribution evolve. Some say that LAN companies have spent considerable time marketing LAN technology itself, instead of developing ways for LANs to do useful work for business. Others say that now is the time to concentrate on developing new applications and distribution channels for LANs, since LANs have experienced a resurgence in the '90s as LAN interconnect was promoted by the RBOCs as a new service offering. However, some believe that, in time, the FDDI will be challenged by new ATM technology fast packet switching to interconnect local and distant LANs. In any event, there are several markets that LAN companies have identified, where many can benefit from LAN technology. The first LAN markets to be pursued were identified as brokerage firms, computer aided design, and the computer aided manufacturing market segments. There also was industry-wide interest in office integration, factory automation LANS, and the health services market.

It's believed by many that new applications in education and other fields will emerge as a strong trend, once the much-awaited distribution channels are open among value added resellers. If users are educated and channels are available, application will continue to play the key role in the '90s. Until now, LANs have primarily been marketed as a means of cutting costs. The new emphasis on LAN marketing will highlight data sharing communications and linking many terminals, computers, PCs, and mainframes together, providing an overlay of internetworking services. Here, considerable effort has surfaced in the mid '90s for new server/client systems, network management systems, and protocol converters to interconnect diverse mail systems, file transfers, document interexchanges, and multimedia workstation interfaces.

In retrospect, LAN vendors have spent a lot of time educating the market. Market acceptance of LANs, as the singular solution, might become a lost point as IBM roles out more elements of its token ring network. The token ring might emerge as a favorite of company management information systems directors, causing the product to flourish with many nodes and totally eclipse Ethernet in the '90s. However, Ethernet will continue to develop using FDDI and FDDI-II for private networking, as well as by using frame relay/SMDS public offerings.

Interconnectivity in the multivendor environment now tops the list of concerns for LAN vendors. As noted earlier by the survey questions, the LAN market has reached the point where there are a multitude of media choices. The user focus will move from wiring to connectivity. DEC and others are preparing a second wave of standardization, which could reduce LAN costs over the long term. There's a new emphasis for OSI compatible products, now that protocols are shaping up. The OSI model of a seven-layer architecture intends to provide the standard method of communication between different types and makes of computers. As specific protocols for each layer of the model are defined, LAN vendors will be quick to offer them as new services from their LAN product base. LAN interconnectivity through frame relay and SMDS technologies have entered the market in the early '90s. However, the initial need for permanent virtual private networks has shifted to dynamically switched virtual private networks with access to the world using ATM nodal switches. Hence, without a clever shift to public data ISDN networks in the late '80s, LANs have indeed enjoyed considerable growth over the early '90s. However, the new interest generated by the presence of national ISDN has refocused attention on switched ISDN data-handling opportunities. This can help existing LANs by enabling ISDN interconnection. It can also make ISDN competitive by offering a directly switched basic and primary rate, addressable, reliable alternative as the ISDN-versus-LANs issue blossoms in the mid '90s.

T1

Since divestiture, more and more large users have followed the T1 transmission route, simply by using one of several 1.54 Mbps T1 channels. These channels can be fractionally divided into several smaller and slower transmission links for voice and data at a lower price than buying separate pieces. This is called fractional T1, or f-T1.

Early players in the market of digital terminal systems (DTS), a form of microwave bypass, are now concentrating on T1 multiplexing and nodal point switching/hubbing products for private users. Centrex, after a shift, made a strong comeback from the late '70s and early '80s, when it fell victim to a strategy to kill off central-office-based switching systems in favor of premise-based private branch exchanges (PBXs). The features that the PBXs could offer, during that time, were technologically superior to anything the operating companies had in their Centrex arsenal. However, since then, they've revitalized Centrex service and are closing the PBX technology gap as new ISDN data-handling Centrex capabilities are available for local business using T1 and T3 facilities.

Many managers of the large networks now look for a streamlined, centralized, comprehensive network management system (NMS). Many of the traditional T1 multiplexer and switch suppliers are vying with each other to provide T1 digital cross connects and network management solutions. Other companies are scrambling to provide network management interfaces and other complements to IBM's Netview software for IBM mainframes and PCs in order to extend network management for the IBM Systems Network Architecture computing environment to include T1 telecommunications equipment. T1 and T3 leased facilities continue to compete with SMDS offerings, as many large users prefer to directly access POPs rather than use LEC-shared transport offerings. However, primary rate ISDN is now becoming a viable alternative, especially since it enables multiple trunk groups (functions) to selectively and dynamically share any channel in the primary rate 1.544 megabit stream.

Multiple networks

We've now entered the world of multiple choices, as both private and public network architectures structure new information networks using multiple media to interconnect multiple user terminals and PCs to multiple databases. (See FIG. 2-15.)

Section three: the competitive marketplace

Economic theory reveals that as information becomes more available, more quickly and cheaply, markets become more efficient. Resources are allocated more rationally and wealth is maximized.

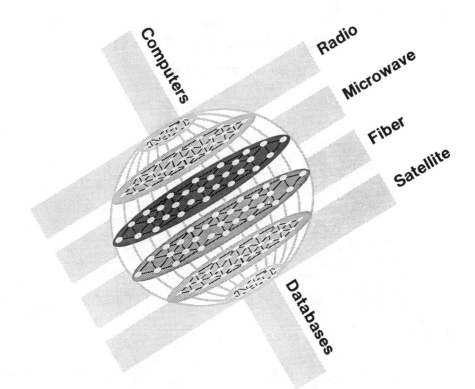

Fig. 2-15. A new world . . . the geodesic sphere.

The information tree

So, after reviewing several years of these diverse strategies, we can't help but ponder where we're going and where all of this activity will end up. So, let's take a moment to summarize what's happened to try to see where we're going or could go if we want to take a different path or different fork in the road. Is the opportunity for ISDN over, or is the real opportunity for ISDN just beginning, now that we have a better understanding of past mistakes?

In reviewing and assessing our helter-skelter movements of recent years (see FIG. 2-16A) it becomes startlingly clear that we've now reached a "crossroad in time." We've indeed arrived at a decision point, where, as FIG. 2-16B notes, two somewhat independent paths lie before us. Considerable money will be spent over the remaining years of the '90s; many believe it will be too late to revisit this crossroad in the next century. For by then we'll be in a different place, in a different time, with different paths and different choices. So let's pause for the moment to now consider what's happening, where we're going and where we want to go.

Figure 2-16A traces the numerous paths the communication industry has taken to lead us to today's somewhat tenuous, precarious position. Here, we see POTS (plain old telephone services) consisting of switched-voice dial tone, nonswitched

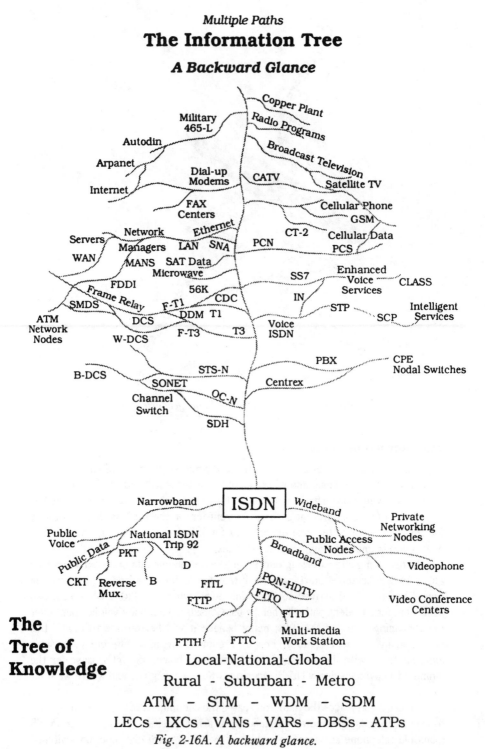

Multiple Paths
The Information Tree
A Backward Glance

Copper Plant

Military 465-L

Radio Programs

Autodin

Arpanet

Broadcast Television

Internet

Dial-up Modems

CATV

Satellite TV

FAX Centers

Cellular Phone

GSM

Servers

Network Managers

Ethernet

CT-2

Cellular Data

WAN

LAN SNA

PCN

PCS

MANS

SAT Data

Microwave

SS7

Enhanced Voice Services

CLASS

FDDI

56K

IN

Frame Relay

STP

Intelligent Services

SMDS

F-T1

CDC

SCP

ATM Network Nodes

DCS

DDM T1

Voice ISDN

W-DCS

F-T3

T3

PBX

CPE Nodal Switches

B-DCS

STS-N

SONET

Centrex

Channel Switch

OC-N

SDH

ISDN

Narrowband

Wideband

Private Networking Nodes

Public Voice

National ISDN Trip 92

Public Access Nodes

Public Data

PKT

Broadband

Videophone

D

CKT

Reverse Mux.

B

FITL

PON-HDTV

FTTO

Video Conference Centers

FTTP

FTTD

FTTH

FTTC

Multi-media Work Station

The Tree of Knowledge

Local-National-Global

Rural - Suburban - Metro

ATM – STM – WDM – SDM

LECs – IXCs – VANs – VARs – DBSs – ATPs

Fig. 2-16A. A backward glance.

A Telephonic
Telecommunications Beginning

A Forward Glimpse

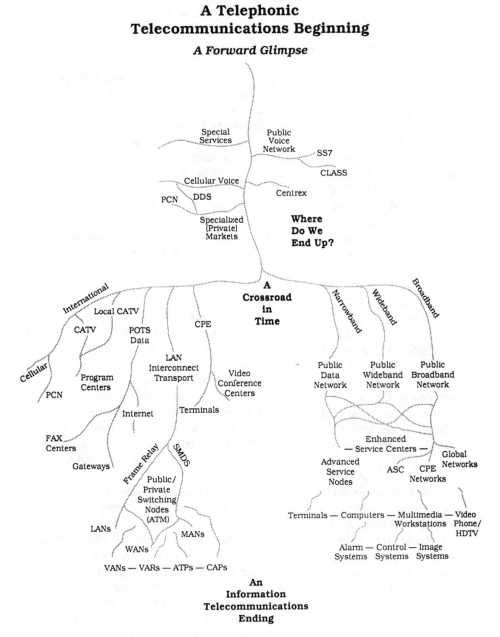

Fig. 2-16B. A forward glimpse.

special services, foreign exchange (FX) lines, private leased lines, slow-speed modems for data transport over analog facilities, publicly shared Centrex, privately owned PBXs, and other voice-based services such as 800, 911, time, weather, audiotex, etc. These singularly voice-based offerings had been the "products" of the telephone company, as they were automated and then automated again over the '60s and '70s.

During the turbulent '80s, many new offerings were visualized, a few were tried, but still fewer were actually available in the early '90s. Of these, we've seen cellular struggle through cost and availability problems, while usage, internetworking, and standards considerations accelerated and blossomed as the industry rivaled with TDMA-versus-CDMA alternative-spectrum coding-transport technologies. European cellular committees commonality standards, known as GSM, have now been called the "camel," while new PCN standards are referred to by some as the "son of the camel." CT-2 teleport abilities are beginning to stabilize. These offer a more limited version of PCN by allowing a user to dial out of the area from a portable unit, without the extensive overhead needed to track the journey every two-hundred feet or so. This blossoming of wireless usage has encouraged some to offer wireless data services so that a PC at home could supposedly communicate with an office over satellite. The arguments over the TDMA/CDMA had led some marketers to cry, "Shoot the engineers and let's get on with it," as market demands increased for more and more radio offerings. However, spectrum is indeed limiting growth, as many vie for it, especially as new forms of satellite TV offerings challenge the use of available spectrum. Many believe there will be a reassessment of what services are delivered over what medium at the turn of the century, once capacity-rich fiber is deployed.

Data needs have continued to change as telex and teletype services were replaced in Europe and America by new data packet networks with Japanese facsimile-type offerings of Group III and Group IV fax. Rates increased from 60 and 100 words per minute to analog 2.4, 4.8, 9.6 Kbps, and on to 56 and 64 Kbps digital bit streams. Here, modems, multiplexers, concentrators, contenders, and cluster controls have played their roles, as multiple users have attempted to use and share first analog, then digital transport.

From numerous data services such as E-mail, electronic funds transfer (EFT), fax, broadcast, polling, personal mailbox, access passwords, security, electronic document transfer (EDT), data inquiry/response searches, data collection, data distribution, transactions, etc., we've seen messaging, file transfer, and database access rise to the forefront, becoming the new "killer services" or "killer applications" that create an ever-expanding demand for new data handling networks.

During this period, due to the lack of a publicly switched data network with universal addressing, routing, and transport error correction and definition architecture, local area data communications were left to their own devices to mature and grow or wither and die. From this came the local area networks (LANs), which used computer manufacturers IEEE agreements in the form of 802.X standards for enabling terminals to talk to computers or other terminals. Unfortunately, each major computer manufacturer usually had its own proprietary version, providing a protocol that didn't specifically talk to another system's proprietary protocol. Hence, bridges were established between LANs, and then routers were added to extend addressing and protocol communications. As diversity became an issue, wide area networks were deployed using public dial-up transport or privately leased facilities; next, metropolitan area networks (MANs) were developed, facilitating higher transport rates in local ring or collapsed ring configurations.

As time passed, more and more sites needed to be interconnected, as firms became more distributed throughout the country and their databases needed to be "networked" together. Initially, digital transport facilities, called T1, operating at 1.544 Mbps, were leased between locations. Next, higher rates, of 45 Mbps became available (provided by T3). Then, fractional rates at subrates of T1 at 384K, 786K, and then multiples of T1 and T3 were provided, as users attempted to construct T1/3 switching nodes at key locations. This enabled dynamic virtual private networking (VPN), where the user can request varying amounts of bandwidth to changeable destinations. Initially, these setups were established ahead of time by operators; actually, they needed to be established directly by the customer at the time of the call, where more or less bandwidth is allocated dynamically during the communication, as needed.

To achieve these transports, the universally deployed twisted copper pair has been provided with new technologies. Digital Subscriber Loop (DSL) has been enhanced and extended by ADSL, HDSL, and VHDSL, as multiple pairs achieved 1.5 Mbps or so transport rates over 12,000 feet with limited repeater spacing. At the same time, these copper-based facilities are being augmented by fiber, as new SONET offerings, based on multiplexes of 50+ Mbps, become available, especially at the universally accepted 155 Mbps rate, noted as OC-3/STS-3. Here, Europe's Synchronous Digital Hierarchy (SDH) of multiples of 2.04 Mbps becomes in sync with multiples of the American transport basic rate of 1.5 Mbps. In this, FITL, FITP, FITC, FITH, FITO, and FITD (fiber in the loop, pedestal, curb, home, office, and desk) deployments will be standardized during the '90s, into the twenty-first century.

Technical connectionless amplitude and phase modulation (CAP) or 2B1Q information transport techniques can achieve up to 3 Mbps over 12,000 feet. ADSL (asynchronous digital subscriber line) will use CAP to enable 1.5 Mbps (video) between networks and customer over a single pair of copper wires. Meanwhile, HDSL (high bit rate digital subscriber line) technology, using 2B1Q standard ISDN BRI coding, will enable T1 rates within 12,000 feet of single twisted-pair and more than 12,000 feet in four-wire to two-wire applications.

Digital cross connects (DXCs) have been developed in the early '90s to enable access to individual 64K bit streams; they combine channels to achieve T1 and T3 rates. Next, wideband and broadband digital cross connects, W-DCS and B-DCS, combine higher and higher transports, either optically as OC-1, OC-3, OC-N, or electronically as STS-1, STS-3, STS-N. In this process, add/drop multiplexors can initially provide access to individual channels (circuits), where full broadband switches will achieve this complete integration as new technologies, such as asynchronous transfer mode (ATM), synchronous transfer mode (STM), wave division multiplexing (WDM), and space division multiplexing (SDM) are deployed.

As these new "killer technologies" search for "killer applications," more and more information service providers (ISPs) and enhanced service providers (ESPs) arise to provide an incentive for customers to use the new technologies in order to access information. In this regard, SS7 signaling enables switching systems to communicate with each other in order to enable access to specialized databases above the network, through STP/SCP centers, where 800 services and special-line database look-ups can be achieved via this intelligent network signaling mechanism.

With this has come a new emphasis on America's open network architecture (ONA) and Europe's open network provision (ONP) interfaces, as new players offer increased, more enhanced services. Even the voice world continues to expand as voice conferencing, voice mail, voice-to-text, text-to-voice, priority message, private message, language prompts, etc., give way to integrated, simultaneous voice, data, text, image, video combinations. This causes further shifts to networks that not only achieve these possibilities, but also offer privacy, security, and survivability.

Hence, information will arrive in bursts of variable-bit-rate (VBR) data or in the continuous-bit-rate (CBR) form for videophone and high-definition TV. It will enable point-of-sale, inventory control, merchandise ordering, financial transactions, transportation vehicle monitoring, and control for commuter traffic, boxcar loading and routing, aircraft safety, alarm monitoring, energy management, meter reading, weather sensory, file transfers, database access, and all forms of information accessing, storing, retrieving, browsing, combining, processing, manipulating, integrating, indexing, translating, transferring, and presenting; this will ensure that information is maintainable, portable, accessible, functional, and available for not only the large business users, but also for the hundreds of thousands of small businesses, individual residences, educators, law enforcers, investors, and state and federal agencies.

To keep pace with this change is essential, lest the United States become a third-world information country in the late '90s. Some say the litmus test for any new service is demand. This leads us to the chicken-and-the-egg scenario. To have demand, a service must be offered, but to offer a service, a network must be constructed; to construct the network, demand for its services needs to be established. Due to this type of thinking, ISDN, a new network that provides the user access to new voice and data networking services, was still not established ten years after its initial announcement. There has been considerable confusion to date of what exactly ISDN is. There have also been a number of technical and network interface issues that have needed to be resolved before full deployment of ISDN. However, the time has come for ISDN to come of age. It has matured in its growth from the hoopla and holler of its birth, through its youth, until its debutante ball. During this period, users have realized that ISDN is more than an expensive interface to an alternative voice line in digital form. (ISDN is defined in its narrowband terms as two 64 Kbps channels that can transport voice or data. It also has a 16 Kbps signaling data packet channel for sending, communicating, and connecting information, specialized sensory signaling, and low-speed packetized text information.)

Although ISDN does indeed provide the application for two high-quality voice conversations or even 7 kHz stereo in high-quality digital form, it does offer direct digital access to a medium-speed 64K or 128K (using reverse multiplexors to combine both channels) public data network. The information can be either circuit switched and/or packet switched using SS7 signaling to ensure transparency. ISDN chip sets are now available for terminal systems. With the advent of national ISDN, interoperability between multivendor systems enables network transparency for CPE. TRIP 92 demonstrated universal accessibility and operability throughout the community and around the globe. In this regard, Bell Communications Research (Bellcore) has established standards for SS7, such as TR905 for SS7 interface with IXCs and TR962, 268, 444, 448, 317, and 374 to ensure ISDN interfaces.

As the marriage of ISDNs and LANs continues to take place, enabling remote terminals to access private LANS using the ISDN public network, we see future public switched offerings enabling access to and internetworking with currently existing terminals, rather than requiring direct replacement either/or decisions.

Data ISDN will also enable LAN-to-LAN connectivity, as multiple ISDN lines are accessible between LANs as well as between PCs and host computers. The new chip sets in CPE will meet the quick "plug-and-play" objectives as the 200,000 or so ISDN terminal connections of 1991 expand to several millions in 1994, and many, many millions by 1999, as ISDN becomes universally deployed throughout the '90s. Japan has found that demand becomes explosive the more universally ISDN is available throughout the country. One past RBOC deployment mistake was to form only islands of ISDN connectivity. Firms don't come in islands, nor are the many users of each industries' community of interest all located on only one side of town. There's a need as well to provide for non–ISDN-to-ISDN connectivity and vendor transparency throughout the entire metro area. The more it's available, the more demand there will be for ISDN. As its public data network becomes more and more ubiquitous across America, it enables file servers, file transfer, remote printing, Group IV fax, off-campus access to on-campus computers, PC-to-PC communications, medical image transfer, slow-speed videophone, video conferencing, and LAN interconnectability; additional marketable services will address mass customization for every aspect of the marketplace. For higher speeds of broadband ISDN, as bandwidth becomes "elastic" or as "rubber bandwidth" becomes available, we can achieve data multiplexing, dynamic bandwidth on demand, Group V fax, and virtual computer configurations.

However, to have continuing market growth success, the "killer issues" of narrowband-broadband pricing conflicts must be addressed, as well as the broadband standards, higher-layer OSI interfaces, and the integration of existing message/file transport systems. Similarly, regulatory boundaries and rulings need to be revisited to allow information services to be deployed from a single inter-LATA service point of interconnection (SPOI) platform to reduce cost and enable rural access to urban services. In this regard, the collocation of multiprovider equipment has been successfully achieved by virtual collocation, enabling access to nearby facilities and ensuring that a single fault or disaster doesn't unnecessarily affect all providers. Similarly, software/hardware fire walls might need to be established to protect the network from multiservice providers who request their own ability to access and control all aspects of information movement and manipulation (IM&M) as we enter multimedia-voice processing, voice messaging, voice mail, interactive voice response, voice recognition, audio information processing (AIP), audiotex, speech-to-text, E-mail, facsimile, client-server computing, graphical user interfaces, image transfer, video conferencing, high-definition TV, message broadcasting, interactive videophone, etc.

There will indeed be competition and bypass as customers use pick-and-choose available transport offerings to construct their own networks and access when and where they want pieces of the public network. Here, we see a wide array of alternative access providers (AAP), alternative access vendors (AAV), alternative local transport (ALT), competing on price, service, and technology. Some existing interchange carriers, perhaps even AT&T, will establish themselves and/ or partnerships with these alternative players in the local arena to bring customers directly to their network, enabling such services as MMDS (MultiMedia Data Services), by establishing a pure megabit (DS1 to 100 Mbps) digital pipe to the customer.

Key technologies to ensure ISDN success will include rate adaptation using standards such as CCITT V.1 10, and V.120 to allow subrates to be packaged within a basic rate ISDN channel of 64 Kbps, allowing interfaces to SNA, API, Northern Telecom's T-Link, AT&T's DM2/3. Similarly, reverse/inverse multiplexing technologies will be needed for allowing interfaces to be sent in parallel over several ISDN B channels at the DSO 64 Kbps rate and then combined into a serial bit stream at the destination. This will go a long way in extending today's copper plant, and so will the very high bit rate digital technologies, as noted earlier.

Besides the previously mentioned services, SS7 will offer further services such as credit card calling, caller identification, caller return, follow-me routing, 800 telemarketing (a 1 billion dollar industry by '95), telecanvassing, and premium pay per use. Similarly, #7 ISDN user part will enable caller identification (ID) before answer, as well as allow selected call waiting, selected call transfer, selected call message, caller ID blocking, call rejection, call trace, continuous redial, last call return, priority call terminal sub addressing (one out of eight), and terminal compatibility confirmation.

Optical fiber will ring the Pacific rim, as transpacific fiber links the United States and Canada with Japan, Singapore, Hong Kong, Sydney, and Malaysia, providing 64K, 384K, 45M, 90M, 140M, 400M, 565M, 1.2G, and 2.4 Gbps, as Japan provides fiber to every home by 2010-2015. The Burns Bill for broadband networks for America promotes a similar time frame. However, for this to be successful, we need a fiber distribution plan, interface standards, and cheaper fiber costs. Here, Bellcore's TR303 and TR909 standards begin to address standards for digital loop and fiber-in-the-loop distribution systems, while Ameritec's deployment plans of 1.5 million fiber line accesses by 1995 attempts to bring down the price of fiber once other RBOCs follow suit.

New telecommunication free trade zones, such as in Chicago, are beginning to span the competitive arena, sprinkling many new local urban telephone companies, thereby further necessitating America's open network architecture (ONA) or Europe's open network provision (ONP) standards. This competitive arena is further emphasized as FCC's video dial tone decision encourages RBOC competition (and partnership) with the cable companies for delivering television programs. However, as noted earlier, numerous other services (such as electronic funds transfer, international money transfer, electronic mail, and fax services having broadcast, delayed delivery, personal mailbox, access password security, alert fax for payer or phone, collective data, etc., capabilities) begin to clearly show the complexity of the interoperability issues of having multiple providers. For, as one provider noted, "the realists among us will not be laying in the champagne for some time yet."

Hence, the interoperability stage for internetworking, interprocessing, and interservices is set. It opens the gate for the entrance of ISDN, a concept that's ready for reality, built on ten years of establishing a detailed construction of standards for both networks and applications. The public network does indeed take longer to define and establish, as numerous time-consuming local and international agreements needed to be reached before deployment. During these years, the private world did indeed travel to the IEEE 802 Committees defining private internetworking standards to more quickly establish access and information exchanges between each of the U.S. computer firms' private systems. However, while this enabled quicker standards, the expanding success of this deployment has caused a level of complexity that's now being extended and addressed via frame relay and SMDS as they layer protocols.

However, this form of layering can increase congestion and inhibit transparency. Many of these store and forward protocol issues can be resolved by a clean, crisp, functional, switched vehicle such as ISDN in its narrowband, wideband, and broadband public network form.

So what is ISDN? What does it offer? Why was it delayed? Does ISDN challenge or enhance LANs? Are we proceeding down two separate paths? Do LANs follow transmission and does ISDN follow switching? Is this a trans-switching issue, a network issue, or a service issue? What is an ISDN network? What services does it offer — data services, digital services — in terms of future narrowband, wideband, and broadband services?

ISDN

As noted earlier, ISDN provides the user with a "2B + D" interface, where B is a 64 Kbps bearer service channel and D is 16 Kbps channel for out-of-band signaling and data packet handling. The 64 Kbps can provide the user with both voice and/or data, for it can transport one voice and one data call, or two voice calls, or two data calls. At the same time, the "D" channel can provide:

- "D" channel signaling for supplementary services and call flow. Here, CLASS-type services can be offered as the "D" channel signaling interconnects to SS7 networks, providing calling party ID.
- 9.6 Kbps packet switching.
- 14.2-16 Kbps data transport.
- Classification information and subaddressing information for enabling up to 8

terminals to share an ISDN B channel port over a four-wire interface to the network terminating unit (NT2).

ISDN effectively provides three separate data networking capabilities, as it offers the user:

- "B" channel circuit switching at 64 and 128 Kbps.
- "B" channel packet switching at 64 and 128 Kbps.
- "D" channel packet switching at 9.6 Kbps.

Note that by using reverse multiplexing techniques, both B channels can be used to achieve 2 × 64 Kbps, or 128 Kbps.

Packet switching

Packet switching originated in the late '50s and early '60s in the military networks, such as 465-L, using frequency shift keying technology in which a start header-information-stop guard tail format was deployed. The length of the information was as short as one 8-bit character and as long as 256 characters. Size varied, depending on content and bursty noise conditions, requiring a number of repeat request retransmissions. In the mid '60s, the Advanced Research Projects Agency (ARPA) of the U.S. Department of Defense embarked on developing a data communications network to link the various universities and applied research. Here, ARPANET was deployed as the prototype packet switching network, based on earlier store and forward techniques developed for the Navy, as well as those by the Air Force on 465-L for S.A.C. and Minutemen.

Subsequent networks were launched in the '70s, as GTE established Telenet and Trans-Canada provided Data Pac. Later, numerous PTTs (Postal Telephone & Telegraphy) companies in France, Great Britain, and Germany provided their particular version of public packet switching. By 1976, the Consultative Committee of International Telephone and Telegraph (CCITT) had established the X.25 standard for user-to-network interfaces, and the X.75 standard for internetworking gateways.

Over the years, packet-handling techniques have matured. Initially, the complete text was continued within the packet, where a header identified where the packet was going and the tail signified the completion of the packet; this single packet was processed as a datagram. Care was taken as the packet was sent from network node to network node between organization and destination to ensure that errors were detected by an elaborate procedure of protocols to acknowledge receipt or request for repeated transfer. Here, error correction and detection was facilitated by hamming-fire codes and other cyclic recovery codes to help identify the incorrect bit or bits without requiring a retransfer of the entire message.

Over time, the message was broken down into smaller and smaller packets. As time progressed, the process of providing a virtual circuit transport to the user to changeable destinations encouraged more and more packets to share dynamically channelable transport. As congestion problems developed, ensuring the flow of messages became the network's prime concern, as it assumed the task of packet sequencing to ensure that a multipacket message, where packets were sent on diverse routes, were provided to the destination user in proper sequential order, especially if there was need for several repeat request retransmissions for several of the packets.

Hence, the header and tail information began to contain more and more transport and error control information, such as leader information in the first block, layered channel numbers, etc. In time, connection-oriented packets were able to set up a virtual path to a destination between nodes, where the nodes were able to remember particulars concerning the origin and destination for a series of packets, thereby enabling subsequent packets to contain less information in the headers and be handled across the network in a faster delivery manner. Connectionless packets always contained all their destination information and appeared to the network as singular, stand-alone package to be transported independent of earlier packages.

From this work came burst switching, which provides a full steam of packet information, while the conversation is present, as a variable length packet. (Some forms are limited but variable up to 64,000 characters.) Next came the fast packet switching of a fixed number of 8-bit bytes (cells) using the principle that the switch can handle any length input as a series of 48-bit bytes as it nibbles away, as long as it's nibbling at a rate faster than that at which the information arrives. This then became the foundation for ATM (asynchronous transfer mode) broadband (fast packet) switching, while STM (synchronous transfer mode) is a circuit-switched offering enabling throughput of X number of fixed channels. In time, the fixed number of channels can be varied, enabling new channel switches to more effectively compete with packet switches, especially for continuous-bit-rate traffic such as videophone versus bursty terminal-computer variable bit rate traffic that can more easily be handled by ATM packet switching.

Two paths

Before we leave our review of current-day strategies, we need to address both the opportunities and the conflicts noted in FIG. 2-16B and symbolically represented at the base of the information tree in FIG. 2-16A. As suggested in the review of the progress of data, as it moved from the mainframe to the terminal to remote terminals to remote workstations, the lack of an existing publicly switched data network has encouraged computer firms to establish private local area networks (LANs), which proliferated once the computer was applied to every aspect of the marketplace. This proliferation of different types of LANs created a complex environment having numerous protocols for enabling numerous forms of terminal-host communications, allowing numerous servers to access numerous databases over numerous networks using numerous network management systems. Unfortunately, we've seen that the more numerous, the more complex indeed.

This path of information movement and management (IM&M) built on private networking tools has been addressed with a vengeance by the entrance of frame relay and SMDS. Frame relay provides a connection-oriented envelope to contain the many forms of variable-length frames of the different LANs as they exchange information between LANs over direct, interconnecting public facilities or private wide area high-speed transport mechanisms such as FDDI. SMDS, on the other hand, is a Bellcore-sponsored MAN-type network that enables connectionless information to share facilities between locations or a ring of locations. Here, information is packetized in the 48-byte text/5-byte header = 53 byte format that can later be switched as an ATM-type fast packet. Hence, ATM cross-connect capabilities are added to SMDS nodes to enable access to broadband ATM switching networks to further universal connectivity.

Many argue that simply (or not so simply) layering private networking capabilities on top of each other without establishing the universal public network is simply an interim solution waiting for fully deployed B-ISDN switched facilities, providing access to full fiber bandwidth. In fact, it's simply more of the same when networking one private solution on another, without taking advantage of the switching, addressing, routing, transferring, error detection/correction, transport, and manipulation services of a full-featured, ubiquitous, public broadband network. One need only to look at the complexity of integrating "nested" layers of numerous dissimilar protocols to better appreciate the advantages of a publicly switched, connection-oriented network — be it narrowband or broadband.

In parallel with this LAN interconnect path is renewed interest in other short-term, financially rewarding, less capital-intensive ventures such as international voice cellular and analog fiber CATV partnerships, selected dense area PCN penetrations, and dial-up "voice-transport-based" service nodes such as analog data fax centers, etc. Unfortunately, these ventures don't establish a solid, supporting, robust infrastructure that another, less traveled path might take a little longer to establish. However, once established, this infrastructure could easily support numerous service platforms that foster an increasingly universal exchange in all aspects of information, creating an entirely different society.

Services

As we look at new computer and communication services, we find a vast array of possibilities and offerings such as: file translation between different operating systems, word processors and spreadsheets, electronic mail, error correction protocols, database searches, auto dialing and auto logon, file uploading and downloading, network handshakes, meet-me conferences, delayed delivery of information, call redirection, calling party identification, virtual networks, voice mail, message telephone services (MTS). There are also videotex interactive communication services such as; electronic shopping, banking, and information access. Some say that voice mail (such as GTE's Telemail, where telephone voice messages are digitized and stored on magnetic disks in the central office or CPE customer provided equipment) is the answer to phone tag.

In time, there will be a new family of teleservices, such as: telewriting, teleauditing, telebanking, telecommuting, telemarketing, television, telefax, teletext, telecontrol, teleconferencing, teleshopping, tele . . . However, these service offerings must become more cost effective and more revenue producing, as noted by many information movement and management (IM&M) business plans based on various market research, market forecasting, and development of the forthcoming information marketplace. The future requires extensive market planning together with network planning. Here, network planning must anticipate revenue opportunities, both from existing and new, forthcoming markets. Decisions must be based on understanding user resistance and predictions of when to have the right product at the right time. To achieve these new information services is a complex and difficult game. It's necessary to plan tomorrow's networks as well as today's, in a manner in which future functionality and feature issues are resolved to ensure that premature obsolescence doesn't occur.

Looking at the service marketplace, one observer noted the following:

"Today there are three general types of interexchange services, Message Telephone Service (MTS) — which can be defined as the ordinary use of voice network; Private Line Service — where special access or dedicated lines are available for specific customers; and Data Services — which shall require higher and higher links of quality transmission and switching. There are three general kinds of interexchange carriers; regional, national (such as MCI and AT&T) and WATS resellers, which buy service in bulk from AT&T and resell it at discount rates to individual residence and business customers. In addition, there are the carrier's carriers that do not deal with individual end users but provide high traffic transmission facilities for resell operators. We must also realize that many providers will be moving into these and new arenas, as transport becomes a commodity and new services begin to grow.

The marketplace is indeed changing, sometimes in a zigzag direction. In some cases, telcos have been outflanking PBX manufacturers with new Centrex capabilities, with local area network access and integrated voice data transmission. However, it now seems that the ability to supply sophisticated Centrex might be outstripping user demand. Users' lack of excitement over the new technology is apparently due to the fact that although customers are moving from an analog environment to the shiny new digital scene, this move in services is evolutionary rather than revolutionary. True, ISDN will bring wonders of voice, data, and video over a single twisted copper pair, representing advanced improvement over today's typical one-line, one-service setup. However, many users perceived digital Centrex as a little more than a stop along the way on a trip that they are not even sure they are ready to make, as the telcos advance to their ISDN Centrex version.

As one person earlier said, 'Customers who are looking long term, want digital, but in the short-term it doesn't necessarily have to be digital.' Still, having digital offers users a future natural evolution to ISDN. The transition of analog to digital Centrex might be a first important step towards their entrance into a digital network, but the user will have to see more data-handling services.

A university communications manager noted that he is looking for data product capabilities in Centrex but not yet looking for ISDN compatibility. 'We're checking specifications for it, but we're being realistic. ISDN is not here yet' . . ."

Fortunately, other users such as Xerox, Eastman Kodak, J C Penney, and numerous department stores and grocery markets are beginning to see the advantage of both the internal and external networking capabilities provided by ISDN,

ISDN-Centrex, ISDN-PBXs, and ISDN-CPE . . . Hence, it's essential to keep the users in mind and bring them to understand and realize that ISDN is now there!

Users

The chairman of the telecommunication chapter of the European Association of Information Services (EUSIDIC) observed, "that pre-ISDN public data networks were not designed with nontelecommunications professionals in mind; that public network interconnection was neither user friendly nor reliable; that tariffs for text services were too high." In summarizing, he noted problems in just doing daily jobs. He recognized that influencing the standards practice for services and equipment might provide another way of achieving some of the goals.

Besides personal communication networks (PCNs), a different PCN— personal computing networks are becoming the game of the '90s, where personal computers are internetworked together, allowing computer linkage to send personal messages and create, change, and send data information from various word processors. More and more users are trying to make their views and needs known as business telecommunication users request a platform or forum in which they can meet on equal footing with service providers and equipment manufacturers' standards-authority regulating bodies. UserCom has been a generally successful attempt to pull many of these threads together. There now are many users groups, forums, and standards bodies. (See chapter 7, case studies one and two.)

"We see users who are reactive, proactive, and leaders. There is a need to educate new users and foster user planning groups to identify, target, and reposition ISDN for various types of users. There is the need to analyze what the competition is doing for the users, to establish credibility with the users, and to incorporate realistic user needs in regulatory rulings. Similarly, we need to launch long lead time systems to meet future user needs."

Small business products and services must bring greater perceived value to the small business user and improve the owner/manager's personal effectiveness. Small business is composed of submarkets having 3.9 million businesses with 19 or fewer employees. Understanding this market requires understanding future benefits against future costs, where features only have value when they're easy to use and increase effectiveness. Most of the enterprises are financed out of current cash rather than long-term debt. Hence, these owners look for immediate return on their expenditures. The new public, usage-based, ISDN data networks will enable companies to access remote databases economically. Hence, small business is fast becoming "the market" for ISDN, as it also enables more large-small business information interexchange.

Governmental users are requesting new networks such as FTS 2000. As we look past 1995, we see that this will drastically change data communications. By 1990, data was nearing 20 percent of network traffic. Some believe that, by the turn of the century, data will surpass voice, although data transmission revenue has remained roughly the same percentage of overall network traffic revenue. For the past 10 years, our U.S. expenditures for computer equipment, computer services, and telecommunication equipment rose 6 times to more than 130 billion dollars.

According to *TE&M,* "Almost 25 percent of corporate telecommunications spending today for customer premise equipment, or a 14 billion dollar annual market, is devoted to data communication related equipment."

In the early '90s, the government spent between 9 billion and 12 billion per year on telecommunication and computer hardware/software services, with 25 percent devoted to transmission. Program development budgets in data processing and telecommunications alone were 1 to 3 billion dollars per year. FTS at 1.5 billion call minutes per year is impressive. The FTS 2000 and its sister programs on the defense switched data network represent an effort similar to NASA's early space program. According to *Communications Week,*"Its participants should find their ability to subsequently sell and capture commercial market share greatly enhanced, as they transfer technology learned from the country's prime beta test site environment in which many new services will be defined."

Protocols will be standardized, voice data networks will be integrated, and operator procedures will become outlined as the government agencies shift to more and more data communications. There are 13,000 separate government computer systems. At last count, there were more than 240 independent, full-blown data networks in operation. These new networks will be good competition when the Department of Energy's OPODEL, a satellite-based integrated telecom network and the Federal Aviation Administration National Data Interexchange Network are in operation. Similarly, there's the need to bring office automation to more than 1.8 million civilian agency employees. Similarly, Internet, established for the scientific and university community with its internetworking TCP/IP protocol, is now turning to more commercial availability. These are truly mind-bending events and tasks.

Therefore, the whole user-supplier-provider relationship, essential for ISDN, is still in its embryonic stage of development in terms of achieving the information marketplace. We're just at the beginning . . . the first step on a long journey!

The missing users

The consequences of underinvestment in telecommunication was not overlooked by the ITU, Plenipotentiary Conference, which established an independent commission for worldwide telecommunication development. According to *Telephony,*

"The commission recognized that, in industrial countries, telecommunications is taken for granted as the 'engine of growth and a major source of employment and prosperity.' However, in most developing countries, the telecommunication system is inadequate or nonexistent, where large tracts of territories have no system at all."

In reviewing common carriers' world telecommunication spending for the '80s, there was an increase from 75 billion dollars to approximately 100 billion dollars. Those who preside over telecommunication networks of developing countries entered the '90s cautiously. The two factors that influenced their telecommunication development were their raw material export demand and interest rates. Both are beyond their control. Depressed earnings offer little hope that these countries can do more than concentrate on their highest-priority projects. For many countries, this is payment on rescheduled loans and crucial services. Long-distance toll networks represent a source of foreign currency. For example, one long-distance telephone company serves a major share of the country's local network and generates 70 percent of its revenues from toll, with 50 percent of the toll from international calls. These dollar earnings could help finance large-scale telecommunication projects. However, funds generated by telecommunication might be given to meet other priorities. In many countries, this is health and education, water and power, utilities and roads. For many, due to limited funds, cellular has begun to play a bigger and bigger role, spurring the wireless-versus-wireline debate.

User interfaces

Many players are involved in establishing standards and agreements for moving information across boundaries. Of particular importance to the future of standards in the United States are bodies, forums, and user groups such as the forum of the Exchange Carriers Standardization Association (ECSA), which came about through strong leadership of the independents, as well as the former BOCs.

As we look at the history of U.S. participation in the International Telecommunication Union (ITU), we can make the following observations. These are based more on the International Telecommunication and Telegraph Consultative Committee (CCITT) rather than the International Radio Consultative Committee (CCIR), and more from the standpoint of a major telephone carrier than a record carrier.

"We have seen tremendous pressure to obtain standards quicker and sooner than previously achieved within the CCITT process. The fact that technology is outstripping established institutions is a worldwide problem, not unique to the United States. Unless some changes in methods take place within the CCITT, an increase rather than a decrease of regionalization of standards and practices will be seen. This will work to the disadvantages of carriers, manufacturers, and customers alike."

Budgets, revenues, markets

Today's business user is on the frontier of an information society. In the early '90s, only two offices in twenty in the United States are equipped with a personal computer. This is expected to grow substantially during the mid '90s, with the voice/data computer-based workstation becoming commonplace.

ICA (international Communication Association) surveys calculated the overall average for telecommunication expenses across the United States industry in the early '90s as .74 percent of sales and .95 percent of expenses, up from .51 percent and .65 percent in the early '80s.

The RBOCs are spending $60 billion during the 1991 to 1994 period to modernize, replace, and expand subscriber (customer) and trunk (network) carrier systems. Of this, approximately $40 billion, or 66 percent, will be used to grow the network; modernization efforts will consume $15 billion, or 25 percent, and $5 billion or so will be for plant replacement. Of the 9,366 network central offices, by 1994, 7,074, or 76 percent, will be digital, and 2,269, or 24 percent, will have ISDN capabilities. Of the 118,961,000 access lines, 68,028,000, or 57.2 percent, are digital; 86,964, or 73.1 percent SS7 access lines are available, and 2,218,000, or 2 percent, of access lines are ISDN, up from 496,000 in 1990. The number of local loop working channels is 135,304,000, while the number of local loop equipped channels is 203,092,000.

Telecommunications carriers spent approximately $25 billion per year in the late '80s. With RBOCs spending approximately $15 billion, independents 5 billion, and interexchange carriers $4 billion. In looking at revenues, a snapshot look at predivestiture reveals that revenues in 1983 were $62 billion, of which $30 billion were local revenues and $29.5 billion were toll revenues. Operating expenses were around $42 billion, and maintenance expenses only $14.4 billion.

Switching and transmission technology dominated the LEC (local exchange carriers) expenditures in the late '80s; switching consumed 28 percent of the total LEC expenditures, while transmission cable took 29.7 percent and fiber optics 3.6 percent.

Although $60 billion over four years in the early '90s is a large number, it's approximately the same amount spent during the later years of the '80s, despite substantial growth in telephone services, where $60 \div 7 = \$8.3$ average per RBOC, or where $8.3 \div 4 =$ approximately $2 billion per year.

SS7 will grow from 33 percent (1990) to 73 percent in 1994, but it will be available in only half of COs; fiber equipped loop channels will increase drastically from only being 3.3 percent of the network. The number of access lines having ISDN capabilities is only 2 percent under 1992 plans, but this will change drastically once all the RBOCs follow Ameritec and Bell Atlantic's lead to launch the public data network from ocean to ocean.

Together, switches and cable account for approximately 60 percent of LEC outlays. Sophisticated digital switches and high-capacity fiber-optic cable hold the keys to the hearts and welfare of demanding business customers. Business customers account for a small portion, 17.5 percent of the total access lines, but they're easily the most important revenue generators. They're also the telecommunications consumers with the most opinions.

Many of the RHCs have decided to bring full digital data-handling capability to business users as rapidly as possible. As noted earlier, the independents also have approximately 9,000 switches, of which 31 percent are digital, while only 6 percent of the RHCs 10,000 switches were digital by 1990. The '90s promise to witness the continuation of the already hot pursuit for both the large and small business customer, but in order to move the business customer's information successfully, the carrier will rely heavily on new digital switches and fiber-optic transmission links.

The business picture looks different from the interexchange carriers point of view. The major five spent $4 to $5 billion per year in the late '80s, with the big three (AT&T Communications, MCI, and GTE) reducing their outlays. Hence, the

'90s appear to be a new phase in establishing service nodes within the local community and forming alliances to bring users to their networks.

For 110 of the Fortune 1,000 firms with an average budget of $16.5 million for telecommunications/information services, telecommunications was 33 percent of the C&C budget, of which voice was 65 percent and data was 29 percent. Personal computer growth went from $5 million (1983) to $18 million (1985) at a 10 percent growth rate. The next-generation PCs in the '90s now have "intelligent modems" and application programs, making it relatively easy to internetwork PCs to foster new business applications using programs such as Appletalk. New fourth-generation PCs will have the power of previous, early-generation supercomputers.

PBX manufacturing revenue was about $41.7 billion in 1990, with vendor revenue at $4.5 billion, serving low-end PBXs (less than 100 stations) and high-end PBXs (more than 400 stations). Looking at business equipment sales by vendor category, interconnect vendors obtained 37 percent of the market, AT&T 28 percent, BOC's 27 percent, and independents 8 percent of a $6.4 billion market in the late '80s.

The answer to future switched data transport budgets lies in the economic realities of production consumption. How far will data transport and switching equipment prices fall once the top market has justified mass production? When will data calling traffic increase sufficiently to justify substantial price reduction, which in turn will simulate increased calling, and so on? There are no easy answers, as both cellular, traditional carriers, and specialist common carriers (SCCS) face these questions. In viewing post divestiture forecasts, we see that there's sufficient competition. This competitive objective that led to the upsetting of the old ways is working. The marketing forces of supply and demand are more or less visible in all market segments. Nevertheless, the local exchange segment is still a bastion of conservative management.

Whether or not the new order will be better than the old are questions that are open to debate. Meanwhile, many telecommunications firms are doing new things and, though inexperienced, some of the players are doing them quite well, but others are not.

The Information Age

Industry watchers have noted the following:

"In his book, *Mega Trends,* John Naisbitt observed that we are living in a time of 'a time inbetween.' The revolution is driven by advances in microelectronics transforming our contemporary world from an industrial to Information Age society. The heart of this revolution is the computer. If information is power, perhaps the best advice to heed is that of a wise ruler of ancient Greece, Pittacus, who said, 'the measure of man is what he does with power.' However, another measurement of a person is how well one keeps up with the others in the race. If keeping up isn't hard enough, being one step ahead of the competition is certainly getting to be next to impossible. It requires intense concentration of effort, resources, and strategic thinking to be a leader. As it is, it will require our greatest efforts simply to stay with the pack. The Information Age has produced global competition, affecting not only national pride, but also economic survival. This requires us to think not only of the opportunities, but also the risk. In reality, it will be the total environment of the universities and technology-based industries working together to make new products in fields of common effort, which will provide the basis for the national economic growth.

The national policy is to foster more competition and less regulation. U.S. experience indicates that the public is likely to benefit with the pace of change. The availability of new service options are determined by the marketplace, which is the "linchpin," with White House administration support for procompetitive deregulatory policies. Both domestically and internationally, there is an increasing interest in the part of major corporations for the development of sophisticated computer/telecommunication networks to manage their overall production processes more efficiently. U.S. military organizations long have employed highly complex systems, which rely on similar technologies that the private sector corporations are now endeavoring to build. The commercial worlds subsequent efforts are based on this military experience. Electronic Data Systems (EDS) is, for example, developing a global computer telecommunication network for its parent firm General Motors, to facilitate a closer coordination of customer orders, inventory, distribution, and other production processes, even though there is much union resistance to automation changes.

Similar enterprises reportedly are being undertaken by other major firms both here and abroad. In addition to such specialized intracorporate communication networks, sophisticated global financial service systems are being developed by most major international banking and financial companies. Similarly, many of the developmental high-definition television standards and the trend towards digital television have future implications in the use of satellite communications. Producers want to have feature-length motion pictures simultaneously transmitted electronically to the diversity of movie theaters worldwide, rather than the present process of 'bicycling' films.

The White House administration policy, regarding separate international satellite communication, will prove a considerable benefit to the American industry and ultimately to the world public as well. If we are able to secure customer benefits, such that our procompetitive domestic satellite policies could deliver, it should prove an effort that was well worthwhile for the future of the Information Age.

Privatization of telecommunications in developing countries is essential for balanced development. No national public sector has been able to develop a technically modern efficient and effective telecommunication provider. One worldwide trend in various stages of implementation is this privatization.

Privatization is the transition from the complete public ownership to either private or a combination of private and public. Partial privatization is probably politically obtainable in the first step. This allows sovereign telecommunications control by the state, but new competition, partners, and owners can streamline operations and increase service efficiency. Several governments, such as the United Kingdom, Netherlands, and Italy, have made privatization a major goal. Efficiency and eventual modernization of global telecommunication will greatly aid interaction between the developing and facilitating countries. The key, however, is held by the planners of the developing countries. Some developing countries do not wish to spend their money on telecommunications. They wish to have other more apparent projects in their country or simply do not wish their people to be able to communicate as much as they would desire because with communication comes education, and with education might come criticism of their governments."

The competitive arena

Financial interests of the '90s have, through continuous monitoring of the budgets, brought projects into near real-time accountability with demand. Projects that can be deferred are being deferred. Consequently, spending is less than the budgeted amount. The risk inherent to this process is the temptation to defer projects that really ought to be done. There's no sign of explosive, runaway demand or early emergence of significant new revenue streams. There's a tightening of financial controls and steady stream of rate increase requests before the appropriate regulatory bodies.

"Many providers' business plans are clearly to minimize costs and maximize revenues. Some RBOCs bombard the court and regulators with requests for waivers for every option that could put the local exchange network at a more competitive advantage, as well as enable their separate subsidiaries to pursue opportunities previously forbidden to the RBOCs. Even the partially deregulated interexchange market segment has new carriers' success depending on market growth alone, where each one expects a share of the growth. Of course, for many new players, while their primary objective is a greater share of both AT&T's and the RBOCs'communication's market, the RBOCs' and AT&T's objective is keeping their market share and shutting off their competitive handicap."

Telecommunication competition is clearly going about its business. Except where regulation says otherwise, competition is driving prices towards cost and shifting cost to cost-causers. Competition is challenging projects, comparing them with demand, approving some and deferring others. It's redistributing market share and shifting some responsibilities to the customer. It's creating and closing markets, evaluating suppliers and correcting over- and under-supply. It's challenging the traditional players, as well as the new entrepreneurs. It is indeed a new game, which we'll call "the information game . . . the ISDN game . . . in the information arena."

Playing the game

As we look at all the new technical possibilities, we need to assess the market opportunities before deploying these new technologies. For example, it's quite evident that there's a need for several new network switches and service platforms to serve both the private and the public arena. We've seen the opportunity for interconnecting LANs on a local basis expand to frame relay/SMDS/FDDI offerings, where variable-bit-rate, bursty data traffic is handled over shared transport mechanisms.

There has been considerable discussion concerning the advantages of fast-packet fixed-cell type ATM crosspoints and switches for handling bursty data versus channel switching STM facilities that support continuous-bit-rate video-phone-type traffic. As users request the ability to access multiple locations on a customer-controlled basis, we need to understand exactly what this means in terms of these new switching capabilities.

Does the user wish to establish a connection for a selected amount of bandwidth, such as a T1, T3, fT1, fT3, OC-1, OC-3 rate and leave it up for a day, a week, a month? Should this destination and transport rate be changeable on a per-call basis? Should the amount of capacity needed be channelable during the call? Should the capacity be varied dynamically as needed — such as when "data content movement" or video "talking heads" require more bandwidth? Should wideband/broadband public data networks be established only for the business community? Is there a need for a dataphone, videophone directory of addresses to enable the ability to dial up anyone located in the city, the state, the region, the nation? Should videophone be available to everyone? Residence and business? If so, do we really need to packetize video, or simply channel switch the information, especially as photonics replaces electronics, as the proton competes for the electronics customer? As we deploy private networking nodes to offer shared transport either by the telecom or the alternative carriers, what should be the new public broadband switching network architecture?

In reviewing these questions, we need to look again at our deployment strategies, both market and network. Perhaps we need a front-end ring switch, which provides switched virtual network services instead of permanent virtual networks so that information paths and capacity can be changed dynamically at the time of call, to any place, any time. This requires more universal addressing schemes than simply using private internetworking routers. New internal CPE information-handling switch/service nodes will be established on customer premises during the '90s, replacing voice grade PBXs as they again challenge traditional Centrex offerings.

Here, network providers need to understand what these new products — voice, data, video, and image offerings — will be, and how they'll use the full range of ISDN capabilities in order to provide a corresponding family of global narrowband-wideband-broadband network offerings. Finally, determining how both CPE and network players achieve private-to-public networking and internetworking will be essential, as both games are played in separate but somewhat integrated and interdependent arenas.

Future telecommunications: a forward glimpse

"With the historic abolition of long-distance charges on 31 December 2000, every telephone call became a local one, and the human race greeted the new millennium by transforming itself into a huge, global, gossiping family."

Arthur C. Clarke
2061: Odyssey Three

We might agree or disagree with Arthur C. Clarke's intriguing vision of the world-to-be in 2061, but it's indeed important to assess the future of telecommunications, especially as it becomes more and more global. So, let's pause, as we did earlier with a backward glance at how we got here, to now obtain a forward glimpse of where we're going, both technically and socially . . .

Let's first begin by assessing the potential of future trans-switching technologies by projecting the direction and impact of SONET, fiber, photonics, switching, support, and ISDN networks. Next, let's look at future services and applications in view of LAN, PCN, and ISDN services; then let's conclude with a glimpse of possible future cities and societies, in light of business divestitures, mergers and acquisitions, alliances and partnerships, noting data networking and imaging, telephone and television, wireline and wireless, and local and global telecommunication opportunities.

Trans-switching

Transmission and switching, previously considered two separate entities, have become more and more integrated as variations of connectionless data transport services are routed here and there, interfacing with connection-oriented data streams. As we look to photonic switching as the next step in the merger of transmission and switching, we see the possibility of transporting numerous wavelengths or frequencies within a single mode fiber. As more and more frequencies (which can be visualized as colors) become simultaneously available, we might move from binary-based communications and computer systems of ones and zeros to other modulo-based number systems, such as decimal. In these domains, information is transported and manipulated with higher and higher degrees of content.

Just as red and green produce yellow, so multiple frequencies can produce a spectrum of colors, enabling new arrays of services. However, to both transport (switch) and manipulate information in the light medium, we need optical memories and optical decision logic. Otherwise, we must return to the binary world of today's electronics of 1s and 0s. As Dr. Ross noted, though we have prototypes of various forms of photonic switches in the laboratories, optical computer engineers are still searching for the optical equivalent of an integrated circuit. However, years of research experience has quelled the high hopes of coherent lightwave techniques boosting sensitivity one-hundred-fold over direct detection. New optical amplifiers now enable direct detection to match the performance of coherent detection. In addition, as the signal in the local area network application is combined and split into multiple channels, the optical amplifier is used in coherent detection to boost power and composite for the loss of the splitting, as the original signal deteriorates. Engineers have found that Erbium-doped amplifiers, operating in the 1.5 micron wavelength added significantly less noise from semiconductor laser amplifiers. Much more needs to be done. We need to find other elements, such as Neodymium, that can operate at an atomic emission line of 1.3 microns, as well as new technologies for transport, such as hybrids that mix direct detection with coherent detection or lithium niobate external modulators to help reduce intrinsic noise additions and signal loss problems. This has led researchers to believe that the commercial availability of pure photonic switches having no electronic-to-optical conversions will remain the dream product of the next century, leaving the 2.4 Gbps world to the '90s.

Copper plant

Similarly, as noted earlier, new technologies that enable the "mining of the copper plant" continue to indicate that expanding transport capabilities over existing plant can be achieved, such as high-speed bit rate digital subscriber line (HDSL), using ISDN's 2B1Q basic rate access technology to transmit 784 Kbps over a 12,000-foot copper pair within a carrier serving area (CSA). This enables two HDSL transceivers to send 1.544 Mbps T1 payloads over two pairs. This then enables users to "plug and play" with a much faster installation that doesn't require conditioning or the removal of bridge taps, which, unless removed in previous T1 installations, causes echoes. In addition, repeater spacing can be substantially expanded. Similarly, asymmetrical digital subscriber line (ADSL) technology links fiber and copper facilities, providing enough capability for customers to receive VCR-quality video along with a regular telephone call, as 1.5 Mbps is available to the customer from the network and 64 Kbps or 16 Kbps is received by the network from the customer. This allows operation "over virtually all the nonloaded loop plant up to 18,000 feet." Bellcore's HDSL Terminal Unit (HTV) is a higher-speed version of pair gain's 2B1Q transceiver for the DSL rate, where it transports 160 Kbps for ISDN BRI over an 18,000-foot copper pair; HTV sends 800 Kbps over a 12,000-foot copper pair — so, in parallel, two transceivers send 1.6 Mbps over two pairs. This then extends the current plant's copper data-handling capabilities well into the next century.

Broadband

SONET (synchronous optical networks), on the other hand, as noted in *Telephony*[10] is "like a railroad track. It doesn't care whether the train is carrying boxcars full of gold, gondola cars full of coal, flatbeds full of lumber, or all those things together. It just takes them from here to there. SONET carries byte payloads of Asynchronous Transfer Mode (ATM) and bitstreams of Synchronous Transfer Mode (STM) all mixed together, as it all goes over the same fiber through the same hierarchy in a very standard way, allowing users to build different cross sections of transport capacity and service types in the same pipe."

The future will see fiber to the curb (FTTC) and fiber to the house (FTTH) competing for implementation in active and passive optical networks (PONs) arrangements, as new network strategies take on high-speed bus and ring configurations with access switches located closer to the user. This will enable private-to-public interconnection, allowing information to be "virtually" transported through multiple survivable configurations controlled by new superbroadband

---

[10]See *Telephony Supercom '93* issue.

switches and routed to information services platforms located within and outside the regulated community. As video services such as videophone are introduced, volumes of continuous-bit-rate traffic will compete with bursty, variable-bit-rate computer/terminal/workstation data traffic for bandwidth on demand, as information is trans-switched over broadband SONET/SDH-ATM/STM-WDM/SDM facilities. Already, CCITT G.707, G.708, and G.709 standards for multiple hierarchies of digital systems are accommodating the merger of North American and European differences, as multiples of the synchronous transport signal (STS-1) at 51.8 Mbps are integrated with the European Digital Multiplexer (DSMX) 34/140 rates of 139,264 Kbps at the Synchronous Transport Module (STM-1) rate of 155.52 Mbps, with STM-4 at 622.080 Mbps and STM-16 at 2.48832 Gbps.

Similarly, Bellcore TR-303 interfaces and full-access time-slot interchange (TSI) capabilities have become the centerpiece for new generations of digital loop carrier (DLC) systems. TR-303 allows a circuit interface of the DLC into the new switches, eliminating the need for additional central office (CO) terminals, main distribution frames, or other terminal gear. Backward compatibility via TR-008 enables working with existing digital carrier systems such as AT&T's SLC 96 DLC. However, the next-generation systems will require flexible bandwidth options to enable LECs to cost effectively offer services from N-ISDN to f-T1, T-1, DS1, T3, 384 Kbps H/O and STS-3/OC-3, OC-1 2, and OC-24 (2.4 Gbps) services.

As Rodney Dangerfield noted, support systems "gets no respect." However, new operating support systems (OSS) will be deployed during the '90s, enabling SONET provisioning, testing, and surveillance features. Management and control will be provided over a new language, ASN.1/CMISE, as a machine-to-machine language platform for exchanging messages. Now, as the '90s progress, support systems, especially network management, customer control, and automated provisioning "gets more and more respect."

Finally, open network interfaces, via Bellcore's TA909 specification for defining fiber-in-the-loop interfaces, will help establish the necessary standard interfaces for both the network and the customer. Other standards are being established by T1 working groups for the Broadband ISDN and OC-1, OC-3, etc. transports via the CCITT-I series, including the I.361 ATM layer spectrum, I.321 B-ISDN protocol reference model and I.413 B-ISDN user network interface for permanent or semipermanent ATM virtual connection and connectionless data services. So, work continues throughout the '90s to set the trans-switching stage for the next millennium.

Wireless

In the shadows of wireline activity, the wireless Personal Communication Network (PCN) progresses as the cellular spread spectrum code division multiple access (CDMA) technology also vies for PCN applications to help resolve frequency overcrowding problems. CDMA is said to boost cellular capacity more than 20 times by allowing more calls to occupy the same space spread over the entire frequency band, as it competes with time division multiple access (TDMA) and enhanced ETDMA technology over the 1850–1990 MHz range. Other equipment is dispersed in the 902-928 MHz, 2.4-2.48 GHz, and 5.725-8.50 GHz radio bands to enable "the ability to make and receive a call anywhere, from anywhere in the world . . . using such systems as future digital wireless PBX systems that have pico cells with a range of 50 to 100 meters, providing seamless hand-over between radio cells, two-way calling, and intrabuilding roaming."

Video

In the video arena, some believe that combining telephony with CATV will do nothing for broadband applications, which will be 99 percent residential; others believe they must combine. Assuming that switched video is provided over fiber, it will take 20 years to replace the metallic loop. There's little commonality between business-oriented, two-way switched broadband service and advanced residential one-way CATV. Others look for LAN interconnection, electronic publishing, and CAD/CAM mapping rather than teleconferencing and videophone to be the global application. However, as passive optic networks are deployed for some broadband video broadcast-type services in FITL applications, CATV providers are overlaying a switched fiber arrangement on their feeder routers, interfacing to their traditional residential tree-branch facilities in an effort to prepare for more and more video-on-demand switched offerings. However, they're still continuing the analog world with interfaces to analog coaxial facilities to the home.

This leads us to the future of video, for not only workstations but also desktop video and PCs will begin to require more and more video communication at higher and higher resolution. Similarly, videophone will come in narrowband, wideband, and broadband versions requiring more and more transport capabilities. In time, we'll see integrated systems of varying degrees of definition/resolution as users interact. Hence, users of the same transport quality can display similar images, while those of lesser capability require less image transport. This "mix-and-match" requirement will be essential over the transition and implementation period of the '90s, perhaps even throughout several hundred years of the new millennium, until adequate areas of the globe have been upgraded sufficiently . . .

According to the U.S. Bureau of Census, in 1990 there were approximately 120 million workers in the United States. Approximately one-third of them worked at a desk, using PCs, dumb terminals, word processors, or typewriters, of which there were 42 million. Fourteen million workers had PCs of one form or another, using LANs or modems to connect them together and to mainframes. One analysis noted "that LANs were deployed, such that: 75 percent of the LANs served general office applications of word processing, accounting, and database access; 8 percent education; 6 percent medical/scientific; 5 percent general; 4 percent manufacturing; and 3 percent other uses." Private LAN interconnect, using fiber distributed data interface (FDDI-II) capabilities of 100 Mbps, operating at 10 times the speed of Ethernet or token ring LANs, was both complemented and challenged by public frame relay and SMDS-ATM switched offerings at speeds of 1.5 Mbps to 4 Mbps to 16 Mbps and 140 Mbps, respectively, to transport LAN data, Group 5 fax, and computer-based imagery, etc. Furthermore, narrowband ISDN (n-ISDN) supports numerous types of data communications services as well as LAN interconnect, such as Group 4 fax, videotex, and computer-based imagery at medium speeds. These digital n-ISDN facilities will be fully, universally deployed with SS7 perhaps by 1995.

Thus, independent of the merger of some telcos with CATV for broadcast analog TV services, we've seen that numerous bandwidth-on-demand services, with many choices for voice/data/video offerings, can be supported by selected high-speed digital transports. These will also serve interactive, two-way videophone conversations at varying degrees of compression and quality resolution, until the fully digital high-definition videophone, television, and computer imagery services can enable "virtual reality" services, video "juke boxes," and image systems to interact with not only businesses, but also home users.

Managing the merger of C&C

As we look at the integration of computers and communications, especially as we view their mergers and acquisitions, partnerships and alliances, and even divestitures, it's of the utmost importance to understand and appreciate the contrasting differences of the players that lead and manage these somewhat diverse but similar endeavors. The computer industry has been built by aggressive management pursuing complex, changing, advancing technology. These managers not only labored to understand the subtle differences of many new technologies, but were also willing to take the necessary risks required to achieve the technology's full potential in the marketplace.

On the other hand, advancements in the communications industry, specifically the telecommunications industry, were achieved through advancements in technologies, but these changes were in part due to harnessing controllable segments and implementing them in five-year increments. In this manner, technology was researched extensively by laboratory personnel, carefully culled and selected, and then established in one or two new products that were then fully tested and operationally procedurized before deployment in the field. This low-risk mode of operation was fostered and supported by a monopoly-based marketplace in which the dominant players could introduce selected new features — when and where they wanted — with little concern for the customer, the ultimate user, and without the normal competitive forces that existed in the computer arena.

Over the years, the communications industry became heavily involved in ubiquitous, common, standardized offerings, while the computer industry continued to pursue, in an unrestricted manner, any new exciting idea or technological advancement. As a result, to succeed in the computer industry required superior technical skills, while to succeed the communication industry required superior political and financial skills; the computer industry wrestled with complex technology, and the communication industry struggled with massive, broad deployment plans, state and federal regulatory issues, and large organizational and personal management challenges. For many, personal advancement was left to the risks of political games, and the operation of the products were left to a few.

As these two industries merge and form partnerships, especially as more C&C offerings become more and more integrated, interrelated, and interdependent, it's especially interesting to observe how the different management styles and cultures have in the past, and most likely will in the future, continue to offset and inhibit each others' advancement. For example, the missing timely arrival of public data network offerings drove the computer manufacturers to create their own specialized local area networks.

We should also keep in mind that the alliances between different types of communication providers also have their problems, as CATV providers were able to quickly establish low-quality transport and program offerings to get anything to the marketplace to make money. This is inconsistent with the high-quality, standardized, long-term telephone providers' mode of operation. So, as the future unfolds, as the various providers merge and form partnerships within the communication industry and between the computer and the communication industries, success will really be tied to resolving the differences between the different leaders' different perspectives, modes of operation, and personal objectives.

Change changing change

The telecommunication odyssey is moving to the phase where a full evolution of the interdependent parts of telecommunication must take place before the major benefits of change can be achieved. This is especially true as we move to the Age of Light in the forthcoming Information Millennium, where fiber optics will play a key role, as light is split, multiplexed, demultiplexed, and switched. As noted, laboratories throughout the world are hard at work on devices such as multifrequency lasers and the optical equivalence of electronic transistors, amplifiers, dividers, and switches. The telecommunication potential of direct optical signal processing and switching is enormous, and the work is continuing. (See FIG. 2-17.)

However, now is the time to slice the analysis a little differently to cut across the functional areas, the technology layers and partitions, to obtain a better focus in specific areas. After taking this closer look at "what's happening," we need to determine "where we're going." This can best be seen by framing our view more specifically in terms of ISDN, C&C, and the new features and services in the information marketplace. From this we might be able to assess the potential outcome of our endeavors and establish a clearer, more specific direction. This might require some redirection of efforts or midcourse corrections to somewhat better channel the forces of change in the direction we want to go . . . (See FIG. 2-18.)

The information society

The early twentieth century fostered rapid growth in the telephone industry as numerous, noninterconnected, separate telephone companies were established in the cities. Now, in the final years of this century, we see the expansion of private local area networks (LANs) searching for interconnectivity, with their terminals and computers searching for interoperability. Hopefully, the future possibilities of

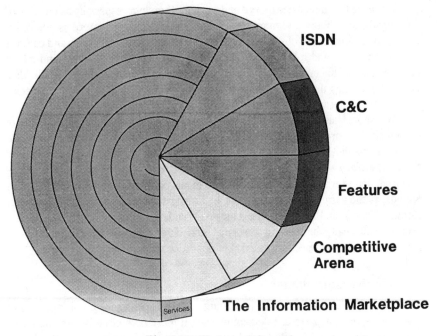

ISDN

C&C

Features

Competitive
Arena

Services The Information Marketplace

Fig. 2-17. Wedges of change.

new public/private switching networks offer an insight into the proper integration of computers and communication so that the appropriate public data narrowband, wideband, and broadband networks can be established in a timely, universal manner. This would diminish the unneeded chaos and complexity of attempting to integrate numerous dissimilar networks without the supporting common information communication infrastructure . . .

To finish our assessment, we need to pause and take a final look at society in America and across the globe. This view of the past and glimpse of the future might indicate that today's civilization has come to a "crossroads in time." Just as past technologies challenged the horse-and-buggy world of our ancestors to advance to the fast-paced, machine-based society of today's high-powered sport cars and jet airplanes, future technologies will have similar, far-reaching effects as we advance to a world based on the creation and use of information. In the past, industrial nations of the world have found their growth in removing farm workers from the harness of the plow to the harness of the assembly line. Both blue-collar and white-collar workers migrated to the factory and office jobs of the cities, causing their extensive growth to form megatropolises, where large labor pools moved from one production line to another. This enabled Los Angeles' military industry, Seattle's aerospace industry, Boston's computer mainframe industry, and Chicago's electronic television/communication industries to flourish and blossom. Subsequent economic forces migrated these industries to every sector of the globe in search of cheaper and cheaper labor.

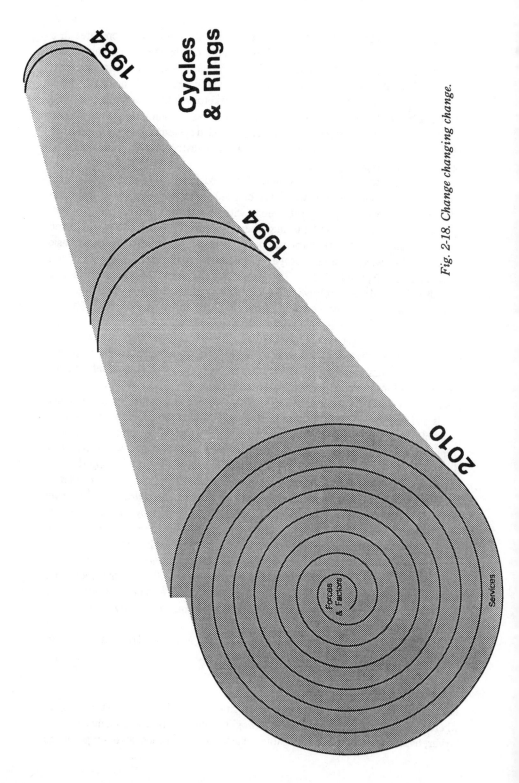

Fig. 2-18. Change changing change.

With the advent of the integrated circuit and its subsequent computer in a chip, a new age had dawned. A shift occurred from hardware assembly lines employing many uneducated people to more automated assemblies using sophisticated equipment to speed the flow of products and improve their quality. Today, computers have entered every aspect of the marketplace; their versatile programming capabilities have changed every form of work. As a result, previous repetitive or complex tasks are replaced by computer-controlled systems. No longer are large labor pools required in centralized locations, as more distributed but more educated forces provide the pieces of the product.

Just as the wild '20s spanned new jobs, good times, excessive income, and questionable morality, so the wild '80s enabled the haves (separated from the have-nots) to experience prosperity, along with considerable wealth and immorality. This has left us with the "morning-after" residue of problems to clean up and resolve in the '90s. Large corporations have begun to refocus on their basic businesses, following years of improper expenditures, reduced products/production lines, closed plants, and high debt. This has caused the work force to find dwindling jobs, dwindling salaries, and dwindling opportunity. Unfortunately, this boom-to-bust scenario is not simply the result of the classic business cycle of expansion and recession. Several key shifts and changes have taken place.

As those within the communication industry know, technology is now able to redistribute the urban work forces back to the rural communities, where smaller groups of workers are networked together by new electronic/optical information highways to form "virtual" assembly lines across the region, nation, or globe, to produce new products from new ideas. With the renewed emphasis on customer needs and new products to fit specific user applications, there will be an exciting array of new services during the next millennium. This will be achieved in a new, competitive, global marketplace, as countries such as Singapore, Malaysia, Hong Kong, Korea, and Japan on the Pacific rim position themselves by leading the way in establishing versatile communication infrastructures to participate in the information revolution. These and other aggressive nations are addressing the many complex issues of today, as they attack poverty and despair by establishing new jobs, providing education for the masses, winning the war on drugs, and encompassing a return to family values and morality. Without addressing these needs, once prosperous countries will diminish, while others will grow stronger. We've seen the rise and fall of many civilizations over the ages . . . So it has been, so it will be . . . Hopefully, these new technologies can provide some assistance as we take our first steps on the long journey back to a vibrant, competitive, strong, and morally sound society . . .

So, let's close with our assessment of what's happening today with a look into the future. It might well be a tale of two cities . . .

A tale of two cities

Infolopolis and Megatropolis are two urban cities located in different states, somewhere in America. Megatropolis is a thriving, hustling, bustling community built on power; here, the decision-makers gather, clustering their headquarters together to influence government policies and procurements. Many of their plants are nearby, while others are selectively located in appropriate congressional districts, where sympathetic congresspeople who concur with their interests prevail. In a different time, in a different place, Infolopolis has risen from the ashes of a decaying city, where new technologies and global competition brought a quick and forceful blow to the city's major industrial plants. However, after a long delay, visionary city and state leadership brought an immediate reversal to a degenerating society, bringing new hope and prosperity to its inhabitants.

Having looked at the possibilities of many new technologies and the opportunities of their new services, let's review the day-to-day activities of these two cities, Megatropolis and Infolopolis, in terms of the modes of operation of their citizens, in order to better appreciate the ramifications of the forthcoming information marketplace.

Megatropolis

Megatropolis is built on the East Coast, in a corridor of large cities. Most of its inhabitants are enclosed within and around an inner core of skyscrapers. The local communication monopoly had been under the stringent control of the local telephone company, which specialized in automating its voice operating systems and deploying accessible LAN interconnect transport. It has entered the television transport in joint partnership with local CATV providers. It didn't offer specialized public networks to facilitate universal data or interactive video; it believed that it was the task of the customers to construct their own networks, using shared bandwidth public transports needed to offset the high costs of privately leased transport. Alternative networks were offered in the wireless domain by constructing an overlay cellular network, and, in the wire-line arena, as a joint offering with the local cable company to enable selective access to "video juke boxes" for pay-per-view services. Due to limited technical needs, little fiber, if any, was deployed in the residential plant for this endeavor; the company relied mainly on CATV's coaxial analog cable transport for delivery, using specialized, selected frequencies for low-speed customer requests or voice conversations. While remote data customers were encouraged to use dial-up analog data modems to access information services providers' databases or gateways to LANs, the main data effort consisted of interconnecting LANs and providing service platforms that provided various protocol and code conversions to internetwork various types of LAN transport.

As time progressed, several alternative "networking" service providers were established to provide similar protocol interfacing software packages. In time, many of the major businesses elected to privately internetwork their own traffic via gateway switches on their premises, using the public network only as an overload safety valve. In this manner, life remained relatively the same within the city.

However, as daily functions began to turn to using the telephone network to transport more and more dial-up data via analog modems, traffic "brown-outs" began to appear during busy hours; the analog, voice-based switching systems couldn't keep up with the excessive number of attempts and short or long holding times required for low-speed data traffic. As time passed, citywide data networks began to appear to selectively remove the various industry-based communities of interest from the public network. In this manner, the local government offices interconnected themselves using LANs within the various complexes, they and established large, survivable, ring-type transports using "dark fiber" (fiber in conduit without public network electronics) that they purchased from the local telephone firm; the government offices added their own transmission electronics with connections to internal nodal switches. Selected locations having specialized nodal switches provided access to the world, allowing direct connection to a particular interexchange carriers' point of presence. They also facilitated limited outside access to their internal facilities via dial-up modems.

In this manner, the city businesses huddled together to create as much efficiency as possible in their use of their private internetworking facilities. Nonelectric, face-to-face meetings continued to be the best form of communication, continuing to encourage local automobile/global airplane transportation. As more time passed, congestion from local traffic growth increased, as the city complex grew and grew until gruesome. Soon it became more economically productive to establish private microwave links between office complexes surrounding the city and downtown headquarters, to enable video conferencing of meetings and cut down on local travel.

However, problems continued to prevail as cross communities of interest attempted to interconnect information. Doctors in one HMO had difficulty sharing information with specialists or doctors in another HMO. Similarly, lawyers had difficulty accessing insurance firms and state law enforcement files, as each was self-contained on its own internal network. As time progressed, addressing problems severely hampered cross-network assessability, as layers of protocols were required to achieve interconnection. Much was accomplished in this regard, but the complexity and congestion factors kept the networks at the edge, leaving users many times more willing to use their automobile transportation rather than communication. In time, Megatropolis living became more and more complex when efforts to offset automobile congestion encouraged the work force to live in the more densely packed high-rises, rather than suffer the long commute times required due to too, too much tollway/freeway rush-hour traffic. As the businesses within Megatropolis became more and more successful, their success generated more and more growth, which generated more and more communication needs that couldn't be fulfilled by the existing local telephone infrastructure, highway transportation infrastructure, or social community infrastructure, causing many to question the quality of life in Megatropolis . . .

Infolopolis

On the other hand, the city leaders of Infolopolis were keenly aware that a new revolution was taking place, as they stared out the city windows at their decaying heavy-equipment-based industries. The industrial revolution was coming to an end, as their large assembly plants, using somewhat unskilled labor, attempted to compete with foreign firms that had more automated assembly that used electroni-cally controlled mechanical devices. As the highly competitive Japanese plants led the way in robotic assembly and "just in time" inventory control, as manufacturing facilities all over the world become more and more automated, the leaders of Infolopolis had indeed become cognizant that a new revolution was taking place — an information revolution. To be part of this change, to harness it and channel it for their own use and advancement, they elected to construct a new communication infrastructure to support new businesses that used information as one of their key tools and assets. The first step was to expand existing facilities by constructing a parallel network to the voice network — a public data network over the existing copper plant. To do so, they used the full capabilities of narrowband ISDN. Every home and business within the entire city, as well as each major town in the surrounding communities, were provided access to the new public data network. Soon, new public "dataphone" directories were established so that every terminal was interconnected. Security and password codes were developed to protect closed user groups from outside penetration. Care was taken to ensure that the new network was equipped sufficiently to robustly handle success.

New shared office work centers were established to ring the city with elec-tronically interconnected facilities, thereby encouraging workers to live nearby and commute to work locally, rather than over long distances. These centers were excellent candidates for the faster information transport speeds provided by first wideband and then broadband publicly switched and addressable facilities. New higher-speed switched public networks were established to enable extensive com-puter-to-computer traffic, video imagery, multinode workstations, video conferenc-ing, and eventually high-resolution videophone capabilities to more fully integrate the remote locations together as one. Access was made to national and global networks with special reduced tariffs to encourage usage.

After the initial years of growth, an interesting phenomenon began to take place. During the fifth year and the years following, new cities began to spring up, and these new cities were quite remote from the initial city. Huge communication highways were constructed to link these cities together, as new, more distant rings of cities began to cluster around the city center. However, these rings didn't develop as an urban/suburban extension. They had sufficient green belts (miles and miles) between them to ensure that the small-town quality of life was achieved, but with electronic access to all the services of a large, urban city. In this manner, satellite work groups could develop their own particular aspects of a particular product, which was then electronically integrated into the total package. Hardware assembly plants did exist, using the latest in automation, but these plants could now be located in more remote communities, because of "online" access to design information from other remote locations. So, as Infolopolis developed over time, many different community-of-interest groups were established using the common public ISDN network, as the basic transport infrastructure. Specialized information service platforms were then constructed to tailor offerings to specific needs. These platforms were established above the network in a layered network's layered services architecture. Cross "community-of-interest" interoperability was achieved using public addressing, switching, and standard open interfaces. As broadband fiber was publicly switched and deployed to every residence, interactive videophone services augmented data services to provide full multimedia capabilities to the new users. The local telephone company became the local information company. Numerous information service providers were now able to provide a growing array of services to meet growing customer needs. Private networks did exist within local complexes, but they used the public network for interconnection, as private-to-public internetworking became quite standard and straightforward using addressable switched offerings.

Cellular and private alternative networks also developed, but selectively, as the massive transport capabilities of the fiber delivered more and more massive data and video offerings, successfully providing a parallel economical alternative to coaxial-based CATV networks. Much was spent on upgrading the local infrastructure, for to go "global" was to create a robust "local" marketplace. It was back to rebuilding the "business of the business." In time, these increasingly high-quality communications were not only available for selective local applications, but were also interconnected to the world through global communications, which, as Mr. Clarke noted, were to be as relatively inexpensive as a local phone call . . .

It was a time of growth. It was a time of improving the quality of life for the citizens of Infolopolis . . .

Part II

The information era

What's happening?
Where are we going?
Where do we want to go?
How can we get there?

3

The ISDN marketplace

*"I'd rather use the feather
than the pencil . . . I don't like change . . ."*

A resistive user, 1898

*"I prefer my good old typewriter rather
than learning how to use a computer
word processor . . ."*

A reluctant user, 1998

Section one: the user

What does the user need? . . . We must meet user needs, not technical niceties! We must be market driven! ISDN is only a technologist's dream, but what does the user really want? These and other statements have become a new, driving force as firms, finding few buyers lined up for ISDN services, begin to probe a little deeper to find justification for various technical possibilities. Unfortunately, when marketing was handed the "decision hammer," the silence was deafening. Many new possibilities, identified by technical breakthroughs, were not further developed, as they waited for marketing to satisfactorily determine an acceptable, true market application for the technology. However, many times marketing couldn't find any market—for anything. Their silence in determining the marketplace was then challenged, after R&D houses waited several years in limbo for the "go/no-go" decision. In most cases, after sending out questionnaires for various possibilities, marketing research teams were unable to justify by definite numbers exactly how many users would definitely purchase a given offering.

This is all very understandable; it's extremely difficult to project a future demand for a new service. Anyone who truly believes they know the future, especially to the point of proving with statistical numbers with any degree of accuracy how some particular offerings will be successful, should reassess their analysis to differentiate what could happen from what will happen.

Over the years, this has become a favorite tactical ploy of many business leaders, who challenged their people to prove to them that one potential product would have varying degrees of success over another. Proof becomes a nebulous thing. In some cases, this simply became a delaying tactic. We can't prove the future. On the other hand, this line of questioning can be an effective tool to cause people to reassess and differentiate between "what's happening" and "what could happen," to try to answer the question . . . "Why?" Why would I or someone else really want to buy this service? Why should we develop this product? Some believe that the "why game" is too negative. An alternative approach tries to move forward more positively by asking questions such as when, where, and how such a product/service can or should be deployed. This is a useful management technique to get out of the negative roadblock mode of operation.

- Unfortunately, the dilemma of the ISDN marketplace is tied to all of these factors.
- Unfortunately, most ISDN products require big financial decisions.
- Unfortunately, all ISDN networks require big financial decisions.
- Unfortunately, expensive financial decisions have risk — sometimes big risk.
- Unfortunately, if management is uncomfortable with what's taking place, they're less inclined to take risk.

Usually, the more information that's known about something, the easier the decision is. As information marketplace forces and factors, drives and shifts were better understood in the late '80s, new emphasis was placed on understanding the users, their needs, and their applications for technology. In many cases, much was learned from the market emphasis to help focus the technology. In some cases, erroneous indicators lead researchers down blind alleys. Reliable statistics became increasingly difficult to develop, especially as cross-elasticity of demand for a new offering had little real basis for association with previous endeavors. Some attempts to relate videophone to TV, etc., had little or no concrete results.

User involvement became a necessary but risky business. As one colleague noted, we sat down with the most sophisticated players and asked them what they wanted. They requested an automatic number identification (ANI) feature on every calling party. I asked why. After a long discussion, we finally found out that customers wanted to use it for security access protection. So, the real feature they wanted was security, not ANI. We then proposed several methods to secure their information — so you must be very careful to ask the right question! Others found users, who had limited understanding of what technical price they would have to pay for a particular feature. A doctor once demanded instantaneous screen fill; he later settled for considerably less when it became a choice of a data packet network over an expensive wideband point-to-point facility. Price does a lot to change "musts" to "wishes!"

Again, many needs can be identified, but if the user doesn't perceive them as being as great and wonderful as the product or service provider claims, then an offering might not be as quickly accepted as initially anticipated. Many times it's not the original idea that creates demand; it's a very slight shift in the feature offering or its combination with other features (packaging) that makes it more successful. In some cases, it's a totally different application to a different market segment that changes a mediocre market to an explosive, expanding one. Finally, some things simply need to be presented in a "Madison Avenue" advertising fashion to convince the users that they need it, or by having a trendsetter lead the way for others to follow, copy, or emulate.

So, when we think of ISDN's potential in terms of the '90s marketplace, it's important to not only be technically driven, but also market driven. However, in reality, what's needed is a "user look" at applying the new technology, where "user application" becomes an essential aspect in determining the feature's requirements.

This approach does lead us to the user. (Many times it changes the technology.) In the world of "reality," it's important to tie down the nebulous, the possible, and the potential into the feasible. On the other hand, to lock one in by looking at an opportunity through a limited "view" might inhibit the more global view that would have identified the "right product" for the "right market" at the "right time," rather than a product for a limited market perhaps at the wrong time.

Yes, the users today are king and queen. However, success will come if and only if we've been able to truly understand what the users really want and where and when they want it! To do this, we must also challenge ourselves to more extensively determine why a prospective buyer would want a service or something else, perhaps a little different. We've then crossed from the realm of technical possibilities to the market-driven domain. We're then able to take technical ideas and translate them to actual, feasible, packaged offerings by first applying them to specific user situations.

User types

A reasonable approach to obtaining these requirements is to review the users in terms of their actual modes of operation. One technique is to take a look at the 18 major industries and review the tasks performed in each industry. These tasks can then be individually reviewed in terms of the types of communication needed to accomplish the task, using both today's and tomorrow's particular technologies. From this will come an understanding of the various types of users, using the various forms of new technologies. (See FIG. 3-1.)

This then sets the stage for establishing classes of user types that are common across the industries, using specific types of technology. The net result will be a list of user types that perform specific types of tasks within all 18 industries in a common manner. This will provide a present and future communication insight into the banking business, the insurance business, and the lawyers' operations, but it won't provide a quantitative estimate of how many would actually use the technology to change their mode of operation. However, it will provide a realistic assessment of the application; for example, if you're a bank in New York City with remote tellers, your communication needs will be solved with these communication features. However, this analysis doesn't indicate how many banks in New York City will actually subscribe to these new services. Identifying the feature is one thing; saying you'll order it is another. If you're a bank, these are the features you'll need,

Fig. 3-1. User features?

but whether you believe that you really need them and are willing to pay for them is indeed another story, isn't it?

People types

This then brings us to looking at the marketplace in terms of the individuals themselves — their motivations, their drives, their courage, their adventurousness and their resistance. Users can be classified in several types, from the high society to the Archie Bunker types. Similarly, the faceless types of users in the various workplace environments can be identified in terms of market segment users, as well as specific people types, who will or will not quickly adopt to new technology.

Market segments

Groups of users can be identified as having particular needs that can be met by different types of technology; for example: people in motion, database managers, home inquiry response, or business transactions. By understanding a particular market segment, a host of features and services can be identified to perhaps entice them to change their existing methodologies and tools for more communication-information-oriented application packages to make their work a little easier, more productive, more secure, and less stressful. A common interest group can be a market segment, such as doctors, drug chains, medical record centers, hospitals, etc.

The purchase/the sale

Only when we can combine all of these factors, along with the Madison Avenue advertisement strategies for enticing a user to want to make the purchase, do we have a reasonable chance for success, but in actuality the extent of the success will always be initially unknown. The offering will have different degrees of success, depending on the extent to which the timing is right, how great the need is, and the impact of other uncontrolled forces (such as war, inflation, etc.) that support the need. One key factor is the sales persons themselves in terms of their understanding of real issues, needs, and the ability to reach "the buy button" of the purchaser. (Past history has shown a lack of technical knowledge and sensitivity in dealing with potential buyers of future information services.)

We must be able to differentiate buyers from watchers: we must be able to understand our buyers' desires as they change from wishes to wants to needs, or as requirement shoulds are changed to woulds and coulds. This brings to mind the story where the smart businessman finally asked the prospective buyer to "himself" define what it took to make the sale. Once this is done and negotiations take place to an acceptable compromise, the decision to buy is already made. At this point, it's determined whether or not the original buyer is just fishing for the sake of fishing with no intention to make a real buy or commitment. For now the prospective buyer has (or has not) become a "real buyer."

Similarly, once the real price is established to make the sale, the provider must now make real commitment decisions and decide if indeed the price is right to provide the offering. Hence, the realities of the marketplace become quite evident to both the provider and the user!

Extended needs

A carefully performed analysis of user needs doesn't necessarily come up with the right solution. One bank firm provided remote teller capabilities throughout a midwestern city. Later, the users told the bank that they would prefer to not only access the bank for transactions through their tellers, but also to access national accounts from other institutions such as Sears, American Express, etc. and perhaps even some other local banks. To meet the needs of their users, the bank obligingly established such services from their remote tellers. However, as time progressed, the expense for maintaining the additional cash for other bank transactions, etc., became considerable. Since the other banks didn't want to pay these expenses, the bank offering the service decided to pass on the increased cost to the users at 50 cents a transaction. In response, the users reassessed what they really wanted. Some left the bank. Others limited their outside bank use to the point that the overhead expense for achieving extended services was quite questionable. The bank had not truly considered what the impact of the success of the new offering could be to their mode of operation. They had to reassess what services they really wanted to provide their users for different degrees of a user acceptance (volume).

In conclusion, the new emphasis on the market can be quite rewarding, if it's accomplished in the light of recursive, deeper interactions between technical possibilities and market opportunities. Here, the future ISDN user will demand more than a 2B + D interface, more than an asynchronous to X.25 protocol conversion. To truly understand not only the basic transport user types but all of the other new types of users, as noted in the case example, we must begin to consider the users in terms of needing higher-level information exchanges that require communications for all levels of computer interfaces that are totally transparent to the users. This then frees us to view new applications in terms of the expanding user needs that are resolved in the upper levels of the OSI model. Finally, statistics must be understood in terms of realistically accessing a totally unknown future market. Projections can only be provided to enhance the comfort level of the decision or denote the risk but can never be used solely as the basis for the decision. The future can't yet be proven—nor should it be . . .

User needs

As we review the brief list of needs shown in TABLE 3-1, it's interesting to note how many firms have constructed their business offerings around one or more of these needs, only to find in time that their product base must expand to meet several needs. Users are quite "fickle." Once one of their present problems (needs) is resolved, then they forget that it ever existed, and they want the next and the next need satisfied. We no longer purchase an automobile for transport. We buy it for comfort, looks, etc. . . !

Hence, it's essential to recognize that drastic shifts will take place once we move the human element off its watching, waiting position to "Inter" the door to new, exciting ISDN services. Once the ISDN infrastructure is in place to provide a framework for PBXs, etc. to interconnect users, those that have been sitting on the fence, watching to see what others are going to do, will now have no (logical) excuse not to enter the game. This type of movement has been amply illustrated by the housing industry. You need only to take an airplane ride to visually see numerous houses clustered together on very expensive land where they're surrounded by vast wastelands of inexpensive land, where only the more adventurous dare to go. However, once a direction has been established, be it west, south, or southwest, this then stimulates an outward migration spike for the others to soon follow. (See TABLE 3-2.)

The '80s were a time for overcoming the human resistance to change. Once the initial resistance is over, the time of waiting will have ended, and the great exodus to the information frontier will take place in vast numbers not initially visualized. The Department of Defense recently noted that the numbers of computers it now has in service are above the original estimates by a factor of 10. TV growth increased by a factor of 4,000 in one year—1949. What, then, is the catalyst to motivate such growth in the Information Era? Let's take a deeper look as we recognize that providers and suppliers have needs as well, and these must also be met to enable them to meet the needs of users.

Table 3–1. User Needs

• Personal Needs —Less Time in Queues —Less Time in Work Commute —Flexible Work at Home • Remote Access to Data —Banks —Stock Exchange —Financial Information • Education at Work/Home —Specialty —Hobby • Entertainment/Amusement —Interactive Games —Movies —International T.V. —Past Events —Travelogs • Research Searches —Medical —Government —Legal • Childcare Assistance —Work at Home —Remote Access to Doctors • Remote Shopping —Goods —Foods	• Business Improvements —Increased Effectiveness —Faster Access to Info —Increased Personal Efficiency —Better Decision —Efficient Operations —Reduced Staffs —Cheaper Operations —Quality Products —Faster Order-Delivery Cycle —Better Planning —Deeper Market Penetration • Computers —Inquiry —Search —Retrieval —Processing —Manipulation —Analyzing —Presentation —Instantaneous —Cheap • Communication —High Resolution —High Quality —Reliable —Available —Accessable —Cheap • Information Exchange —Voice —Video —Data/Text—Image

Table 3–2. A Time for "Inter"

The Human Element . . .	
Intervention	Intermediary
Intermix	Interlock
Intermingle	Interlude
Interrelations	Intermission
Interdependent	Interregnum

The new features and services must be based on understanding the needs of both the suppliers and providers and their customers as well. The new services must be properly packaged to make them truly attractive and acceptable to all the users. This then requires an extensive requirement analysis to enable a more realistic identification of user needs and translation of them into very specific requirements. This more rigorous approach requires some process such as the

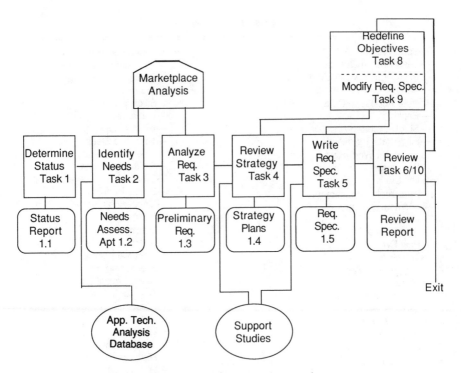

Fig. 3-2. Requirement phase task.

requirement phase task described in my book *Telecommunication Management Planning.* (See FIG. 3-2.)

Features and services

Besides the user's personal interest in making a job easier, having more achievements, and appearing successful, there's the company's interest in improving operations, increasing efficiency and productivity, and enhancing its product quality. This then leads to numerous features and services that can meet both personnel expectations and corporate objectives. No one buys a product just to own the product. This was the mistake of selling ISDN as a 2B + D interface. ISDN must be sold on the basis of its features and services. We've not yet seriously addressed features and services as products, especially to market the full potential of the "S" of ISDN in terms of ISDN.

Features = functions, enhancements, techniques, conditions or variations.
Services = enhanced operations, packaged offerings or packaged features.

Features usually pertain to some particular capability that a product provides to a user by extending the performance of the machine to meet a user need. (See TABLE 3-3.) In some cases, new features are simply variations of an existing feature

Table 3–3. Suppliers' and Providers' Needs

• Visions/Architecture	• Multiple Databases
• Standards	• Trials
— OSI Levels	• Phases of Offerings
— IEEE 802	• ISDN Networks
• Gateways	— Overlay
— Regional	— C&C
— National	— Wideband
— International	— Narrowband
• User Packages	— Broadband
— Features	• Internetworking
— Services	— Private-Private
• Usage Growth Pricing	— Private-Public
• Responsible Tariffs	— Public-Specialized
• Financial Partnerships	• Commitment
• Joint Ventures	— Risk Takers
• Competitive Rulings	— Agreements
• User Participation	— User Purchasers

to provide some new aspect to the marketplace, such as: a different type of button for a clock watch or replacing two buttons with one button that's pressed two times. Thus, a feature becomes more an operational technique. On the other hand, a service usually means more than a feature, it usually denotes a complete packaged offering that's self-sustaining. One form of service providers, for example, are those who provide a database containing lists and lists of a particular type of information. Since they're a basic form of service, they've become known as sink providers to differentiate them from higher-level service providers who search through the lists for the specific relevant information that the user requests. There's a growing trend for higher levels of service providers to take the relevant information and mix and match additional user requirements to provide a more complete picture of the information, perhaps going to higher levels of service provisioning by presenting more expansive graphic displays of the material. Still more extensive services further up the scale will require more detailed analyses of the information in order to present the user with conclusions and recommendations based on material obtained from dynamically changing databases.

As expert systems are deployed, we might want to allow the computer to not only provide recommendations, but also develop future scenarios, based on implementing various proposed alternatives, to enable the user to appreciate the full significance of the data. As artificial intelligence enters the world of fuzzy logic, parallel processing of thousands of nodes, neural processing, etc., we might be able to allow the computer to dynamically make real-time decisions and directly apply control to some crucial but dangerous or boring operations. This relieves the human from being part of the direct implementation process—thereby changing the human role to one of monitor or overseer.

In this chain of progress, we move from features to services based on packaged features, and on to packaged services where:

Packaged features = F (layered features F (products F (price F (design/manufacture/support))))

Packaged services = F (layered services F (networks F (price F (product costs plus operational support))))

Features are usually grouped in clusters layered on top of each other with clear demarcation points that separate them into various classes of offerings. These offerings are usually time-phased to extend the life of the product. These classes of features are based on a pricing structure that many times is quite independent from actual cost (for example, Touch-Tone service). Some offerings require extensive design support as more and more features are layered on top of each other. (For example, an original PBX was designed by five people providing 30 features, but now it has 200 features that require a design support team of 60).

As designed features become delivered services to the user, they're provided in packaged form to take into account the layering of services on top of phases of network products. Offerings are differentiated by the pricing structure to encourage usage at all levels. These packages should take into account the various amounts of operational support required to maintain and update existing versions with enhanced capabilities.

Voice/data features

Hence, it's important to review the potential lists of voice, data and video feature possibilities and distinguish those that will be provided by each of the various phases of ISDN. Packaged service offerings are based not only on the layering of features subject to the supplier's pricing strategies, but also on the provider's networks and services' pricing strategies. In reviewing the C&C features and services in TABLE 3-4, we can see that there are many types of data network user features that affect the overall network's operational performance requirements. Hence, it's essential to determine the set of product features that enable the network providers to operate more efficiently and successfully, as well as to determine the set of features which, when packaged into services, enable the providers to meet the expanding needs of their users.

Therefore, offerings will be packaged first from the supplier to meet the provider point of view as layered features. Then they're provided from the provider to the user in a layered service form to attract, retain, and increase the user's desire to use them. If successful, the users will request many expanding sets of features and services to assist them further in the performance of their operational tasks, such as those shown in TABLE 3-4.

Section two: information cubics

The information world has opened up a new game for telecommunications—the feature game. No longer are we simply concerned with technical operational

Table 3 – 4. New Features

Calling Number Display
Distinctive Ring for Call Waiting
Selective Call Forwarding
Automatic Call Back Recall
Call Management for Variable Bandwidth
  • For N Number of Digital Channels
  • For Automatic Reconfiguration of Internal Network
  • For Automatic Change of Features
  • For New Class of Service
Polling of Data Terminals
Delayed Delivery of Data Messages
Broadcast of Data Message
Protocol Conversion for Different Terminals
Code Conversion for Different Terminals
Barred Access to Data Networks
Encryption of Data
Security Levels of Information Transfer
Short Call Setup
Remote Terminal Identification
Bit and Byte Interweaving for Error Control
Format Transformations
Attempt Limit
Speed Conversion
Error Rate Quality Grade of Service
Data Formatting
Data Structuring
Classes of User Services
Administrative Billing "online" Services
Operator Assistance/Information Services
Video Teleconferencing
Compressed Video Display
Flexible Call Routing
Customer Database Information
2400 or Less Data Features (Switched)
  • Point of Sale Transactions
  • Electronic Funds Transfer
  • Inquire/Response Packets
2400 – 9600 Data Features (Switched)
  • Electronic Mail
  • Facsimile Med Speed
  • Sophisticated Workstation
  • Internal Data Transfer Networks
9.6K – 64K Data Features (Switched)
  • Computer Aided Design
  • Distributed Processing
  • High-Speed Facsimile
  • Graphics

Table 3 – 5. Data Features

Broadcasting	Call back (Automatic)
Delayed delivery	Redirection of calls
Packet interleaving	Speed/format transforms
Byte interleaving	Multiple lines
Code conversion CCITT codes	Abbreviated address call
Polling	Packet switching
Inquiry facility	Re-try by network
Three attempt limit	Store and forward
Low error rate	Short clear-down
Data collection service	Manual/automatic calling
High grade service	Manual/automatic answering
Standard interface	Data service classes
Data tariffs	Direct call
Access to lease line	Network to subscriber interface
Duplex facility	Barred access
Bit sequence independence	Remote terminal identification
Short setup	Multi-address call

features such as network attempts, connect time, holding time, and signaling systems. We now have several users: the provider, the provider's customers, interexchange firms, intermediaries, the private network customers, etc. (See TABLE 3-5.)

To visualize new needs, requirements, and opportunities, we can look at this new world in terms of several three-dimensional cubes. (See FIG. 3-3.) In effect, it's a four-dimensional problem that can best be seen by two three-dimensional views.

The new requirements are like a bottle of champagne. (See FIG. 3-4.) The bubbling features have been bottled up for many years, waiting for an opportunity to escape. The divestiture breakup has shaken up the bottle and released the cork, enabling the bubbling features to fizz out! As they begin to emerge, various corks

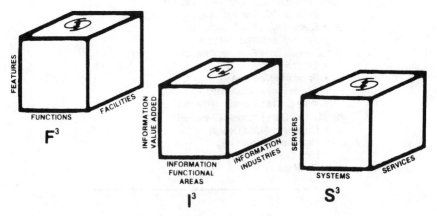

Fig. 3-3. Information cubics.

Fig. 3-4. It's time for a "feature" party.

have been reapplied to the bottle, such as the MFJ, the conclusions of Inquiry II, Inquiry III, the appeals, and open architecture considerations. The strategies of AT&T and IBM, as well as the CCITT standards groups have attempted to control the flow and direction of the new energy and life that has been breathed into the world of telecommunications, especially as it integrates with the world of data processing. Finally, removal of information services restrictions sets a "midcourse correction" to enable the telcos to participate in the formerly very restricted "content" world. Earlier inquiries were used as a delay tactic for non-telco players to prepare for the game. (See TABLE 3-6.)

It's indeed a new game, where the whole will be greater than the sum of the parts, as the two giant C&C industries join together. There was a definite "pop" on Jan. 1, 1984, when divestiture took place. Since then, there has been a flow of smaller "pops," as bubbles of opportunity begin to flow and burst into new ventures. Now, ten years after divestiture, indeed, it's time for a party—so let's play the game and see what kind of party it will be.

Table 3 – 6. Service Applications

Service applications	Peak bit rates Kbps
Energy management	.3
Slow facsimile	1.2
Low-speed data entry	1.2
High-speed data entry	9.6
Home information systems	9.6
Communicating home computer	9.6
Remote job entry	9.6
Inquiry response	9.6
Point of sale verification	9.6
Audio/graphics conference	9.6
Fast facsimile	32/64
Electronic mail	64
Communicating word processors	64
Integrated work stations	64
Electronic filing system	64
Timesharing	64
Batch processing	64
Communicating minicomputers	64
Computer interactions	64
Voice communications	64
Compressed video	1.544 Mbps
Mainframe interactions	1.544 Mbps
Variable graphic-video	64K to 90 Mbps

First we must ask ourselves, "What kind of game will it be?" "Where will it be played?" Figures 3-5 and 3-6 indicate that it will be a world of many new features that will be provided by many new systems. The figures also note that the game

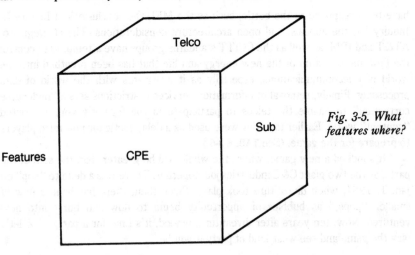

Fig. 3-5. What features where?

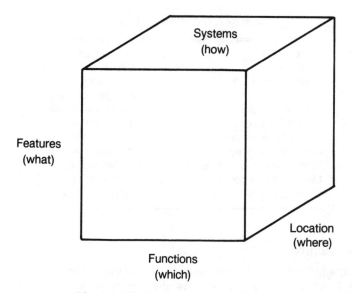

Fig. 3-6. The business of the business.

will be played on at least three, if not more, arenas: the customer-provided equipment (CPE) market, the subsidiaries of the regional telcos, and the regulated and nonregulated divisions in what we'll call the basic information distribution firms (the former BOCs). Though this appears to be a reasonably complex three-dimensional problem, we'll see how another dimension, called functional areas, further complicates the picture. (See TABLE 3-7.)

Never in the decades of defining, designing, supplying, and providing new products have we seen such an involved overlay of special requirements to meet the concerns of the government (Inquiries, MFJ, Waivers, and then midcourse new freedoms, etc.), for meeting the needs of potential new customers (who aren't yet really customers) for a new industry that's really just beginning. Yes, it's a challenging world for those who dare to play the game.

Recall the saying:

The strategy of the strategies:

a twist here . . .

a turn there . . .

Positions . . .

The business of the business:

Strategies . . .

Goals . . .

Objectives . . .

Emphasis . . .

We'll see that requirements are not only greatly linked to strategic direction, but also to the strategies of the various teams playing the game.

Table 3–7. Data Network Parameters

Transfer time	Format structure
Rate structure	Network
Route selection	synchronization
Modes	Data call processing
Network interface	Transmission limitations
Speed conversion	Network signaling
Class of user services	Call clear-down time
Category of error rates	Call request time
Type of network switching	Numbering plan
Overall grade of service	Inquiry handling
Overall quality of service	Usage recording

The big picture

They say a picture is worth a thousand words. The bigger the picture, the better. The F^3, I^3, S^3 cubics are big pictures that show the many facets of the new game. Let's pause and take time to understand these views from every angle and perspective that we can: first, from afar to see the forest, and then up close to see the beauty and complexity of each tree.

The feature game

Figure 3-7 shows the future voice, data, video, text, and image world in terms of features. The vertical axis breaks features into six groups as it extends through several levels, adding more and more value to the service:

I/O The I/O level is the terminal area, where any form of input/output (I/O) device can be connected to the network. No longer are the dial pulse and Touch-Tone telephones the only reigning sovereigns. Terminals must meet not only voice, but also data and video needs. Depending on where the game is played, terminals can also be the interface points to private networks or new data networks, where local area networks (LANs), private branch exchanges (PBXs), key systems, computers, printers, modems, and concentrators exist.

Basic These are the traditional transport features such as plain old telephone service (POTS), as well as new transport features for data switching and wideband switching. Here, data can be switched on circuit switches, packet switches (packet, fast packet or burst), or megabit broadband switches.

Level one: extended information transport In this case, more and more capabilities are added to the transport of information. As noted, custom calling and extended custom calling features are available, as well as, a new family of transport features for various grades of service, levels of maximum error rates, and different types of protocol conversions. Also, transport considerations for security and levels of quality would be available as offerings above the basic level. Note that the new family of CLASS features, based on receiving the calling party identification number, are available here.

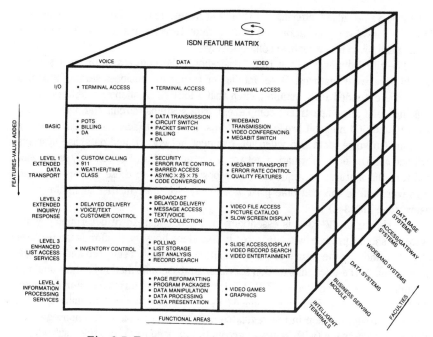

Fig. 3-7. Features/functions/facilities — the F³ cubic.

Level two: extended inquiry   As we enter the new Information Era, there will be a great need for inquiry response interactions. Information will be moved by remote data distribution and data documentation systems. This "F³" figure indicates an extended world of new service offerings, as information is requested and exchanged from various sources.

Level three: extended list access services   Not only must we access lists, but we must be able to search through masses of information. Only then will the computer be a tool for society. Using more and more artificial intelligence, it will acquire reams of information and search through it for relevant data.

Level four: information processing services   The information found in level three is processed, analyzed, manipulated, and prepared for presentation. At this level, the computer is able to truly solve complex problems by using its fully developed multiprocessor's capabilities operating at several hundred millions of instructions per second (MIPS), preparing answers to questions in real-time applications (weather, control systems, etc.).

You can see the type of work that becomes more and more useful, as well as more complex, as you progress through the various levels. The providers of database services will use numerous versions of new families of product offerings. The government will devise many playing-field questions, such as, "How will the information distribution companies be able to provide for the masses using public common carrier 'integrated network' offerings?" "What will their subsidiaries or unregulated divisions be providing to the more sophisticated customers as an enhanced value added offering?" "How will a new feature be competitively offered?" "How will collocation and open architecture be available to ensure that anyone can provide the feature competitively?"

The third dimension, the right axis, shows the complexity of what system should have what features. Here, intelligent terminals, business serving modules (from the extended PBX or info switch that's located in shopping centers, office buildings, and large apartment complexes), data systems (circuit and packet), 1.5, 45, 140 and 564 megabit broadband systems, 2.2 gigabit facilities, access gateway systems (to voice, data and video interconnect networks), and database systems will become the new information networks systems. Thus, the strategy is to twist and turn the features or requirements to position them to these various systems. However, before this can take place effectively, we must further understand the game. (See FIG. 3-8.)

I^3, shown in FIG. 3-8, is essentially an F^3, but instead of determining what systems should provide what feature, it considers how we'll offer what feature! Here, we address the future of the distribution firm (in its regulated and nonregulated arenas), the telco information services/database information centers, and the customer provided equipment (CPE), such as intelligent terminals. For example, the future features to be provided in a data switch should be carefully understood in terms of providing them in the regulated distribution company, the nonregulated distribution company (with separate accounting procedures), the telco subsidiary, or in CPE nodal switches. With future DOJ/appeals court decisions on freedoms for

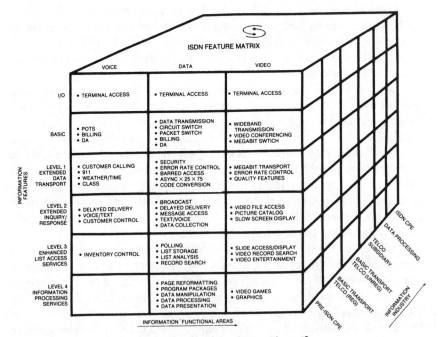

Fig. 3-8. The information cubic — I^3.

playing the game in the value added, information, and manufacturing world, the arena will become more of a public network versus private network business, requiring decisions such as: "What unit will provide what services and features for basic public transport?" In so doing, we must also consider what the user needs and wants, today and tomorrow, as the marketplace develops for the extended features. This type of investigation should become an integral part of the equation that determines strategies. Indeed, it has become a four-dimensional problem:

1. What functions (voice, data, video).
2. What level of features (IO, basic, 1, 2, 3, 4).
3. Provided by what system (data, wideband, access . . .)
4. How, in what arena (distribution company, subsidiary, data center . . .).

The two different third dimensions of the problem, noted in the I^3 and F^3 cubics, become the vertical and horizontal axis in the S^3 cubic shown in FIG. 3-9. This shows the servers, from pre-ISDN CPE through the telcos, their subsidiaries, data processing firms, intelligent customer terminals, and nodal point switches (ISDN CPEs). The central, horizontal axis displays new potential systems for voice, data, and video functional areas. The depth axis will now be the features, noted earlier, for each functional area in the I^3 and F^3 cubics.

It's this future world in which the users, providers, and suppliers must play the new game under the challenging and changing rules and guidelines of the FCC and

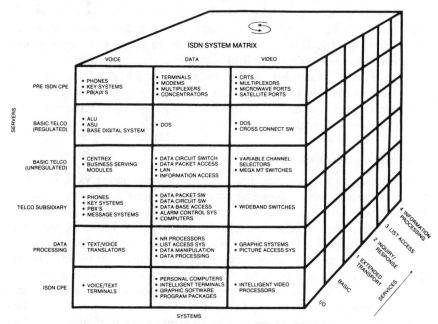

Fig. 3-9. Servers/systems/services — the S^3 cubic.

DOJ. It's the world where, if you want to win, much must be totally understood in order to position you firm in a specific area with the right product, or the right service. This can best be demonstrated by again considering the "packet switch" for the "new data networks." For the collection arena, it can be positioned as a public network, first-level switch in the unregulated telco with separate accounting, or in a fully market-oriented, advanced-services subsidiary unit as a specialized, common unregulated network, or even as a shared private network offering, where it can interface to the "office-of-the-future" internal networks of large businesses, shopping centers, and clusters of small businesses.

There it can provide an unlimited, continuously changing, enhancing, and expanding array of new features that aren't delayed through the waiver processes or limited by appeals. However, it could also be a public data network second-level switch, used as an access switch to the world. Here it could exist in the basic transport telco in an unregulated portion of the firm (with separate accounting to ensure that facilities and switches aren't subsidized by the local voice plant), enabling direct interfaces from private local networks to more global data inter-exchange carriers.

Alternatively, it could be in the regulated portion of the telco, enabling universal access by all, but with only a limited set of transport features. Additional features can, perhaps, still be provided on a waiver basis, tariffed, or detariffed (depending on existing governmental restrictions, which come and go). Also, it could be the network entrance level switch of a special carrier. As noted, synchro-nous conversion pads can exist in the basic telco. Initially, they were marketed from the subsidiary, until later governmental decisions. Hence, the initial access system might in actuality provide limited enhanced features, but it will mainly provide basic transport to the new interconnect interexchange international data networks to the world. However, Judge Greene did provide some transport feature freedoms when he encouraged the RBOCs to offer a new videotex network.

The S^3 cubic shows that not only for packet switches, but also for other numerous opportunities, the task is to map the right feature into the right system located in the right server. This is the "masters game" for the players of "the strategy of the strategies!"

Information features/services

As we attempt to put our arms around the new features and services, let's first take a moment to assess these information cubics. Here we see that features extend through several levels as they provide more and more value to the user.

However, due to initial political regulated and unregulated arenas, it was many times questionable what level of features could be offered where. Hence, a packet switch located in an unregulated entity of the information distribution company (IDC) in the public network might only be allowed to offer level one and two capabilities, while an IDC in an advanced services parallel network of a telco subsidiary might be able to offer up to level three features with the exclusion of list analysis, leaving level four features to be provided by non-telco providers. This demonstrates the need for several types of packet switching systems capabilities, depending on who is providing the service. Of course, these are only features until they're packaged into services, which then brings us into the full arena of offerings from various providers using their particular pricing structures. (See TABLE 3-8.)

Table 3 – 8. Integrated Networks' Integrated Services

Telephone . . .			
Teleshopping	Telepolling	Videotext	Datainquiry
Telecommuting	Telewriting	Videograph	Datasensor
Television	Telecontrol	Videophone	Database
Telebanking	Teleaccounting	Videoimage	Dataprocessing
Teletext	Teledoctor	Videoconference	Dataexchange
Telefax	Telemessage	Videoradiology	Data . . .

Information features, as noted in FIG. 3-10, become truly dependent on the integration of computers and communications, as features from both worlds become package services that are overlaid on the new information network infrastructure. To be of any real service to the user, much must be added to basic transport features to make them easy to use, transparent, and as acceptable as possible. As we stop and pause here to reflect, let's take a moment to jot down all the tele, video, and data services that we've seen targeted for the user during the past three years. We can't help but note how communications is being integrated into an ever-increasing array of applications for every aspect of our day-to-day home/business world, from ordering medicine at the pharmacy to having a pre-shopping tour of what sales are currently available at the local shopping center, to moving inventory control information around a factory floor.

Many of the services are time dependent, location dependent, or more geographically applicable in one location of the country more than another; for example, teledoctor might be a national full-time service in Australia's outback, or

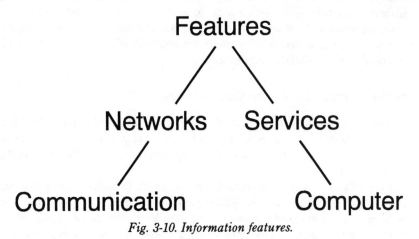

Fig. 3-10. Information features.

perhaps a night-time service in New York City's tougher neighborhoods. On the other hand, some services — such as video radiology and video conferencing — are quite dependent on cheaper wideband capabilities. However, once cheap wideband capabilities are truly available, this would short-circuit other services — such as telefax and teletex low-speed services — because economical high-speed bandwidth was not initially available. Alternatively, the greater bandwidth might cause these low-speed services to change and become high speed — for example, going to high-speed fax, as its mode of operation is changed with cheaper technology. Hence, many services are actually quite dependent on other services in terms of prices and availability of inexpensive transmission capabilities. These servers will do well to add more enhanced value to their offering by having the computer process, manipulate, and present the information in more extensive forms to the user. This then would remove the "transport-only" aspect of the service and extend the service into a truly functional offering.

As transport becomes more and more a commodity, we'll see many supposedly transport-only features slip back into the lower levels of basic network offerings. Hence, levels one and two features of the feature matrix will retrench back into level zero and level one, respectively.

This also applies to private offerings. We've seen the C&C philosophy, established by NEC, attempt to denote layers of manipulation of data files as they're moved around office facilities. Similarly, as new LANs and WANs are established, they'll begin to have their PBX counterparts provide more and more internal features such as voice mail, fax mail, and text mail as they add delayed delivery services, based on store and forward capabilities, to their basic ring, bus, and branch transport features. At this point, let's take another brief pause to appraise what offerings are and aren't available in the middle of the '90s. Let's see how we're entering the Information Age through the first wave of offerings of its formation phase. It's interesting to note how interwoven computer interworkings have become. In fact, the late '80s and early '90s were the period for the computer to recognize that it's no longer an island unto itself. It must communicate with its neighbors to the point of working intricately together to provide a reference point to establish where we're going in the service arena. This will enable us to reflect on where we're going in the technical arena and establish where we want to go in terms of the potential ISDN marketplace . . . !

Section three: ISDN service phases

As we revisit our earlier analysis of ISDN and consider not only the three pillars but the services they support, we need to ask ourselves what this figure really means in light of the overlaying of data and video capabilities on the IDN voice world network. (See FIG. 3-11.)

Especially as we look at the dotted lines around the Business Serving Module, class-five-level switch, and access switching system, we need to further determine how integrated must/should our network be in order to attract data users. Most data offerings are based on a medium-speed data packet/circuit type network that

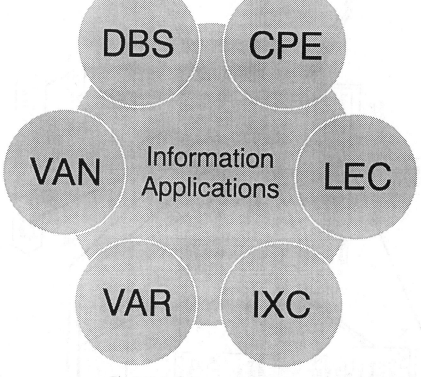

Fig. 3-11. Infrastructure applications.

enables multiple processors of different vendors to interconnect together. You might then ask what new exotic network is really needed? Should it be different from this straightforward overlay approach that quickly provides user access to data-handling transport capabilities. It offers several high-level features (noted in the previous figures) such as: broadcasting, polling, code conversion, delayed delivery, etc. What more is really needed from technology? What is the marketplace ready to absorb? However, look at the potential future technological arena, indicated by FIGS. 3-12A and B.

We can't help but see the achievement of the "seamless transporting" of voice, data, and video images at much higher transmission rates than initially required for the first wave of new users. We'll need these faster rates to move larger quantities of lower-speed users, once the many new, potential low-speed services are a success! This point is extremely important to grasp!

Remember that the French network went down for three days, due to operating system changes for controlling, routing, and limiting traffic in order to handle its huge success (it couldn't carry high-volume calls at intersecting nodes). Any data transport network based on one set of "queing" tables for a particular volume of calls will have to be redesigned (or restricted at access nodes to limit volume)

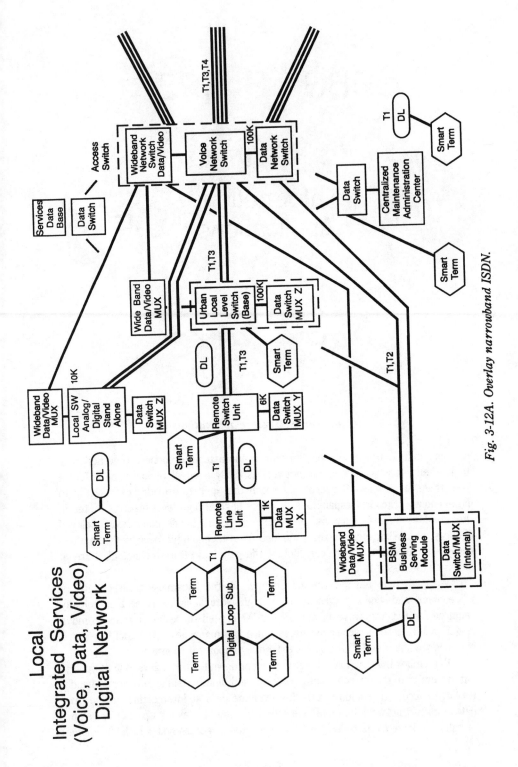

Fig. 3-12A. Overlay narrowband ISDN.

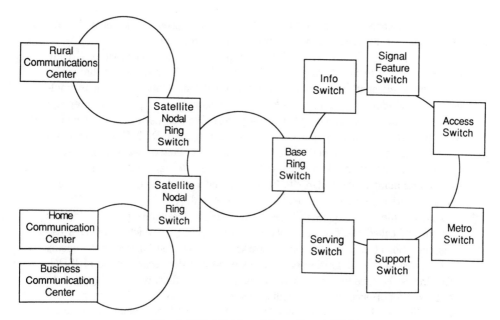

Fig. 3-12B. Wideband/broadband ISDN.

due to its vulnerability for being able to provide real-time responses, if indeed its traffic growth is overwhelming. Hence, the overlay network is, in effect, a "beginner network" in one sense. Its presence is there to enable users to begin interexchanging data and video messages. However, as their acceptance increases and resistance decreases, causing an increase in volume, we must provide a completely new network based on wideband/broadband technologies to handle the high volume of message exchanges that success will bring.

If we don't have the wideband network in place at the time it will be most needed (end of the '90s), we've simply created a new lifestyle in a new society, which will change from a futurist's dream of a higher quality way of life to one of Edgar Allen Poe's nightmares. The network will collapse on itself due to its own weight. Unfortunately, as society becomes more and more dependent on the computer, everything comes to a halt when the computer no longer functions. As we go to more intelligent services in which the computer takes control of daily decisions, we become more and more dependent on these systems for crucial operations that must not go down. (Note the 1987 stock market crash.)

This can be prevented by providing first the overlay ISDN network, which is soon followed by broadband ISDN to enable multiple computers to perform shared tasks and absorb work loads from nonfunctioning systems. Hence, when we address the dotted lines around the system boxes, it's not really important during the ISDN phase how integrated the devices are at these low-speed transport rates. In actuality, it will usually be done for ease of design rather than anything else or to keep the evolutionary stages of a particular existing system active as long as possible. However, it's essential that we differentiate evolutionary changes from revolutionary changes to ensure that we "cap" existing product lines near the late '90s in favor of the more robust next wave of ISDN products.

Conversely, we need the overlay ISDN products now. Today, we're already ten years late in terms of what technology could have been doing for the world. The "human element" needs time to learn and feel comfortable with new technology, to break down resistance to old ways, to allow the computer to enter the marketplace in various aspects of their daily lives. We also need time to allow the wideband facilities to be deployed, to provide the $2B + D$, $23B + D$, and NB interfaces to the user. We need time to determine whether we want to operate at 64K or a variable-length kilo/megabit or byte rate. We need time to enable the tremendous number of standards to be defined and agreed upon, as well as ensure that a new pricing structure is identified and deployed.

This "time for using ISDN" has been noted as a separate phase in ISDN's growth. It's called the transition phase. It's the phase in which computers use communications (the overlay ISDN network) to achieve their "networking" needs. As indicated in the integration of C&C, especially in the second phase of ISDN-C&C, this is the time for not only tying computers together, but enabling them to work together. Hence, we're providing networks that foster interprocessing and interservices as they tie numerous interfaces together ("interconnection"), based on the IEEE and OSI models layers to achieve true internetworking of both private and public networks. In this manner, we'll provide layers of services based on the basic backbone network offering.

Basic transport will become the "infrastructure" on which to overlay layers of expanding, new packaged offerings. These offerings will not only enable transport to become more versatile, error free, and dynamically network manageable, but it will also ensure the tying together "internetworking-interworking" of these many complex networks, so that the first evolutionary phase of ISDN will indeed integrate nicely into the subsequent revolutionary phase of ISDN. This will allow its services to expand and grow into not only the local, regional, and national marketplace but also into the global international arena. Here, phases of ISDN will differ as different countries are out of sync with their particular entrance into the information world.

By understanding how to link the N-W-B ISDN phases of the ISDN's together, both countries can coexist for a long period of time until, eventually, economics and technical achievements dictate movement to the full photonic/superconductive light switching networks of the future. This will be the fifth and final stage of this round of technologies' development. So, now let's take a deeper look at ISDN in terms of its "S" services and see how they relate to the transitional pillar — the time of C&C integration.

Integrated services

As features become packaged into services, as services become more and more overlaid on each other, as users begin using the computer for more applications, the formation phase of the ISDN has yielded a variety of offerings, many of which were initially autonomous. The '90s is now the time to integrate them together. As indicated in FIG. 3-13, integrated services means integrating word processing with

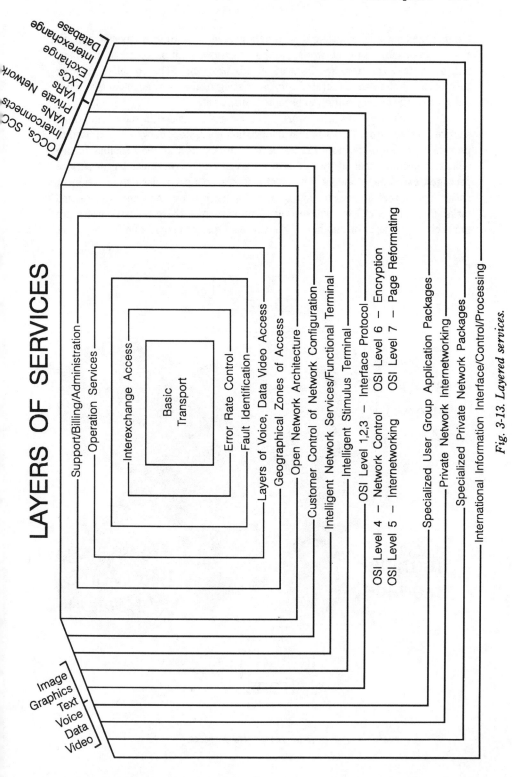

Fig. 3-13. Layered services.

file management and coleasing it with data presentation to form specific application programs by using network transport services such as terminal interface, data/image/text transfer, and network access programs. The complete package then becomes the true integrated service offering to the user, enabling the entire machine-to-machine operation to become transparent.

As we ask ourselves what work functions are contained in these integrated services, we see from FIG. 3-14 that information is created, deployed, and used to provide a variety of services to aid specific entities such as the hospitals or law offices to perform their daily routines. As noted earlier, we must target service packages, based on providing clusters of features, to a particular market segment consisting of specific information user types performing their industry-related tasks. (See FIG. 3-15.) It's interesting to observe that these industry users are themselves one form or another of the various types of people who are or aren't

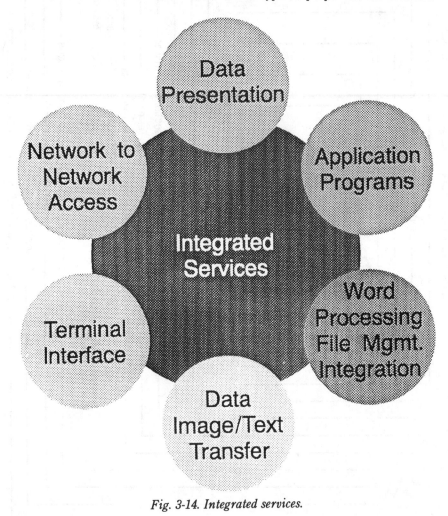

Fig. 3-14. Integrated services.

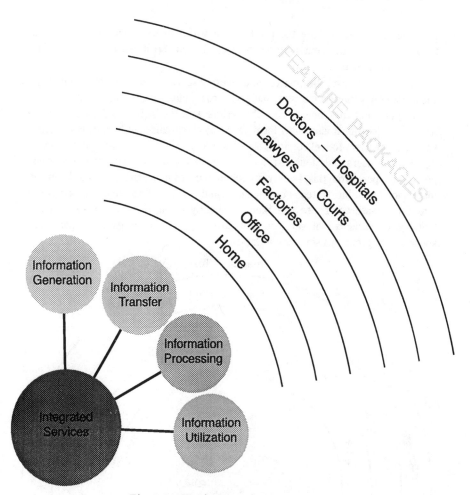

Fig. 3-15. The information marketplace.

interested and/or capable of using the integrated services efficiently and effectively. Hence, much must be done to tailor the services as much as possible for these potential users to meet their real needs.

For example, once an outdoor festivity had many types of food dispensaries. One was cooking bratwurst in direct competition with one cooking hot dogs. As the buyers arrived to place their order and pay for their bratwurst, they were quickly handed their order and directed to a nearby relish mustard bar. However, one individual placed his order, but asked that the bratwurst be well done, and he was quite willing to stand aside and wait for it to cook. This caused considerable resistance by the stand's providers, until the customer indicated that since it didn't fit with their operation he was willing to go elsewhere. This caused the stand's providers to stop and think. They were there to make money from customers by providing a food service. If their inflexibility inhibited them from keeping their customers, why were they there? Hence, a variation was added to enable customers to obtain different degrees of cooked food. So it must be in providing information services . . .

As we become a little smarter in delivering services, we'll be able to integrate them not only within an industry, but also across industries, where a word processing arrangement from one office will interlink with the factory and eventually the home. Services must also allow for differences or variances of operation to enable the different users to feel comfortable with the system. In the case study concerning the new users, only four attributes were used to differentiate potential transport user types. From this, twenty-six common user types existed across the many, many industries. Integrated services has a similar potential to provide a base set of integrated features. These can then be slightly changed to provide specialized features or variances of services that customize the offerings for a particular specific user group or user. (See FIG. 3-16.)

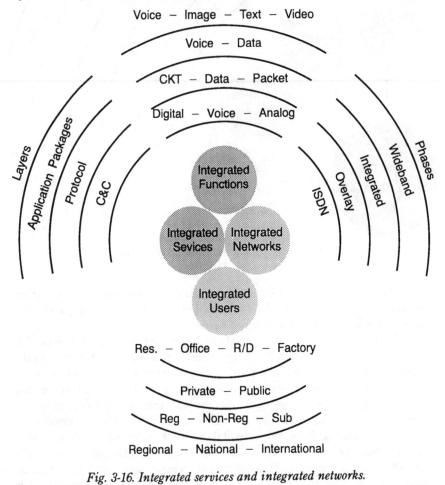

Fig. 3-16. Integrated services and integrated networks.

Integrated services' integrated networks

As services and networks are integrated closer and closer to the users to provide functional solutions in the form of voice, data, video, image, and text offerings, we see a further merging of the two industries (computers and communications) in terms of their layers and phases. This is where the game becomes a little complex. As noted earlier, it's the "master's arena." It's no place for the amateur or novice. Here, protocols are established for different forms of ISDN, from narrowband to broadband phases. However, they aren't just formulated for one particular aspect, but must be resolved for more universal applications such as private-to-public electronic mail systems, employing multiple addresses, security, access codes, error recovery, and delayed delivery mechanisms for use within a factory, an office, a region, a nation, or around the world.

This is indeed complex but necessary in order to be competitive enough to move parties off of private, self-contained, controlled networks to a more general-purpose but cost-effective, ubiquitous network. As users demand more overlaying of services on each other, they also require more interprocessing and interservices operation. By obtaining fully integrated services from integrated networks, we've moved them further and further into the networking-internetworking world of the C&C phase of ISDN.

This then places the providers (and suppliers) in a difficult and somewhat undesirable position of establishing standards that can be used to bypass their existing networks and products, but which at the same time promote connecting to their network for its particular array of features and services.

Figure 3-17 again emphasizes the ISDN marketplace's dependence on the central pillar to achieve the transition from stand-alone private networks connected by bridges and gateways to wideband ISDN-based networks interconnected together — using the IEEE standards — overlaid on top of the ISDN OSI model. If this structure is not quickly and effectively achieved by the end of the '90s, then the future of a public/private network homogeneous "interworking" operation is indeed questionable. Throughout this decade, emphasis must be placed on bringing the two in line with each other. The computer industry can't go off by itself, establishing its own architectures that are independent of the public domain's forthcoming ISDN communication structure, nor can the public domain continue to ignore the private networks and the needs of the computers.

ISDN is based on having a rigid set of standards for interconnecting terminals and networks together. In the other case, LANs and WANs were established without rigid standards for connecting multiple terminals and products together or LANs with other LANs. As a result, nonstandardization has developed in the LAN, WAN, MAN industries so that LANs implemented by one manufacturer are different from LANs implemented by another. They don't talk to each other. This can't be allowed to continue unchecked during the '90s or, indeed, the formation phase will not yield the needed solid, supporting infrastructure. This is essential in order to have a basis for providing the many potential ISDN services that can greatly benefit society. (See FIG. 3-18.)

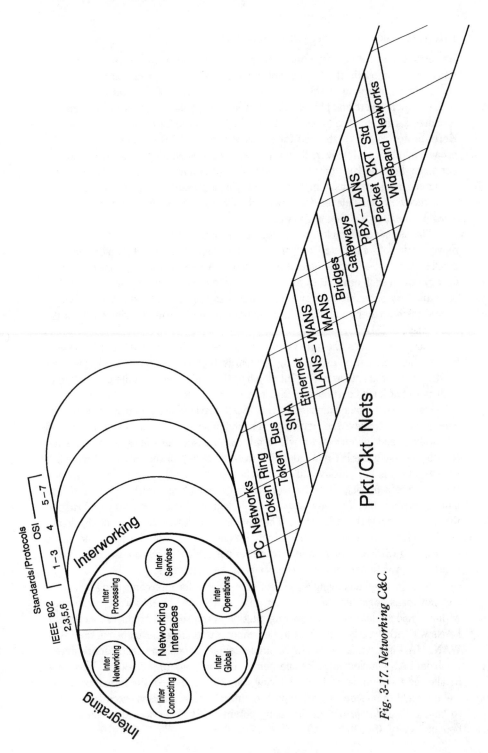

Fig. 3-17. Networking C&C.

Fig. 3-18. ISDN: a service game.

ISDN must then be structured to perform as an easy medium to move newer and better services to the marketplace. Also, its implementation must become more a game than a gruesome task (it grew and grew until it became gruesome). In order to have a real, not artificial, marketplace, new services must be easily and quickly deployed. This then requires a framework that enables, encourages, and supports rapid growth. If not, then parallel networks will soon develop to bypass ISDN to formulate their particular version of integrated services.

ISDN society

As FIG. 3-19 notes, the basis for society's real growth will be an internetworking of integrated services. A supporting structure must be constructed in which services are overlaid on each other, enabling them to expand and develop until they spread throughout the world, integrating remote societies together.

In a sense, the train first linked the eastern United States with the western part of the country; then came the car. Similarly, ships linked Europe with the Americas, the Far East and Africa. Later it was the plane. Now, as travel becomes expensive and prohibitive due to the high cost of fuel and economic currency fluctuations between countries, robust, inexpensive high-capacity information

Fig. 3-19. ISDN: future society platform.

exchanges can bring the great and emerging nations closer together. However, this does require an infrastructure to support this accomplishment — a new monolith.

As FIG. 3-20 demonstrates, the fiber will be the long-term basis for bringing the new and exciting services to the marketplace. Without this conduit in place, services will not have a path on which to travel. They need a path that's illuminated all the way to the marketplace, lest they become lost or waylaid, especially as the competition becomes a little rougher and more formidable. A public roadway for new services would prevent players from becoming too dominant.

These questions must be addressed and resolved. Some solutions will require risks and safeguards. However, without a public infrastructure that enables both worlds — the private and public — to expand and grow with new technology, little real progress can be made in achieving a truly ubiquitous information society. See the chapter 8 workshops for a detailed assessment and possible solution that enables the RHCs to participate in but not inhibit the competitive information services marketplace.

Pricing

Also, we cannot move forward without revolutionary (not evolutionary) changes to the pricing infrastructure. Today, telephone service has been based on flat rate local calling by both the business and residential community, with business paying a high rate for bulk interstate and intrastate services. There are numerous incentives supplied by various WATS and "CALL PAC" packages for greater-volume users. Alternatively, phones can home directly on foreign exchanges at fixed monthly rates to enable flat-rate calling within the foreign community of interest. There are also special services for point-to-point facilities that have different degrees of conditioning to enable more error-free movement of data and video information.

This entire pricing structure was established by tariffs, based on two assumptions. The first assumption was that a resident made 4-5 calls per day (consisting of three minutes per call) and business generated 20-30 calls per day (amounting to five minutes per average per call). The second assumption was that data should be charged so that increments of 1200 bit/sec rates were considered big advances in throughput, causing big changes in pricing. Hence, since basic stored program machines were "attempt limited" due to earlier limiting processor capacity, it was essential to not have explosive growth in usage. It was more desirable to have line growth over line use. Thus, businesses were encouraged to add more lines as their phone use increased (even for incoming usage). Touch-Tone, which actually reduced the switched cost by reducing call-handling time, was priced to obtain revenue as a service as well as delay excessive demand for the Touch-Tone offering. There was also a strategy that long-distance facilities were expensive and the local plant was cheap. This was reversed over time as long-distance capacity economically increased.

Data users were charged excessively for modem attachments. They required a second line that couldn't be time shared with the phone. Subsequently, the users turned to acoustical connection and/or dial modems using the same flat-rate facility

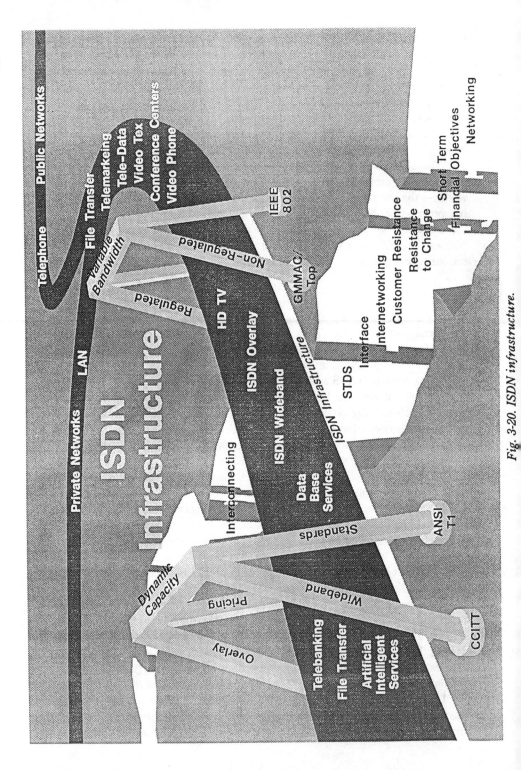

Fig. 3-20. ISDN infrastructure.

for voice or data calls. (Unfortunately, if 10 percent of the calls to a voice switching system are short-duration data calls using voice-grade facilities, this requires deloading the switch from potential voice capacity to the tune of several million dollars, as well as prematurely changing out the switch to obtain bigger, high-capacity systems.) As users came to recognize the potential of bulk-rate T1 facilities, they elected to multiplex lower subrates onto a shared T1 facility, bypassing the public network for the movement of voice and data traffic. (See FIG. 3-21.)

This caused an exodus of large business users, leaving the small-business and residential users to share the costs of sustaining the network. This put upward pressure on residential flat-rate charges, and legislators then intervened to suppress increases.

However, with the advent of gigabit facilities, megabit memories, and parallel processors, it's now time to reassess the basic assumptions underlaying the public pricing structure to determine what has to be done to encourage and sustain growth of the public domain data networks. Today, users pay for originating the calls unless they use 800-type inward WATS numbers. They also have unrestricted calling availability within a community of interest. They pay flat rates for services such as custom calling, while business users (and in some cases residential users) are provided various high-volume accesses, using tariffed feature group services A through D to reach specialized or traditional long-haul carriers. Access charges to the interexchange carriers have been shifted from the carriers to the users as one- and two-dollar fixed charges were assessed to the user. Specialized carriers who performed switched data transport networks have encouraged regulators to consider basic network access techniques as a value-added service, requiring an extensive tariff and waiver process to obtain basic access protocol conversions at the lower OSI levels in order to inhibit the IDCs from supplying free access to their own BOC future data networks and thus potentially inhibiting users from selecting their specialized parallel network operations. This then reveals the complexity of the issue as we move to the potential high-throughput networks, which can provide greater bandwidth on demand and almost unlimited capacity.

In reviewing the pricing strategies of the past, we should note the regulator's concerns for ensuring that the poor, residential, and small businesses don't pay excessively for their basic phone (limited data) services or that cross subsidization of new services doesn't exist to inhibit new competition. It should also be noted that the desire of the telcos is not to kill their cash cows or tamper too much with pricing structure to seriously inhibit cash flow while waiting for new demand for new services. With this background, we see that we must overlay the revolutionary change strategy on top of an evolutionary strategy and ensure that it doesn't destroy the existing supporting structure.

Most observers can see the strategic advantages for a country having an economical information transport infrastructure. This can be conceptually visualized by the example of a cheap ride on the bus versus an expensive seat in a private cab. Whereas gigabit facilities are made available and voice calls are reduced to a few kilobits, many users such as the poor will be able to obtain an economical seat on the high-capacity buses, perhaps even a free ride; otherwise, as users leave the

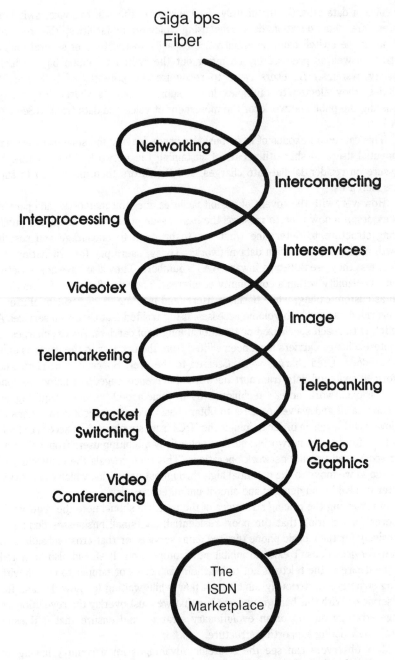

Giga bps
Fiber

Networking

Interconnecting

Interprocessing

Interservices

Videotex

Image

Telemarketing

Telebanking

Packet
Switching

Video
Graphics

Video
Conferencing

The
ISDN
Marketplace

Fig. 3-21. A spectrum of services lighting up the marketplace.

slower-speed, uneconomical public network those remaining might have to pay more and more for a seat, for example, on a small, half-empty bus or even a private cab.

Similarly, special network providers that today only handle a few users must come to realize that the more users that can be provided their more specialized value-added services, the more their overall revenue picture will increase. Therefore, instead of delaying public offerings to handle the few that can afford their high prices, they should be adding more value-added services to their network and encouraging overall growth by having more public network access points to their network. Finally, the problem surfaced by Germany's ISDN tariffs must be resolved. This is the one in which pricing emphasis on broadband rates penalized low-speed, short-holding-time calls, inhibiting the growth of the narrowband data industry. Both low- and high-speed data services must be encouraged to grow to their full potential.

Also, the distance component must be removed, as CEI and ONA connections take place without requiring physical collocation. Here, facilities are extended to locations where alternate providers house their switching systems. However, with all said and done, pricing must be used to attract and encourage the new users to trade in existing techniques (many of which are manual or use car/plane transport) for the more effective, electronic form of information exchange.

One such technique that has been proposed is usage pricing and price caps, in which customers pay for only the bits or packets transported. Over time, this might require extensive billing programs, as electronics systems spend considerable overhead attempting to keep track of who did what with each bit. Also, some algorithms seriously inhibit one portion or the other of the spectrum of users. Some models might be more expensive to implement across the various situations. One technique that might be applicable would be to divide the users into twelve or so tiered classes such as: res (basic service), bus (basic service), res voice/data types 1–4, bus voice/data types 1–4, res total information service, and bus total information service. Usage counters within each class can denote volume of information transferred and only note exceptions that are more than the tiered selected rates.

This example is only to identify the complexity of the issue requiring extensive RBOC and industry study to provide a basic, full-spectrum service-pricing model that encourages use of the network for both short-holding-time calls and high-bandwidth, longer-holding-time information transfer, so that high bandwidth is not priced to discourage extensive use and growth (see chapter 9).

Intelligent services

Once price enables narrowband and broadband data to be transported economically, we can then, on a network basis, take advantage of moving a great deal of information, which can be reviewed and processed by intelligent nodes on or associated with the network. The power of computers is still doubling every 18 months or so, and silicon has a long way to go as it's used to achieve densely packed logical units. We therefore have the operational capability to achieve parallel

Table 3-9. The ISDN Marketplace

Integrated Networks'
Integrated Services . . .
Intelligent Networks'
Intelligent Services . . .

processing of information in a manner that allows us to make "if then else" decisions using expert systems' analyses. Computers can then provide us with better "real-time" decisions, using past history and dynamically changing, sensed information.

Where do we want to go?

Later, as more and more information is accessible within large databases and as human-machine interfaces become less inhibited by more functional and friendly input output mechanisms, we'll be able to make full use of the search and analysis capabilities of computers to aid us in shifting through the mountains of information, that will be generated by a more information-oriented society. (See TABLE 3-9.) Otherwise, as one programmer noted in Australia, the computer building should be located near the opera house so that the reams and reams of data can flow out through an open window into the harbor in synchronism with the music from the night opera . . . never to be seen again . . .

For further analysis, see the chapter 8 workshops.

4

The integration of computers & communications

"Computer interconnection breeds computer usage,
which breeds computer interconnection,
which breeds . . ."

After reviewing "what's happening," we should take a moment to assess the effects of current strategies. As we enter the mid '90s, it's time to ask and address the question, "Where are we going?" To do this properly, a review of both ISDN and C&C will help show us our "potential" destination. This then can help formulate the basis for establishing new strategies and directions, which will further integrate C&C within ISDN, as we position ourselves for the forthcoming, crucial stages of the information game.

Section one: ISDN checkpoint

In looking at ISDN, we see that it has become a broad concept that represents much more than just standardization activities for interconnecting users to networks. ISDN has become a framework within which existing networks can evolve to meet changing user needs by providing flexible, new arrays of expanding services. C&C, on the other hand, has indicated the increasing dependency of computers on communications, as more and more computer applications enter every segment of the marketplace. This has been more clearly demonstrated as computer processing capabilities are distributed closer and closer to the user. There, these capabilities can be used to access local, as well as multiple, remote distributed database systems for specific functional information. Similarly, we've seen the need for more network control and error-rate transparency. These needs have encouraged front-end computer systems to assume more and more network management functions. As one reviewer noted, this then "fostered a call for 'seamless interfaces' between computer and communication systems." (See FIG. 4-1.)

However, progress is often slower than initially visualized until the particular cause of a resistive block is diminished. A review of RBOCs by one researcher noted the following views of ISDN:

- ISDN is being implemented systematically to sample test the new technology.
- ISDN is viewed as a technology aimed more at cost reduction than at meeting customer needs.
- ISDN is a technology in search of customers.
- ISDN technology is in the driver's seat, but the market has yet to be defined.
- The introduction of services based on ISDN technologies will be slow.
- One watcher said "I'm up in the air on ISDN. I don't know if there's a market . . . what kind of features it will, deliver or who will buy it . . . Our firm will stand back and watch what develops!"
- RBOCs have many concerns about ISDN (other than who will purchase the services they might deliver). These concerns include:
  a. Standards — In the absence of standards, the manufacturers are going to have to build specialized, individual machines.
  b. Software-RBOCs want to be software independent.
  c. Customer Premise Equipment (CPE) — interfaces between network channel terminating equipment and the network are becoming increasingly difficult to resolve.
  d. Regulation — the ability to provide various value-added services within the network as well as information services still remain unresolved issues.

This then leads to the need to truly understand ISDN . . .

Understanding ISDN

The integrated services digital network (ISDN) is really a merger of several concepts from IDN to ISN. IDN — Integrated Digital Network — is the program to change the existing plant from analogue to digital using stand-alone or distributed systems to formulate digital islands. This will enable the traditional analog network to become digital during the next twenty years. In this manner, analog voice is sampled 8,000 times per second and encoded using pulse code modulation. It's then digitally transmitted on 64-kilobit channels throughout the network. Subsequent techniques are deployed to use adaptive pulse code modulation and only use 32 kilobits of the information channel. As more and more becomes known about voice recognition and synthesis, recognizable voice might be eventually sent at 9600 bit-per-second rates. In any event, over time, the existing voice network will

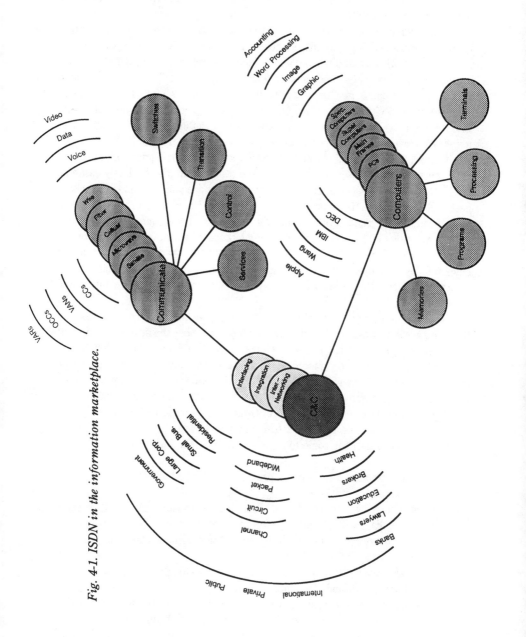

Fig. 4-1. ISDN in the information marketplace.

become fully digital to move digitized voice, data, and video information using distributed switching by remote switch units, homing in on control base units.

DN (data networks), PDN (public data networks), (PSDN) (public switched data networks, or PPSDN (public packet switched data networks) have not been introduced ubiquitously by the BOCs throughout their states, except by other common carriers (OCCs), specialized common carriers (SCCs), or by value added networks (VANS) such as Tymenet and Telenet. In reality, the world is starved for a good, inexpensive, public, universal data transport medium. This then has created a buildup of demands for the "data networking" aspects of ISDN, but due to regulatory protocol restrictions and universal flat-rate pricing strategies across the LATAs, both the providers and users have been reluctant to push for public data networks. However, the suppliers see it as an essential offering of ISDN.

Services (S) can't really be considered without a supporting network structure for integrated network services (INS). On the other hand, it's absolutely essential for ISDN to have services in order to succeed. As more and more is known about potential new services, the more integrated they become with the network, and the more layered they become on top of other services. Today, many "private networks" are being overlaid on each other and integrated with the public network to provide numerous new exchange services. These offerings are becoming part of new, multilayered packaged offerings, as C&Cs become more and more integrated. Hence, ISDN could have been called INIS or "Integrated Network's Integrated Services."

To understand the potential of these services, we must take a closer look at the framework on which they rest as they attempt to meet the new, changing, but more realistic user needs. The key elements of ISDN have been defined as: architecture, structure, interface, standards, network control, services offerings, and tariffs. Each country will, no doubt, have their own form of ISDN within some variance of the generally accepted view. Interconnecting agreements will enable countries to interface with other ISDNs through gateways. ISDN will provide a new, exciting chance for the world to communicate together on a grand scale. Hence, for some, ISDN has come to mean a conceptual architecture that:

- Standardizes user interfaces by providing a clear demarcation between the network and the station.
- Constructs a digital network that allows higher transmission speeds, greater switching capabilities, better error rate performance and throughput, as well as lowers costs (both intercity and intracity) and enables the provision of many more services.
- Integrates access to simplify the network control for the movement of voice, data, image, text, and video information.
- Offers transmission capability to meet the potential of the fiber in RBOC's main central offices by passing it all through an intelligent switching matrix of lenses without changing the data (or digitizing voice) from light to electrons. Because of this capability, such optical processors could run large networks.

- Provides a single path to the user to not only reduce the proliferation of wires and costs, but also to provide the transport media for a multitude of application services.
- Redefines the special ordering, design, and installation of multiple networks, removing delays in offerings and providing capabilities for customers to be able to easily tailor their services as their needs change.
- Provides better network use by reducing call setup time and increasing interface availability by 20 to 50 percent. This is accomplished by time-sharing facilities during dead time in conversations, or sharing work time of processors, as well as increasing efficiency through dynamic adaptive bandwidth, adaptive traffic capacity, and dynamic adaptive performance improvements.
- Enables dynamic network management for changing user configurations, providing a virtual network to the customer that includes problem management such as surveillance, diagnostics, maintenance, and usage control.
- Provides call management during setup, involving multiaddressing, clearing, logon, handshaking, and deliverance of the call using, if necessary, alternate routing and ensuring connections, establishing authorization, and providing billing for voice, data, and video messages.
- Ensures network transparency so that users don't have to worry about idiosyncrasies such as losing synchronization if more than 15 zeros of data are present in the content.
- Achieves network internetworking or connectivity between autonomous networks and services to increase the scope of the communications universe.
- Obtains flexibility for ease of new service offerings and making the network robust to changes.
- Provides standards, enabling multiple terminals to communicate through multiple networks to multiple computers and multiple databases.
- Achieves cost control, thereby reducing access costs and providing for growth of new features, services, and offerings.
- Provides secure, high-speed, high-quality, reliable, error-free communications without requiring specialized redundancy, encryption, etc., alternatives.
- Formulates the infrastructure on which to base economical services, meeting realistic user needs, taking advantage of the exciting advances in new technology.

These aspects of ISDN then translate into various forms of benefits for both users and providers. As we review what has happened up to the mid '90s for both the computer and communication industries, it's quite apparent that high profits for the players was an initial, immediate, and prevalent goal. This was achieved temporarily by reducing operating personnel and long-term expenditures. Some providers attempted to enter other businesses outside the C&C industries, while others attempted to buy out those, who had achieved a small edge in the marketplace.

However, the easy decisions are over as we reassess and refocus on the new questions and decisions that center on overall structure. New services have not been offered because separately they can't grow and be profitable without a supporting infrastructure.

Almost all new ISDN services require this shared structure. An example is the videotex Minitel Network of France, which uses France's public packet transport network to move its information. Thus, when we review ISDN for benefits, we must address its long-term strategy. It's important to look at the total benefits of several services collectively. Their cumulative accomplishments should be viewed over a 10-year period to note the impact of the supporting infrastructure. This structure will become a catalyst for encouraging new players, such as database sources, to use the network to provide many new service offerings, from which additional transport revenue will be obtained.

Finally, it should be noted that ISDN is different from the past because it separates itself from the old "attempt-limited" service structure, in which only a few offerings occurred. ISDN will encourage usage and growth of numerous services at more reasonable, economical prices by multiple vendors providing gigabit transport facilities. It will encourage high-volume traffic, more dynamic use of its bandwidth, and the interconnectability of all types of terminals to promote further growth of the computer industry. This ISDN is truly a supportive solution to advancing computer needs.

User needs and ISDN services

User needs can be summarized by the following observations. End customers are already pushing for greater information productivity by making information work smarter for them. They're beginning to demand easier access to the network, plus a wider variety of digital services, increased control over their communications, and, of course, increased data transmission speed. They also want lower costs, better performance, greater flexibility, effective disaster recovery systems, and improved data security.

As new services become widely available, they become less costly to the end user, the vendor, and the manufacturer. Many new alternative services can be provided by ISDN to meet the needs of both the users and their providers. Here, voice calling services are enhanced with class-type extensions, where use is made of the calling party identity for call waiting, call transfer, call pickup, and call coverage. Similarly, personal computers, TTYs and integrated voice data terminals (IVDTs) obtain access to both premise-based host computers and external data networks. For messaging, terminals need access to message desk services to send or retrieve mail, while high-speed facsimile devices are required for image information transfer between remote locations.

At these higher speeds, graphic display terminals can more easily access sophisticated CAD/CAM systems. Similarly, providers need the capability to quickly and easily provide call management functions, facility management features, account and authorization codes, moves, changes, and access to multiple services.

New needs will arise, so that:

- Tariffs need to be established that encourage the use of ISDNs' various high-speed transmission rates, but that don't penalize slower, short-duration calls. Both will be areas of major growth of the information industry.
- ISDN's 64-kilobit channel capacity will have to be integrated into new PBXs' data movement, filling, and storage capabilities, as simultaneous voice and text conversations exist.
- Dialogue, message, and retrieval services will need to be integrated on baseband and broadband facilities, where dialogue services provide a means for bidirectional communication with real-time, end-to-end information.
- Transfer will occur from user to user or between user and host (e.g., for data processing), so that the flow can be bidirectionally symmetric or asymmetric, such as video text, video conference, and high-speed data (radiology). Messaging services offer user-to-user communications via storage units with store-and-forward, mailbox, and message-handling functions (e.g., information editing, processing, and conversation).
- Retrieval services will allow users to retrieve information that's stored in information centers — information such as broadband video text films, static pictures, and radiology films.
- Distribution services without user control, or broadcast services, will provide a continuous flow of information from a central source to all authorized receivers, such as broadcast TV and high-quality stereo TV. where the user can't control the start and order of the information being broadcast. Those distribution services with user control will also transmit information from a central source to large numbers of users, but the information will be provided as a sequence of entities, or frames, with cyclical repetition. In this case, the service received will have the ability to individually access and control the start and order of presentation, such as cable text. Due to the cyclical repetition, the information will always bepresented from its beginning.
- Video using current NTSC (National Television Standards Committee) signal format can be achieved by codecs operating at about 6.3 megabits per second. However, to obtain high-quality video (HQV) or high-definition TV (HDTV), the extended-quality television (EQTV) scheme requires a codec operating between 40 and 140 megabits per second. Hence, high-definition TV, (HDTV) will require (need) broadband switching networks at the 140 megabit rate.
- The fundamental nature of data emphasizes the need for low-error-rate, high-capacity systems.
- New customer service needs can be met by 64K facilities to transport slow scan video, bulk data, high-speed fax, computer graphics, encrypted voice or data, and limited motion video (such as head-to-head video conferencing).
- We need the ability to send two messages at one time so that the computer terminal can send a message that can be viewed and discussed simultaneously.

- Some ISDN services have been visualized as transport oriented. They're considered as fundamental (telex, facsimile), sophisticated (video text and video mail) or special (alarm, telemetery). These services will provide the user with broader communications among different terminals and better exchange of information using out-of-band signaling channels to achieve shorter transmission time by providing single access and handling, independent of the terminal, with great flexibility.
- For the large user, ISDN needs to reduce the number of special networks. An observer noted that a large manufacturing firm had 20 special networks in use for product control, inventory/material control, telephone, CAD/CAM, machine control, word processing, electronic mail, engineering records, cost accounting, timekeeping, payroll, purchasing, financial, marketing, etc., and these networks were not interconnected except in isolated cases.
- To reduce the amount of voice information transfer, we need to understand the ears' cochlea, where acoustic signals are converted into neural signals. For efficient coding, we need to know just how much of the speech signal's information is required for the acoustic-to-neural transformation. For example, Bell Lab's Multipulse Linear Predictive Coding Algorithm (MPLPC) will perhaps, in time, commercially enable speech to be recognizable, encoded in 9600 bits instead of 64,000.
- Similarly, interexchange carriers' (ICs) tests show the need to improve connect time, first-try call complete, error rates, signal-to-noise ratio, and to reduce phase jitter and impulse noise problems.
- One step to achieving true office automation is to enable the user to access various facilities by switching the type of needed connection, with maximum network transparency, enabling voice and data switching, store and forward, electronic mail, switched LAN, text messaging, file retrieval, and private wide area networking.
- Many of the new services need to be supported and encouraged to grow. These services include teleshopping, video-interactive marketing at home or at the shopping mall, telemetery, home banking, telemonitoring . . .

Finally, we have the "internetworking" need. As Arno Penzias, the Nobel Prize winner of Bell Labs, expressed so eloquently, "Tying it all together seems to be the name of the game!"

Models and standards

Two ISDN architectural models have emerged over the '80s and have been embraced by most standard-setting groups of the world as the framework on which to hang or cross-relate their network architectures. These are the Open Systems Interconnect Model (OSI) depicting seven overlaying layers of operations and the user terminal-network model depicting five points of interface to the network (R, S, T, U, and V).

OSI

The Open Systems Interconnect model's three lower layers have been adequately defined for narrowband (less than 1.5 megabits) transport movement of data. Analysis is progressing for the broadband movement of high-speed data, text, image, graphics, and various degrees of video (from slow scan to high-definition TV). Work in the U.S. is mainly taking place in IEEE 802 and ECSA's T1 working groups. The main international effort is taking place in CCITT working groups such as Working Groups XVIII, XI, and VII.

The net result of this effort is a set of recommendations and positions that adequately define a particular interface, method, or technique. However, it usually takes eight years for a recommendation to become a standard. It will become defined in one of CCITT's I series, X series, or V series, etc., standards that relate to ISDN, data protocols, video transport interfaces, etc. (See the chapter 7 case study, "The standards game.") Let's now assess where we're going in ISDN standards. (See FIG. 4-2.)

Terminal-network interface model

In the fall of 1984, the International Standards body of CCITT issued a set of ISDN recommendations. A key recommendation was the standard format for the *Digital Subscriber Line (DSL)*. This is the facility that connects to the network. The DSL is described as having two physical interfaces, the T and the U.

The basic "T" interface (no relation to T1) provides two clear (no in-band signaling) 64 kilobit "B" channels for voice or data and one 16 kilobit signal "D" channel for a total of 144 Kbps. It's a 4-wire interface between the customer set and the network, providing the full 2 B + D access for a subscriber terminal.

The primary "U" interface supports large business customers. It's a two-wire interface that operates on the standard unloaded telephone loop plant. This service consists of 23 "B" channels of 64 Kbps and one "D" channel of 64 Kbps for a total of 1.544 Mbps as 23B + D. This format is essentially the same as the T1 format. In Europe, the primary service is defined as 30B + D to be compatible with Europe's 2.048 Mbps CEPT trunk standard. The T1 carrier form of the digital subscriber line is the *Extended Digital Subscriber Line (EDSL)*. The EDSL could be used for switching systems such as connecting PBXs to central offices, as well as supporting LANs.

The "D" channel is purely a packet-switching channel. It can be thought of as a 16 Kbps or 64 Kbps data link. It's used to transmit network control information between the network user and the service provider. A CCITT protocol (LAP-D) facilitates this interface by supporting: signaling information (s-type data); telemetery information regarding the status of the terminals and the network elements (t-type data); and low-speed interactive data in packet form (p-type data) in X25 format for advanced ISDN features. CCITT Signaling System 7 (SS7) has been accepted as the interoffice signaling system to support communications between network switching facilities.

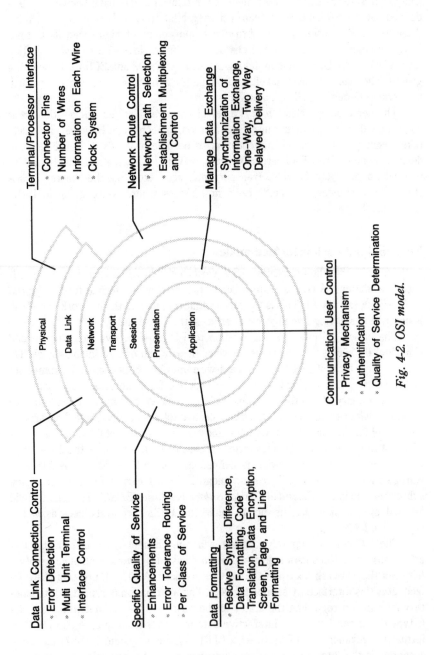

Fig. 4-2. OSI model.

In order to achieve a content-independent 64 Kbps data channel without losing synchronization, there's a need to remove inband signaling and be independent of data content. Tins is called *clear channel capacity (CCC)*.

There has been difficulty in implementing CCC because of the "ones" density required in hardware used to regenerate digital signals. Virtually all existing digital hardware has a density requirement that can't accommodate more than 15 binary zeros in a row. CCC compatible hardware is only now being introduced. For in-band network signaling to be converted to out-of-band, this requires some form of common channel signaling in the local network. Clearly, a transition to ISDN is dependent on the development of this standard.

The U.S. Exchange Carriers Standards Association (ECSA) T1X1 and T1D1 technical subcommittees have resolved the 64 Kbps CCC "ones" density problem by developing a practical standard for U.S. carriers. Here, the T1X1.4 digital hierarchy working group sought a standard for 64 Kbps clear channel capability (64 CCC) on DS1 1.544 Mbps facilities. Two alternatives were selected. One was the bipolar with eight zero substitution method (B82S), while the other was the zero byte time slot interchange (ZBTSI). They recommended B82S, which was accepted as the preferred standard for North America and is referred to as 64CCC. However, present equipment that's not compatible must be bypassed; therefore ZBTSI is considered by some as an interim strategy for sites that aren't yet compatible to B82S.

Basic access interface standards today involve both technical and regulatory issues. The Federal Communications Commission (FCC) has ruled that a network interface is required at the unstable U reference point (an interface here depends on the type and characteristics of local loop facilities). As a result, the ECSA T1D1 3 subcommittee devoted a tremendous amount of time to developing a recommendation. This was particularly difficult because two-way basic access interfacing technology was still evolving.

Fundamentally, the ISDN architecture will offer several information channels that can be combined with one another in several configurations: the B 64 kilobit per second (Kbps), the H-0 channel at 384 Kbps, and the H-11 channel at 1536 Kbps. Regardless of how local loops will be accessed, standardization of interfaces is essential. Access configurations are 144 Kbps (2B + D), 80 Kbps (B + D), and 16 Kbps. For primary access, user arrangements for the United States are 1536 Kbps or subrate configurations. These will include multiple B channels with a D channel up to 23 B + D, multiple H-0 channels, and H-11 channel. Pre-ISDN 56 Kbps will continue to be supported during this transition period. SONET B-ISDN will grow in 50 Mbps rates.

The physical and electrical specifications for the ISDN interfaces are described in the CCITT recommendation I.430 (basic access) and I.431 (primary access). The recommended basic access bit stream is being designed to operate at 192 Kbps regardless of the configuration of B and D channels. Similarly, the United States recommended primary access bit stream is being designed to operate at 1.544 Mbps (as does today's T-1 digital carrier), regardless of the configuration of B, D, and H channels.

The basic access interface connector will be similar in appearance to a modular phone jack, only (as one observer noted) slightly larger. The difference is that the ISDN interface will be an eight-pin connector, where the typical telephone jack today has four or six pins. The U.S. proposal to CCITT for the primary access interface is that the connector be identical to the basic access interface as an eight-pin modular connector. (See FIG. 4-3.)

Specifically, four CCITT standards interfaces have been defined:

- The "R" interface (comparable with many accepted interface studies established by RS-232C, RS-449, V.35, etc.)
- The basic "T" interface between terminal and NTI is 192 Kbps (1 kilometer).
- The basic "U" interface between NTI and the network is 160 Kbps (1,800 kilometers).
- The primary interface to network (23B + D).

Three of the key players have formulated their plans around these interfaces.

One manufacturer's description of this structure is as follows:

"In the ISDN Basic Access configuration, shown in FIG. 4-3, the important, new functional groupings on the subscriber line are represented by NT1 and NT2. The NT1 builds up the interface to the loop, handling the OSI model's layer 1 functions, such as transmission, remote power feeding, activation/deactivation

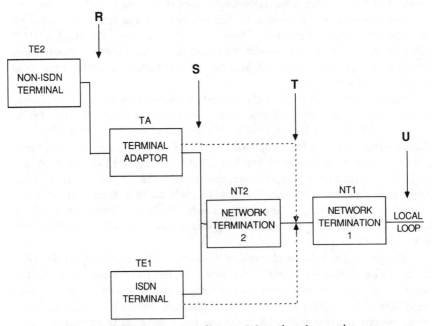

Fig. 4-3. ISDN reference points and functional grouping.

and maintenance. NT2 forms the S interface to the subscriber terminals, including maintenance and local power.

For standard basic access, NT1 or NT2 don't handle the protocol associated with OSI layers 2 and 3; their functions are limited only to layer 1. As a result, there's a tendency to combine NT1 and NT2 into one unit, NT12 (S-U). Individual subscriber terminals communicate directly on level 2 and 3 with the corresponding exchange termination (ET). Line termination (LT) has functions similar to NT1.

The S-interface is the most important interface in the present global ISDN concept, since it would function as the one access point for all network services. The present S-interface concept envisions a worldwide standard using communication OSI layers 1, 2, and 3, enabling compatible terminals to be developed for all services that could be terminated on the same S bus. The S-interface will be implemented using point-to-point and point-to-multipoint configurations; its range is approximately 500 feet in the point-to-multipoint mode on a passive bus.

The S-interface circuitry multiplexes the two B-channels, the D-channels, and some additional bits for framing and balancing into a gross bit rate of 192 Kbps. From the NT12 to the terminal equipment, an echo channel for D information is used to achieve contention resolution at the terminal site. The terminals constantly monitor this channel. The frames in both directions have an offset of two bits to achieve correct/abort mechanisms should different terminals gain simultaneous access to the D-channel.

Terminals are connected to the S-interface by transformer coupling. Power feeding of simple communication terminals is accomplished via phantom circuits. The loop interface "U" is designed for transmitting the basic access bit rate over the subscriber's conventional copper pair network. "U" differs from S only in level 1.

An adaptive, digital-hybrid method employing echo cancellation is used for transmission using the 4B3T transmission code. Effective ranges of 2.5 miles, using 26-gauge lines, and 5 miles, using 22-gauge lines, are achievable using the echo cancellation method at the U-interface.

Activation/deactivation of the U-interface is accomplished by a handshaking procedure. Subscriber access is activated and deactivated in two steps: ET NT12 (U-interface) and NT12 terminal (S-interface). The procedure can be initiated from both ends. For maintenance, and for fault localization and transmission measurement, test loops are used in the LT and NT12 units. Primarily, they involve detection and localization of faults between the subscriber premises, the loop, or the exchange.

To control the maintenance and loop tests at NT12, special information bits are defined at level 1 of the U-interface. There are the three additional interfaces R, T, and V.

- R is an existing standard interface derived from present data terminals (X.21 or X.25, for example). Via proper terminal adapters (TAs), these terminals could be connected to the S-interface.
- T is an interface between NT1 and NT2.
- V is an interface between LT and ET and represents the dividing line between the transmission section (LT) and the switching (ET) sections.

The V-interface, has been widely discussed in the international community with regard to whether it should be an external interface. Those favoring its uses as an external V-interface see the need for having different LT equipment, depending on the transmission standard and loop technology (copper or optical fiber) used.

In line with the CCITT reference model, the D-channel protocol structure composes layers 1–3. Signaling (as it relates to setting up and clearing down the B-channel connections, and controlling service and user facilities) is as follows:

Layer 1 functions involve the transmission of the D-channel multiplexed with the B-channels, activation/deactivation, power feeding and, at the S-interface, contention resolution of the D-channel access from terminals. The contention resolution mechanism uses the D-echo channel on the S-interface and is activated-based on the method of carrier sense multiple access with collision detection (CSMA-CD) by the terminals.

Layer 2 implements the HDLC protocol based on an LAPD of X.25 (multiple LAP). One link is established for each active terminal. By the terminal end-point identifier (TEI), layer 2 separates the control classes (e.g., signaling and telemetery) from the class identifier (CI) and one terminal out of several belonging to the same class.

Layer 3 controls the ISDN signaling (ISDN user part). It's envisioned that different signaling protocols might exist (e.g., for subscriber or PABX access) and that layer 3 messages that exceed the maximum length (e.g., 32 bytes) should be changed. To permit this, a user part identifier (UPI) and additional data bits will be included in the special header field.

D-channel messages can be transmitted not only from a terminal to the first exchange, but also end-to-end between terminals or PABXs. This can be accomplished by adding routing information (TY) in a special additional header; several simultaneous signaling processes on one terminal are separated by the transaction code (TC).

A special task handled by the D-channel protocol involves control of terminal portability on the S-interface. To accomplish this, a newly activated or temporarily deactivated terminal can "ask" for allocation of a new terminal identifier (TEI) at the exchange. The chosen TEI is then stored in the identify allocation data field within the exchange and in their terminal. Addressing a terminal in the ISDN is done using the normal subscriber number, a service indicator, and the terminal end-point identifier. For calling a number with identical terminals (e.g., all telephones in one location), a global cap procedure is used."

Communications between central offices in an ISDN network will be provided by Common Channel Signaling System #7. In North America, a version known as SS7 has been developed. SS7 contains capabilities over and above those originally defined by CCITT.

The protocol used in CCITT SS#7/SS7 is similar to the one used in the Primary and Basic Rate Access D-channel in that both are message-based common channel protocols. However, at the application layer, the format and content of the call signaling messages are different.

One manufacturer has displayed FIG. 4-4 to indicate the types of standards for each of the three transport layers of the OSI model that their system handles for the various basic, primary, signaling, and packet interfaces.

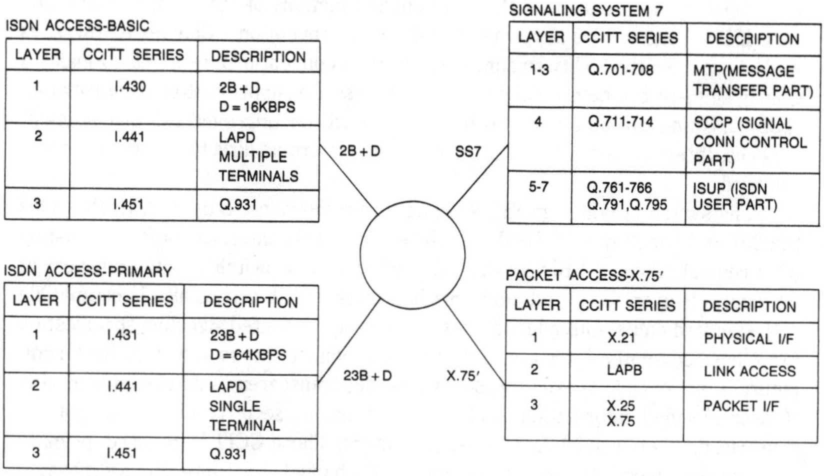

ISDN ACCESS-BASIC

LAYER	CCITT SERIES	DESCRIPTION
1	I.430	2B+D D=16KBPS
2	I.441	LAPD MULTIPLE TERMINALS
3	I.451	Q.931

SIGNALING SYSTEM 7

LAYER	CCITT SERIES	DESCRIPTION
1-3	Q.701-708	MTP(MESSAGE TRANSFER PART)
4	Q.711-714	SCCP (SIGNAL CONN CONTROL PART)
5-7	Q.761-766 Q.791,Q.795	ISUP (ISDN USER PART)

ISDN ACCESS-PRIMARY

LAYER	CCITT SERIES	DESCRIPTION
1	I.431	23B+D D=64KBPS
2	I.441	LAPD SINGLE TERMINAL
3	I.451	Q.931

PACKET ACCESS-X.75'

LAYER	CCITT SERIES	DESCRIPTION
1	X.21	PHYSICAL I/F
2	LAPB	LINK ACCESS
3	X.25 X.75	PACKET I/F

Fig. 4-4. ISDN access network interfaces.

Another manufacturer has noted the following to show conformation to ISDN interfaces:

"Four distinct application areas are being planned for the initial ISDN implementation: Centrex services, PBX and host-computer interconnect, private networks, and operator services.

ISDN offers simultaneous voice and data services to Centrex users over the basic rate 2B + D access with either the T-SDL (Digital Subscriber Loop) or U-DSL interface. For ISDN voice users, the network switch must support the full range of Centrex voice features using ISDN out-of-band message signaling. ISDN Centrex data also offers circuit-switched and packet-switched data services. Basic rate 2B + D access can provide simultaneous voice and data services in several ways, giving users flexibility for configuring their services. They might use a B channel for voice service, circuit switched data transport or packet switched data services, or the D channel might carry packet-switched data, interleaving data with the signaling packets.

Circuit-switched data services include 64 Kbps clear and restricted data transport as well as 56 Kbps digital data transport. The 56 Kbps capability can be used to communicate with existing circuit-switched digital capability terminals in a data-only mode. Both 56 Kbps and 64 Kbps data transport can also be used for accessing host computers via a host computer interface. Packet-switched data services include X.25 local area network services from the switch and access to external public packet networks via a gateway. X.25 is the CCITT recommendation for access to packet-switched networks.

In addition, the ISDN network switch should offer modem-pooling capability for data access and communication with existing customer terminals through the conventional public network. ISDN Centrex improves on conventional multibutton key system services in several ways. The simultaneous voice and data capability of the access simplifies premises arrangements, eliminating the large bundle of wires needed in non-ISDN key systems. The out-of-band message signaling capability of the D channel also enhances the call control functions of ISDN multibutton key sets. ISDN Centrex also supports the full set of conventional Centrex features, as well as provides the ability to communicate with conventional terminals. Finally, a display element can be provided on the station set to supply customer information about calls and can be controlled from the switch for improved call management services. Interworking with message desk and electronic directory services is also provided.

The switch provides an ISDN primary rate interface to users with PBXs via the 23B + D or 30B + D EDSL interface. The EDSL interface supports existing (CO) central office to PBX services as well as circuit-switched data transport at 64 Kbps, clear or restricted, and 56 Kbps rates. EDSL access also is compatible with standard digital multiplexed interface message-oriented signaling specification for a host computer interface and can interconnect the switch with host computers. A set of Q.931/I.451 messages provides transparent, end-to-end transport of user-specified information such as caller name, security check, or feature transparency between PBXs or host computers. These CCITT standard, primary rate signaling messages are carried on the D channel. Real-time facility management also uses these signaling messages to allocate facilities dynamically, call by call, giving users more per-call control. With this capability, an EDSL B channel can be assigned to a particular service for one call and to a different service for the next call. The service-independent interface leads to more traffic-efficient use of access channels and reduces the number of channels.

The ISDN network switch can be deployed in private network applications both as PBXs serving individual end users and as tandem switches interconnecting PBXs. The ISDN applications for public networks are also being used in private networks to meet similar needs. For example, ISDN Centrex services provide PBX-like voice and data features to individual end users over the ISDN standard, basic rate interface. Similarly, the ISDN host computer interconnect capability provides an effective interface to host computers for PBX data services, and PBX interconnect features provide tandem switchlike features for interconnecting PBXs with ISDN primary rate interfaces.

The operator services position system, which provides directory assistance, toll and assistance, and coin services, is based on the ISDN implementation, demonstrating the flexibility of simultaneous voice and data capabilities. The operator service functions include switching a caller to an operator position via an automatic call distributor, switching the caller to an automatic announcement system, and switching data from an operator to databases, and vice versa. These functions use ISDN Q.931/I.451 messages to control B-channel circuit-switched and D-channel permanent and virtual circuits for voice and data needs. As a result, the ISDN Operator Services System implementation minimizes interfaces and fully integrates voice and data.

The T interface implements the CCITT I.430 recommendation for specifying layer 1 of the basic rate user-network interface. It provides a 4-wire connection to ISDN station sets, has a 1-km distance limit, and is used in a protected environment. Because overvoltage protection has not yet been specified, the T interface is not suitable for outside plant distribution. The T interface will be offered directly from the switch and from its remoting vehicles.

The two-wire U interface is not specified in the CCITT recommendations. (Practices such as loop bridging that impair transmission quality aren't global.) The

U-DSL interface must be used if the distance from the switch exceeds 1 km or if the transmission facility is in the outside plant. The CCITT standard T interface can be derived from the U interface at the user's premises through NT1 network terminating equipment.

The network switch's U interface will incorporate echo-canceled, hybrid circuitry to transmit full 2B + D on a conventional, unloaded two-wire subscriber loop. Very large scale integration technology is used to integrate echo canceling, clock recovery, equalization, and scrambling or descrambling of circuitry in tiny, singular custom chip sets. Although a technology-related distance limit exists, the 2B1Q U-DSL offering will meet the carrier serving area range.

The EDSL offering supports a 23B + D or 30B + D channel format, with one channel of the DS1 facility serving as a 64 Kbps D channel that carriers signaling information for the 23 B channels. The EDSL uses the existing DS1 carrier, which meets the CCITT I.431, layer-1 recommendation for an ISDN primary rate, user-network interface. In addition, the EDSL interface supports the existing, domestic DS1 framing and line formats for those users or regions that don't support 64 Kbps clear channel transport.

ISDN services can be provided to distant customers using several remoting vehicles. For high-density clusters of users, remote switching modules can be deployed to provide ISDN interfaces to individual users. The remote integrated services line unit can be used for smaller clusters of users. Additional flexibility to serve dispersed customers is provided by ISDN access in SLC carrier systems. These remote vehicles, which are transparent to end users, provide remote users with the same features and services as local users."

Similarly, providers are teaming up with suppliers to demonstrate ISDN capabilities to their users. One supplier supplied a digital adjunct switch, four NT units, five TA units, two Group III facsimile units, two integrated voice-data terminals (IVDTs), four personal computers, software, and miscellaneous cabling for an ISDN demonstration system, such that:

"The ISDN demonstration system provided the first application of ISDN architecture over the public telephone network and the first demonstration of full Centrex capabilities over ISDN. The Centrex connection was crucial to ISDN plans.

The demonstration system consisted of a small stand-alone ET equipped to serve four ISDN basic access lines. The system provided full data switching capabilities up to 64 Kbps over the B channel within the ET. Voice calls were routed through a Centrex switch. On both voice and data calls, all incoming and outgoing signaling between the ET and the station took place over the D channel.

Furthermore, the system adhered closely to the ISDN basic access line standards adopted by the international Telegraph & Telephone Consultative Committee (CCITT) as issued in the I.430 recommendation. The ET signals to and from the host Centrex system used standard loop-start supervision, dual-tone multifrequency addressing, and conventional ringing.

The station equipment used in the system was configured into four workstations. The first two contain IVDTs connected directly to the network termination using the short, passive bus concept. In ISDN standards terminology, the terminals' type TE1.A terminal adapter was bridged on the same bus and connected a conventional facsimile machine and a standard analogue telephone to each workstation.

The other two workstations consisted of conventional personal computers and standard telephones, both connected to the network termination through a terminal adapter. The TA provides standard RJ-11 and RS-232C connections, providing the ability to connect multiple vendors' voice and data equipment to the demonstration system. The RS-232C port could accommodate asynchronous terminals up to 9.6 Kbps and synchronous terminals up to the full 64 Kbps capacity of the B channel. Rate adaptation was accomplished within the terminal adapter.

The demonstration was not done on a self-contained or closed demonstration system. The four stations, when modified to ISDN access lines, maintain the usual Centrex calling capabilities, including four digital dialing and custom-calling features."

ISDN standards

By the mid '90s, standards had become the most important driving force of ISDN, providing the gateway to future ISDN networks and services. Bellcore, the major suppliers, and many new providers have recognized this and have placed increasing resources on resolving future ISDN standards. These standards are the key to broadband/wideband ISDN products as numerous vendors attempt to understand and standardize various interfaces for the exchange of integrated voice, data, and video information in the form of bursty, fast-packet, circuit, and channel type transmission and switching.

The BOC providers have an excellent representation by the Bell Communication Research Standards Analysis and Management Division, which is one of the most fruitful and key activities of Bellcore. To be most effective, the BOC providers need to participate with their Bellcore associates, providing whatever resources are necessary to enable the various working committees, such as T1, to advance these standards in U.S. positions as rapidly as possible. These standards are essential to the success of the U.S. ISDN network.

By the late '80s, almost all suppliers had accepted the need for ISDN standards. As one supplier (AT&T) observed:

"The ISDN concept calls for:

- Uniform national and international standards that support open customer interfaces.
- An open network architecture.
- Simultaneous and integrated voice and data access.
- Out-of-band signaling.
- Universal ports for homes and offices that will permit end customers to "plug in" any terminal or other application device.

ISDN standards are being aimed toward describing the function of a piece of equipment or a system, not its design. Each manufacturer then is free to implement these functions any way it chooses, allowing maximum freedom for implementation.

To ensure that the separate developments of ISDN services, customers' equipment, and network facilities are aided and not impeded by standardization, AT&T supports the Open Systems Interconnect model, which calls for seven separate and independent layers of protocol for communications from terminal to network to terminal. The first three layers define access to the network and define and describe the service characteristics the network should provide for each service or feature. The last three layers suggest how to define and describe the way users can communicate with each other. The fourth, middle, layer defines the bridge between the higher-level user protocols and the lower-level network protocols.

This seven-layer approach will permit terminal and network technologies to advance in harmony with one another. As a result, the ISDN networks will be able to act as an economical test bed for vendors' services that can be developed independent of network and equipment limitations and permit a faster, more economical introduction of new customer services."

ISDN phases/stages/steps (1994-2014+)

Where is ISDN going? We've seen the tremendous amount of change taking place in technology. We've seen a movement to digital voice networks paced by a movement to digital data networks. We've seen ISDN defined in terms of maturing user services, advances in society, implementation steps, and ISDN stages, but where is the "ISDN Network" going?

Indeed, we're faced with not only an evolution but a revolution, and it's extremely important to know at any given point in time which game we're in and what game we should be playing in order to not only survive but also be successful in this period of intense change. (See FIG. 4-5.)

Hence, let's consider ISDN in terms of three phases: The first is evolutionary, the second is transitional, and the third is revolutionary. During the first phase, we see user needs established as technology extensions, additions, and modifications are overlaid on the existing network, as we move from analog to digital, from the traditional provider needs to the competitive marketplace user needs, from point-to-point special services to switched private networks, and onward to the overlaying of data and video on the voice world. Thus, this first evolutionary progression of changes, this identifying of new user needs, this overlaying of new capabilities to attract more and more new users, is the ISDN overlay phase . . .

ISDN overlay phase (1994-2004+)

As we all know, technology is moving very quickly. During the first phase, there was a shift to IDN (integrated digital networks), from analog to digital, which uses remote line units and remote switch units homing in on a digital base. These are deployed as direct replacements for analog switches in the rural/suburban environment, where clusters of areas are replaced by creating digital islands. In addition, digital switches are also used as new central offices to handle suburban growth, using remote switch units at shopping centers and office complexes. These switches are also used as adjunct switches in the metro environment to serve the

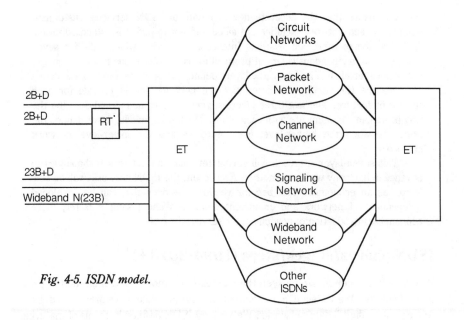

Fig. 4-5. ISDN model.

business communities' digital facilities, providing new services such as customer control of virtual networks. (See FIG. 4-6.)

The second stage of ISDN technology is the overlaying of circuit and packet data switching systems on the voice facilities to access databases. This is followed by their integration as well as the overlaying of adjunct ATM/STM systems to serve as trial applications for high-speed data movement and video conferencing. Many of the data applications initially are in the private community, as special services move from point to point to switched multipoint services provided by value added networks (VAN) and specialized common carriers (SCCs).

The third stage consists of integrating access to voice data and video networks using ISDN $2B + D$ and $23B + D$ (European $30B + D$), pre-ISDN England's $B + D(80K)$, or Japan's $B(64k) + B'(16K) + D(16K)$ offerings, in which various countries provide ISDN or pre-ISDN interfaces to ISDN users in their metro communities.

During these initial phases, various techniques are deployed to increase the transmission capability of "the last mile" of the distribution facility to the new users (customers, not subscribers). T1 first enabled 24 channels of conversation at 64 kilobit rates on a twisted pair. Then, burst switching increased this capability to 256, and ADPCM adaptive compression techniques, enabling voice at the 32K subrate, increased this to 512 channels, reducing a single voice message to require only one percent of the original facility. As we move to 9.6K voice, we can see where substantial reduction is taking place to enable the facilities to become integral parts of full information, voice, data, and video distribution. (See FIG. 4-7.)

There's a continuous sharing of loop facilities using various pre-ISDN alternatives such as frequency shift multiplexing, time compression, multiplexing, and

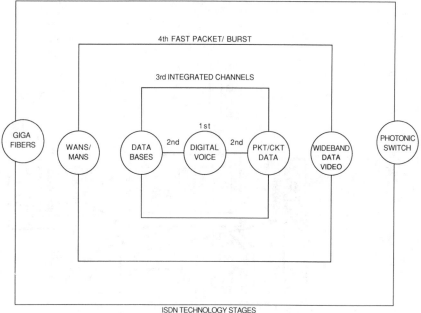

Fig. 4-6. ISDN technology stages.

echo cancellation techniques. From a service standpoint, the public packet switched networks support the newly emerging CCITT standards for network interfaces such as the X25 standard packet mode interfaces and X28 and X29 protocols for communication between dumb terminals (asynchronous ASCII start/stop devices) and host computers. Billing systems are also deployed to handle multiple vendor assistance on a single call, as well as short-holding-time packet calls. Other services, such as ISDN operator services, provide integrated voice data capabilities that enable data search and retrieval simultaneously via operator inquiry response. Digital access and cross-connect systems (DACS) have been reevaluated in terms of integrating voice and data and sending different content bit streams to different systems, denoted by out-of-band signing channels to differentiate the type of information coming down the "digital pipe." These use such systems as AT&T's D5 channel bank, fiber SLC, and SLC series 5 carrier systems. These trends set the stage for extending digital transmission throughout the loop plant, making wideband digital switching services economically more attractive. This, along with new local area signaling services such as AT&T's LASS, CCITT's No. 7 signaling and D channel signaling, enables more and more functional and stimulus communication between networks and terminals to extend customer control into the network as well as deliver more call information to the receiver.

Similarly, maintenance and operations become more automated during this first phase of ISDN, as data packet switching enables the fully automatic movement of traffic statistics, office dependent data, and network statistics; data packet

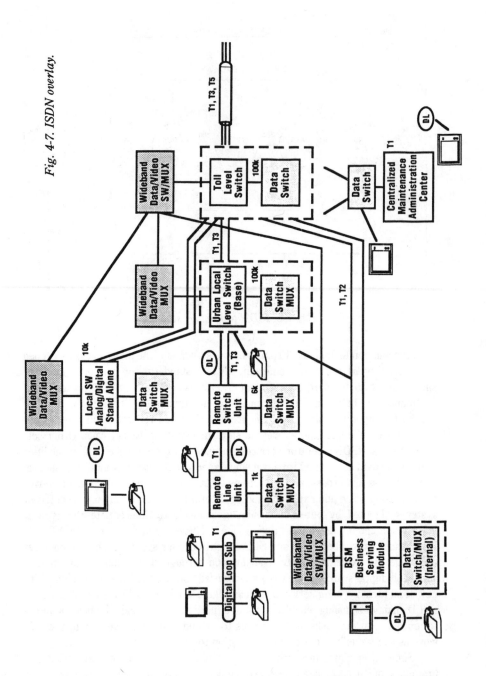

Fig. 4-7. ISDN overlay.

switching can also program recent changes and version update releases for voice data and video software control programs.

These new capabilities extend the world of Centrex; it becomes enhanced with new data-handling capabilities that enable it to challenge customer-owned PBX systems and compete for shared services in the small business community. However, in retrospect, during this overlay phase of ISDN development, a great "happening" will be in seeing the power of the fiber as it achieves more and more capabilities and reaches the 2-, 8-, and 48-gigabit transmission objectives; this will challenge the limits and expertise of new switching systems, where armies of programmers attempt to make these complex, large public systems provide more shared services by using intelligent, smaller nodes to do specialized, functional work and provide competition with customer-owned PBXs' that support private LANs, MANs, and WANs.

In this regard, we saw Japan's Information Network Services initially begin with pre-ISDN B + B' + D' interfaces that achieved digital data-handling capabilities, overlaid on their recently completed analog network. This was followed by their new plans to use the Tokyo suburbs to determine the realistic narrowband and broadband needs of their new users as they move toward a fully integrated ISDN environment. Similarly, the Germans have made bold moves as the German (PTT) Bundspost—together with Siemens, ANT, SEL and Nixdorf—introduce 140 Mbps services to their customers, dropping to 2 Mbps rates where required.

In this arena, we saw 10 Mbps Ethernet LANs (unidirectional token bus schemes operating at 140 Mbps (Fasnet) for MANs and high-speed variable channel (bits) burst switching schemes) as we moved from T1 (24 channels), T2 (96 channels), T3 (672 channels), T-3C (1344 channels) to T4 (4032 channels) and T5, as extremely fast GaAs multiplexers for SONET metro area networks using rings and collapsed rings in star configurations.

During the end of this period, a 40-line private customer branch exchange PABX could be achieved on a single silicon chip that's no larger than a baby's fingernail. This enables further movement to the Hub-type structure, where bursts of information at variable-bit lengths are provided to neighborhood link switches, where, as one person noted: "These hubs originate information, receive information off incoming channels, terminate incoming channels, and imply intelligence to reshape or manipulate the information and control and assist in the decision making of network control." Here, fiber has made substantial advancements in handling hundreds of megabits per second of information, using LEDs, light-emitting diodes.

Later in the '90s, by using economical laser sources, they'll provide gigabits-per-second interoffice trunking operating at tens of Gbps. Therefore, the complementary nature of gallium arsenide and silicon foster new developments and great achievements, where GaAs is 10 times as efficient at higher speeds, providing the speed and power for fiber application to extend the capability of single-mode fiber to 10 gigabits and above; the high-density functionality of silicon enables processor power and memory capabilities to continue to double every 18 months, as desk processing capabilities compete with older IBM mainframes. This moves us into the "soft technologies" used to provide control and movement of information to ensure security, integrity, and flexibility.

Hence, by the end of the '90s, this overlay phase of ISDN should be near completion in the metro environment. It might still be used in some more rural communities because data-handling networks can be overlaid on facilities that are uneconomical to totally change out until near the turn of the century.

In looking at the future, the third phase of ISDN can't be achieved unless the users accept and embrace the movement of data and video information into their daily lifestyles. This is essential for ubiquitous deployment. Otherwise, change will occur only in the private arena of corporate networks, specialized defense networks, or specialized residential applications. In one respect, key catalysts will be the FTS-2000-type networks, in which government agencies shift to more fully integrate their communication on private networks and extend their capabilities to off-net suppliers and users.

In any event, it's the second phase that's the true, pivotal point of ISDN, once these three technology stages are complete. The second phase is the transitional phase, where ISDN matures out of childhood. It's the phase that offers the user the capabilities needed to make communications and computers become the truly reliable, effective tools of the Information Age, much as the automobile, train, and plane became the tools of the Industrial Age.

ISDN-C&C phase (1995–2005+)

Beginning in 1990, it became clear that "computer talk" must be transparent to the average user. This realization has become the driving force for a new form of information exchange. Numerous avenues will be pursued to make the user feel more comfortable and in control of the machine, as internetworking of new services become available, economical, and "friendly." This then presents a challenge to the computer industry to move from the more comfortable arena of closed user groups, which are islands to themselves where captured users have become more and more dependent on a single vendor's programs and systems, to the new world of interconnected multiple vendors that provide integrated services to multiple users. The ISDN overlay network enables firms to become "physically" distributed throughout the world. In many cases, this then puts the users in the environment of using several vendors' products and several providers to interconnect their distributed plants and offices together.

As we left the '80s, the struggling computer industry realized that their users were requesting universal access to multiple databases; industry leaders began embracing the OSI model to connect their SNAs, token rings, and Ethernets together, using first OSI's lower layers for information movement and then its higher layers for information generation, storage, retrieval, processing, and manipulation. As these tasks are accomplished, we'll have successfully increased the use of our overlay networks and whetted the users' appetites for more dynamic and universal integrated voice and data, data and video, voice, data, and video high-quality communications. Then we'll move through the fourth stage of the technologies' evolution into the integration of LANs, PBXs, Centrexs, and databases that use more integrated, fast packet/burst systems. Then it's on into the world of broadband ISDN. (See FIG. 4-8.)

Networking

Computers and terminals are locked in an ever-widening struggle to communicate better. Their new needs and requirements have become increasingly more demanding as computers have entered every aspect of the business marketplace. Unfortunately, communications firms have remained preoccupied with digitizing their voice networks as they added more versatility in control and operation. However, computer companies, recognizing their communication "networking" needs, have turned to the private arena to construct specialized networks, enabling their closed user groups to interexchange information.

The expanding environment for new, interrelated applications for enabling multiuser, multitask distributed systems to access multiple remote databases has moved computers into a more dependent relationship with public communications. This is one in which communication and computer interfaces with different vendor systems are established to integrate NEC, IBM, DEC, Apple, etc., terminals together and access the many different suppliers' mainframes throughout the

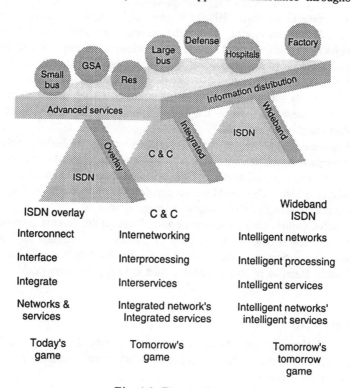

ISDN overlay	C & C	Wideband ISDN
Interconnect	Internetworking	Intelligent networks
Interface	Interprocessing	Intelligent processing
Integrate	Interservices	Intelligent services
Networks & services	Integrated network's Integrated services	Intelligent networks' intelligent services
Today's game	Tomorrow's game	Tomorrow's tomorrow game

Fig. 4-8. The platform.

world. Emphasis on IEEE 802 interfaces and protocols (physical, MAC, and LLC) were overlaid on the first three levels of the OSI model (physical, data link and network) using an array of techniques, from dedicated transmission systems to switched T1 and DS3, Bridged LANs, PBX-LANS, and switched data packet networks. (See FIG. 4-9.)

Thus, C&C, in its initial step for achieving "integrated-interworking" systems, was forced to spend the bulk of its activity in the areas of "internetworking and interprocessing" before it could venture into the more lucrative world of "interservices."

The "networking" of systems to connect processors and terminals together in point-to-point, bus, and ring configurations requires using various types of media, from copper wiring to co-ax to fiber. Technology is providing many new techniques and capabilities to network a user's facility and then internetwork this network with others within and outside the area. Various media have been used for providing new machine capabilities, such as: AT&T's 1 Mbps Starlan using existing wires, Northern Telecom's 2.56 Mbps Meridian LAN, and IBM's 4 Mbps Token Ring, which uses twisted-pair, 3-grade (only 22- and 24-gauge wire). This then leads to co-ax and, of course, to the fiber. Hitachi has developed a 1 Gbps local area network using optical electronic integrated circuits (OEIC) that can handle a number of data communication applications in a space no larger than a dime.

Some have noted that: "Hitachi is now marketing a third-generation laser diode of 1.55 micron design, where the second generation was a 1.3-micron wavelength laser diode. At the 1.55-micron wavelength, we can send information 5 times further than its predecessor to achieve greater distances for transoceanic fiber cables. With LM Ericsson's 8 × 8 optical switching matrix, which can switch 8 optical channels into 8 receptors on a lithium niobate chip, this moves internetworking into a new dimension — 'the age of light,' which Einstein's theory says is the fastest thing in the universe."

Meanwhile, Bell Laboratories and several universities are seeking to develop a general-purpose optical machine that would process huge chunks of data in each cycle. Components would transmit light between lenses without wires or even fiber-optic structures. This would permit parallel operations, useful in manipulating arrays or in processing all the pixels in an image at once.

As noted earlier, such a computer could process traffic from large converging bundles of fibers in main central offices by passing it all through an intelligent switching matrix of lenses without changing the data (or digitizing voice) from light to electrons. Because of this capability, such optical processors could run large networks.

Linking LANS

Per James E. Heaton, "the topology of a network describes how the network media are configured." The four major topologies include point-to-point, star or radial, ring, and bus/tree types:

A point-to-point network links two stations along a single communication channel. Radial topology is used in traditional time-shared computing, control

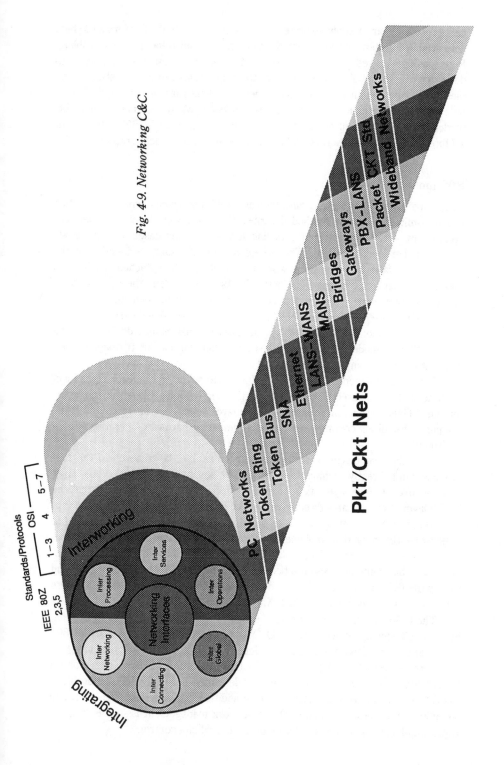

Fig. 4-9. Networking C&C.

data-processing, and telephone system layouts. A central controller forms the hub, with attached systems interconnected via dedicated point-to-point wire or cabling. Ring topology is used almost exclusively with "token" access methods. The medium must be joined at its ends to form the ring. Buses are logical, straight-line media with runs and taps for terminal connections. Trees are logically equivalent to buses from a communications procedures viewpoint. Many, but not all, bus networks can be configured as trees. For example, neither IEEE 802.5 baseband/ 1 Mbps networks nor Ethernet-802.3 can be used in a tree configuration.

802 model

Access methods constitute the rules by which LANs determine when each station can transmit. The access method describes the two lowest levels in a network architecture — the physical and data link levels. In some cases, it will include several higher-level functions. The access method is usually a function of the network interface and/or the network tap, enabling the attached machine to "speak" the language of the local network. As noted earlier, the open systems interconnection model (OSI) is a conceptual framework for defining and implementing generalized communications interconnections between differing types and brands of equipment. Formulated by the International Standards Organization (ISO), OSI is a model (not a detailed specification) for having two significantly different machines communicate via a network.

Since the OSI model divides the problem into seven layers, each layer functions as if it were directly connected to the corresponding layer in the other machine. Thus, application programs (above layer seven) can be written as if the computers had direct communications and a compatible hardware/operating system environment.

Since the two machines are actually incompatible, layer seven in the first machine can't directly communicate with layer seven in the other. Thus, layer seven invokes its own layer six instead. This basic process of pretending that the "N"th layer communicates directly with its counterpart in the other machine (but by having it in fact communicate with the next lower layer) iterates downward to level two — the layer that implements conventional link-level communication protocols. Layer one is the actual physical medium with rules for driving and interfacing to it. While some progress has been made on firm standards for layers one and two by the IEEE P-802 committee and on layers three and four by the NBS, layers five through seven now have FTAM, X.400, X.500 and VT.

The P-802 specification consists of subparts numbered 802.1-802.6. In defining the relationship between the ISO OSI reference model layers and the 802 specification, the committee split OSI level two, the data link layer, into two sublayers referred to as Logical Link Control (LLC) and Media Access Control (MAC). 802.1 is an overview document that describes more fully the relationship of the 802 specification to the OSI model. In addition, it discusses internetworking (communicating between networks) and network management issues. 802.2, the Logical Link control document, discusses the logical link control.

The remaining four specifications define specific and different physical network techniques: 802.3, a bus using CSMA CD as the access method; 802.4, a bus using token passing as the access method; 802.5, a ring using token passing as the access method, and 802.6, a metropolitan area network.

The LLC layer is the common denominator between the various 802-specified media access control/physical layer alternatives and level III of the OSI model. Thus, in any local area network design where 802.2 is taken as a base, higher layers (OSI 3-7 or equivalent) can be built on it with little or no regard to the actual physical network.

More and more local area networks (LANs) are being installed by U.S. corporations. The Yankee Group, a Boston-based market research firm, noted that at the end of the '80s, the value of the LAN market has more than $4 billion. According to Strategic Inc., a market research firm based in Cupertino, Cal., that figure represents about 125,000 local area networks, each interconnecting LAN stations. Collectively, groups of LAN stations are used for many applications, including office automation, factory automation, research, and engineering.

Many of these LANs at scattered locations will themselves be interconnected via such public communications networks as the telephone system or through private or public satellites or microwave systems. While communications on a single LAN is reasonably straightforward, LAN interconnection might not be. Companies that have not planned for inter-LAN communications will find that interconnecting LANs with stations of different architectures from different vendors over multiple media can be a difficult task.

There are currently three classes of devices that provide LAN-to-LAN interconnection. These are gateways, routers, and bridges. The functions of each one can be defined in relation to the seven layers of the international Standards Organization (ISO) model.

A gateway operates in the higher layers (above layer three, or the network layer) of the ISO model. A gateway interconnects users (terminal operators, applications, and so on) of different architectures (for example, DECnet, SNA and X.25). The protocols used to carry the user information are different in each of the architectures. A gateway translates these different protocols from one architecture to the other, so that the users can communicate. Because more than three layers of protocols are involved, gateways are required to perform substantial processing of information. Gateways are "visible" devices; that is, the user station protocols must communicate with the gateway in order to use the gateway's services. This requires each station that wants to use gateway services to have knowledge of the gateway device and its protocol in order to maintain a compatible protocol.

Routers work at the network layer of the ISO model to interconnect LANs by using an internetwork protocol. Like gateways, routers must be visible to user stations. Unlike gateways, routers are used to interconnect architectures that are similar. Stations without a compatible internet protocol layer and software release version can't use the router. So, whereas stations of different architectures might share the transmission capacity of a LAN, they might not be able to share the internetwork transmission capacity provided by a router.

Bridges operate at the data link layer (level 2), where the Ethernet and IEEE 802.3 standard protocols themselves exist. Bridges store and forward entire LAN frames. A bridge, therefore, is able to filter and discard messages addressed to local stations, keeping local traffic on one LAN from congesting the interconnect media or the remotes LANs. Filtering allows bridges to use substantially lower link speeds than those used on the LAN.

Because bridges work at the data link layer, their operation is "transparent" to the LAN station; that is, LAN stations on different LANs interconnected via bridges appear to be on the same LAN. Regardless of respective locations, stations simply address the data link frames to other stations; they never knowingly communicate with a bridge. This is true for both single destination and multicast/broadcast-destination frames.

Additionally, because bridges work at the data link layer, they have less processing overhead than routers, which operate at the next higher layer, or gateways, which operate above routers. Consequently, bridges are able to transmit messages at higher rates than can routers, typically several thousand frames per second. As a result, bridges are capable of using very high bandwidth links between LANs."

LANs

Per Mr. Koshy: "The merging trend is toward the existence of multiple local area networks (LANs) within one organization—each one catering to the needs of a specific operation or a functional group. Multiple LANs within an organization need to be interconnected so that all users can communicate with all others if necessary. The devices that perform the interconnection are called bridges, providing high throughput and low delay so that users don't experience any significant performance degradation when communicating with other users attached to the conglomerate of LANs. Local area network products available today don't conform to a single standard. They exist on a variety of media, such as twisted pair, coaxial cable, and optical fiber; use two signaling schemes (baseband and broadband); and work with a variety of media access techniques such as carrier-sense multiple access with collision detection (CSMA/CD), token passing, time-division multiplexing, and so on. There's wide support among all segments of the computer industry for the Institute of Electrical and Electronics Engineers (IEEE) 802 standards, and it's expected that within the next few years most LAN products will conform to one of these standards. Currently, IEEE 802 standards support the following schemes:

- CSMA/CD on baseband cable.
- CSMA/CD on broadband cable.
- Token-passing bus on broadband cable.
- Token-passing bus on baseband cable.
- Token-passing ring on baseband cable.
- Frame relay on broadband cable.
- SMDs on broadband cable.
- ATM-switched trunking.

Internetworking

We've entered the world of internetworking as we attempt to have IEEE 802-compatible LANs operating at 4, 5, or 10 Mbps work with lower-speed wide area networks whose maximum throughput is normally 48 or 56 Kbps, or as we attempt to have more and more physically interconnected LANs located in clusters. Hence, technical leaders of the computer industry have begun to identify solutions for internetworking. Weissberger, Stein, and Chapin noted that:

"Standards bodies concerned with fleshing out the Open Systems Interconnection (OSI) model are also tackling the associated problems of internetworking — that is, communications between an interconnected set of networks. The seven-layer model from the International Organization for Standardization (ISO) has become a familiar model within the industry. OSI provides a framework for the interaction of users and applications in a distributed data processing environment, which can include a wide variety of both computer and terminal equipment, as well as many different communications technologies.

The term OSI refers to the seven-layer architectural reference model and to a set of standards that describe how to provide communications among computers and terminals. To examine internetworking, one must understand OSI terminology. For each of the seven layers, a layer service is defined that identifies the set of functions that the layer provides. Layer services in OSI are of two general types: connections oriented and connectionless, which allow the service users to exchange information without having to establish a connection.

Within each layer, protocols operate to provide the services defined for that layer. As a number of protocol selection options exist in some layers of the reference model (for example, the transport layer defines five distinct connection-oriented protocol classes), conformance requirements are specified by each of the layer protocol standards. When in compliance with the required set of standard protocols prescribed for OSI, configurations are considered to be open.

The lowest two layers, physical and data link, provide technology-specific access to the media that's used to interconnect the network equipment. While the third layer (network) performs data routing and relaying, the fourth layer (transport) provides for the reliable, error-free, end-to-end delivery of user data. An equally important and often overlooked function of the transport layer is to determine the most cost-effective means of providing data transport service. Given specific quality-of-service (QOS) constraints by the higher layers, the transport layer matches a transport protocol to the network layer service provided. (The QOS is defined by the characteristics of a connections-oriented or connectionless transmission as observed between the end points.) Thus, the requested QOS is satisfied in the most expedient and cost-effective manner.

To be a successful standard, OSI must provide a homogeneous environment in which information can be accessed and exchanged independent of the immediate network to which corresponding users are attached. Network interconnection, or internetworking, has thus become a most important issue. The advent of local area network (LAN) technologies has lent new urgency to this effort. Part of the world treats LANs as a sophisticated, multipoint data link; the remainder, as merely one more type of subnetwork (OSI reference for a network that's part of an internetwork) that must be accommodated by OSI.

The problem of interconnecting networks to form a single 'global' network is an inevitable consequence of the recent explosion of network technology. Network designers have investigated and implemented a number of interconnection strategies that attempt to facilitate communications among computers and terminals connected to different networks. While all create a homogeneous networking environment by resolving differences in network technology, access method, address structure, and administration, two appear to be most applicable to an OSI global network.

In the first case, the networks to be connected:

- Offer predominantly connection-oriented services.
- Exist where close cooperation among the network administrations can be achieved and enforced.
- Exist where the extent to which the individual network services differ is limited.

With this approach, connection-oriented internetworking can be achieved by relaying the services of one network directly onto corresponding services of the other networks. An underlying assumption of this network interconnection strategy is that it's easier to solve the problems associated with subnetwork interconnection when the services that the networks offer are the same than when they're different.

In the second case, the networks to be connected offer a mix of connection-oriented and connectionless services and exist where network administration is largely autonomous. The extent to which the individual network services differ can't be predicted or controlled. In such configurations, connectionless internetworking preserves individual network autonomy and service characteristics of the networks to be connected. This is achieved by conveying the information necessary to support a uniform network service in an explicit internetwork protocol (IP). This protocol makes minimal assumptions about the services available from each of the interconnected networks.

In the first case, gateways (network layer relays) perform a mapping of the service offered by one network onto another. In general, the gateways don't add services. Rather, they perform the relaying and switching functions necessary to bind the individual subnetworks into a unified or global network. A consequence of this approach is that either all of the subnetworks must inherently provide equivalent services, or each must be enhanced to some common level of service.

Interconnecting

To best appreciate the "degree of connectivity" for allowing PC users to have concurrent access to either an IBM Token Ring or another local network, as well as enable IBM processors to interoperate with non-IBM processors over the IBM Token Ring physical network, we must understand the "degree of complexity" in which users can and cannot easily obtain inexpensive chip sets, boards, and small control (7 Kbyte) programs to accomplish these interfaces.

To understand what's open about IBM's Token Ring and what's not requires a layer-by-layer analysis of IBM's Token Ring implementation, starting at the bottom physical level in reference to the Open Systems Interconnection (OSI) model of the International Organization for Standardization (ISO), where IBM transmits information at up to 4 Mbps rates over a variety of copper media. (See IBM's "Blueprint for the future" vision in chapter 1.

Interglobal

NASA's satellite-to-satellite networks are providing a new generation of tracking and data-relaying satellites (TDRS) that move us another step further into global internetworking at 300 Mbps rates. The initial TDRS networks will cover 85 percent of the earth's surfaces.

These satellite networks — together with the high-capacity, marine-type fiber networks described earlier — will begin linking the world together, eventually offering gigabit-rate communication at cheap rates. This will enable the linking of the ISDNs of various countries together into a world globalwide network. (See TABLE 4-1.)

Interworking

As we consider expanding user needs, we can't ignore the new networking requirements that are driving computers to enter the world of "inter." Once the subsystems' modules are networked together, the users will be able to use various automatic processor capabilities to obtain new, interdependent services. This is the second step of the C&C phase. It's one in which interprocessing achieves interservices using ISDN interfaces to provide layers of value-added features to meet the new needs of the information users. (See TABLE 4-2.)

Interprocessing

As microprocessors are used in smaller applications — such as the home — to perform various tasks, from environmental control to alarms to TV monitoring, several interprocessing buses have been proposed, such as the IEEE 100 bus that enables different processors to directly communicate with each other. One author has noted the need for an asynchronous nine-bit interprocessor protocol (NBIP) to allow flexible system configurations for both low-end performance (dumb terminals) and intelligent stations. The home entertainment bus is a typical example of this application.

Data terminal equipment (DTE) devices and data circuit terminating equipment (DCE) use RS 232-C type signals in which an asynchronous terminal might be running at 300 b/s or 1.2 Kbps, requiring different settings from a modem running

Table 4 – 1. A Time for "Inter"

The C&C Element . . .	
• Interfacing	• Internetworking
• Interlacing	• Interprocessing
• Interconnecting	• Interservicing
• Integrating	• Internationally

Table 4-2. The New User Needs

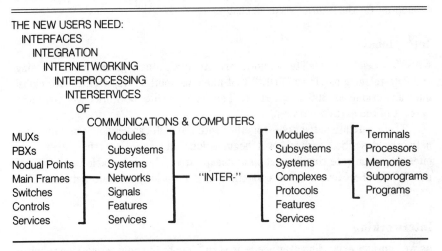

THE NEW USERS NEED:
  INTERFACES
    INTEGRATION
      INTERNETWORKING
        INTERPROCESSING
          INTERSERVICES
            OF
              COMMUNICATIONS & COMPUTERS

MUXs	Modules		Modules	Terminals
PBXs	Subsystems		Subsystems	Processors
Nodual Points	Systems		Systems	Memories
Main Frames	Networks	"INTER-"	Complexes	Subprograms
Switches	Signals		Protocols	Programs
Controls	Features		Features	
Services	Services		Services	

at 19.2 Kbps. This brings us into the area of network management and control of the exchange of information, where, for example, Ethernet employs one form of collision control and retry, and token ring uses another.

Contention-based systems are inherently more robust than collision avoidance schemes. Ethernet's algorithm provides for retries after collisions, but there can also be collisions on subsequent tries; hence, it can't necessarily be used for networks where messages must be delivered within a fixed period of time.

As we move into the world of using LANS to interconnect processors and we attempt to manage traffic, we must use different network management tools than the traditionally switched star networks. LANS use distributed topologies such as the bus or ring as opposed to the star. Connectivity in LANS is usually achieved through packet switching instead of circuit switching. This has lead to higher-level protocols, while circuit switching data through the traditional communication network typically only employs data link level protocols.

Multiple local networks are being used increasingly to solve global network problems. In these networks, management tools must be transparent across multiple networks and interface with local packet switching protocols that are used in the basic local area network. In cases where standard, high-level protocols are used, products from multiple vendors can communicate effectively by using TCP/IP (Transmission Control Protocol/Internet Protocol). However, rarely do products from multiple vendors cooperate in the management of the network, due to the lack of standardization. An IEEE 802 committee has been working on standardization of network management for the lowest two levels of the ISO model, and there's work being done by the GM MAP (Manufacturing Automation Protocol) task force.

Currently, security promises to be an aspect of interprocessing and network managing that will receive increasing attention in the '90s. Fiber-optic technology is already providing enhanced security at the physical level. Subsequent local area networks and public information networks will focus on user authorization and unauthorized access detection with audit trail type features. Hence, obtaining new standards for interprocessor communication will be the major task for C&C during the '90s.

Interservices

IBM's Distributed Office Support System (DISOSS) package for exchanging documents from different vendor systems is expanding to provide new capabilities, such as the ability to exchange "revisable form" information. Using an IBM host computer, DISOSS documents enable users to work on DEC networks to exchange documents with users on IBM networks, and vice versa.

Similarly, Professional Office System (PROFS) is the office automation package for the virtual machine (VM) operating system for the 9370 line. This product line is targeted to compare with DEC's VAX line, where 15 VAX processors can be clustered to share resources. This ability for pooling of VAX processors, the recognition of IBM's mainframe dominance, and the existence of SNA has encouraged DEC to provide its users with a wide variety of IBM-compatible networking and interfacing tools, which have made DEC the envy of the industry because they were the first to recognize the need for internetworking, interprocessing, and interservices.

Interservice Standards will play an increasing role in the '90s — for example, for electronic mail. The standard for plug-compatible electronic mail will be based on the message-handling X.400 series recommendations of the International Telegraph and Telephone Consultative Committee (CCITT). However, the degree of achievement might be a matter of interpretation due to contentions over message naming and addressing that describe the contents and particular data formats of each message, text, graphics, and facsimile. There are also deliberations on message heading information, which notes such things as multiple destinations or carbon copy.

The naming and addressing are included in the X.400 series P_2 application layer protocol, which rides on top of the recommended X.25 network protocols. Other considerations for standards are the Message Transfer Protocol (P_1) and the Reliable Transfer Service (RTS), which are a series of intermediary communication commands that act as buffers between the presentation and session layer.

Other aspects that must be considered in obtaining standards (especially across private networks such as IBM's System Network Architecture (SNA)) is the need for some form of gateway to transform IBM's Document Interexchange Architecture/Document Content Architecture (DIA/DCA) multimedia message contents to whatever form X.400 allows. As various vendors provide electronic mail offerings such as AT&T Mail, Easy Link, MCI Mail, Quick Comm, TeleMail, etc., we'll require other standards such as X.500, and X.409 a subset of X.400 to obtain full interservices.

Therefore, this transition phase (the ISDN — C&C pillar) can be best summarized by the following observations. In the mid '90s the transition from the first step of networking and internetworking system to the second step of proving new services and interservices occurred by focusing new computer architectures around the higher layers of the OSI model.

This is adequately demonstrated by one observant group, who had tracked the first step of C&C by providing training seminars on IBM's SNA in the early '80s. Subsequently in the late '80s, they moved to reviewing IBM's System Application Architecture (SAA) for product planners, network designers, product development managers, marketing managers, MIS managers, system analysts, and system programming managers to demonstrate how SAA involves all of IBM's key communications technologies—APPC, APPN, DIA, DDM, SNADS and ECF. It's believed that this new communication strategy was adapted by IBM to support networking of distributed applications. These new distributed applications required network services such as: peer-to-peer communications, program-to-program communications, remote file access, electronic mail, remote database access, and enhanced LAN and WAN connectivity.

Their SAA umbrella supports a migration strategy from central host to distributed networking, as well as the ability to achieve multivendor network management. SAA provides a networking model for application services, session services, networking, and data link connections to achieve distributed services for distributed office applications using SNA Distribution Services (SNADS) and the Document Interexchange Architecture (DIA) by having a Distributed Systems Architectures (SNA) based on Distributed Data Management (DDM) and Enhanced Connectivity Facilities (ECF) for strategic data streams consisting of Document Content Architecture (DCA), Intelligent Printer Data Services (IPDS), and 3270 Data Services. The SNA architecture can achieve communications services such as Local Unit Type 6.2 session services, employing the networking technologies of Low Entry Network PU 2.1, Advanced Peer to Peer Networking (APPN), and X.25 Product Switching Networking. These enable data link connections to SDLC, Token Ring, and other LANS. Network management can use IBM's multivendor approach, Netview, and Netview/PC, as well as SNA management services. This then leaves non-IBM systems to determine how they can coexist with SNA, as well as provide better or equivalent offerings to achieve networking of their products and internetworking across autonomous product lines.

Hence, we see the transition to integrating layered communications with various computer services, as the second step of the integration of computers and communications begins to develop in sync with overlay ISDN technologies. Q.931 (I.451) out-of-band signaling, X.121 data, ISDN E.164 (I.331) numbering plans, Q.921 (I.441) descriptions of link access procedures on the "D" channel (LAPD), and basic and primary rate interface recommendations I.430 and I.431 are further defined using such things as adaptive echo cancellation hybrid and coding techniques to achieve 64 Kbps clear channels, etc., etc. This then paves the way for wideband ISDN.

Broadband ISDN (1996-2014+)

SONET-based ISDN or broadband ISDN (B-ISDN) is no longer an evolutionary change but a revolutionary change. We've left the evolutionary arena, as we move into the fast packet/circuit switching stage of communications followed by the more profound fifth-stage light switches that will first appear as hybrids before the turn of the century and later become multilevel logic systems, perhaps using higher number bases than binary.

However, they'll still use, as Dr. Rose once noted, "The expanding functional power of silicon." Therefore, it's important for both the providers and suppliers to play two games at the same time. They might indeed be playing all three; but for now let's only discuss broadband ISDN.

In reviewing the potential of new technology, we see that technology developed for the movement of high-speed facsimile systems and high-definition TV have lead firms such as NEC to construct multiple-node system network concepts "using 1.2 Gbps optical loop LANs, which logically support 700 Mbps networks containing 100 Mbps circuit channels and 400 Mbps multiaccess networks, where every signal is packetized. As for the local loop applications of optical transmission, 565 Mbps transmission over 5 km of single mode fiber, using 1.3 um mesa structure surface emitting LEDs are possible, while bit rates of 140 Mbps are achievable over a 35-km span and are stable at ambient temperatures up to 60° C." Satellite communications systems have a smooth ISDN interface at 64 Kbps SCPC channels and 1.5 or 2 Mbps TDMA channels, having been mainly used in the '80s as a backup for terrestrial systems. Future satellites, having more than a hundred transports enabling switching between satellites, will be internationally used as a major information media. Similarly, Digital Microwave Radio, (DMR) "using NEC's cochannel dual polarization transmission methods to provide fourfold frequency reuse can achieve 400 Mbps capabilities." Finally, with the advent of long wavelength devices and low-loss single-mode fibers, the 400 Mbps transmission systems with 30-km repeater spacing will come into commercial use. (In the laboratory, NEC and other vendor firms have successfully transmitted 4 Gbps over a 123-km length fiber, based on direct intensity modulation of a laser diode and using coherent communication systems.) Above 10 Gbps transmission capacity, wave length division multiplexing (WDM) techniques are quite promising.

Thus, there will be a tremendous increase in transmission capability together with the increase in switching capability using VLSI technology, where a GaAs 8×8 functional block matrix can operate at 1.65 GHz and can cope with about ten H4 channels or almost the equivalent of a thousand H1 channels. When applying this technique to the packet movement of information, using a high-speed-oriented network protocol with separate signaling and network control from data transfer and network hardware switching, we can provide fast, high throughput reaching 3 Gbps for data packets with reliable transmission and provisioning for cap control. This then enables us to enter the arena of intelligent communications services for picture transmission and processing, protocol conversions, database accesses, media conversions, and automatic translations for VAN interfaces to achieve teleconferences, remote mechanizations, home banking, home health care, multimedia mail, radiology consulting, etc. . .

Therefore, as many have prophesied, ISDN has the potential to become a multimedia, intelligent, reliable, secure, friendly, personalized, broadband communication digital information network that provides layers and layers of transport services.

Now, what does this mean in terms of where we're going? It means that we must accept the end of evolutionary changes to our current network and at some point "cap" overlay offerings by limiting new switch features in order to enter a new arena. We must plan for the wideband/broadband arena while playing the overlay game. Hence, we must plan for new, revolutionary changes. (See FIG. 4-10.)

Rings on rings

New facility deployment plans must be generated. These include: ringing cities, using various ring star type structures, homing in on distributed nodes, perhaps having a two-level type of hierarchy in the metro environment to enable universities, shopping centers, and small towns in the vicinity of the ringed metro cities to access these high-speed transport mechanisms. They'll process variable-length packets, circuits, or channels of voice, data, and video information. These facility access distribution switches will most likely use some form of survivable technology to provide an infrastructure to move gigabits of information around the metro community.

They'll replace automated mainframes by providing intelligent analysis of the type of information being handled, and they'll appropriately route information to internal, functionalized, specialized system complexes. Alternate routing, security, reliability, and flexibility for growth will be essential aspects of these structures as the ring switching complex is deployed over the late '90s, enabling LANs, MANs, and WANs to tie to the high-speed public information network. Depending on the regulated/unregulated forces and factors, this structure can be initially developed for RBOCs (and other open network architecture providers), or the structure can be shared service or private networks, enabling new information services to be provided in the unregulated arena. (See FIG. 4-11.)

The info switch

Using the ring information splitters, partitioners, distributors, or directors, information can be transferred from the ring to functional work areas such as an info Switch, which can be located appropriately in the network so that portions of its structure can be physically distributed in the home or business communities. The remote unit will then home in on the base unit for shared services. Thus, the access to specialized content-dependent or protocol-dependent programs is achieved within the info switch, much in the same manner as using a PBX to handle information services for a LAN. This can be the new Centrex, but it will be much more than simply extending existing Centrex systems to handle a few ISDN data features.

This system can address service centers for more specialized open system vendor programs, as well as various open operator services that employ both voice and text operations. In essence, the info switch will compete with the new distributed computer branch exchanges (CBX) and information branch exchanges (IBXs)

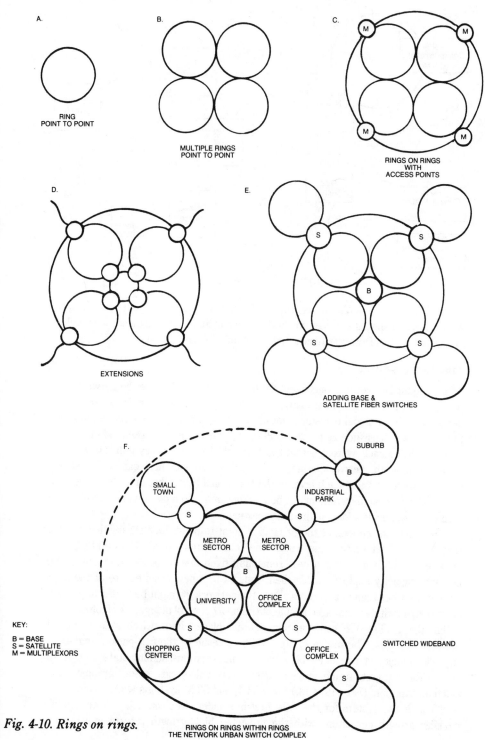

Fig. 4-10. Rings on rings.

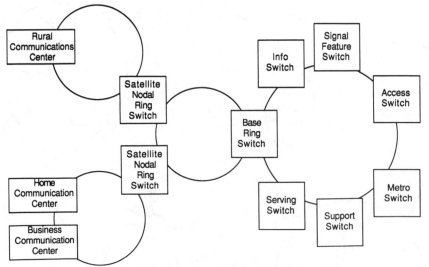

Fig. 4-11. Ring switching complex.

in the '90s. In the public arena, the info switch will provide specialized features with access to special services for both the small and large businesses, as well as interested parties from the residential community. (See FIG. 4-12.)

The metro switch

As Intelligent Networking (a concept for features provided above the network) was being developed in late '80s, many new features could be brought up above the network by using signal transfer point (STP) centers to access specialized systems to provide services such as extended 800, etc. These services then didn't have to be provided by each system within the network. However, they didn't have to be provided above the network either. As Huber pointed out, there can be a proliferation of feature nodes at each level of the traditional hierarchy, or, as Ross pointed out, the traditional hierarchy might be restructured into a two-level structure with three new sublevels added at the customer level.

Similarly, as we look at the expanding point-to-point fiber capabilities, we see that a single fiber system can handle the conversations of all 100,000,000 lines in America. With installation cost remaining fixed due to poles and labor costs, but with capacity exploding, this then leads us to a new architecture of the local network. Rather than put features above the network, it might be better to provide large metro switches that are capable of transport control of gigabits of information within the LATA. We can use strategically placed info switches to extended network services. The metro system will be a result of the fast-packet, high-density silicon logic, which can enable numerous information-handling state changes to ensure the integration and movement of voice, voice/text, image, graphics, and video information. (See FIG. 4-13.) Both ATM and STM systems will prevail.

This is the system for the '90s, first in smaller sizes that are able to employ modular growth consistent with the projected high growth rate of information

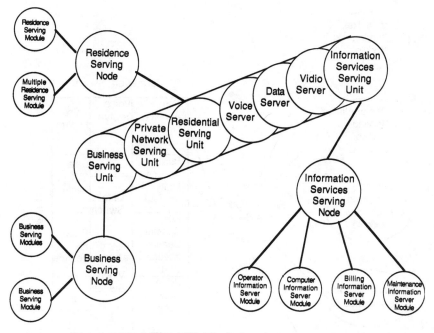

Fig. 4-12. The info switch.

movement. The switch will encompass narrowband services with broadband capabilities and enable both to progress using, if necessary, specialized matrixes dedicated to particular types of functionality. It should be supported by a local service center to provide the extensive maintenance, operations, and administration control needed to facilitate an information network in terms of usage billing and customer control of various network services. (See FIG. 4-14.)

ISDN network architecture

As IBM's SNA embraces X.25, as PCs use AT&T's Unix and IBM's MS-DOS Systems, as we move from 262.44 Mbps in increments of 4.076 Mbps to 16.777 Gbps, the resulting ISDN network by the year 2010 will be composed of the narrowband ISDN switches using the overlays of the early '90s, integrated with the broadband ISDN switches of the late '90s. They're tied together by digital ring switches, enabling access to ICs, SCCs, VANs, and RCCs from home communication centers, business complexes, and private LANs. The essential aspects of this architecture are the integration of variable-bit-rate streams of voice, data, and video (perhaps in strings of ISDN 64k bytes), using out-of-band signaling. They're routed by transport switches on fiber rings to large transport metro switches that enable access to numerous services provided by info switches or feature/service switches. The architecture obtains automatic network control and dynamic transmission allocations via service centers supported by intelligent workstations.

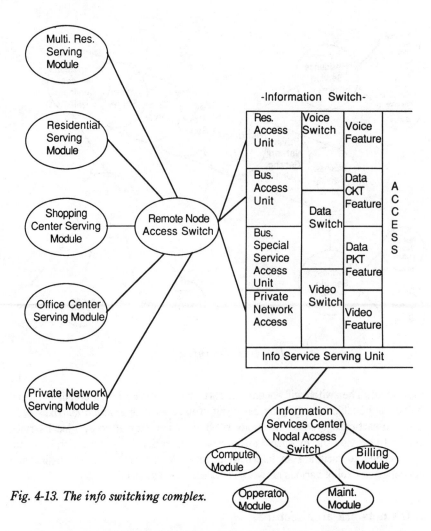

Fig. 4-13. The info switching complex.

In terms of open network architecture and comparable efficient interconnection, this structure supports entrances and exits of multiple vendors at the services communication center, info switch, and feature switch, and enables multiple providers' entrance and exit access to the ring. This allows multiple providers to establish parallel networks within the "local monopoly" and furnish their users with access to services provided by the traditional provider, new database sources, or feature providers. Having this infrastructure in place, it should be easier to separate the "service access aspects" of the competitive arena from basic transport. For "the common good" of society, the ring is "regulatory-wise" encouraged to grow and handle gigabit traffic at reduced costs for simple, basic voice services. In any event, this structure will be able to support the ultimate movement of the new users to the many new types of services of the new information game. (See FIG. 4-15.)

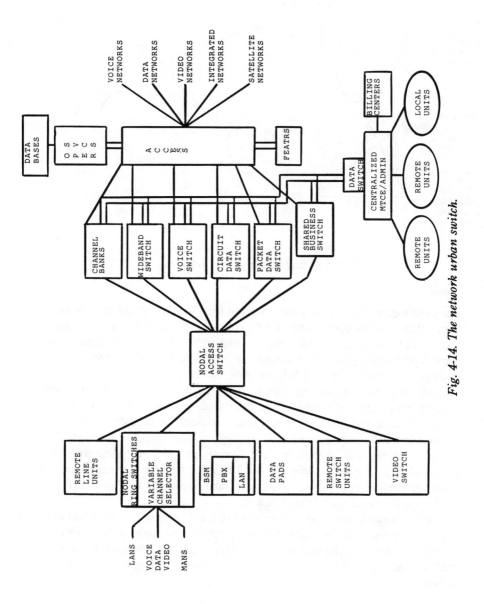

Fig. 4-14. The network urban switch.

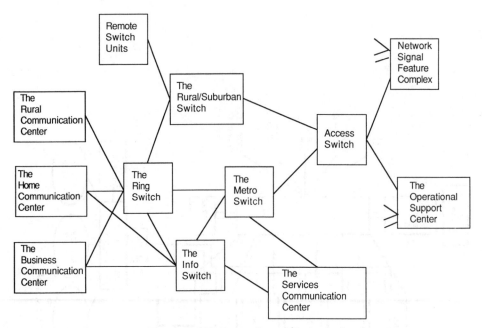

Fig. 4-15. The network architecture.

C&C

As noted earlier, C&C is the pivotal point of ISDN, as its massive infrastructure forms three pillars supporting the platform on which residential, business, government, and defense entities will obtain exciting new features and services. As we move from today's networks to tomorrow's integrated networks and on to future intelligent networks, we can't help but note that this communication movement coexists with the computer movement, from the basic services of stand-alone computers to integrated services, from distributed systems to intelligent services, to international databases using specialized artificial intelligence or expertise. These information advances and exchanges help reduce repetitive tasks, assist in searches, enable data comparisons, and perform exciting, new state-driven sequences based on dynamic changing data. Thus, we "inter" into the new world of "integrated network's integrated services" and eventually to "intelligent network's intelligent services." (See FIG. 4-16.)

We're actually progressing down the two C&C axes, where our actual existence is somewhere on the playing field at a particular (computer, communications) coordinate. Here, we change from having POTS (plan old telephone services) to PANS (positively awesome new services) as we achieve the transition to intelligent network services.

Integration of C&C

Computers have progressed from the internal payroll/accounting departments to various aspects of the business community, from sales to inventory control and on

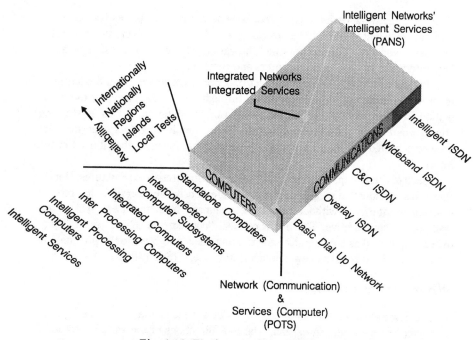

Fig. 4-16. The integration of ISDN-C&C.

into all aspects of the banking and securities industries, and there's been a change from "batch processing" to remote front-end, pre-mainframe work using "remote job entry." This was the beginning of connecting multiple machines together to perform different functions of a task. Thus, the university-type "ARPANET" networks came into existence, where specialized computers for particular types of analysis were used to solve specific portions of scientific experiments — for example: using superdistributed computers to solve matrix-oriented problems, (ILLIAC IV).

Next, computers were used in numerical control of specialized systems for tool-and-die work, using optical sensors for part placement; then it was on to graphic design of automobiles, where background systems performed high-speed manipulations and front-end processors controlled graphic displays and provided the interactive manipulations with the user. Finally, with the advent of microprocessors that have the power of minicomputers (recent minicomputers have the power of earlier mainframes), the computer is able to perform almost every aspect of the business operations. As the typewriter was replaced by the word processor, the need for "intercommunication" between different vendors' systems became quite apparent. Therefore, with all this taking place around them, the new users entered the world of C&C by way of the door marked "inter." It's the new, essential aspect of C&C.

As both the computer and communications worlds have become more versatile, they've employed many vendors' subsystems. Terminals became interconnected to processors, to memories, to modules, to protocols. Similarly, switching systems, already vastly interconnected, became more so, as pieces become more remotely distributed to be closer to clusters and users. However, this generated new user needs for "internetworking" the various elements to provide new exciting "interservices" between computers and communications.

Figure 4-17 shows the advancement of services concurrent with the advancement of networks. As society progresses through the various phases of the Information Era, we see the various coordinates of the different phases as stepping stones where users have stopped to rest. Here, they learned to appreciate what they've achieved and then formed new requirements for what they'll need in the future.

Each of these steps require considerable implementation expenditures. Hence, there was considerable resistance to providing extensive new services that require costly new interfaces without considerable demand from the users. Telcos are traditionally conservative. There is a residual "connect-and-collect" mentality to overcome, as well as considerable new training needed to educate the providers of the expanding needs of the new communication users. (See TABLE 4-3.)

Where are we going?

This review has shown the complexity of today's game as the compressed springs of change are beginning to expand. The new directions of the various protocols, interfaces, and technologies have shown that each phase of society is dependent on its previous phases to push, expand, and open the constraints to achieve new opportunities. C&C will be the integrating, internetworking, interprocessing, interservice phase in which many new users begin to expand their computer usage throughout all the industries. They'll be using the computer in many new endeavors to achieve value-added services, provided as interservices from multiple systems on multiple networks throughout the world.

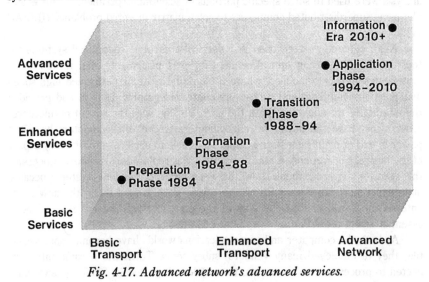

Fig. 4-17. Advanced network's advanced services.

Table 4 – 3. Evolution/Revolution

Evolution	Transition	Revolution
Age of Learning	Age of Knowledge	Age of Wisdom
ISDN Overlay	ISDN C&C	ISDN Broadband
Human Resistance	Human Use	Human Dependence
Needs	Understanding	Change
Traditional Rates	Service Rates	Service Usage Bit Rates
LANs	MANs	Switched WANs
Stimulus	Functional	Intelligent
Services	Integrated Services	Intelligent Services
Local	National/Regional	International
Manual/Auto	Partially Distributed Auto	Fully Distributed
Separate Networks	Integrated Networks	Intelligent Networks

As we look at the various types of potential services that ISDN networks might support, we see an ever-increasing need to fully identify these services and overlay them on the higher-level layers of the OSI model to obtain interservice standards, which enable interconnectability to the multiple private and public networks of the world to fully achieve the potential of the integration of C&C. This is the task of the '90s. It's to encourage the growth of multiple users to create the information flow that will justify and support the "broadband ISDN" of the twenty-first century.

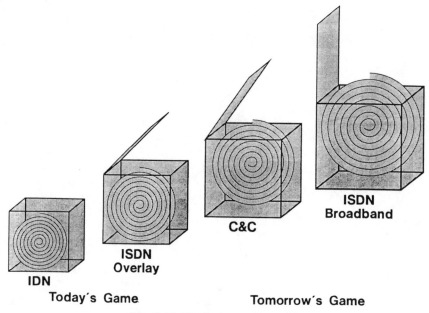

Fig. 4-18. The information game.

As usage increases, the need for higher bandwidth and switching capabilities will provide the economic basis for positioning ubiquitous broadband ISDN networks. They must be available in a timely manner to provide new arrays of wideband services — economically, efficiently, and effectively.

Hence, let's turn from where we're going in networks to where we want to go in services today and tomorrow to justify ISDN expenditures, based on the further integration of C&C in the marketplace. For further analysis, see the chapter 7 case studies and ISDN-LAN networking. (Also see FIG. 4-18.)

5

The information game

How do we play the game?
How do we get to the Information Era?

The crucial step

Having stopped for a moment to first look at "what's happening" and review "where we're going" in terms of technical possibilities and marketplace opportunities, we've been able to assess the importance of each of the three phases of ISDN, the need for extensive involvement in timely standards, and the urgency of establishing a new pricing structure that encourages growth in wideband services and short-holding-time baseband data transports. Those assessments and the expanded look at the available and potential services indicate that the trend to providing internetworking and interprocessing solutions in LANs has now extended into the ISDN arena. This requires more complex private-to-public interfacing solutions. The analysis of "where we want to go" indicated the need to achieve an ISDN marketplace, one in which integrated networks provide a supporting infrastructure for present and future layers of integrated intelligent services. At this checkpoint in time, let's now ask ourselves how we'll get to where we want to go.

In reviewing the potential of ISDN and the tremendous movement of the players as they push and expand the boundaries of their regulatory and political containments, it's evident that we've advanced to the next crucial step of the formation phase of the Information Era. (See FIG. 5-1.)

The information baby is on its feet, just beginning to walk, but where it walks will determine its existence for many years to come. It might venture into deep waters, dangerous to its health and well being, or it might frolic and play in the sunshine, growing each day to maturity.

As we look at the phases of the Information Era, as we move from the formation phase to the transition phase and on to the application and eventual utilization phases, it's these crucial steps in the transition and application phases

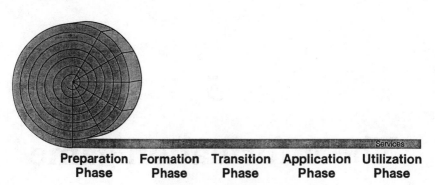

Preparation   Formation   Transition   Application   Utilization
   Phase   Phase   Phase   Phase   Phase

Fig. 5-1. The Information Era.

that are most important. Without constructing the infrastructure to support the movement of new services, the transition will be short-lived for the public arena, with emphasis shifting to the private domain. Hence, it's essential that we, the players, determine how we can integrate and achieve the goals and objectives of both private and public offerings in order to achieve the home, office, hospital and factory of the future. Interprocessing and interservices, based on advanced networks' advanced services, will be the new playing field for further integration of computers and communications. (See FIG. 5-2.)

As we look at the opportunities for having fully functional hospital-doctor patient information habitats, more automated factories, from order to design to inventory control to product assembly, as well as having a variety of changing offerings for the home of the future (depending on social status and economic means), we need to formulate plans and strategies on how we can progress from ISDN's basic transport to its enhanced advanced network, as well as participate in the computer's movement from providing basic services to more advanced and intelligent services. This progression and movement must be locked in sync with the marketplace, as customer resistance diminishes and growth occurs. Thus, this time between the application and transition phase is the stepping stone to move from basic transport's basic services to enhanced transport's enhanced services.

To accomplish this, we need to structure the overlay ISDN as the initial, beginner networks to nurture and foster growth—to provide our "information baby" with a playing field upon which to grow to maturity. It's this playing field that's supported by the ISDN pillars. We must not let our preoccupation with being market driven translate into waiting for yet-to-be identified customers to create a sufficient demand. This might cause extensive delay in establishing this overlay (relatively minimum investment) network that will be required for whatever type of new services we might want to choose. Note that many of these services are now being implemented in the private domain, but could (and should) now be applied to the public arena. (See FIG. 5-3.)

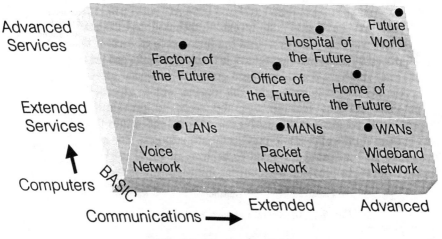

Fig. 5-2. The playing field.

The information marketplace

In reviewing the office communication center (OCC) and home communication center (HCC) future potential services, it's evident that we must understand user needs in terms of the user's answer to, "What should the packaged service be for the customer to use it?" As we consider previous trials, tests, and offerings such as Japan's Information Network's Mitaka trial, France's Minitel network, Britain's Pretzel network, and the United State's Videophone attempt (see the case study on Videophone), it's further evident that we must formulate and base these offerings on a backbone data network structure that enables layers of transport vehicles to interconnect efficiently and cheaply. It must enable multiple terminals to easily "talk" with each other. The rate of communication doesn't initially have to be faster than 64 kilobits to achieve an extensive array of services. This will enable new service providers to the network to access their potential customers via an open ISDN interconnection.

We must also recognize that the information marketplace exists in a changing society, where 88 percent of the new jobs are in small business; 60–70 percent of women will work full time outside the home; six jobs will be average in a lifetime; flex-time will become a norm; pension portability will enable movement from job to job; 40 percent of the work force will only work part-time. Similarly, manufacturing facilities might become geographically dispersed, changing more and more to strictly assembly-type operation, as foreign corporations meet trade restrictions by simply slipping in piece parts for assembly. (See FIG. 5-4.)

Hence, as American industry turns toward more service industries, what will

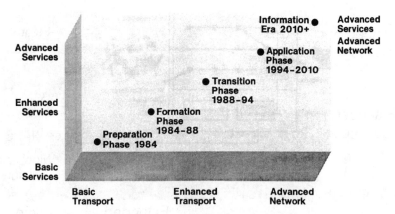

Fig. 5-3. Advanced network's advanced services.

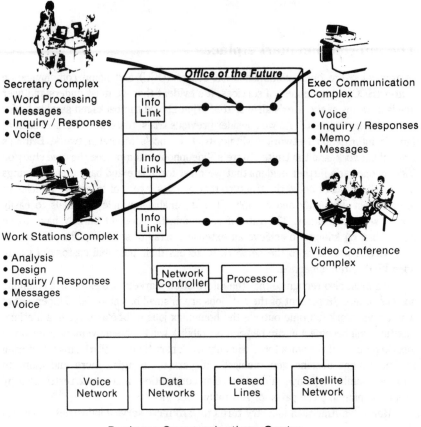

Business Communications Center

Fig. 5-4. Office of the future.

be the actual outcome as corporations become more like financial houses? What type of information management systems will be in vogue after the turn of the century? Will the home of the future actually require extensive wideband communications, or will narrowband networks be adequate? What will be the impact of international trade wars as more and more countries are able to acquire competitive expertise in information generation and processing? What will happen to multinational corporations as the demand for large, complex products requires more highly sophisticated technical managers that have considerable depth in research and development and knowledgeable laboratory personnel to draw upon — especially as these firms no longer spend much effort on acquiring skills for the long term, by emphasizing only short-term projects? Will this change as the technologies become extremely complex, as the marketplace heats up, and as the competition becomes more intense? Why should a product manager emphasize a new product that will have a period of slow market acceptance — especially when it might endanger or even destroy cash flow achieved from existing products? Why move from evolutionary to revolutionary product planning? . . . At what risk to the product manager? (See FIG. 5-5.)

Can we remain sitting on the fence until these and other questions become resolved, or continue to wait for the point where risk has been reduced to the level to ensure full success for any major commitment of funds and resources? Many firms have done just this over the initial four years of the formation phase. Can they continue to watch and play "wait and see what ISDN turns out to be?"

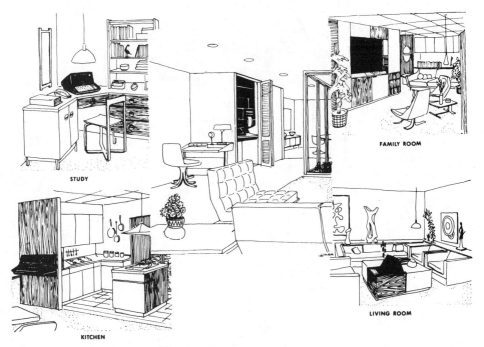

Fig. 5-5. Home of the future.

Well, the clock is ticking. The game is being played with or without various players. As we look at the future in light of the present business climate, we can see the pent-up demand by the new generation of players to have their own piece of the action, especially noting the dwindling number of positions at the top of large corporations after restructuring. The younger, more adventurous people are forming their own companies. With minimum overhead and limited finances, they're able to obtain sufficiently powerful computers and programming tools to develop software that's quite competitive with many of the larger firms' internal developments. As we look at the forthcoming "global integration of information," tied together by high-capacity, cheap bandwidth, we might observe that as the information marketplace develops over the next 20 years, it's actually restructuring society to its own image. As it provides the capabilities for remote software houses to interconnect and interexchange information, this enables these software houses to blossom and grow quite independent of the large corporations and their geographic locations. This then takes work away from a large product development unit because it's more economical to subcontract out the pieces of the development to these smaller design shops. The result of this expansion to smaller entities will result in more program/project-oriented controlling firms, which we'll call infocorps. (See FIG. 5-6.)

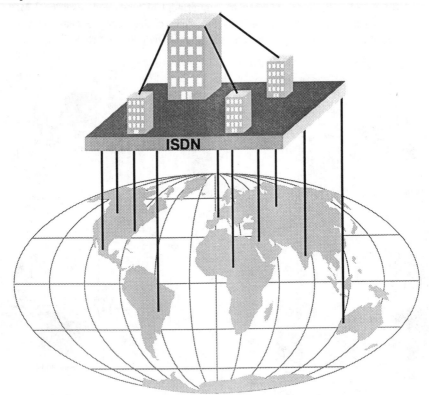

Fig. 5-6. Infocorp's infoworld.

By the turn of the century, an expanding number of infocorps will be organized to manage medium to large projects by developing their products by using subsystems provided by a multitude of smaller firms. The large 110,000-size multinationals will be reduced to half their size, as they restructure to use these smaller $10 million to $100 million firms. The interesting fallout will be that as the information networks transcend country boundaries and artificial barriers, this will enable these firms to be more international than ever before, as small businesses around the world are internetworked together. Perhaps in time the geodesic network that Huber once noted will traverse the global arena, supporting the many new planning/program/project management firms that erect these complex information systems. This arena will enable firms to provide all types of vertical services. This will encourage many new forms of alliances and partnerships among the players, as noted in FIG. 5-7.

This then leads us into two issues: How can we achieve the Information Era? What will we be like when we achieve it? For to achieve it, we'll have to change our own current mode of operation, to be in sync with a changing society, which is

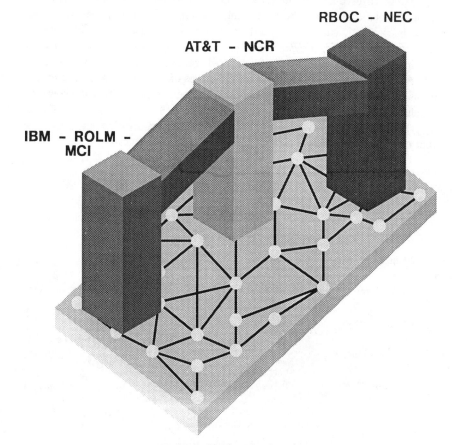

Fig. 5-7. Vertical integration.

changing as a result of our efforts to provide network products and services for the ever-changing information marketplace. This recursive cycle is an integral part of the information game—for those who dare to play it . . .

The information game

We now know where we want to go, so let's take a look at how we want to get there. It's in fact a game, a somewhat complex game, a somewhat deadly game, a somewhat enjoyable game, but when all is said and done, it's a game and should be played as one.

We first have to separate the players from the watchers. Next we must identify the officials and their rules. Occasionally, a brisk walk around the "playing field" is in order to understand its boundaries and limits, as well as to be able to note where it's changing. With this in mind, an assessment of the other players is a must in order to determine their positioning strategies, not only in terms of today's game but also tomorrow's. (See FIG. 5-8.)

We've covered a lot of material in our previous analysis to draw on and help formulate our conclusions. Since this information is constantly changing as the game is constantly changing, a yearly review of past articles from *Communications Weekly, TE&M, Telephony, Data Communications*, etc., magazines will help in assessing who is doing what, when, where, and how. (See TABLE 5-1.)

A second look at ISDN in terms of the stages of technology is then needed in terms of where your own firm's networks and products are positioned, showing a detailed assessment of features and services. Figure 5-9 clearly (but only figuratively) shows various player's positioning (today and tomorrow). Mark it to show your own location in today's game. (Hopefully not in the bleachers.)

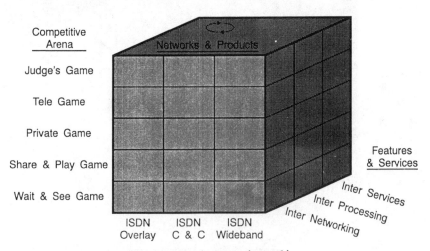

Fig. 5-8. The information cubic.

Table 5–1. The Information Game

The "Player's" Strategies	The "Official's" Strategies
• Managing	• Rulings
• Planning	• Boundaries
• Providing	• Agreements
• Positioning	• Controls
• Using	
	The "Playing Field"
The "Viewers" Strategies	• Changing
• Observers	• Maintaining
• Spectators	• Replacing

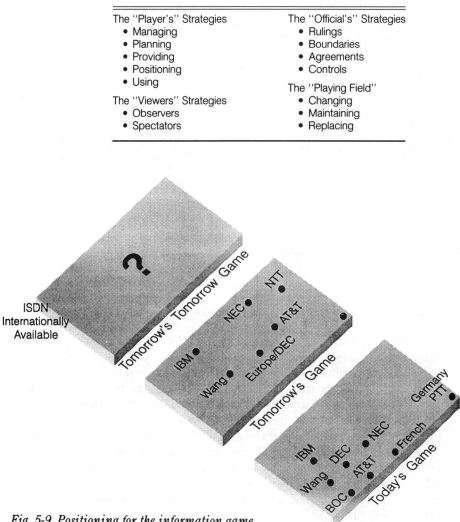

Fig. 5-9. Positioning for the information game.

With this accomplished, our next step is to specifically define and pinpoint where we want to be in two four-year plans or four two-year plans, whichever is easier and clearer. This analysis must take into account the current stage of technology and the changing phases of ISDN, as well as the "heartbeat" of the marketplace in terms of the stages of user resistance and acceptance to the technology. It must also include the impact of the competition to meet new user needs with the new products and service. (See FIG. 5-10.)

At this point, we enter the game of games. By now we should have an understanding of ISDN. We should realize it's not only a technology, but transcends

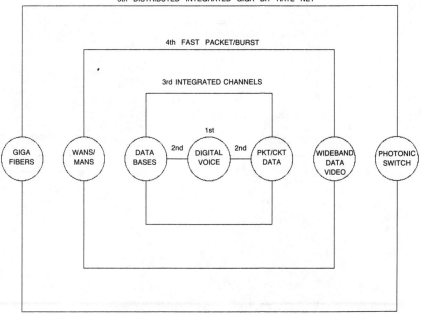

Fig. 5-10. ISDN technology stages.

into many areas. For every time we attempt to grasp it in one endeavor, it pops out in another. As we open the many boxes to find out what ISDN is, we're drawn into one arena after another, where, as FIG. 5-11 notes, we move from the business game to the regulatory arena and on into the market game. However, in a final perspective, ISDN is the accomplishment of integrated networks' integrated services that in time will become intelligent networks' intelligent services as more and more computer-to-computer operations take place without human intervention. Here, the computers use dynamically using changing information as they assess and make decisions in every segment of the marketplace, requiring new network configurations for providing new services. Hence, no longer is a service on a single axis of C or C. Services now exist at a coordinate point on the new C&C playing field. (See FIG. 5-12.)

As noted in *Telecommunications Management Planning*, it's essential to play the information game based on layers of strategic strategies. Mark-tech strategies are tied to business strategies, which then formulate the basis for financial strategies. These are then in concurrence or cause change in governance policy strategies. It doesn't matter whether we move from governance to the market or from market to governance. What's important is that one can change the other, as the analysis recursively cycles through these levels until "where we want to go" is established from all three—marketing, technical, and management perspectives!

With this accomplished, we're ready to use the management planning process (see *Telecommunications Management Planning*) to more specifically identify

Fig. 5-11. The game of games.

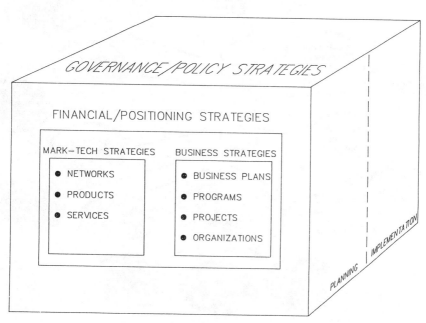

Fig. 5-12. Strategies.

and define our networks, products, and services. The process enables us to formulate ideas into concrete concepts, which are then detailed in requirements and specified in specific product definitions. The product analysis has a corresponding program plan for its achievement. This consists of the project development plan, system design plan, market plan, financial plan, manufacturing plan, and deployment plan. They're defined at a realistic, reasonable level (at the end of the product definition phase) to the extent needed for obtaining a management decision to commit full resources to the venture. (See FIG. 5-13.)

It's interesting to note the maze through which we've progressed in order to be able to formulate such plans. It's further interesting to note how others have failed because of not having taken the time to think out the game before attempting to play it. As FIG. 5-14 indicates, we've moved from strategic planning through an interesting mix of endeavors before finalizing our strategic strategies to play the information game.

Now we're ready. As was once said, "We don't plan to fail; we fail to plan." We've now achieved all that can be accomplished at the pregame planning point. It's now time to play the game:

- In the standards arena—both overlay ISDN and wideband ISDN standards must be defined in terms of C&C.

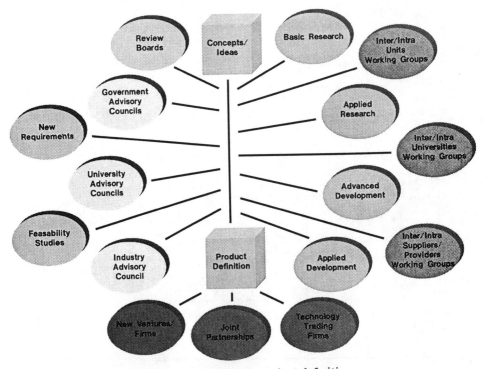

Fig. 5-13. From concept to product definition.

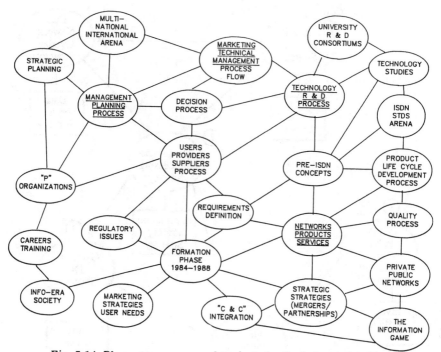

Fig. 5-14. Plans, programs, and projects for the Information Era.

- In the pricing arena — both for today's and tomorrow's services in order to achieve the transition from narrowband (3 kilohertz) features to baseband (less than 1.5 megabit) features to broadband (greater than 1.5 megabit) features and services.
- In the evolution arena — for enhancing existing products and services with new features and extensions.
- In the transition arena — for the integration of computers with communications to form layers of protocols and application programs above the transport interconnect world to enable interprocessing and interservices.
- In the revolutionary arena — by introducing wideband facilities and switching transport capabilities to ubiquitously meet expanding classes of users from large business to small business to residential.
- In the products arena — as we take advantage of the stages of technology, by defining and designing new families of products to achieve the three (evolutionary, transition, and revolutionary) strategies in concert with the three phases of ISDN.
- In the new features and services arena — by identifying, testing, procuring, deploying, supporting and modifying offerings until successful packages of them are achieved in the marketplace.
- In the organizational structures of providers and suppliers — enabling them to change with the changing world, which is changing as a result of their own networks, products, and services.

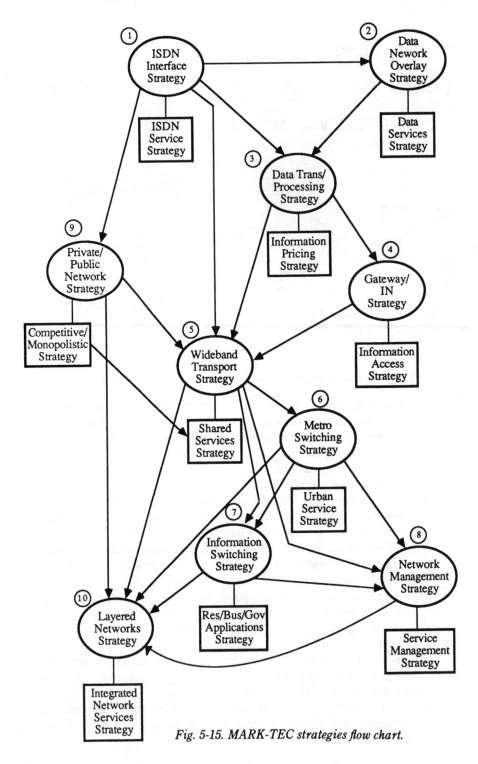

Fig. 5-15. MARK-TEC strategies flow chart.

- In the pricing arena—to achieve a usage incentive pricing structure for encouraging tremendous growth of all types of services.
- In ourselves—as we attempt to accept change and leverage change as a part of our daily life.

Thus, we've identified the new users and established ISDN networks, products, and services to meet their needs in the information marketplace via the information network. (See FIGS. 5-15 and 5-16.)

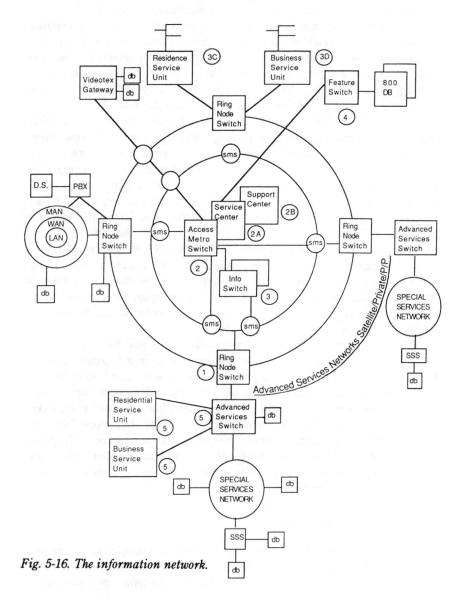

Fig. 5-16. The information network.

The missing infrastructure:
differing views, differing perspectives

Different views, different perspectives, and different goals have led different players to different networks with different services, as they provide different solutions to address different needs. Over time, these differences and somewhat difficult choices have become more complex and more crucial, as the forces for the merging and integration of the computer and communication (C&C) industries intensify, thereby becoming more massive and explosive.

To best understand and appreciate "what's happening," it's time to step back from our active involvement in playing the information game and take a broad view, encompassing the full scope and range of not only today's perspective, but also tomorrow's, to review "what has happened" to bring us to this juncture in time. In so doing, as we assess how we came to this particular game, we might wish to reassess the game itself, redefine it, or not continue to play it at all . . .

Some might say "what's the difference; all roads lead to Rome." Perhaps they did for the weary traveler some 2000 years ago, when one ruler could extend his or her influence over many diverse groups. However, today, it's a different story. Today, there are many paths and they all don't lead to Rome or some mecca or Shangri-la depicting success, fortune, peace, and comfort. Today, the issues have become multifaceted. In today's competitive arena, no single leader, such as AT&T in communications or IBM in computers, is alone able to set direction. Today, the human and C&C elements have grown quite complex. In fact, they "grew and grew until gruesome." We've entered "intered" a new arena, where C&C considerations now require interfacing, interlacing, interconnecting, integrating, internetworking, interprocessing, interservicing, internationally . . . while the human element notes the need for intervention, intermixture, intermingling, interrelations, interdependencies, intermediaries, interlock, interlude, intermission, and interregnum (the period between kings) . . .

For many, it has been difficult to put their arms around the key strategies needed for successful play. Some have simply moved from game to game, such as at the Mad Hatter's tea party, leaving things in a worse state than before. So what has happened to the national information networks and services, which many believe will have a monumental effect on our society, bringing about great social, economic, and cultural changes as the various countries throughout the world position themselves as major players in the global information game in the global information society. Indeed, what has happened to the missing information infrastructure? What's happening today? What could, would, should happen to achieve the information society in the not-too-distant future?

A different perspective

It's time now for a final look at the telephone, dataphone, videophone, and personal phone. What should we be doing differently from what we're doing now? It's time to reevaluate what we're trying to accomplish today for tomorrow's information society. Do we want to achieve a new data-handling network, similar to the voice telephone network, but specifically for data — so a dataphone can talk to any other dataphone anywhere, anytime? What are we doing to deploy videophone in its narrowband, wideband, and broadband forms? Unfortunately, these network offerings don't exist today. By the early '90s, enhanced service providers have not yet established large numbers of switched data customers. This has made it difficult for the traditional RBOC. It usually prefers to enter previously defined markets with an established, identifiable customer base so that its particular offering can be more easily targeted to specific customers. In this, the RBOC faces less risk as it attempts to encourage the customers of the other providers to shift to its new services. Without a precedent, the RBOC's new products and services will have to be more strategically planned and carefully developed, as there's always more risk in deploying totally new endeavors.

This is something that the telephone providers of today have not had to "deal with" since the early days of their founding father, Alexander Graham Bell. Since the '30s and '40s, the "baby bells" operating companies were simply told "to operate." They were given products from their "mother bell," AT&T, whose systems planners conceived the new products, which were designed by "brother bell" — Bell Laboratories, and manufactured by "father bell" — Western Electric. Over the years, their "Dutch uncle" — the U. S. government, protected them from competition by fostering and protecting their communication monopoly. Here, AT&T only deployed technology in controllable five-year windows to mainly provide for automation of network operation and maintenance. Then, in the mid '80s, along came divestiture, deregulation, and competition.

So, after approximately ten years of being on their own, after divestiture, we've seen the babies grow up into their teens. During these years, they pursued their sparkling toys, sometimes spending vast sums to acquire them, and then quickly discarding them when they became soiled or tarnished in their hands. As time progressed, they needed more and more funds to support their growing appetite to acquire more and more new objects, especially their more expensive international endeavors. In time, forced by economic necessities, they began shrinking their size as they attempted to become "mean and lean," for they already were "hungry" for more and more . . . of this and that . . .

To maintain their revenues (funds), they then elected to offer their previously "full-time" leased transport facilities on a "usage basis," hoping to encourage greater and greater usage to keep their funds (customers) from shrinking. However, they began "giving away the store," as they had to provide more and more transport at cheaper and cheaper rates to meet the new competition; for over time, they saw their competitors match their offerings with newer, better, cheaper technology. Rather than fight them, some "baby bells" joined them, providing offerings to transport broadcast television and movies to the home in a quick and less expensive manner, using modified old analog facilities with new hybrid analog/digital coaxial/fiber transport techniques. In a like manner, other RBOCs encouraged dial-up voice-grade data usage on previous network systems that were originally designed specifically for analog voice traffic, with little understanding or regard for overall transport performance and throughput efficiency impact. For some, the battle cry became more desperate—being "milk it or sell it." Some babies decided to get out of the public network business and take their money to cellular, tetherless opportunities, or elsewhere . . .

While elsewhere, a new "daddy" government developed more and more aggressive strategies to foster a competitive marketplace; such as enabling full interconnection of many new local providers by removing limiting restrictions for private-world offerings. Many in Washington and throughout the country visualized a fully competitive marketplace "with or without" a common public carrier. It's the "without" impact that brings questions to mind. Here, if the RBOCs no longer pursue telephone, dataphone, and videophone, but instead elect to provide telephone, bandwidth, and cable vision, then islands of private overlay networks will develop here and there, interconnected by selectively channelable, variable-usage, point-to-point or point-to-multipoint, publicly shared bandwidth transport facilities. Thus, hundreds or thousands of isolated private networks will be established, requiring interconnection via layers and layers of protocols, thereby further fostering the "internetworking multiprotocol nightmare."

In like manner, a video network can be established for broadcast or dial-up video services, using very limited interactive selection mechanisms (low-speed request/high-speed response); this will enable revenue streams to be maintained over the remaining '90s, as these numerous private networks use their variable-bandwidth transport facilities. In this manner, many specialized networks will be established to handle closed user groups for selected communities of interest, such as: the medical community, education, state agencies, apartment complexes, and shopping centers. However, in this approach, little effort is expended on planning, developing, and implementing the needed universally available, publicly switched dataphone and videophone networks. Hence, the telephone company remains "the telephone company" instead of progressing to become "the information company."

In like manner, IBM and the other computer firms, sometimes referred to as Snow White and the Seven Dwarfs, have experienced a similar history in a somewhat volatile and changing marketplace. With the entrance of intense competition from the microchip personal stand-alone computer, and the absence of the national public data-handling telecommunications infrastructure to enable "networking" of dissimilar terminals to the dissimilar large mainframe computers of traditional computer manufacturers, Snow White (IBM) began showing blemishes, as she laid off thousands due to billion-dollar losses, while her Seven Dwarfs (Wang, National Cash Register (NCR), Burroughs, Honeywell, Control Data, DEC, . . .) began shrinking or simply faded away. Traditionally, IBM set the standards and the "others" followed with their own particular version or emulation. Some did strike out on their own into new worlds, as DEC led the charge for "internetworking" and Wang for "word processing," but most early offerings from the '60s to the '80s were based on providing specialized services to closed user groups, each with their particular "family" of offerings. Still others simply participated by "cloning" terminals or "emulating" systems/software to enable their specialized product service to be used as part of the extended family of data processing systems. Then, as noted, along came the integrated circuit with its VLSI computer-on-a-chip technology, as well as ergonomic concern for user-friendly interfaces. From these new aspects and considerations came the personal computer and the Apple "mouse," enabling anyone in any industry to use the computer for any application.

If only the somewhat "resistive-to-change" communications industry had not ignored the changes within the computer industry, much would be different. For by ignoring the needs of computers, the communication industry drove Snow White and the Seven Dwarfs to establish private data-handling internal local area networks connected by leased lines. Later, private networking nodes emerged to integrate bridges and routers, using shared high-speed transport capabilities. However, the telecommunications industry, even by the mid '70s, had not offered the crumbling large mainframe computers access to remote terminals located in distant homes, small businesses, etc. What was missing was a universal public data network that interconnected on a publicly switched addressable basis, any terminal to any terminal to any computer.

However, what if one, just one, public provider (such as a "baby bell" with newfound wisdom teeth) elected to provide the new infrastructure for delivering a full array of successful information services? Then the others would soon follow! . . . So what indeed must be done to achieve a public data network and a public broadband network that support dataphone, videophone, . . . imagephone? Let's first begin by considering the public data network. What is it? What should it be? What services should it offer? Where?, When?, Why? . . .

A public data network

Let's begin by noting that the public data network will eventually exist as part of a fully serviceable information network in its narrowband, wideband, and broadband forms. However, it's important to differentiate the initial narrowband data offering from the others, as specifically being a public data network — one that's carefully designed and structured to transport data. In this, it's different from the more versatile and expanded wideband and broadband offerings that address video services, requiring varying amounts of bandwidth and specialized imaging features.

Some believe a data network is simply connecting two terminals together and transporting the data from point to point. They really don't care if the transport vehicle (the network cloud) is the slow 100-words-per-minute Western Union telegram delivery vehicle, or a dial-up 2400 or 4800 bit per second voice-grade data modem, as long as the transport mechanisms are performed electronically and are rapidly available to compete with the existing manually performed Federal Express package or cross-town messenger delivery systems. They ignore the somewhat difficult and complex data-handling requirements that provide unique attributes and characteristics for specifically handling data.

When defining a public data network, we can't help but note that a key ingredient is the dialable, accessible, public dataphone number; just as everyone on the public telephone network has a number, so every terminal on the public data network must have an identifiable number. However, this doesn't mean simply going to a specialized offering such as "Internet" and obtaining one of their limited numbers for access to other analog dial-up voice-grade terminals or LANs.

The public data network, in its medium-speed form, must be universally available. It will most likely be deployed initially in the major cities and then in the rural county seats. The key to its success will be to have it available universally and ubiquitously, as quickly as possible, with minimum expense. To accomplish this, worldwide plans are to use existing copper plant facilities at narrowband rates of 64,000 and 128,000 bits per second. It will offer the agreed universal data-handling capabilities of universal addresses, polling, broadcast, delayed delivery, protocol conversion, and code conversion, as well as the transport throughput features of fast data call set-up and take-down capabilities (100 millisecond fast connect/200 millisecond disconnect) and low error rates. It will achieve high survivability and performance objectives by offering bit and byte message inter-leaving, error detection and correction, cyclic coding, and routing capabilities to enable alternate routing, specialized store and forward, connection-oriented packet transport mechanisms, inverse/reverse multiplexing, packet sequencing, three-attempt limit, etc. The data network must ensure high throughput and traffic loading capabilities that enable substantial and sustainable growth with limited blockage and congestion problems. Similarly, privacy and security must be assured by using access passwords, terminal verification, audit trails, call backs, attempt limits, encryption, etc., mechanisms.

Much can be done to establish a robust public data network in both its circuit switching and packet switching forms. In this, ISDN provides layers of transport and data application services, as its higher-layer standards, X.400 and X.500, offer message delivery and directory capabilities. More and more computer application program software will be introduced to the public data network, as its interfaces foster point-to-point or point-to-multipoint access for computer-to-computer, computer-to-terminal, or terminal-to-terminal networking, thereby enabling client/server, host/remote, base/satellite, and front-end/back-end processing of data information.

As ISDN chips are inserted into computer terminals, as more sophisticated data handshaking mechanisms are designed for a high-performance transport, as applications enter every aspect of the marketplace, data usage will expand and expand again, thereby providing a growing need for higher- and higher-speed transport mechanisms. These expanding information-handling facilities need to be designed, developed, and phased in, parallel to the narrowband public data network.

Dataphone: ISDN public data network issues and strategies

As noted in *Future Telecommunications*, there are 32 or so tasks for achieving a narrowband public ISDN-based telecommunications network for delivering moderate-speed data and video image communications. The tasks indicate the need for ubiquitous deployment, at least throughout the major cities and rural county seats so that small business have the ability to internetwork information and access large businesses and governmental databases. Similarly, 10 to 20 percent of the residences desired "data networking" capabilities, thereby enabling doctors to review X-rays from their home, managers to access company files, and marketing and design personnel to remotely perform their work functions.

To achieve success in ISDN, it's therefore necessary to implement these 32 tasks. In fact, depending on the degree and extent of availability, not only do we need to implement them for narrowband offerings, but wideband and broadband ISDN networks need to follow a similar methodology for their successful deployment.

In reviewing these endeavors, several aspects need to be highlighted in this regard: pricing, addressability, CPE, robustness, ONA standards, network management, and deployment availability — not only locally, but regionally, nationally, and globally . . . These, together with customer understanding, appreciation, and acceptance will foster ubiquitous use of ISDN technical possibilities in the forthcoming information marketplace . . . As we look to the future, we need to address and resolve the following issues:

Pricing   To encourage universal acceptance and use of narrowband ISDN, we need to immediately address ISDN pricing for a public data network offering. Narrowband ISDN delivers three networks: A — 64,000/128,000 bps data circuit switched transport, B — 64,000/128,000 bps packet switched data transport, and C — 9600/16,000 bps packet switching data and signaling transport. These networks need to be deployed ubiquitously and priced so communities of interest will use them to exchange the full range of information transport. Hence, ISDN shouldn't be sold as an interface, but as a series of networks that support higher-level services at prices that will attract users to the new data-handling networks and away from dial-up voice-grade data modems on the existing flat-rate voice service network. Some believe these prices need to be tiered, depending on use, so that initial offerings are as low as $16 per month for certain amounts of use and local area wide access.

We also need to deploy switched wideband and broadband offerings so that videophone, for example, and high-definition videoconferencing and television can be economically accessible to all, thereby shifting our pricing, based on bandwidth, from simply relating it to the equivalent number of voice conversations to pricing the service independent of the required bandwidth. In this manner, videophone could be available ubiquitously for $30–$60 per month. As we've found in Germany, we must be careful in separating these narrowband and broadband services to ensure that each doesn't inhibit the other from flourishing. There's a need for considerable work in this regard to ensure that an appropriate, new pricing structure is effectively established to accomplish growth.

Addressability   Full data movement will be achieved only when there's a similarly available dataphone directory that's equivalent to the telephone directory. Each RBOC and independent carrier, as well as the private carriers, must all work together to obtain not only interconnectability, but also a universally available address directory for their data customers. This is key to the success of future public data networks.

CPE   As today's customer-premise equipment begins to use ISDN chips to replace low-speed modems, there's a pressing need for these systems to change their transport protocols to the newer protocols that are based on the higher-speed, less-error-rate, digital data ISDN network capabilities. As rate adapters and inverse multiplexers enable asynchronously disparate terminals to access these higher-speed synchronous ISDN networks, we need to develop more sophisticated terminals that use functional/stimulus "D channel" network interfaces to enable more sophisticated network and CPE operations.

Robustness   As we encourage computers, which have entered every aspect of the marketplace, to interconnect and exchange information, we need to prepare a network that can successfully handle more and more traffic. The worst scenario would be to encourage the hospitals, doctors, police, government, and other society-supporting agencies to shift from private networks that use leased lines and trunks at 99.95 percent operational availabilities to a public data network that then can't handle the increased traffic load. When throughput loads for increased traffic reach unattainable network operational objectives and they can't handle these increased traffic loads, they go down, causing disruptions at critical times; this happened in France, causing three days of data network outage. In this, the latter state might be worse than the former. This is similar to encouraging the people in Los Angeles to use their cars so that they can sit in traffic jams on freeways that can't handle the growth in traffic, thus causing them to go nowhere. Better to not only have automobile transport, but trains as well. Similarly the shift from narrowband to wideband to broadband must be timed appropriately to facilitate growth.

ONA standards   Past endeavors in ONA have reached stumbling blocks, as well-meaning parties attempted to open up the switching systems so that multiple providers can provide multiple services without being inhibited by cumbersome procedures, standards, and delays. To obtain a competitive marketplace, it's indeed essential for numerous diverse services to successfully grow and flourish. In this regard, the Information Networking Architecture (INA) by Bellcore promises to provide a desirable standard interface for exchanging services; one system can offer customers to another system for enhanced information networking and layered service offerings, using the global telecommunications layered network's layered services model. This model enables functional separation at universal interfaces, so that each layer can enhance the next for both private and public offerings; this enables not only LECs and IXCs, but also VANs, VARs, CAPs, ATPs, and SPSs to participate effectively without danger of bringing the network down. This model needs to be challenged and used to its fullest, as numerous firms throughout the world are now exploring not only the local ONA interface possibilities, but also its global networking aspects.

Network management — OAM&P   When all is said and done, it's essential to be able to manage the movement of information. By reviewing the layered networks' layered services model, it's quite apparent that not only do CPE systems have their network management capabilities, but local exchange carriers (LECs) also have their network management capabilities, and interexchange carriers (IXCs) and value added networks (VANs) have their network management capabilities as well. So, as we enter a more global community, the global networking aspects must be integrated into our network management hierarchies. Similarly, we must construct appropriate network management, operations, maintenance, administration, and provisioning mechanisms not only for today's voice traffic, but also for data and video. Thus, we must resolve who the "keepers of the network" are. Who will ensure that the layered networks' layered services model can be successfully implemented? Is this a task for Bellcore? Is this a national standards challenge? How can we ensure that all networks function together appropriately when we have multiple service providers hanging here and there on this or that network? This is indeed the challenge of democracy, where everyone can do their thing without affecting the freedoms of others.

Availability   Availability will not be an issue once the other six items that we just discussed have been resolved. RBOCs are very good at deployment once the risks are reduced and the customers needs are understood. However, we do need to shift emphasis from short-term, fast-revenue nearsightedness to full-service, full-deployment, long-term visions. We need to address not only the narrowband OAM&P deployment strategies using current upgraded plant, but we also need to develop the more expensive, fiber-based OAM&P deployment strategies needed for high-resolution, high-quality video.

In conclusion, while addressing these seven key issues, telecommunications firms' market units need to concentrate on the customer. They need to educate the customers on the technical possibilities that will be available to them. This will require, as noted in the 32 tasks, extensive advertising to clearly demonstrate what the technologies offer and how the customer can use them to obtain a better quality of life. All factors and facets of the industry need to work together, all of us together! The information service providers (ISPs) and enhanced service providers (ESPs) can't offer their services if these public networks aren't available (as we see the problems that IBM and Sear's Prodigy Services are having today). We, the telecommunications industry, need to ensure that private networks flourish, as customers use shared public offerings to achieve their individual tasks. We need to work together, using front-end planning processes, to determine where we're going and how we'll get there. For these reasons, a series of tasks have been provided for the industry to address this forthcoming information marketplace, showing what needs to be done and how we can work together to successfully accomplish these exciting goals and objectives of the Information Age . . .

The public broadband network

Indeed, there's also a need for a fully fiber-based broadband network infrastructure that's in place in the twenty-first century. This must be available to not only meet the needs of these dynamically increasing dataphone users, but also the new users that will require interactive videophone, video windows, video vision, imaging, high-definition television, and . . .

We've seen the progression of digital transmission from T1/T2 at 1.544/6.03 Mbps over copper facilities to fiber-based T3 at 45 Mbps. Just as these public "leased-trunk" synchronous transmission (Syntran) networks were being accepted by the private community to form private T1 and T3 networking hubs, new capabilities were being constructed to enable valuable "usage-based" offerings, where information was transported in the form of packetized, connection-oriented or connectionless datagrams. Here, frame relay technologies "relayed" variable-length packet messages from LAN to LAN over copper plant, upgraded to handle 1.544 Mbps, while SMDS technology offered 4, 16, 32, . . . , and 100 Mbps capabilities within the T3 and SONET umbrellas. Then, the somewhat fickle, private community quickly turned to the "variable destination" switched offerings provided by asynchronous transfer mode (ATM) technology; this technology was soon embraced by bridge, router, cluster controller, and PBX suppliers.

In lock step with these proceedings, digital cross-connects were established to provide dial-up T1 switching, fractional T1 switching (384 Kbps (H0), 1.536 Mbps (H11)), primary rate ISDN switching, fractional ISDN switching, T3 switching (1.544, 2.02, 6.3, 10, and 45 Mbps) and fractional T3. Users next attempted to switch a variable number of 64 Kbps channels in a synchronous transfer mode (STM) type, circuit-switching manner: this provided the shift to channel switching, as wideband switching (WSM) and broadband switching matrixes (BSM) paved the way for the central offices' main distribution frames to be automated and physically located closer to the customer. Here, "gigabit"-handling, survivable ring switches provide local access to the private networks. Therefore, in this new trans-switching technology, developed the access node, located away from the central office, nearer the customer, allowing the economics of shared transport and private accessibility to not only public networks, but also to the points of presence (POPs) of local VANs, VARs, IECs, and DBSs . . . Thus was born a new network access switch — Class 6, as a new private/public information networking platform to switch wideband/broadband facilities and broadcast offerings, and provide wireline interfaces to wireless personal communication services. Here, Broadband ISDN — with its network interfaces of 622 million bits per second to the user and 155 million bits per second from the user — provides an exciting new infrastructure using the internationally agreed American SONET and European Synchronous Digital Hierarchy (SDH) standards.

In this manner, full broadband services (such as interactive videophone, video conference center), choice/selected (entertainment/educational), and broadcast (HDTV)) will develop — and not just for large, singular central offices with fiber transversing directly to every shopping center, business office, and home, but as a multilevel switching hierarchy with a front-end network node that's physically located closer to the user; this will enable user access to multiple, higher-level switching networks, both public and private, and thereby provide accessibility and survivability protection. In time, a multilevel switching structure will also reside on customer premises, as the LANs give way to physically distributed, fiber-based broadband switching structures to take full advantage of gigabit trans-switching technologies. This will therefore establish new class-level network nodes within the customer environment, which can be called Class 7s. In time, to complete this picture, new service nodes, also called application service centers, will be located above the network and accessible via information switches. They'll provide specialized programming and service enhancements for videophone, imagephone, dataphone, and high-definition television.

Videophone: future video services

Regarding possible future video services for the mass market, these services can be broken into the following three categories: interactive, choice (selection), and broadcast. Once the specific services are identified, they can be further segmented into narrowband, wideband, and broadband varieties; for example, videophone is an interactive service that could be provided over the existing copper plant at 64K and 128K narrowband ISDN rates in a flicker mode, as well as in a compressed mode at 1.54 Mbps, and finally in the high quality 45–50M broadband rate. Of course, it might be delivered in the high-definition high-quality 155 Mbps version. With this in mind, here's a possible list of video service offerings:

1. Interactive
   - Videophone
     a. Personal conversations
     b. Medical consulting
     c. Shopping
     d. Computer imaging
     e. Newspaper delivery
   - Video conference (two-party to four-party split screen)
     a. High-resolution still graphics
     b. White board camera (encryption secure)
   - Video conference center (Bellcore Video Windows)
   - Multimedia/computer terminal
     a. Handicapped (specialized terminals for toes, pencils, speech-activated, etc.)
     b. Work at home
   - Education (classroom)
   - Program instruction (multiple paths depending on answers provided by student)
   - Computer aided education (CAE)
   - Video database
   - Computer aided design (CAD)
   - Computer aided manufacturing (CAM)
   - Electronic photograph storage
   - Medical imaging
     a. PACS-Picture Archiving & Communication System
     b. Remote CAT scan (RCS)
     c. Magnetic resonance imagery (MRI)
     d. Computer aided tomography (CAT)
   - Video mail

- Video messaging
- 35mm slides
- Video storage/retrieval
- Hyper media
  a. Graphic displays
  b. Windows
  c. Indexed full text
- Computer imaging
- International video gateways
  a. International databases
- Computer art
- Holographic imaging
- Holographic discussions/conversations
- Variable transport bandwidth
- Personalized education from home to home

2. Choice
   - Selected sporting events
   - Selected retail catalogues
   - Selected entertainment events
   - Selected educational courses (canned)
     a. Cooking
     b. Hobbies
     c. Specialized training
   - Selected movies (rated G or PG)
   - Shopping from home/work/office
   - Video libraries
   - Video advertising
     a. Sales
     b. Mall sales for the day
   - Browse
   - Travel logs
   - Cultural events
   - International databases

3. Broadcast
   - Network programs
   - University lectures
   - International news
   - Specialized events
   - Video advertising
   - Advanced television (ATV)
   - High-definition TV (HDTV)
     a. Access to all channels
     b. Dial up (4)
     c. Browse
     d. Picture in a picture
   - International programming

In conclusion, these services can be further subdivided, grouped, and categorized; for example, "interactive services" can be grouped in terms of the operative functions: conversational, search, browse, executable, and inquiry/response. In further investigating market opportunities in terms of technical possibilities, it will become clear that data will drive the narrowband/wideband copper-based networks, using circuit and packet switching/ATM type technology, while videophone, video conferences, and high-definition TV, and computer graphics and imaging will be the drivers of the new fiber-based, broadband networks; these will use channel switching/STM/WDM/SDM technologies.

We can then realize the "visions of the future" offered by the communications and computer industries' leaders such as Tom Bystrzycki, U S WEST's senior executive, Dr. John Mayo, President of Bell Laboratories, and IBM's chief architects of their future computer networks. As we deploy their visions of new technologies, new architectures, new topologies, new switches, new transports, new protocols, and new services, we enter the world of telecommunications information networking, where, indeed, not only dataphone, but also videophone and videowindows can become commonplace . . .

Who is to say what the future will hold? In the past, some have resisted new technological advancements; they believed that "transportation" would remain the horse and buggy. Others set their store in the bicycle, while still others continued to pursue more and more advanced technology to achieve high-performance automobiles, high-speed trains, large commercial jet airplanes, and comfortable space vehicles for going to distant planets, distant worlds.

Risks and rewards

So it is with computers and communications. The technical possibilities of the future are indeed quite intriguing. Similarly, the forthcoming information market opportunities are now becoming quite evident. However, the "reality of achievement" is many times left to the marketers, who, depending on how they promote, advertise, foster, and nurture these new offerings, determine their ultimate outcome of success or failure.

As we've seen the results of "Watergate" in the political arena, so there has been a varying form of "Telegate" in the information-handling arena.

After ten years after divestiture, the RBOCs had not developed the needed data networks and video networks to support dataphone and videophone offerings anywhere, anyplace. For ten years after its exciting announcement, ISDN remained an illusive mystery to many, as its pricing and availability remained out of the reach of most users. Although there has not been a deliberate cover-up of the lack of these offerings, there has been a deliberate effort to ignore the need for their existence. There indeed has been an indifference, an ignorance, a lack of understanding, and a lack of desire to take risk. Similarly, there have been few financial incentives for RBOC marketers and management, and therefore little desire, to take the time to truly understand the data users' needs and provide more functional, versatile computer communications services. Some RBOCs have pretended to offer "data-handling" solutions that are in most cases either another form of high-priced transport or dial-up voice-grade data-transport band-aids.

Data and video service offerings will require new pricing strategies. Many planners believe that a dataphone network will only be successful when it's priced very economically and is ubiquitously available in order to encourage a major shift from dial-up services over low-speed voice-grade facilities—especially when there's a change from flat-rate to measured-rate services. Some suggest a multitier pricing "usage" strategy, based on initial offerings as low as $15 with $10 increments per tier. These services will require massive advertising to show usage applications to undo the damage of past voice-grade data promotions.

The information game: a crossroad in time

There are several options for the future of the Information Age, depending on the information game that we might elect to play. (See FIGS 5-8 and 5-15.) Note that there is no such thing as no game; the default is game five (wait and see), which is indeed a game itself, with definite consequences. So, what game do you want to play? (See the chapter 8 workshops.)

In conclusion

You'll need a vision indicating the strategic direction of your entrance into the Information Era, based on the following strategies that have been discussed throughout this book and shown in TABLE 5-2. (Also see FIG. 5-17.)

With information comes knowledge; with knowledge comes understanding; with understanding comes the power to better control our destiny and make technology do for humanity only what we want it to do. We must establish the controls and self-checks to channel technology in the particular direction we want to go, so humanity doesn't become lost in the tide of technology, but rides its waves to new lands and new places . . .

Table 5-2. Ten Strategies

Market strategy	Technical strategy
1. Data Services Strategy	— Data Network Overlay Strategy
2. Information Pricing Strategy	— Data Trans/Processing Strategy
3. ISDN Service Strategy	— ISDN Interface Strategy
4. Information Access Strategy	— Gateway/IN Strategy
5. Shared Services Strategy	— Wideband Transport Strategy
6. Urban Service Strategy	— Metro Switching Stragegy
7. Res/Bus/Gov Applications Strategy	— Information Switching Strategy
8. Service Management Strategy	— Network Management Strategy
9. Competitive/Monopolistic Strategy	— Private/Public Network Strategy
10. Integrated Network Services Strategy	— Layered Networks Strategy

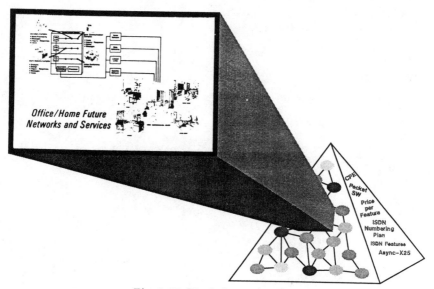

Fig. 5-17. The Information Era.

Real change requires real commitment to address real issues to make real decisions to take the real risks to achieve real successes. Hence, different visions from different perspectives provide different networks and different services, as different providers, making different choices, pursue different paths, where fortunes and destinies are made or lost by these differences . . .

Who is to say —
What the future will hold,
What path will be taken —
Where, when, by whom . . .
"The answer is . . .
blowing in the wind . . .
The answer is . . .
blowing in the wind . . ."

6

The information society

What . . .
    could have been . . .
    Would have been . . .
    Might have been . . .

In looking back over the last hundred years of the twenty-first century, it's difficult to grasp how much change has taken pace. They say the twentieth century had considerable advances and changes as the global wars were played out with increasingly dangerous technology. During this period, space was penetrated as expeditions ventured further and further from planet Earth. Technology played a leading role as computers were first introduced in the payroll-accounting arena and then permeated into every field. Computers replaced the typewriter with word processing, assisted the pilot with feedback control systems, etc. However, in hindsight, these advances were only the forerunners of the tremendous changes that took place in the latter portion of the twenty-first century.

Having the unique distinction of being the first baby born (at least by current-day records) on January 1 in the year 2000, and still being alive, of sound mind, and well in the year 2100, I've been asked to describe how society changed during the last hundred years. In looking back, I believe that a dozen or so key communication/computer technologies provided the platforms from which numerous major advancements in society were made, changing forever our way of life, providing some changes for the better, some for the worse . . . as we gained a higher living standard but lost some personal obscurity.

So, what were these technologies that formed these platforms? Let's begin by taking a look at them individually and then collectively as we view life in the resulting society — as lifestyles changed, as nations changed, as we all grew a little closer to each other on this unique and lonely planet in a distant galaxy in a foreboding universe of galaxies . . .

Platform technologies — past building blocks

In the late twentieth century, scientists and engineers were pursuing several technical possibilities that would forever change their lives, as they established the building blocks to create a new society . . . an information society in the Information Millennium. These technological advancements have provided an ever-expanding range of market opportunities.

So, let's take a moment to evaluate the effect of voice recognition, videophone, video conference windows, artificial intelligence, virtual reality, public data networks, flat screen display, gigabit storage, broadband fiber networks, high-definition television, wireless personal communication, supercomputers, and knowledge workstations.

Let's begin by reviewing our first "baby steps" into the new era of voice, data, text, image, and video information, where these various forms of communication were destined to be ubiquitously available to anyone, anywhere, anyplace, anytime . . . all the time. We need to visualize what changes and effects these technologies could/would/should have provided (but in some cases didn't) in order to see if we appropriately positioned and adequately paced ourselves during these hundred years. As noted in an earlier analysis, *Future Telecommunications*, the twenty-first century was to be the entrance into the Information Millennium. Never before had so much technology been available for consumption, enabling marketers to wrestle with difficult decisions of "what change (service/product) to provide, where, to whom, and for how long?" — such as a particular narrowband videophone service or an overlapping broadband videophone service, or perhaps both. So, let's pause and see what these building-block technologies offered at the beginning of the twenty-first century. (See FIG. 6-1.)

Voice recognition

We've all experienced the "talking" this or that . . . , as elevators now tell us what floor we've arrived on, to watch our step as we exit, or to look out for a closing door. The friendly elevator operator who used to open the brass cage doors is forever gone, perhaps for the best, as their world was controlled by continuous ups and downs. Now, voice synthesis chips enable telephone operators to be assisted by computer database search programs that find the desired number and "speak it" to the caller in any language. Similarly, toys talk to children, numerous audio response devices answer questions, provide weather and flight information, or move the caller through a series of questions, proceeding down the many different paths, depending on the users' Touch-Tone responses.

In time, voice recognition techniques would become sufficiently available so that numerous types of devices were "educated" to recognize key words from any individual. Problems of background noise (for example, in pay phones) or various dialects and accents were overcome as individuals taught their devices to recognize their personal instructions. As recognizable vocabularies increased from ten words to several thousand, enabling short-sentence recognition, machines were no longer

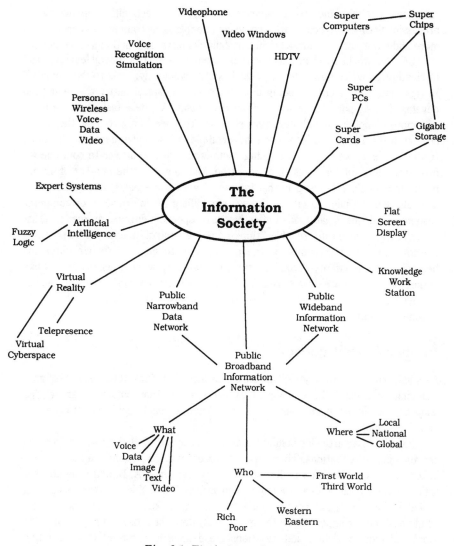

Fig. 6-1. The information society.

limited in functionality. We've seen how buttons and functions were reduced or removed, as added capabilities oftentimes extended the usage complexity to the point that customers couldn't even turn off the blinking time/set light indicator on their VCR.

So, as we not only enabled "machines to talk to us, but us to talk to the machines," we could then enable our factory workers to perform quite versatile tasks, as they were provided step-by-step instructions from computers that interactively responded to their questions. No longer must they access large, complex procedure documents, now they could more easily jump from assembling automobiles to airplanes. In a similar manner, voice recognition enabled word processing without keyboards to become commonplace, as computers responded to more and more verbal input, as their vocabularies increased, and increased again.

So, the world of interactive verbal communications is indeed exciting and fascinating, as we're now able to, as Dr. Doolittle would say, "talk to the animals." In this case, the "animals" being any electrical/mechanical entity that had been developed to support one or more of our daily tasks. As these tasks became more and more complex, so had our support tools. You need only to visit the pilot's cockpit of the 1970s and '80s to see how complex these instruments had become. In the late '90s, we began an ongoing commercial effort that was to continue for fifty years until fully successful, as we attempted to reduce the number of instruments to a single video display that interacted with numerous system computers. This allowed the pilot to talk to the system, calling for information or computer response, and this greatly aided effectiveness, especially during emergency situations. In the future, safe, reliable "think response control" might yet be possible, but for now, verbal response is the proven way to go . . . As we enter the beginning of this twenty-second century, we can only wonder what life was like without voice response devices that now enable us to not only talk to machines, but to anyone, as devices translate our words into any language in the world . . . to anyone . . . anywhere . . .

Artificial intelligence

As some pursued "fuzzy logic" to enable products to think their way through a changing situation, others achieved expert systems that obtain a "knowledge transfer" or "information transfer," from a knowledgeable performer to the less knowledgeable.

Experts in a particular field are tapped to describe what they would do given certain inputs or situations. Their thought processes and decisions are then defined in terms of logical decision tables, such as — where given A, B, and C inputs that satisfy particular situations or events, then actions X and Y would take place, or if A and B don't occur, Z action would take place. In logical design, these "else conditions" are as important as the more easily described, desired happenings. As more and more variables and situations are defined in terms of their resulting actions, these responses will usually cause changes to inputs or introduce new inputs, thereby requiring new actions, causing new inputs, etc., etc. Hence, an input/output decision-making program can be established based on the experts' decisions and responses. These programs can then be provided to the less knowledgeable to assist them in performing similar tasks under similarly varying conditions.

With these tools, doctors can perform more complex analyses, robotics can leave the welding and spraying manufacturing arena and enter the full marketplace of human assistance or replacement by performing repetitive or dangerous tasks. We've seen where the Japanese have introduced robots to paint the huge water towers or gas spheres. Using advanced communications techniques, this work can be controlled remotely, as we integrate more and more of these advancements together. Over time, we've seen robots driving high-speed freight trains in tunnels, mining for coal or precious metals, directing traffic during rush hour, performing repetitive precision laser eye surgery, cutting lawns, controlling elevators, and maintaining intelligent buildings. In this, we've seen a fine line arise in determining the difference between feedback response control systems and robotics. Hence, we've continued to differentiate entities by noting moving versus nonmoving capabilities. However, over time this has become a blur, as sensing and decision-making functions became more and more advanced.

Virtual reality

After attempting to create machines that think, the second wave of artificial intelligence was to create environments that respond to our thoughts. Here, we could create worlds of colors, shapes, sounds, and feelings that allow the human mind to better absorb, manipulate, process, and interpret information more quickly and completely, as many believe that the brain can reason better through sight, sound, and touch instead of just text and numbers. As a visionary once noted, there's a substantial difference from just looking at an aquarium rather than putting on your scuba gear and swimming in it.

As we became able to not only look at a two-dimensional picture, but also enter the scene and walk around it to see each side from a different perspective, we had stepped into the world of Cyberspace. In this electronic ether, we're able to see 3D X-rays and hear 3D sound. As we don our data gloves, power gloves, eye phones, and data suits, we can not only overlay our personal image in an old John Wayne movie, but also act in the visual theater where our characters move as we move, talk as we talk. Here, we feel what's touched in virtual space, as our artificial life is finely tuned for sensory and psychological responses, enabling virtual perceptions to be obtained from the different virtual worlds created by complex, realistic graphs or motion. We can manipulate devices remotely or respond to simulated situations, enabling us to provide a telepresence — here, there, anywhere . . .

Designers have become able to create personalities in animated characters, so people can relate and identify with them. This enables various role-playing to better address phobias and fears. Just as in the early Star Trek movies, whose players were able to create their own simulation to represent a past event or future situation, so virtual reality enables designers to put together automobiles, airplanes, office buildings, and homes to see how the pieces fit, or what life would be like in different sizes of different structures. So it was . . . in the twenty-first century.

Gigabit storage

In the last half of the twentieth century, scientists used IBM cards, relays, cores, disks, drums, bubble memories, and integrated circuits (ICs) to store information. Over time, we progressed and changed from read only (ROMs) to write once read many times (WORMs) to numerous diverse, dynamically changeable read-write devices. One such device, the IC, expanded and expanded again as the 256,000-bit chip became 512,000 bits, a million bits, etc., and on to achieve packages of multiple arrays of 50-million-bit chips. We also saw the analog record industry shift to digital players using the 5 1/2-inch and now 3 1/2-inch CDs. Similarly, the computer PC went from floppy disks to megabit hard disks, from single-sided to double-sided disks.

The video industry adapted better and better video tapes in its shift from analog to high-definition, high-resolution digital television. As the demand for more and more video increased, the entertainment world completed its move from various forms of analog storage devices to fully digital disks. Video travel logs, sporting events, musical players, and movies were stored on digital video juke-boxes, offering gigabit storage for ready access to not only these endeavors, but also to medical imaging (X-rays) archives, business data, educational lectures, and book libraries.

Once everything was digitalized and stored, information on any subject could be easily accessed, searched, indexed, tabled, collected, coalesced, manipulated, and presented. As we entered a world of transferring every item, geographic area, event, and image, to storage, we were then left with the reality of archiving and real-time updating. This required significant advancements in display systems, supercomputers, and workstations to better process and use both the old and the new information . . .

Supercomputers

We've seen computers expand and expand again from the days of the "bootstrap loader" that accessed and executed primitive mathematical programs written in the ones and zeros of machine language. Computer processing power developed from the execution of a single program to simultaneous front-end/back-end processing, where new programs were being read into the computer as earlier programs were being executed. Over the 1960s and '70s, the computer advanced from fixed-partition to variable-partition systems, from offline tape storage to online drum/disk access, from card deck input to remote keyboards and printers, from low-level assembly languages to specialized languages for list processing and data-base access to highly sophisticated high-level compilers that enable the creation of a multitude of programs with different object codes for a multitude of different types and sizes of processors.

After Control Data led the change, which was initially established by the University of Illinois' scientific multiprocessor Illiac IV and IBM's military SAGE systems, a new player, Cray, established new heights, new possibilities. Their successes then fostered subsequent spinoffs and international competition, as numerous computer firms throughout the world, such as Japan's NEC, rose to address this "superchallenge" of the century.

In time, we moved from processing binary ones and zeros to optical systems that could manipulate information in higher number bases such as octal and decimal (or whatever), as more and more information was processed faster and faster. PCs became minis and minis became mainframes, until PCs achieved the power of previous mainframes, where millions of instructions per second (MIPS) capabilities grew from 1 to 10 to 100 to 1000 MIPS, as arrays of personal computers (PCs), logically or physically distributed, operated in parallel to increase the overall power of the computer.

As new languages and programs became further advanced to enable more and more parallel processing, we were able to take a further step—enabling rapid manipulation of image and video information, processed online in real time and obtained from both online and offline gigabit storage. With this increased computer power, dynamically changing weather, airplane, train, automobile, and human status conditions, requiring thousands of sensors, could be accessed more quickly; this helped identify changing weather conditions and aided traffic control by enabling information to become more visual, more real-time, more friendly, more personal. These capabilities have enabled traffic controllers to have greater versatility and better data, to achieve greater safety, etc. Over time, these advanced information-handling capabilities have been applied to every sector of society . . .

Flat screen display

The computer then entered every aspect of the marketplace, bringing with it the cathode ray display tube with its concerns of eye fatigue and radiation. Numerous tubes permeated to stock brokers' desks, financial analysts' offices, student dorm rooms, bank teller locations, and manufacturing workstations. With the advancement of flat screen displays, enabling high-quality resolution to be achieved for varying-sized displays, we then had a safe device for faster laptop computers (or even hand held). This then became the tool to achieve the home communication center, the office communication center, the video conference window, videophone, and the knowledge workstation, as we moved from 500×500 to 1000×1000 to 2000×2000 to 4000×4000 high-imagery, high-resolution, high-definition displays.

Knowledge workstations

Computer terminals became highly sophisticated as they proceeded from 2 to 20 to 200 to 2000 MIPS (million instructions per second) systems, enabling users to, for example, design the front end of a new car at a remote workstation. Then, after the design was completed, it could be returned to the main computer for full integration, using virtual reality to remotely sense "merging resistance" as it's coaxed into place.

Designers could, over time, become more and more physically remote, as large communication systems enabled their work locations to interact here, there, and everywhere with more and more powerful computers. These stations incorporated not only the communication networking technology, but also local gigabit storage devices, high-quality, flat screen displays, and supercomputer power. As they accessed and manipulated more and more information, these work areas obtained more and more locally stored knowledge — hence, the term for this workstation became the "knowledge workstation."

As we look at the applications' arena, be it the airplane cockpit, the automobile driver seat, the student desk, the designer's office, or the megamall operations center, we see an overlapping of automated computer control systems, online control systems, workstations, robotic units, and archiving systems, as all accessed more and more information.

Videophone

To appreciate a lack of vision, a two-hour blindfolded walk along your favorite street should enhance your perspective and appreciation. Unfortunately, for those who have never had sight, have never had the opportunity to see the street as it really is, have experienced it only through sounds, touch, and smells, this does limit their full understanding of sight. So it is with videophone. How many arguments could have been prevented by seeing the person at the other end of the telephone. Seeing the reaction (once called body language) to a person's thoughts, ideas, and opinions helps to steer the conversation. How many family problems developed in the twentieth century from not having eye-to-eye contact with a mother-in-law or child? How many sales were lost by simply talking to a "dead phone" and not seeing the prospective customer's response to one "sales approach" over another?

Videophone is a tool that can help in this regard. Some said, "Who needs it? I don't want anyone to see me at 7:00 a.m. unless my hair is just right," etc., etc. The truth is that, once deployed, every communication device simply becomes an extension of our effort to communicate. Just as the cellular phone provided embarrassing conversations to eavesdroppers, so television talk shows, newscasters, and children's show participants become oblivious to the camera. Indeed, there is, as always, the need for privacy and security as well as personal discretion, but the videophones in their flickering narrowband form, compressed wideband version, and full-resolution broadband capability were welcomed and used in every sector of society, once they were priced as a reasonable alternative to the telephone.

Video conference windows

When we deployed wall-mounted, flat screen displays in the conference room, with surrounding sound, and eye-to-eye cameras, we had indeed entered a new phase in human interaction. Over the years, business planning and decision making had continued to progress down the corporate hierarchy, as more participation-management techniques enabled workers to provide their inputs to create new concepts, resolve complex problems, and provide the right solutions.

However, time and travel were still the limiting factors. Not enough time to travel to all the meetings remained a fact of life for many employees. Similarly, time for being with one's family continued to be more and more precious, creating the need to work from home while caring for children or the elderly.

As firms became multinational, where global locations required adjustments for jet lag and different working hours, the need became ever so great to enable employees to be fresh and alert by using the capabilities offered by electronic meetings. A five-year stint in any global, international, multinational firm bore this out, probably in the second month on the road.

Finally, in the latter half of the twenty-first century, once the broadband infrastructure was in place, the exodus from the congested megatropolis to the more distant towns and villages was accomplished by establishing firms in the more rural environments and using high-speed communication highways to provide video windows, interconnecting remote offices to urban conference tables.

Public data networks

The proliferation of local area networks (LANs) in the 1980s and 1990s required substantial interconnection to enable internetworking, interprocessing, and inter-services. This menagerie of local buses and rings demonstrated the need for a ubiquitous public data network — one that enabled any terminal's address to be (if desired) accessible from any other terminal, as were telephones. Earlier systems elected to use dial-up voice networks to send low-speed data over analog modems, but call setup time, transport error rate, network congestion, and expensive computer input/output delays made this approach unsuitable, even though some providers offered protocol interface conversions for dissimilar systems to help facilitate these interconnections. Though these value added services were highly desirable, building them on top of a voice-based infrastructure proved to be an unfortunate use of technology. It caused serious blockages and brownouts of the voice network as more and more data usage occurred. A new, robust network was required that specifically catered to delivering data services. Here, addressing, routing, path selection, alternative routing, and even delayed delivery, priority interrupt, and selected call blocking services once offered to the military data world were needed for commercial data, but at the higher transport rates established by international Integrated Services Digital Network (ISDN) standards groups.

Using these special data-handling services, "data dial tone" was readily provided to universal terminals, identified in data directories, to quickly interconnect terminals at low error rates and high data transport speeds that encouraged usage without network throughput congestion penalties. Specialized, closed user groups flourished, but they were still accessible to the full community through protection mechanisms using passwords, audit trials, designated terminals, call backs, and terminal verification procedures.

Eighty percent of our daily operations require some form of data exchange involving inquiry/response, data collection, data distribution, data documentation, and data presentation. Eighty percent of these data-handling services were initially provided by the public data network operating over existing twentieth-century copper facilities. The remaining wideband/broadband services grew at an increasing rate, provided by the new fiber-based networks deployed throughout the twenty-first century . . .

Broadband information networks

There had been much talk of fiber over the '80s and early '90s, as designers discussed "protons versus electrons" in terms of: signal mode versus multimode, 13 and 15 nanometer wavelength bands, optical amplifiers, optical logic, optical electronic interfaces and trade-offs, asynchronous transfer mode (ATM), synchronous transfer mode (STM), wave division multiplexing (WDM), space division multiplexing (SDM), packet versus circuit versus channel switching, etc.

However, without getting into the specifics of the user network interfaces (UNI) of 155 million bits per second and 622 million bits per second for broadband ISDN, it was important at the turn of the century to ask, "What are we going to really do with this much transport capacity? Who needs it?" Where? When? What exactly is a broadband network and what will it do for us?

The broadband information network took the next step (which was indeed no longer a "baby step") beyond the narrowband public data network, which was based on existing facilities and limitations. Whereas narrowband data (though considered high speed over previous analog dial-up rates) could only be transported at speeds of 64K or 128K bits per second. The next advances occurred through special conditioning, where multiples of 64K up to 6.24 million bits per second were achieved over the copper plant. In this, we actually began entering the wideband, prebroadband arena, where broadband, based on multiples of 50 megabit rate SONET building blocks, would be virtually unlimited. There, the "switched" transport network, operating at these broadband rates would, in time, eclipse the lower narrowband and wideband networks, as the infrastructure for affordable, addressable, routable, survivable, securable throughput became available with virtually unlimited capacity.

However, what is to be done with this capability? We need only to browse through what has just been discussed—artificial intelligence, virtual reality, gigabit storage, flat screen displays, supercomputers, knowledge workstations, videophone, video conference windows, high-definition television, voice recognition, and wireless personal communication. We indeed were moving into a fully functioning global world of information creation, transfer, manipulation, and presentation. Success begets usage, which begets more success and more usage. If, as in electricity, the demand for more and more, cheaper and cheaper communications, drove us to switching or transport brownouts (similar to power outages) we would have created a worse situation than the one from which we started. People in the twentieth century failed to achieve highly efficient, safe, and secure nuclear power plants that didn't harm the environment. This drove the power companies to offer incentives to not use electricity during peak-load days, hours, or minutes. They would even pick up older, less efficient air conditioners and furnaces and pay the owner incentives to purchase newer ones. They did anything they could to limit their customers' power consumption. This was a drastic reversal from initial plans to encourage customers to cheaply connect any device to their network, to use it as long as they wanted, consuming as much "cheap, affordable electricity" as they could.

Similarly, the telecommunication industry providers couldn't encourage hospitals to drop their leased lines (which offered 99.9 percent reliability) to go to a "switched" network that could indeed go down. If this network were successfully accepted by the public, this would cause a situation where external demand for more and more communication capacity couldn't be fulfilled. In time, to prevent this from happening, narrowband and wideband capabilities were to be "mapped" into broadband offerings, but to achieve this, providers needed to begin establishing the fully switched fiber broadband network to each and every location. This was to be accomplished over the first fifty years of the information century in order to have it available as the baseline supporting infrastructure by the year 2050 (original government targets had been as early as 2015). During this period, there was considerable struggle to fully deploy these capabilities. Indeed, it took the first 20 years to convince the financial community to allow the network providers to get started.

Videophone in its highest resolution form couldn't be available to replace the telephone unless such a network was ubiquitously available. Fortunately, there remained the opportunities created by numerous parallel technologies that helped encourage the establishment of the broadband network to service videophones. These parallel opportunities were found in the high-definition television market, as well as the computer networking and data networking arenas.

High-definition television

The significant increase from 526 to 1100 lines enabled such high resolution and definition that, although it was a continuum of existing technology, its advancement was so substantial as to present a completely new media to the customer. However, it required a substantial upgrade to achieve either the wire-line or wireless broadcast distribution network, requiring, respectively, digital fiber or digital satellite capabilities. This upgrade of distribution plant expenses required additional revenues to justify replacement. As noted, the data networking/computer networking markets were expanding. In time, new video service revenues came from selected programming of global sports events, movies, and educational programs. Competitive alternatives included advanced TV (ATV), which used existing facilities and analog programming. ATV was to be provided over selected hybrid fiber/coax routes. At the time of these difficult decisions, who was to say when the public demand was to respond to this significant advancement in offerings? Would it be supported by the cable industry, by an alternative, digital, fiber-based television industry, by direct broadcast, or by a local network provided by the equipment suppliers themselves? In time, many of these alternatives took place in the mad race to fiber every home, every office . . .

Wireless personal communications

Cellular phones became cheaper, lighter, and smaller, with additional car mounting and cigarette lighter battery plug-in capabilities and better low-battery warning light features. As this occurred, the providers' attention shifted to operational concerns such as finding a roaming user in a distant city, traveling across the country, and interfacing with remote databases in "real time" by resolving update problems between cellular providers. As their technologists wrestled with TDMA and ETDMA versus CDMA technology trade-offs, different firms chose different alternatives, causing difficult interface problems. Security and privacy issues rose to the forefront in light of revelations made by scanners of conversations, who eavesdropped on exchanges ranging from drug deals to business plans to improper relationships.

As the mobile cellular standards across Europe attempted to be better resolved, the low-wattage personal communication network with its array of personal communication services (PCS) tickled the imagination of marketers worldwide. However, there were substantial problems in achieving universally accepted interface standards (having the complexity of "ISDN with wings"). Also, spectrum availability issues caused many PCN/PCS suppliers to consider different spread-spectrum technologies. In addition, the complexity of universally achieving the "large database in the sky" that tracked users' movements every 400 feet or so was indeed not trivial. Alternative capabilities enabled the paging of a customer in an area and provided a calling number that the personal phone could recall. This became a more realistic alternative for many urban city applications. Even today, the totally personal phone that locates anyone, anyplace, remains an illusive dream.

In time, wireless cellular data would remain a viable extension of the public data network for small business/tradespeople (such as builders) who worked out of their mobile trucks. Versions of the "Dick Tracy" watch did come to pass, at least in sections of densely populated cities, especially the third world and Eastern blocks, where access to global networks remained a premium, except in the newly formed, planned cities. On the extremely rural side, wireless communication continued to make deep inroads, as the cellular phone replaced the radio. However, some in Australia's outback still prefer the shortwave radio to the phone; on shortwave, all can listen in and add their two cents to the conversation . . . even in the twenty- second century . . .

The information society

So, what happened with all these technical possibilities and market opportunities? In looking at the past hundred years of the unfolding information society, what was it like? Was life a little bit better, a little bit worse? (See FIG. 6-2.)

Having grown up in this century of information, I can say that it did provide me with an exciting profession, which had been performed in previous periods but was never really formally pursued and executed in the same manner and with the same intensity. I became a planner of new cities in the new century. After fifty years as the master planner of new cities of third-world countries, enabling their belated entrance into the information marketplace, I can honestly say that in these endeavors, life is indeed better and will be much better in the next century, not only for the industrial nations, but also for those that have not been as fortunate. For life today uses many exciting building-block technologies to provide for the

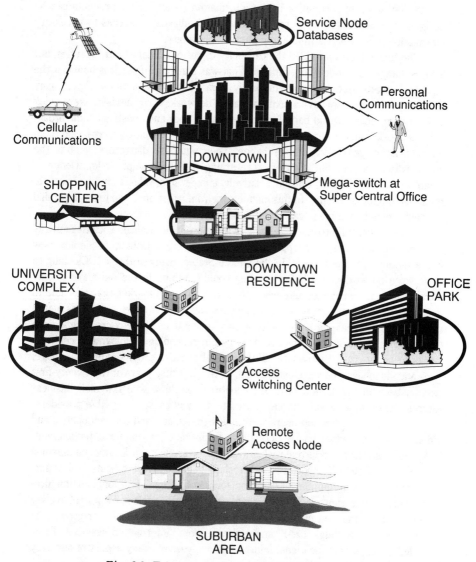

Fig. 6-2. Telecommunications information society.

growing presence of a growing world population, especially in sections of the third world, where these pressures have become explosive.

We all know from the days of one-factory towns that a single industry can create enough wealth to sustain an entire area. As was once said in the days of silver dollars, "Dollars are round to go around." For each person who brings in fresh money to a local community, five to ten other people obtain a living, as the butcher, the banker, and the candlestick maker provide their services. So it is with new cities and their new information-handling technologies and services, which create new work opportunities in the information society. New products can be designed and manufactured in remote towns and villages, as access to necessary information is no longer a function of physical proximity.

The technologies provided the capability to not only change our lifestyles, but also to change our mode of operations. What was startling to see was how fast the new tools were used in the traditionally nonindustrialized nations. Since many countries didn't initially have a communication network, smart advisers were quick to help them obtain world bank funding to deploy fiber and construct their broadband networks. As countries went about building their new cities, they based them on information generation and exchange. Their sons and daughters went to the industrialized nations' finest colleges, returning with the computer knowledge to establish businesses that offered relatively inexpensive value-added services to their larger nations' clients. In this manner, their information usage grew in parallel to their clients and in many cases outgrew them.

It was interesting to see that some of the more industrialized societies initially resisted much of the new opportunities. They were unwilling to deploy new infrastructures for the masses. In the United States, many of the RBOCs clung to their voice networks, still believing they could continue in the old ways of only introducing a little change, only when they saw a proven market that was able to guarantee enough usage to quickly support the new service. Some, as noted earlier, used the voice networks to transport analog data, thereby creating serious congestion and blockage problems. This gap in technology deployment could no longer be suppressed. By the late 1990s, new, alternative providers of data, image, text, and video services were established, so the first fifty years of the twenty-first century became a battlefield of total competition, as those who saw their business futures tied to information services shifted to many of these alternative providers.

These new information users were quick to demand and use videophone and video windows to reduce travel, obtain high-definition television for entertainment, and provide imaging and virtual reality systems for product marketing and personal educational updating. Consortium partnerships began delivering hosts of new services from a growing number of database sources (DBSs). Traditional communication switching and transmission equipment suppliers also became owners of overlay networks, using the best of their features and services for special user groups. As everything became "digitalized" and archived, new "information services" firms provided (from remote locations) information analyses of every aspect of our daily lives.

Multinational corporations became more information product oriented, as they linked together their global companies to offer layers of new information services. In time, the exchange of information between countries was no longer controlled and regulated, as each local economy became tied to their multinational partners' economic futures.

Creating a north/south contrast, as well as internal economic classes, the haves continued to separate from the have-nots. However, in between sprung up a new subgroup tier, so the society was not sharply divided. The subgroup in time grew to limit the expeditious growth of the haves, as more and more subgroups obtained a "piece of the action" from their many small businesses. As information education began to take hold in the underdeveloped countries, it was used to increase their food production. Also, yes, many third- and fourth-world wars took place as the land barons were forced to give up half of their land holdings to enable a growing, more educated society.

Thus, the century was spent in tremendous global economic wars, as countries fought in the streets of the global marketplace to gain control, to capture a foothold with different products and services. The tools of this war were no longer guns and tanks, but communication networks and communication terminals that enabled businesses to better compete and flourish.

Yes, systems became more automated . . . Yes, robots helped perform dangerous and repetitive tasks . . . Yes, virtual reality enabled simulated environments for businesses and recreation . . . Yes, videophone and video windows enabled us to be there—face-to-face, with eye-to-eye discussions . . . Yes, voice recognition eliminated intermediate communication devices such as keyboards . . . Yes, different languages no longer created communication barriers, as machines translated one language to another in real time . . . Yes, supercomputers sensed more, manipulated more, provided more visionary solutions immediately, if not sooner . . . Yes, countries now have strategic plans that are more realistically addressed and implemented, protecting not only their people and their environment, but also the unborn generation of future children . . . These economic pressures and global competition continue to encourage us to better channel the use of our technological building blocks to obtain a better world for our children and our children's children.

Hence, we'll build on new technologies, again and again, in ways yet to be visualized and yet to be understood, for in using these past technologies, my grandson today crossed a new frontier by taking another small step, which is indeed another great leap for humanity—his expedition from planet Earth landed on planet Mars . . . With this appreciation and understanding, I look forward to the twenty-second century and the centuries to come, and I thank all those who worked so hard in the twentieth century and its preceding centuries to enable us in the twenty-first to establish the supporting infrastructure for the Information Millennium . . .

> The fruit has bloomed and blossomed;
> It has ripened for the picking;
> The harvest will be great,
> Unless ignored and left behind,
> To wait for yet another day,
> Another harvest, another time . . .
> "Where young men dream dreams,
> Of what could be . . .
> While old men see visions,
> Of what could have been . . . "
> So it could be . . .
> So it might be . . .
> So it will be . . .
>
> Robert K. Heldman

Part III

The inform
marketpl

*"There is a tide in the aff
which taken at the flood
leads on to fortune;
missed, it ne'er comes i*

William

Part III

The information marketplace

"There is a tide in the affairs of men
which taken at the flood
leads on to fortune;
missed, it ne'er comes in again."

William Shakespeare

7

Case studies
Networks, products,
& services

*"The empires of the future
are the empires of the mind."*

Winston Churchill

The following viewpoints have been presented during the formation phase of the Information Era. They're referenced here to note the players' perspectives on several of the more complex issues. These studies have been selected from the thousands of views provided in industrial journals such as *Data Communications, Telephony, TE&M,* and *World Systems Communications.*

Case study one: The standards arena

A twist here,
A turn there.

The standards arena is described by Phil Davidson in the following analysis on the I-Series as a framework for tomorrow's digital networks.

Towards the end of the 1976-1980 CCITT Study Period, Study Group XVIII on Digital Networks, having established the principles of an Integrated Digital Network (IDN) for telephony, started considering the next stage of evolution of digital networks. At the same time, Study Group XI on Telephone Switching and Signaling was finalizing the specification of a new common channel signaling system (CCITT Signaling System No. 7), which would be used in IDN to convey signaling for both telephone and data services.

The 1980 CCITT Plenary Assembly recognized the very strong interest in the ISDN concept and gave Study Group XVII the mandate to produce overall guidelines and recommendations on ISDN within which the technical studies in a number of areas, such as user-network interfaces, switching, and signaling systems, might proceed. Questions on ISDN studies were also introduced into the work of Study Group VII on Data Communications Networks, which considered the impact of data services in an ISDN. Study Group XI considered digital switching, common channel signaling, and customer access signaling issues. Study Group II also dealt with ISDN numbering issues.

At the end of the 1980-1984 CCITT Study Period, a number of ISDN Recommendations were agreed on at the Plenary Assembly. These recommendations are contained in the I-Series of Recommendations, which contain all relevant ISDN recommendations produced by all of the study groups.

The concept of ISDN was originally built on the evolution, in the various countries, of the Integrated Digital Networks (IDNs), where the term *integrated* refers to the commonality of digital techniques used in transmission and switching systems. In particular, the telephony IDN, based on the 64k b/s adapted for the encoding of speech, was considered to be a powerful means of conveying other services in addition to voice, such as data and video. Hence, the integration of different services onto a common digital capability. The original idea of a 64k b/s circuit-switched ISDN has more recently been expanded. It now includes a more general concept of ISDN to allow networks to evolve in the shorter time frame and, in the longer term, to include packet switching capabilities and circuit switching capabilities at rates above and below 64k b/s.

These concepts form the basic principles of an ISDN and of its evolution. They're included in Recommendation I.120 and can be summarized as follows:

- The main feature of the ISDN concept is the support of a wide range of voice and nonvoice services in the same network. A key element of service integration in an ISDN is the provision of a limited set of multipurpose user-network interfaces as well as a limited set of multipurpose network connection types, each of which support a wide range of services.

- An ISDN might support both nonswitched and switched connections; switched includes both circuit and packet connections. As far as practical, new services introduced into an ISDN should be arranged to be compatible with 64k b/s switched digital connections.

- An ISDN will be based on and evolve from a telephony IDN and might evolve by progressively incorporating additional functions and network features, including those of any other dedicated networks so as to provide for existing and new services.

- The transition from an existing network to a comprehensive ISDN might require, in some circumstances, one or more decades. During this transition period, arrangements must be developed for interworking of services on an ISDN and the services on other networks.

- In the evolution towards an ISDN digital network, end-to-end connectivity will be obtained using plant and equipment in existing networks such as digital transmission, time division multiplex switching, and/or space division multiplex switching.

The ISDN Recommendations are contained in the I-Series of Recommendations and are structured so that new recommendations can be easily included in the appropriate sections. Recommendation I.110 describes the structure. (See FIG. 7-1.)

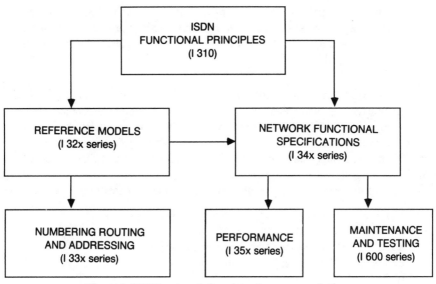

Fig. 7-1. ISDN network I-series of recommendations.

In the 1980-1994 CCITT Study Period, it was agreed that work should be concentrated on those issues relating to access to the ISDN, and, as a consequence, recommendations were produced on the user-network interface, service aspects, network aspects, and, of course, on ISDN general issues.

Initially, there were no recommendations on ISDN maintenance principles or internetwork interfaces, and work on these has commenced in the present study period. In the present structure of the I-Series Recommendations, six parts have been identified and allocated a series number. Three recommendations cover the results of the work to date in describing the support of services of ISDN, including I.210 — Principles of Telecommunications Services.

By definition, ISDN was conceived to support a wide variety of services, from the "existing" services such as telephony and data communications, to "new" services for text and graphic communication (teletex, videotex, etc.) and to also include, in the longer term, the broadband services for video communications (visual telephony, videoconferencing, etc.). Some of these services are already defined by CCITT; some are under definition, while others are likely to emerge in the future.

CCITT has defined two broad categories of telecommunications services — Bearer (I.211) and a host of Teleservice (I.212):

- Bearer Services supported by an ISDN provide the capability for information transfer between ISDN user-network interfaces and involve only low-layer (OSI model) functions. The customer can choose any set of high-layer protocols for communications, and the ISDN doesn't ascertain compatibility at these layers between customers. An example of bearer services is a switched 64 b/s circuit mode, unrestricted service.

- Teleservices provide the full capability for communication by means of terminals, network functions, and possible functions provided by dedicated centers. Examples of teleservices are telephony, teletex, videotex, and message handling.

Teleservices are characterized by a set of lower-layer attributes, a set of high-layer attributes, and operational and commercial attributes. Recommendation I.212 details the work to date on teleservice, but it's not so complete as I.211 on Bearer Services. I.212 contains a framework for describing Teleservices and a list of attributes and their characteristics. Specific Teleservices and their support by the ISDN have not yet been agreed upon.

The I.300 series is composed of the following recommendations:

I.310 — ISDN Network Functions and Principles
I.320 — ISDN Protocol Reference Model
I.330 — ISDN Numbering and Addressing Principles
I.331 — The Numbering Plan for the ISDN era
I.340 — ISDN Connection Types

The ISDN functional description defines a set of network capabilities that enable Bearer and Teleservices to be offered to customers. The services require two different levels of ISDN capabilities: low-layer, which relates to Bearer Services, and high-layer which, together with low-layer capabilities, relates to Teleservices.

I.320 describes a protocol reference model for ISDN. It's based on the general principles of layering given in the X200 series of Recommendations, and has been developed to model the information flows, including user information flows to and through an ISDN, taking into account the separate channel signaling nature of the ISDN. In order to construct the ISDN protocol reference model, a fundamental generic protocol block has been identified based on the seven-layer OSI model.

In particular, the model has been designed so that protocols in an ISDN can be studied in a structured and uniform way, taking account of the wide range of communication modes and capabilities that can be achieved in the ISDN:

- Circuit-switched connection under the control of common channel signaling.
- Packet-switched communication via the circuit-switched or packet channel.
- Signaling between users and network-based facilities.
- End-to-end signaling.
- Combinations of the preceding in multimedia communications.

ISDN numbering and addressing principles are detailed in Recommendation I.330, and Recommendation I.331 (E164) describes the numbering plan for the ISDN era. It has been agreed that the ISDN numbering plan should be based on and evolve from the existing telephony numbering plan, and therefore the telephony country code is used to identify a particular country. The principles relating to an ISDN number in relation to the user network reference configuration are that an ISDN number shall be able to unambiguously identify a particular:

- Physical or virtual interface at reference point T, including multiple interfaces.
- Physical or virtual interfaces at reference point S, including multiple interfaces for point-to-point configurations.
- Interfaces at reference point S for multipoint configurations (e.g., passive bus).

An ISDN provides a set of network capabilities that enable telecommunications services to be offered to customers. ISDN connection types are described in Recommendation I.340 as a way of referring to and describing ISDN connections. The attributes of connection types are defined in Recommendation I.130.

An ISDN connection is one established between reference points, thus, it's the physical or logical realization of an ISDN connection type. Each ISDN connection can be categorized as belonging to a connection type, depending on its attributes of information transfer rate, signaling access protocol, and performance, which are all examples of ISDN connection-type attributes. (See ISDN user types.)

From a user's perspective, an ISDN is completely characterized by the attributes that can be observed at an ISDN user-network interface, including physical, electromagnetic, protocol, service capability, maintenance, and operation and performance characteristics. I.410 lists the requirements of the user-network interface and outlines the scope to be covered in defining the interface characteristics and capabilities.

A key objective in the definition of ISDN has been that a small set of compatible user-network interfaces can economically support a wide range of user applications, equipment, and configurations. To assist the definition of ISDN user-network interfaces, CCITT has produced a reference model for user-network terminal arrangements. This is described in Recommendation I.411.

The ISDN user-network interface Recommendations apply to physical interfaces at reference points S and T. At reference point R, physical interfaces in accordance with existing CCITT Recommendations (e.g., X and V series) or physical interfaces not included in CCITT Recommendations can be used.

The NT1 functional grouping includes functions equivalent to layer 1 of the Open Systems Interconnection Reference model and are associated with the proper physical and electromagnetic termination of the network. NT1 functions are: line transmission, maintenance functions and performance, monitoring, timing, power transfer, multiplexing, and interface termination, including the possibility of multidrop termination employing contention resolution.

The NT2 functional grouping includes functions equivalent to layer 1 and higher layers of the OSI Reference Model. PABXs, local area networks, and terminal controllers are examples of equipment or combinations of equipment that provide NT2 functions. The NT2 functional grouping can include: protocol handling, multiplexing, switching, concentration, maintenance functions, interface termination, and other layer 1 functions.

The Terminal Equipment (TE) functional grouping includes functions equivalent to layer 1 and higher layers of the OSI Reference Model. Digital telephones, data terminal equipment, and integrated workstations are examples of equipment or combinations of equipment that provide TE functions. TE1 functional grouping might include: protocol handling, maintenance functions, interface functions, and connection functions to other equipment. Two types of TE have been categorized.

- TE1 is an ISDN terminal equipment with an interface that complies with the ISDN user-network interfaces.
- TE2 is a terminal equipment with an interface that complies with non-ISDN Recommendations (e.g., the CCITT X and V series interfaces) or interfaces not included in CCITT recommendations.

The terminal adaptor (TA) functional grouping includes functions equivalent to layer 1 and higher layers of the OSI Reference Model, which allows a TE2 terminal to be served by an ISDN user-network interface. Interface structures and access capabilities for ISDN are described in Recommendation I412. A set of channel types have been defined for the ISDN user-network interface.

Examples of channel types are the "B-channel," which is a 64k b/s channel intended to carry a wide variety of user information streams and provide access to a variety of communication modes within the ISDN (circuit switching, packet switching and semipermanent connections), and the "D-channel," which can have the values of 16k b/s for the basic access structure or 64k b/s for the primary rate interface structure. The D-channel is primarily intended to carry signaling information for circuit switching in the ISDN and, in addition, it can also be used to convey packet-switched data services.

The basic interface structure is composed of two B-channels and one D-channel, 2B + D. The B-channels can be used independently, i.e., in different connections at the same time. With the basic interface structure, two B-channels and one D-channel are always present at the ISDN user-network interface. However, one or both B-channels might not be supported by the network.

The primary rate interface structures correspond to the primary rate of 1544k b/s and 2048k b/s. At the 2048 primary rate, the interface structure is 30B + D, although one or more of the B-channels might not be supported by the network. Channel types at rates higher than 64k b/s have been defined, and interface structures of these channels are described in I.412.

The CCITT "brand" name for the basic access interface is I.420, and for the primary rate interface, it's I.421. These recommendations simply refer to those recommendations that contain the detailed specification for those interfaces. For example, the basic user-network interface is described in I.430 (layer one), I.440 and I.441 (layer two), and I.450, I.451 (layer three).

In I.430, the layer one specifies the services required from the physical medium and also the services provided to layer two. The services required by the layer one from the physical medium of this interface are a balanced metallic transmission medium, for each direction of transmission, capable of supporting 192k b/s. The services provided to layer two are:

- Transmission capability by means of appropriately encoded bit streams for both.
- B and D channels and any related timing and synchronization functions; the signaling capability and necessary procedures to enable customer terminals and/or network terminating equipment to be deactivated and reactivated when required.
- The signaling capability and the necessary procedures to allow terminals to gain access to the common resource of the D-channel in an orderly fashion, while meeting the performance requirements of the D-channel signaling system.
- The signaling capability and procedures and necessary functions at layer one to enable maintenance functions to be performed.
- An indication to the higher layers of the status of layer one.

The details of I.430 for layer one of the basic user-to-network interface covers frame structures, coding rules, frame alignment, electrical characteristics, D-channel access control, and activations/deactivations. Similarly, contained in Recommendations I.440/1 and I.450/1 is the information that defines and describes the layer two and layer three of the ISDN network access protocol.

It was recognized in CCITT that there would be a requirement for the ISDN to support terminals operating to existing interface standards, and that in the early years of ISDN the majority of terminals connected to the ISDN would be via existing interfaces at the R reference point.

To ensure that terminals connected to the ISDN would interwork correctly with each other and with compatible ISDN terminals connected via the ISDN interface at reference point S or T (i.e., TE1 terminal) it was necessary to standardize the terminal adaptor (TA), which converts the protocols to be used at the R reference point to those operations at the S or T reference points. These specifications are contained in the I.461/2/3 Recommendations.

In addition, to meet the requirements of existing PCM transmission equipment, which is used in some overseas countries and which restricts the number of contiguous binary zero bits that can be transmitted, Recommendation I.464 was produced. This Recommendation specifies the requirements on the rate adoption procedures when working with such a "restricted" 64k bps transfer capability.

Work in the present CCITT study period is aimed at consolidating and expanding the text of the recommendations described here. Proposals for new recommendations on topics not yet covered have been made and, by the end of the study period, significant advancements and definitions of additional ISDN capabilities will have been made. (Communications Systems Worldwide.)

Case study two: The standards game

Standards, bodies, forums, and groups

The T1 Standards Committee provides the industry with national standards for telecommunications and offers consensus positions for submission to CCITT through the U.S. Preparatory Study Groups. The formulation of ISDN standards presently is a major activity of the committee and its subcommittees. (See TABLE 7-1.) Paul Hughes provides the following assessment of the "standards game."

Table 7-1. ISO and CCITT Data Communication Standards

APPLICATION LAYER
- ○ ISO XXXX—Common Application Service Elements (CASE)
  - ISO 8650/2 (Association Control Service Elements)
  - ISO 8650/3 (Commitment Concurrency & Recovery Protocol)
- ○ ISO XXXX—Authentication Service
- ○ ISO XXXX—Management Information Service
- ○ ISO XXXX—Directory Service
- ○ ISO 8571—File Transfer, Access & Management (FTAM)
  - File Transfer Service Class
  - Reliable Service Type
  - File Management Service Class
  - File Access Service Class
  - User Correctable Service Type
- ○ ISO 8831—Job Transfer and Manipulation
  - ISO 8832—Basic class
  - Full class
- ○ ISO XXXX—Virtual Terminal Service (VTS)
  - ISO 9040/9041—Basic class
  - Forms Class
  - Graphics Class
  - Image Class
- ○ EIA RS-511—Manufacturing Message Service
- ○ CCITT X.400—Message Handling System (MHS)
  - CCITT X.410—Reliable transfer service
  - CCITT X.411—Message transfer service (MTS)
    - SDP Submission & Delivery Protocol
    - MTP Message Transfer Protocol
  - CCITT X420—Interpersonal messaging service (IPMS)
- ○ CCITT X.3—Packet Assembly/Disassembly (PAD)
  - CCITT X.20—Asynchronous DTE Interface
  - CCITT X.29—PAD to Packet-Mode DTE Protocol
- ○ CCITT T.73—Document Interchange Protocol
  - CCITT T.5—Group 4 Facsimile (G4 FAX) (TIF.0)
  - CCITT T.60—Teletex (TTX)
  - CCITT T.72—Mixed G4 FAX and TTX (TIF.1)

PRESENTATION LAYER
- ○ ISO 8823—OSI Connection-Oriented Presentation Protocol
  - Kernel—connection establishment/termination
  - Context Mgt.—context selection/deletion

- Context Restoration — on resynchronization or activity resumption
- X.410 — MODE — X.400 compatible
○ CCITT X.410 Section 4 — Use of Presentation and Session Services
SESSION LAYER
○ ISO 8073/AD2 — Class 4 Operation over Connectionless Network Service
○ ISO 8073/CCITT X.224 — OSI Transport Protocol
- ISO 8073/AD3 — Transport Encryption
- Class 0 — Simple Class
- Class 1 — Basic Error Recovery
- Class 2 — Multiplexing
- Class 3 — Error Recovery and Multiplexing
- Class 4 — Error Detection and Recovery
○ ISO 8073/AD1 — Network Connection Management Subprotocol
○ ISO 8602 — Connectionless Transport Protocol
NETWORK LAYER
○ ISO 8208/CCITT X.25 — Packet Level Protocol
- Optional User Facilities
- ISO 8208/AD1 — Alternative Logical\Channel Number Assignment
- Optional CCITT-SPecified DTE Facilities
○ ISO 8473 — Internetwork Protocol
- Inactive Network Layer Protocol Subset
- Non-Segmenting Protocol Subset
- Full Protocol
○ ISO 8473/AD1 — Provision of Underlying Service Assumed by ISO 8473
○ ISO 8878 — Use of X.25 to Provide Connection-mode Service
○ ISO 8880/2 — Protocols to Support OSI Network Service Connection-mode
○ ISO 8880/3 — Protocols to support USI Network Service Connectionless-mode
○ ISO 8881 — Use of X.25 PLP in LANs
○ ISO 9068 — Use of X.25 to Provide Connectionless Network Service
ES to IS — Routing Exchange Protocol
- Configuration Information
- Roude Redirect Information
○ CCITT T.70 — Minimal Network Layer Protocol
○ CCITT I.451/Q.931 — ISDN Network Protocol
○ CCITT Q.704 — Signalling System No. 7 Network Functions and Messages
○ CCITT Q.710 — Signalling System No. 7 PABX Application
DATA LINK LAYER
○ IEEE 802.2/ISO 8802/2 — Logical Link Control
- Type 1 — Connectionless Service
- Type 2 — Connection-Oriented Service
- Type 3 — Single Frame Service
○ IEEE 802.3/ISO 8802/3 — CSMA/CD Media Access Control
○ IEEE 802.4/ISO 8802/4 — Token Bus Media Access Control
○ IEEE 802.5/ISO 8802/5 — Token Ring, Media Access Control
○ FDDI Token Ring-Media Access Protocol
○ ANSI X3.107 — LDDI Data Link Protocol
○ ISO 776/CCITT X.25 — Multilink Procedure (MLP)
○ ISO 776/CCITT X.25 — Single Link Procedures (LAP/LAPB)
○ ISO 8802/6 — Slotted Ring Media Access Control
○ CCITT I.441/Q.921 — ISDN Data Link Protocol (LAPD)
○ CCITT Q.703 — Signalling System No. 7, Signalling Link Protocol
○ CCITT T.71 — Half Duplex LAPB Extension (HDTM)

Table 7 – 1. Continued

PHYSICAL LAYER
- ○ FDDI Physical Layer Protocol — Fiber optic cable 100 mb/s
- ○ FDDI Physical Media Dependent Interface
- ○ ANSI X3.108 — LDDI Physical Layer Interface (coaxial cable 50 Mb/s)
- ○ ANSI X3.109 — LDDI Physical Layer Protocol (CSMA)
- ○ Under Data Link Layer, IEEE 802.3/ISO 8802/3 CSMA/CD, Media Access Control
  - • Ethernet
  - • Cheapernet
  - • Broadband
  - • StarLan
- ○ Under IEEE 802.4/ISO 8802/4, Token Bus Media Access Control
  - • Broadband
  - • Phase Continuous FSK
  - • Phase Coherent FSK
- ○ Token Ring
- ○ ISO 8802/6 — Physical Interface
- ○ ISO 8877 — ISDN Connector
- ○ CCITT X.22 — Multiplex PDN Interface
- ○ CCITT X.24 — PDN Interchange Circuit Definitions
- ○ CCITT X.50/X.50bis — PDN Rate Adaptation and Multiplexing
- ○ CCITT X.51/X.51bis — PDN Rate Adaptation and Multiplexing
- ○ CCITT G.736 1.544 — Digital Multiplex Equipment
- ○ CCITT G.737 — PCM Multiplex Equipment
- ○ CCITT G.738 — Digital Multiplex Equipment
- ○ CCITT G.739 — External Access Equipment
- ○ CCITT X.21 — PDN Interface
- ○ CCITT X.21bis — Use of V-series Modems on PDNs
- ○ CCITT v.24 — PSTN Interchange Circuit Definitions
  - • CCITT v.22 — 1200/600 b/s FDX
  - • CCITT v.22bis — 2400/00 b/s FDX
  - • CCITT v.23 — 1200/600 b/s HDX
  - • CCITT v.26 — 2400 b/s 4W
  - • CCITT v.26bis — 2400/1200 b/s HDX
  - • CCITT v.26ter — 2400/1200 b/s FDX
  - • CCITT v.27 4800 b/s 4W
  - • CCITT v.27bis — 4800/2400 b/s 4W
  - • CCITT v.27ter — 4800/2400 b/s FDX
  - • CCITT v.29 — 6900 b/s 4W
  - • CCITT v.32 — 9600/4800 b/s FDX
  - • CCITT v.35 — 48 Kb/s 4W
  - • CCITT v.36 — 48 Kb/s 4W
- ○ CCITT v.25/v.25bis — PSTN Automatic Answering and Calling Equipment
- ○ CCITT X.32 — Accessing a PSPDN through a PSTN or CSPDN
- ○ CCITT I.430 Basic (144 Kb/s) ISDN Interface
- ○ CCITT I.431 — Primary Rate (1544/2048 Kb/s) ISDN Interface
- ○ CCITT I.436/v.110 — Support of V-series DTEs by an ISDN
- ○ CCITT I.460 — ISDN Rate Adaptation and Multiplexing
- ○ CCITT I.461/X.30 — Support of X.21/X.21 bis DETs by an ISDN
- ○ CCITT I.462/X.31 — Support of X.25 DTEs by an ISD
- ○ /CCITT I.463/v.110 — Support of V-series DTEs by an ISDN

T1

American National Standards Institute (ANSI) accredited Committee T1 develops technical standards and reports supporting the interconnection and interoperability of telecommunications networks at interfaces with end-user systems, carriers, information and enhanced-service providers, and customer premises equipment (CPE). T1 consists of members from the telecommunications industry, grouped into four categories: exchange carriers, interexchange carriers, manufacturers, and users and general interests. There's a requirement that membership is balanced among these groups in order to prevent dominance by any one group. Membership allows one vote on every standard developed in Committee T1. The T1 Committee Advisory Group (T1AG) is responsible for managing the T1 standards process, identifying future needs, performing preliminary investigations and ensuring communication and coordination of technical committees and other standards organizations. T1 has six technical subcommittees, and each recommends standards and develops technical reports in its area of expertise. The subcommittees also recommend positions on matters under consideration by other North American and international standards bodies. Committee T1 is the primary developer of United States positions.

T1A1 performance and signal processing

The Performance and Signal Processing Technical Subcommittee Develops and recommends standards and technical reports related to the description of performance and the processing of voice, audio, data, image, and video signals within the U.S. telecommunications networks. The Technical Subcommittee also develops and recommends positions in, and fosters consistency with, standards and related subjects under consideration in other North American and international bodies.

> T1A1.1 Network Performance for Voice and Voiceband Data
> T1A1.2 Survivability Performance
> T1A1.3 Packet Data and ISDN Performance
> T1A1.4 Digital Dedicated and Circuit Switched Performance
> T1A1.5 Audio Visual Communications Coding and Performance

T1A1.6 specialized signal processing

1. T1A1.1, through its Loss Subworking group, has submitted to ANSI a draft standard on a Transmission Plan for Evolving Digital Networks. This plan is important in that it was developed in concert with switch manufacturers and equipment vendors as well as Interexchange Carriers and all RBOCs. This plan greatly enhances new services and products (e.g., BISDN, ATM, etc.) because they'll be supported and facilitated by the same industry participants represented in this standards process. In addition to the Loss Subworking group, the Voiceband Data and Voicegrade Special Services Subworking groups developed a standard to provide transmission performance objectives for voiceband data, switched and special

access. This standard will address many of the questions asked of us by modem users and manufacturers as relating to transmission performance and expectations of our network. The focus of the group is to draft a document that will provide customer satisfaction. One of the many specifics being addressed is modem speed. Until recently, in view of recent modem performance developments, this was unheard of in our network.

2. The T1A1.2 working group provides a Network Survivability Performance technical report. This report is a valuable technical reference for network survivability plans as well.

3. The T1A1.3 working group develops performance values for packet data and ISDN frame relay.

4. The T1A1.4 working group, Digital Dedicated and Circuit Switched Performance, has been actively involved in drafting CCITT recommendations such as those relating to facsimile transmission under certain transmission impairments.

5. The T1A1.5 Audiovisual Communications Coding and Performance working group is involved in the standardization of video teleconferencing and video telephony.

6. T1A1.6, Specialized Signal Processing, is progressing on a draft supplement to ANSI T1.302-1989 on channel-control templates and robbed-bit signaling alarm transmission.

1.2 T1E1 interfaces, power, and protection of networks

The scope of the work undertaken by the Network Interfaces Technical Subcommittee is in a state of change, with the addition of the four environmental groups that were in T1Y1. The new T1E1 scope includes:

- Development of standards and technical reports for the interfaces (and interface functionality) involving access to telecommunications (including data communications and integrated services digital) networks by end users, enhanced-service providers, and carriers.

- Development of proposed United States contributions to the related work of international standards bodies, e.g., CCITT. The work will include the mechanical, electromagnetic, and optical characteristics of the interfaces, and might include aspects of the physical layer transmission and signaling protocols.

- Environmental Standards for Exchange and Interexchange Carrier Networks. This includes but is not limited to specialized environmental subjects such as: protection, power, compatibility and interfaces to telecommunications equipment. Electromagnetic compatibility, operating temperature and humidity, fire resistance, contaminants, grounding, physical parameters, power systems, and related measurement techniques and test methods.

T1E1.1 Analog Access
T1E1.2 Wideband Access

T1E1.3 Connectors and Wiring Arrangements
T1E1.4 DSL Access
T1E1.5 DC Power Systems
T1E1.6 Language for Accessing Power Systems
T1E1.7 Electrical Protection
T1E1.8 Physical Protection
T1E1.9 Wireless Interfaces

T1E1.2 participated in the development of the DS1 Standard and the ISDN Primary Rate Interface Standard. T1E1 is developing a BISDN Carrier Customer interface for OC-3 and OC-12, with options for adding other rates, including OC-1. Upon completion of the BISDN work, focus will move on to the project of writing a SONET-based, non-ISDN standard for the same rates as BISDN.

Current work in the environment groups T1E1.5, 6, 7, and 8 includes environmental aspects of central offices such as electrostatic discharge (ESD), fire resistance, temperature and humidity, and earthquake protection. This group also works on power-related issues such as electromagnetic protection, dc power protection and voltage levels, valve-regulated, sealed, lead-acid batteries, and human-machine language commands for accessing power plants. To give the wireless standards development the attention that it needs, the T1E1.9 Working group was established from work previously done in T1E1.4.

T1M1 internetwork operations, administration, maintenance and provisioning

The Internetwork Operations, Administration, Maintenance and Provisioning Technical Subcommittee develops technical standards and reports for internetwork planning and engineering functions such as traffic routing plans; measurements and forecasts; trunk group planning; circuit and facility ordering; network tones and announcements; location, circuit, equipment identification and other codes; and numbering plans. The Technical Subcommittee also develops technical standards and reports for all aspects of internetwork routine maintenance, fault location and repair; contact points for internetwork operations; and service evaluation. The work of the Technical Subcommittee includes standards and reports regarding test equipment and operations support systems together with the required network access and operator interfaces. Further, the Technical Subcommittee is concerned with administrative support functions such as methods for charging, accounting, and billing data.

T1M1.1 Internetwork Planning and Engineering
• Common Language Data Representation
• Credit Cards
T1M1.2 Internetwork Operations
• ISDN Maintenance
• SS7 Maintenance
• Tones and Announcements

T1M1.3 Analog/Digital Testing
T1M1.5 Network Management

T1P1 System engineering, standards planning, and program management

The Systems Engineering, Standards Planning, and Program Management TSC provides overall planning and program management of projects involving multiple technical subcommittees. Standards, technical reports, and proposed contributions are under development in the following areas:

- Systems engineering functions that might include high-level overviews, architectures, and service descriptions; systems objectives and requirements; reference models and definitions;
- Standards planning functions that might include standards program development; program endorsement and liaison activities;
- Program management functions that might include responsibility for standards development, program monitoring, schedule change impact assessment, and liaison facilitation.

The initial project with T1P1 focuses on personal communications, including Universal Personal Telecommunications and wireless/wireline access aspects.

T1P1.1 Program Management
T1P1.2 Systems Engineering for Personal Communications: Functional and Physical Layer Analysis, Requirements, Modeling and Technology
T1P1.3 Systems Engineering for Personal Communications: Definitions; Service Descriptions; Numbering, Addressing, and Routing; Services and Systems Objectives

T1S1 services, architectures, and signaling

The Technical Subcommittee develops and recommends standards and technical reports related to services, architectures, and signaling. The TSC coordinates and develops standards and technical reports relevant to telecommunications networks in the United States, reviews and prepares contributions on such matters for submission to United States CCITT/CCIR Study Groups or other standards organizations, and reviews for acceptability the positions of other countries in the related standards development and takes or recommends appropriate actions.

T1S1.1 Architecture and Services

- Supplementary and Bearer Service Descriptions
  Intelligent Networks
- ISDN Networking (Switch Computer Application Interface (SCAI))
  T1S1.2 Switching and Signaling (Packet-Mode and Frame Relay)
  Generic Services

- Circuit-Mode
  T1S1.3 Common Channel Signaling
  Non-SDN Services
- Message Transfer Part/Operations and Maintenance Applications Part
- Signaling Connection Control Part
- ISDN-User Part
- Transaction Capabilities Application Part and Application Signaling Network Interconnection
- Services/Network Capabilities
  T1S1.5 B-ISDN
  Asynchronous Transfer Mode (ATM)
- ATM Adaptation Layer
- Interfaces Aspects

1.6 T1X1 digital hierarchy and synchronization

The scope of the work undertaken by the Digital Hierarchy and Synchronization Technical Subcommittee includes the concept, definition, analysis, and documentation of matters pertaining to the interconnection of network transport signals. All theoretical and analytical work necessary to support the documented results is generated or coordinated by the Technical Subcommittee.

The International Telegraph and Telephone Consultative Committee (CCITT)

The International Telegraph and Telephone Consultative Committee (CCITT) is responsible for the international standardization of telecommunications.

SGXI Intelligent network (IN)

CCITT Study Group XI prepares Recommendations on general aspects of intelligent networks and switching technologies. There's a working party on new technologies, especially in the area of intelligent networks recommendations. Other areas covered in this study group include: network routing aspects of UPT, SS7 signaling, ISDN services, and Broadband ISDN (BISDN) protocol requirements. The U.S. position on IN has been to do all the work in a single arena — CCITT. Special adaptations for American standards will be made based on the CCITT Recommendations.

SGXV transmission systems

CCITT Study Group XV prepares detailed equipment recommendations on telephone transmission systems. A working party is preparing SONET equipment recommendations. There's no corresponding American standards organization.

ISDN and digital networks

CCITT Study Group XVIII prepares recommendations on general aspects of ISDN and digital transmission systems. One of the working parties is responsible for

SONET recommendations. SONET has been accepted on a worldwide basis as the next-generation transmission system. This concept has been reinforced through the adoption of SONET as the transmission system for Broadband ISDN. Imbedded in this is the implied commitment that the American standard will conform to the international standard, even if the existing American standard has to be changed due to CCITT activity.

The International Radio Consultative Committee (CCIR)

The International Radio Consultative Committee (CCIR) is responsible for the development of international standards recommendations for radio communications, and for the allocation of radio frequency spectrum on an international basis.

SGXIII Task Group 8/1: Future Public Land Mobile Telecommunication System (FPLMTS)

CCIR Study Group XII prepares recommendations concerning mobile, frequency determination, amateur, and related satellite services. The group has four working parties (8A, 8B, 8C and 8D), and a separate task group known as TG 8/1. This task group is responsible for developing recommendations for a third-generation wireless network, which it has labeled Future Public Land Mobile Telecommunication System (FPLMTS). This system is comparable to the Universal Mobile Telecommunications System (UMTS) being studied in Europe by RACE, COST, and ETSI. It's also very closely related to the development of personal communications services (PCS) in the U.S. The work of TG 8/1 is focused in ten main areas: project management, terminology, services, security, satellite interworking, architectures, network interfaces, radio interfaces, quality of service, network management, and use in developing countries.

X3 information processing

X3 establishes standards for information processing systems. This includes computers and other office equipment, peripheral equipment, programming languages, networking, document interchange, databases, graphics, and a host of related information technology. X3 consists of members from the producer, consumer, and general interest categories from the information processing industry. There's a requirement that membership is balanced among these groups in order to prevent dominance by any one group. Membership allows one vote on every standard developed in the X3 arena. There are three standing committees that report to X3:

- The Standards Planning and Requirements Committee (SPARC),
- The Strategic Planning Committee (SPC), and
- The Secretariat Management Committee (SMC).

X3H2 database

This technical committee is responsible for establishing standards in the area of databases. The committee is currently developing standards for Standard Query

Language (SQL) and Remote Data Access (RDA). It also establishes the U.S. position for work in the international standards arena.

X3H4 Information Resource & Dictionary System (IRDS)

This committee works on the Information Resource Directory System and associated service interfaces. It also defines and represents the U.S. position on IRDS in the international standards arena. Databases that support business systems usually describe objects in the real world (e.g., customers, employees, etc.). For IRDS, the real world consists of information resources (e.g., files, records, elements, programs, disk drives, etc.). An IRDS is used to store and maintain descriptions of those resources.

X3J16 C++

The goal of this committee is to define the standard C++ language. The work of this technical committee will affect the work in the international standard arena.

X3S3 data communications

This technical committee addresses the lower four layers of the OSI model. The lower four layers provide reliable data transfer services. They're working on the data link layer, network layer, physical layer, and transport layer. This committee defines and represents the U.S. position for the international arena.

X3T2 data interchange

This committee addresses the syntax and semantics of exchanging information between different computer systems and even different processes on the same computer. It's also responsible for defining and representing the U.S. position on data interchange to the ISO. At the present time, different computers represent data using different formats and recognize different types. The objective of the X3T2 work is to standardize these formats. It's not enough to provide a communications path between computers—if they speak in different codes, they'll be unable to exchange any real information.

Having data interchange standards is crucial in providing advanced information services. Information gateways, for example, will be taking data from many different information providers and passing it on. The gateway will not work unless the information is in a common representation that's understood by all participants.

X3T3 Open Distributed Processing

This committee is responsible for preparing U.S. contributions toward the development of international standards for Open Distributed Processing. The committee represents the U.S. in ISO/IEC JTC1/SC21/WG7, where a joint ISO/CCITT standard for a Reference Model of Open Distributed Processing (RM-ODP) is being developed. The RM-ODP will provide a conceptual model for reasoning about distributed processing in general, as well as a framework for the development of specific standards for open distributed processing. These standards will promote interoperability between heterogeneous computer systems and network elements.

X3T5 Open Systems Interconnection

This technical committee is responsible for establishing the upper three layers of the Open Systems Interconnection (OSI) reference model. OSI is a seven-layer reference model for communications architecture standards. This reference model involves interactions between adjacent layers in executing their tasks, as well as the protocol actions within each layer for processing the transfer of information. Together, the seven layers of the architecture cooperate to provide an environment that enables heterogeneous end-user systems to communicate fully and meaningfully. OSI will provide benefits throughout data processing, process control, communications, office systems, and all aspects of worldwide distributed information systems.

X3T9.5 Fiber Distributed Data Interface (FDDI)

FDDI is a high-speed, token ring LAN. A subworking group is specifying the transport of FDDI over telephone transmission facilities, specifically SONET.

X3V1 Text: Office and Publishing Systems

This technical committee focuses on the interchange and presentation of text and text-related information. Four areas of work are of major interest right now. The first is the development of two interface standards for voice messaging. One project is concentrating on the human interface to voice messaging services. The second project is working on standards for the interchange of voice messaging between voice messaging systems.

The second major area of work of this technical committee is the area of electronic mail, including multimedia mail. This project has had responsibility for liaison with CCITT and ISO on the Electronic Messaging standard best known by its CCITT name, X.400. The ISO name is Message Oriented Text Interchange Standard (MOTIS).

The third major area of work involves the interchange of documents using the Standard Generalized Markup Language (SGML). Bellcore has adopted the SGML as the preferred way to distribute its documents electronically.

The fourth major area of work is the standard known as Office Document Architecture or Open Document Architecture, depending on whether you read the ISO or CCITT version. This standard defines a single interchange architecture designed to facilitate the interchange of multimedia documents between office systems. It's designed to be used in conjunction with MOTIS to encapsulate multimedia documents and their layout information.

These technical committees support voice messaging, fax store and forward, and information gateway, as well as future products such as multimedia services, electronic messaging and information content management and access.

The International Organization for Standards (ISO)

ISO is the umbrella organization that oversees the international computing standards effort. Membership in ISO is composed of national standards organizations such as the American National Standards Institute (ANSI). The purpose of ISO is to ensure that there's international interchange of goods and services and to encourage the cooperation in economic, intellectual, technological, and scientific endeavors.

International Electrotechnical Committee (IEC)

This committee, founded in 1906, is one of the oldest international standards bodies. It's responsible for international standardization in the electrical and electronics fields. There are currently more than 200 technical committees and subcommittees working within IEC.

ISO/IEC Joint Technical Committee 1 (JTC1)

This committee was established in 1987 to coordinate the efforts of both ISO and IEC. There are 40 nations represented in JTC1. It's responsible for international standardization in the field of information technology. The work is carried on in 17 subcommittees and 80 working groups.

ISO/IEC JTC1/SC18/WG9 User-System Interfaces and Symbols

This committee is responsible for developing international standards for open distributed processing. The committee is working jointly with CCITT on a reference model of open distributed processing (RM-ODP). The RM-ODP will provide a conceptual model for reasoning about distributed processing in general, as well as a framework for the future development of specific standards for open distributed processing.

X12 Electronic Data Interchange (EDI)

X12 has developed a format for the electronic exchange of information via computers. There's a generic format for invoices, shipping notices, payments, purchase orders, etc. Each industry has further developed the specific content needed by them, e.g., telecommunications, transportation, chemical, automotive, aluminum and steel, etc. Doing business using EDI saves a large amount of paper handling, reduces errors caused by humans, and speeds up processes. EDI is currently being used by BRI to place equipment orders with vendors such as AT&T and Northern Telecom.

EIA — Electronic Industry Association: CEBus Consumer Electronics Bus

This group is responsible for the development of standards to facilitate communications between various home automation devices and appliances. The standard defines media specifications, including: power line, twisted pair, coax, fiber, infra-red, and radio frequency. The standard also specifies a common object-oriented language used by devices to communicate over the bus.

FO2 fiber optics

This group is responsible for the development of fiber-optic standards. Involvement has been in the area of methods and procedures for the placement and protection of underground fiber-optic facilities.

IEEE — Institute of Electronic and Electrical Engineers: Power Systems Communications Committee

This group develops standards related to the protection of wireline communication facilities serving electric power stations. This type of circuit often requires special high-voltage protection against the effects of fault-produced ground potential rise or induced voltages, or both. RBOCs use these standards in the design and installa-tion of wireline communication facilities serving electric power stations.

802 Local Area Communications

The responsibility of this group is the development of local area communications standards for the lower two OSI layers, within the scope of data link control, media access control, and physical control. The 802.6 working group is responsible for developing metropolitan area network (MAN) standards for interconnecting differ-ent LANs over a wider area.

1003 Portable Operating System Interface

Software for network and computing applications must be developed for the spe-cific environments in which they'll operate. The components of an environment are referred to collectively as "systems software," and the single most important component of an environment is the operating system. Today, we have a wide variety of proprietary operating systems. Because of the variety of systems, we're limited in how widely we can deploy an application. In some cases, we're forced to develop the same application several times for different environments. The work of this committee also deals with the portability issue. If a POSIX conforming operat-ing system is used, then application software should be portable between hardware environments using a POSIX conforming operating system. The initial work was based on UNIX System V.

1201.1 Application and User Portability

This committee develops standards that support portability for both applications and users. Much of the work concerns user interfaces and windowing systems. A window manager provides an application program with a standard high-level inter-face for the display of both text and graphics on a user's terminal and provides a user with the ability to interact with several applications simultaneously from a single terminal.

The 1201.1 Layered Application Programming Interface (API) group addresses the incompatibility of user interface toolkits. This incompatibility is apparent in the X Windows family of toolkits (e.g., OpenLook and Motif) as well as between X Windows and other user interfaces (e.g., Mac, Presentation Manager, MS Windows).

This work is important in order to simplify and reduce the cost of internal applications in general and is crucial for the information gateway. Standards in this area will allow the gateway customer to use equipment from a variety of vendors and allow information providers to write software to a standard user interface that's an essential element of our open network architecture. Addressing the incompatibility of user interface toolkits is crucial in achieving application portability.

Industry forums

The following forums are of interest to both providers and suppliers. Forums are formed by members of industry to address specific issues, with some results being contributed to a standards body.

ATM Forum The ATM Forum is a recently created industry consortium interested in promoting rapid standardization and implementation of asynchronous transfer mode (ATM) technology for both local premises and wide area applications. The initial objective of the ATM Forum is to define cell-based bidirectional point-to-point permanent virtual connection bearer services for both bursty, variable-bit-rate (VBR) and nonbursty continuous-bit-rate (CBR) traffic classes. The results of the ATM Forum's work in important because it will be a primary factor in defining customer equipment, architecture, and the associated customer base for planned public services based on SONET/ATM and Broadband ISDN (BISDN).

Frame Relay Forum The Frame Relay Forum is an industry consortium interested in promoting rapid standardization and implementation of frame relay technology and services. While the previous work of the Frame Relay Forum has, of course, been focused on development of the user network interface (UNI) for frame relay permanent virtual connections (PVCs), the current work is focused on the development of network-to-network interface (NNI) requirements and protocols. The NNI defines interface standards for interconnection of frame relay network switching nodes.

Government Open Systems Interconnect Profile (GOSIP) GOSIP is the OSI implementation specification for the United States Government. This profile was developed by the Government OSI Users Committee. The committee, started by NIST, was organized to carry out policies within the federal government for implementing OSI. It's increasingly important to meet these specifications, since they now appear in government Request for Proposal (RFPs).

National Institute of Standards Technology (NIST), Implementors Workshops The NIST hosts implementors workshops in several areas (e.g.,

OSI, ISDN). Participation in these workshops will provide a better understanding of how vendors and users plan to implement national and international standards. The value of this participation increases our ability to influence those implementation agreements and provide products and services that meet our customers' needs.

North American ISDN Users Forum (NIU-F)   Various standards bodies have either approved or are in the process of completing standards for ISDN. The objective of these standards is to provide a basis for the development and implementation of compatible ISDN services and equipment. Several options are typically provided within these standards as a result of the compromises made during the standards process and the needs for varying applications. The purpose of the NIU-F is to refine these documents, restricting options, allowing for the unique needs of specific application and equipment requirements.

The actual work of the NIU-F is accomplished in two workshops: the ISDN Users Workshop and the ISDN Implementors Workshop. The IUW produces application requirements that describe potential applications of ISDN and the features that might be required. The IUW develops application profiles, implementation agreements, and the conformance criteria that provide the detailed technical decisions necessary to implement application requirements in an interoperable manner. The activities within the two workshops are coordinated by the NIU-F Steering Committee.

Open Software Foundation (OSF)   The Open Software Foundation is a consortium made up of computer vendors and users. It was started by a group of large corporations such as, IBM, HP, and DEC. Their mission is to develop and evolve an open software environment that guarantees portability, interoperability, and scalability. OSF is committed to implementing existing agreed-to standards; as such, they're a member of the X/Open consortium. They also may provide new technology in advance of the formal standards process, and they will adapt these new technologies to comply with the standards as they're established. Through their innovative request for technology (RFT) approach, OSF is in the process of delivering several potentially important technologies. Additional work is in the areas of the Distributed Communications Environment (DCE), the Distributed Management Environment (DME), the Architecture Neutral Distribution Format (ANDF), and their micro kernel operating system.

Telecommunications Industry Forum (TCIF)   The purpose of the Telecommunications Industry Forum is to enhance the effectiveness associated with the provision, procurement, and use of telecommunications equipment, products, and services through a cooperative effort among purchasers, manufacturers, and suppliers. The group agrees on industry-wide coding and electronic interchange as a basis for recommending standards development. Product identifier codes are currently being developed to standardize product identification. This holds down costs to manufacturers. Currently, manufacturers use different identifiers for various corporations. This also allows a common electronic reference to facilitate EDI. Date-of-manufacture codes were developed to allow ease of warranty registration and claims.

UNIX International (UI)   Unix International is also a consortium of computer vendors and users. It was started by a group of large corporations such as AT&T, Sun, Amdahl, and Unisys. Its mission is to direct the future of Unix System V by defining a roadmap of enhancements needed to ensure that Unix meets the computing requirements of future open systems, while protecting current user application investments. The UI also sees their role as providing a unified voice for the worldwide user community so they might also be involved with the future of Unix. Many see Unix System VR4 as the operating system of choice for the next several years. Other key technologies for UI to bring to market are: ATLAS, their distributed computing framework that will support both of OSF's DCE and DME and distributed transaction processing.

Videotex Industry Association (VIA)   The VIA addresses requirements necessary to expand user access to videotex services by way of gateways. These requirements provide a common approach in a number of areas, including: access; directory structure and contents; user interface activities and functions; connectivity specifications; gateway-to-gateway interconnectivity; user authentication; system messages; billing formats; and notices such as trademarks, copyright, and disclosures.

X/OPEN   X/OPEN Limited was started in 1985 by a group of European vendors. It has continued to grow from that beginning to be an international open systems leader. X/OPEN is currently made up of the world's largest system suppliers, user organizations, system integrators, and software development communities. X/OPEN is not a standards body, rather it's a joint initiative by members of the business community to adopt and adapt existing standards into a consistent environment. Where there's an agreed, official standard, X/OPEN adopts it; where there's no agreed, official standard, X/OPEN adapts *de facto* standards to provide a comprehensive environment. The specification for this environment has been published, and the current issue is called X/OPEN's Portability Guide (XPG), Issue 3. In addition to this specification, X/OPEN has developed a test suite to brand conforming vendor implementations.

Case study three: National ISDN

Perspective from the North American ISDN Users' Forum on Global Standards Alignment

Donald E. Auble
Chairman of the ISDN Implementors' Workshop
North American ISDN Users' Forum

The Integrated Services Digital Network (ISDN) is defined in a group of international standards for a worldwide communications network for the exchange of all information (voice, data, and image) among all users, independent of any manufacturer, service provider, or implementation technology.

ISDN standards are being developed by the International Telephone and Telegraph Consultative Committee (CCITT), and for North America in particular, by the

Exchange Carrier Standards Associations' accredited standards committee, T1, under the umbrella of the American National Standards Institute (ANSI). For a complete discussion of the ISDN standards and technology, as well as the relationship of various key standards implementor organizations, a recommended reference is the *Telecommunications Technology Handbook*, published in 1991 by Artech House, Inc., and authored by Daniel Minoli of Bell Communications Research, Inc. and New York University. The Library of Congress catalog card number is 90-26023.

The result of the ISDN standards process is one extensive standard with a tremendous variety of options and parameters. This is necessary to meet all the possible needs and applications for which the standards could be used. However, to ensure interoperability, interworking, and terminal portability for a timely, cost-effective, marketable offering, a uniform subset of options and parameters must be selected. Also, each application usually requires only a subset of functionality, and in order for products to work together in a multivendor environment, common subsets of options must be selected.

To cope with this proliferation of choices and to provide practical products and services that meet users' needs, the specification process must be extended to include application profiles, implementation agreements, and conformance tests to promote interoperability. In the U.S., these issues are being addressed by Bellcore and their client companies (BCCs), including the Regional Bell Operating Companies, in conjunction with their ISDN switch suppliers and in cooperation with the North American ISDN Users' Forum (NIU-Forum) and the Corporation for Open Systems (COS).

Bellcore and its client companies developed and published a robust set of ISDN implementation agreements in 1988 and 1989; these were identified as technical requirements (TRs). In cooperation with the emerging subset of implementation agreements being developed by the NIU-Forum and through successful negotiations with their predominate switch suppliers, namely, AT&T, Northern Telecom, and Siemens Stromberg-Carlson, Bellcore and the BCCs finalized plans for a deployable 1992 multivendor interoperable ISDN. This plan, known as National ISDN One, was announced by COS at a February, 1991 press conference in New York.

Both the NIU-Forum and COS are essential for completing the full spectrum of post standards work needed to realize the introduction of standardized ISDN products. Standards begin the process and COS contributes the final step of verifying that a particular implementation conforms to the standards-based time-sensitive implementation of ISDN. COS specifically develops the downstream executable tests and tester specifications and offers a COS Mark program for ISDN customer equipment certification.

The NIU-Forum addresses the user need for standards-based, complete applications and contributes publicly developed implementation agreements and conformance test specifications. The NIU-Forum's principle objectives are:

1. To promote an ISDN forum committed to providing users the opportunity to influence developing ISDN technology to reflect their needs.

2. To identify ISDN applications, develop implementation requirements, and facilitate their timely, harmonized, and interoperable introduction.
3. To solicit user, product provider, and service provider participation in this process.

Although the NIU-Forum focuses on the requirements of the ISDN users in North America, participation and membership is open to anyone.

The users and implementors in the NIU-Forum have been working since the first meeting in June, 1988 to realize the user agenda of standardized, interoperable application profiles operational over the ISDN platform. The NIU-Forum has created a user voice in the implementation of ISDN and ISDN applications and has helped to ensure that the emerging ISDN environment meets users' application needs. The NIU-Forum is sponsored by the National Institute of Standards and Technology (NIST). The actual work of the NIU-Forum is accomplished in two workshops: the ISDN Users' Workshop (IUW) and the ISDN Implementors' Workshop (IIW). These workshops, which consist of various working groups and special project teams, meet several times a year and develop various products. The IUW produces application requirements that describe potential applications of ISDN and the features that might be required. The IIW develops application requirements, application analyses, application profiles, implementation agreements, conformance criteria, and an applications software interface.

The following are the key ISDN standards on which the majority of standards and implementation harmonization efforts are taking place. Also included are the related Bell Communications Research, Inc. (Bellcore) and North American ISDN Users' Forum (NIU-Forum) implementation agreements that are aligned and form the 1992 multiswitch vendor ISDN implementation known to the industry as national ISDN.

Physical Layer 1 — Basic Rate
- CCITT I.420,I.430 (four wire)
- ANSI T1.601 (two-wire U.S. "Uninterface")
- ANSI T1.605-1989 (U.S. S/T)
- Bellcore TR-TSY-000397
- NIU-101 (two-wire "U"), NIU-105 (four-wire S/T)

Physical Layer 1 — Primary Rate
- CCITT I.421,I.431
- ANSI T1.403 (U.S. "U-interface") and T1.408 ("U", S/T)
- Bellcore TR-TSY-000754
- NIU-103 and NIU-103R1

Link Layer 2 — "D" Channel, Basic and Primary Rate
- CCITT Q.920 (I.440) and Q.921 (I.441)
- ANSI T1.602-1989 (U.S.)
- Bellcore TR-TSY-000793
- NIU-210

Network Layer 3 — "D" Channel, Basic and Primary Rate
- CCITT Q.930 (I.450), Q.931 (I.451), Q.932 (I.452)
- ANSI T1.607-1989 (U.S.) (basic call control procedures)
- ANSI T1.608-1989 (U.S.) (packet mode bearer services control)
- ANSI T1.610-1990 (U.S.) (supplementary services control)
- Bellcore TR-TSY-000268
- NIU-301 (BRI/Class 1), NIU-302 (PRI/Class II)

Rate Adaption
- CCITT V.110 (Red Book), V.120 (Blue Book)
- ANSI T1.612 (U.S.)
- NIU-91-0001

The NIU-Forum's ISDN conformance test group has coordinated with NIST and ANSI to contribute its conformance test specifications as U.S. positions into CCITT's test specification developments. Considerable international ISDN test standards harmonization has begun as a result of these efforts. Progress to date has been at the layer two Link Access Procedures. Layer one harmonization is addressed. Harmonization at this level of downstream implementation detail have made great strides towards a truly international, interoperable and conformant ISDN.

The process of setting ISDN standards and then getting from there to a readily available, interoperable ISDN commercial introduction is a complex trip indeed. It's worth the trip and worth completing the job so that the end users of ISDN can reap the full benefits of the standards promise. Unchartered cooperation among standards and standards promotion bodies are necessary to achieve the promise of ISDN. That cooperation is happening in the industry today.

U.S. ISDN standards interoperability

In an effort to achieve standard, compatible interfaces, RBOCs and Bellcore have been working with switch vendors to achieve an initial platform for standardization and multivendor interworking, to achieve transition from vendor-specific interfaces. Since 1988, Bellcore has issued technical references (TRs) known as Phase 1.1 and 1.2, which are designed to:

- Standardize the network-to-user interface.
- Standardize the network interoffice interface.
- Provide for ISDN CPE portability.
- Provide supplementary services uniformity.
- Provide a standard billing format.
- Provide ISDN packet interworking.
- Provide for uniform operations.

In 1990, the standard 2B1Q line code became available as well as ISDN/CCS (#7) internetworking and switched 56 Kbps interfaces. In addition, ISDN provides links for services such as electronic key for Centrex, along with data and voice channels for voice messaging units and automatic call distributors (ACD). Vendor proprietary ISDN interface differences were resolved with a National ISDN-1 (NI-1) to achieve multivendor internetworking compatibility. Here, AT&T-NTI-Siemens agreed to provide interoperability in their 1992 switch generics (5E8, BCS-34, APS10), with subsequent additional capabilities in 1993–1994 for N12, N13, etc.

The baseline capabilities for NI-1 include:

- A standard network interoffice interface that supports interswitch and internetwork connectivity via SS-7 for circuit mode connections based on TR-444.
- A standard network-CPE interface that provides for CPE to work on any network switch and access the services provided by that switch, thus obtaining protocol portability.
- The ability for the ISDN terminal to access all analog POTS and Centrex features.
- A minimum set of basic rate services and features for circuit mode and packet mode are provided using the standard protocols and which internetwork with prestandard services.
- A primary rate interface and a set of required services and features that can be provided in a vendor-specific manner initially using proprietary protocols until Bellcore TRs are finalized by the mid '90s.

Case study four: Global ISDN

Terry Kero

The concept of a global integrated services digital network (ISDN) extends the complex end-to-end interworking of ISDN terminals from a multivendor, multicarrier domestic environment to a multinational environment. In this new environment, standards and the ability to operate at user-to-network and network-to-network interfaces are crucial.

Although ISDN was designed initially to be an international standard, it has evolved differently in the United States, in Europe, and in the Pacific Rim. As an international carrier, US Sprint is examining these differences to determine how to interconnect U.S. and foreign networks for ISDN trials, and, ultimately, for service. That examination extends to the role of the synchronous optical network (Sonet) optical transmission standard and the impact of broadband ISDN (B-ISDN) on current narrowband ISDN (N-ISDN) technology.

Two significant changes are occurring in the standards arena. First, a movement is under way to make the standards creation process more responsive. Second, globalization is beginning to take precedence over nationalization. The latter movement began with the formation of the European Economic Community and the worldwide opening of telecommunications markets to foreign suppliers. With the 1988 formation of the European Telecommunications Standards Institute (ETSI), and its subsequent NET standards, Europe set the example for the kind of conference test standards that are crucial to the realization of global ISDN.

Since then, the movement has spread beyond Europe. The Interregional Telecomm Standards Conference, also known as the Standards Summit, was held at Fredericksburg, Va., in February 1990 and drew all the major standards bodies from the U.S., Europe, Japan, Taiwan, and Korea, as well as the CCITT and CCIR international standards organizations.

The Fredericksburg Plan was drafted to support the Spirit of Melbourne directive drafted at the last CCITT Plenary in Australia. This plan expedites and restructures worldwide standards activity. It concludes that market-driven standards with specific requirements are needed quickly.

For global ISDN to become a reality, the U.S. and foreign networks that interconnect must both be integrated digital networks (IDNs), with both digital switching and clear-channel digital transmission facilities. US Sprint operates such a network and supports clear-channel transmission via B8ZS (binary 8 zero substitution) at the T-1 level.

Under current standards, there are two common anchor points for ISDN worldwide. (See FIG. 7-2.) The lower anchor point is at the ISDN basic rate interface (2B + D), with the U.S., Japan, and Europe committed to the I.430 standard with a full-duplex 192 Kbps digital rate. The upper anchor point is at the Sonet OC-3 network-node interface operating at 155.520 Mbps.

Between these two anchor points the hierarchies deviate. (See TABLE 7-2.) Direct internetworking between the U.S. T-1 and European E-1 interfaces for primary rate requires conversion between the bit rates, compounding laws, and channel structures. Voice compounding follows separate logarithmic laws in Europe (A-law) and the U.S. (mu 255). The channel structure is 30B + D in Europe, with line rates of 2.048 Mbps, and 23B + D in the U.S. with line rates of 1.544 Mbps.

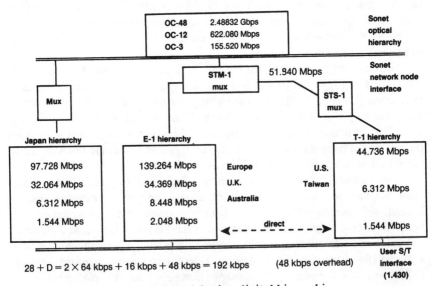

Fig. 7-2. U.S. and foreign digital hierarchies.

Table 7 – 2. Physical Interface Standards

BRI Interface (2B + D)	Europe	United States
Line coding	4B35	2B1Q
User S/T interface		
Rate	192 kb/s	192 kbps
Standard	1.430	1.430
PRI Interface	E-1	T-1
Line coding	HDB3	B8ZS
Rate	2.048 Mb/s	1.544 Mbps
Format	30B + D	23B + D
Framing/CRC	TimeSlot 1	EST-8 kbps
Standard	1.431	1.431

Conversion from the U.S. T-1 rate to the European E-1 rate can be accomplished in dedicated transcoders, T-1 network multiplexers, digital circuit multiplexing equipment (DCME) or digital cross-connect (DCS) equipment. DCS is the preferred implementation at the gateway for US Sprint ISDN links. DCME is good for voice compression and lower-speed analog data on non-ISDN digital links. However, it would require separation of voice and high-speed digital data trunks.

The degree to which European PTTs have converted their analog networks to IDNs varies greatly, and this could cloud the ubiquity of global ISDN access in Europe. France Telecom, for example, has a very high penetration of digital switching, whereas the Deutsche Bundespost still has a large amount of analog switching.

Last-mile access problems for two-wire basic rate interface (BRI) transport are less prevalent in Europe than in the U.S., however. The European loop plant consists of much shorter loops with fewer bridge taps. Load coils are rarely employed.

In the U.S., there's concern over that last-mile connection. This is not a direct problem for interexchange carriers (IXCs), since their ISDN service is derived from four-wire primary rate interface (PRI) or four-wire trunks from local exchange carriers (LECs). However, global ISDN access to U.S. residential and small business customers via LEC's local loop plant might encounter longer loops, more severe bridge taps, and load coils in less urban environments.

A high percentage of the long-haul interexchange plant in both the U.S. and Europe is digital, but coaxial cable is employed to a higher degree in Europe than it is in the U.S. While the long-term interconnection standard in Europe is Sonet OC-3 and above, substantial pre-Sonet fiber and coaxial digital systems have been deployed. This could slow the widespread deployment of B-ISDN based on Sonet.

Signaling

Given the IDN, global ISDN requires that the proper out-of-band signaling be established through the user D channels and transported or mapped correctly across the appropriate out-of-band common channel signaling networks. The importance of common channel signaling to ISDN networking can't be overemphasized.

Three types of out-of-band signaling must be considered for success of global ISDN, particularly in the context of global virtual private networks (VPNs) with PBX interworking through PRI access facilities. First, there must be user-network signaling, following the Q.931 and Q.932 standards for both BRI and PRI. Second, there must be network signaling via signaling system 7 (SS7) deployment. Finally, there must be user-to-user signaling based on the user-to-user information (UUI) standard.

The Q.931 standard for user-to-network signaling on the D channel for basic call setup and tear down is rapidly reaching stabilization in both Europe and the U.S. The Q.932 signaling extensions to Q.931 for supplementary services involved third- party control and standardization of the user interface for keypad or functional key control of services. The interworking between the supplementary services adds to a situation that's already complex. The Q.932 recommendations and implementation standards are far from mature in both Europe and the U.S., although Europe leads the U.S. in this regard. If ETSI can make Q.932 a reality in 1992 within the European Community, this should push the U.S. to accelerate its Q.932 efforts.

The wide disparity among customer-premises equipment (CPE) vendors in the implementation of Q.931/Q.932 standards led US Sprint to create a multivendor ISDN laboratory complete with both network equipment and CPE. End-to-end testing has demonstrated key differences in vendor implementation of Q.931. Similar Q.932 testing and evaluation is planned.

Network signaling

The signaling standards for support of ISDN between switches within a network and between networks is ANSI SS7 in the U.S. and CCITT #7 (SS#7) in Europe. Though similar, there are key differences between U.S. and European network signaling. (See TABLE 7-3.)

The major signaling standard difference between the U.S. and Europe is in the call signaling application part. The European SS#7 most commonly uses the older telephony user part (TUP), which is quite limited compared to the later ISDN user part (ISUP). ISUP is supported in Germany and the Netherlands. TUP is maintained in the United Kingdom and France. France and the U.K. might skip ISUP and go to the more recent open systems interconnection-based ISUP.

The operations, administration, maintenance and provisioning part of SS7 and SS#7 is far from being stabilized as a standard. Also, network management standards for ISDN are quite immature, and major issues such as the choice of either Q.940 or the OSI/Network Management Forum standard as the key recommendation have yet to be resolved. UUI can be passed via the D channel and SS7/SS#7 from user terminal to user terminal or from channel and SS7/SS#7 from user terminal to user terminal or from PBX to PBX through the global ISDN network. UUI can be passed within Q.931 messages in three ways: during call setup or

Table 7 – 3. Differences in Network Signalling

	European CCITT SS#7	U.S. ANSI SS7
Routing label/point codes	32 bits/14 bits	56 bits/24 bits
Message length	60 octets	256 octets
Signaling user part	TUP (TUP+)	ISUP
TCAP – 800 + credit card	no	yes
Signaling links	4.8 – 64 kbps	56/64 kbps
Relevant standards	Q.701 – Q.713	ANSI T1.111.3 – 112.3

tear-down, during a call, or on a noncall associated basis. This is useful for support of PBX-to-PBX networking.

In addition, Q.932 messages such as FACility and REGister can convey status and other relevant information between PBXs without necessarily requiring use of any B channel connections. Both UUI and Q.932 messages, properly mapped into and transported across SS7/SS#7 networks, are useful in PBX networking. Such ISDN capabilities make special links or protocols between distributed PBXs unnecessary for feature transparency. The lack of progress in standards for private networks and supplementary service protocols will continue to hamper the interworking between PBX vendors for anything but the most basic bearer services. ETSI in particular moved to address this issue, with resolution ostensibly in 1992.

Service

There are three categories of CCITT ISDN services: bearer services, supplementary services, and teleservices. Within the bearer service category, there are two additional types of services: circuit-mode voice and data, and packet-mode data, which includes frame relay. Circuit-mode voice includes voice and voiceband data (3.1 kHz). The support of 7-kHz audio has recently been included, since ADPCM technology can provide this within a 64 Kbps channel. For circuit-mode digital data service, rate adaption between data terminal equipment is a key issue, since not all of that equipment operates synchronously at 64 Kbps. While several proprietary rate adaption schemes exist (DMI mode 2, T-link), the U.S. is moving toward the V.120 standard, while Europe supports the V.110 standard. There's a movement in Europe toward V.120, but V.110 might be retained where minimum transit delay is required. In packet-mode via ISDN, considerable effort has been directed at a frame-relaying bearer service standard. Wide area networking is one major application for a high-speed (up to 1.544 Mbps) frame-relaying service across PRIs. US Sprint supports dedicated and dial-up access to its SprintNet packet data network and is committed to frame relaying.

Supplementary services depend on bearer services and often provide the platform for specific teleservices or applications. The complexity of these services and feature interworking between services poses difficult standardization problems

Table 7 – 4. Initial Supplementary Services

Number identification	Community of interest
Direct dialing in	Closed user group
Multiple subscriber number	Private number plan
Calling line identification	**Call Completion**
Connected line identification	Call waiting
Multiparty	Call hold
Conference calling	Call completion to busy subscriber
Consultation hold	**Charging**
Call Offering	Credit card calling
Call transfer	Advice of charge/reverse charge
Call forwarding	
Call deflection	
Line hunting	

in a multivendor, multinational environment. Considerable engineering design and cooperation among all participants will be needed. TABLE 7-4 shows a summary of the initial supplementary services being addressed by CCITT and ANSI T-1 committees.

In European and CCITT terminology, teleservices represent specific applications riding on the lower-level supplementary and bearer services. The six teleservices identified in standard I.240 are telephony, teletex, telefax4, mixed mode, videotex and telex.

In the U.S., the concept of teleservices has not been officially adopted. Telephony in Europe is a teleservice; in the U.S. it's simply voice service. In the U.S. the emphasis is on supporting advanced 800 services, virtual private networking, and digital Centrex-oriented services riding on the ISDN bearer and supplementary services.

In the U.S. and Europe, the major applications of interest that can be transported by the basic bearer and supplementary services are high-speed file transfer, Group IV facsimile, desktop video, image transfer, and video-teleconferencing. This interest is stimulated by the proliferation of low-cost personal computers, improvement in video compression technology, cost, and the development of imaging equipment including PC image cards. In Europe and the U.S., the most popular initial use for ISDN seems to be for simply hooking up PBXs to public networks to provide inter-PBX signaling.

France Telecom's experience with Minitel videotex terminals might lead to a major residential service begging for ISDN. Europeans feel that imaging might be the "killer application," particularly if it can be provided cheaply in the ubiquitous PC, which is considered the "killer platform."

Networking concepts

A global ISDN for an IXC such as US Sprint must support private networks, public networks, and interworking between public and private networks. While large, multinational companies are obvious candidates for global ISDN, smaller companies and residential users must also be supported.

US Sprint is examining three different ISDN configurations. A dedicated ISDN connects two or more PBXs in a multinational company private network with back-to-back, clear-channel PRI links via international digital private lines. There are three configurations for ISDN access for global VPNs. (See FIG. 7-3.) The objective is to offer VPN features developed for the U.S. market internationally.

Finally, there's a global public ISDN configuration that would support European public BRI users interworking with direct US Sprint terminations for inbound 800 services. European public ISDN subscribers and U.S. public ISDN subscribers also would be able to call one another with US Sprint and the European PTT interworking via SS7 to SS#7 and US Sprint interworking with the LEC networks via SS7. This is the stage at which ISDN is not just global but also ubiquitous.

In FIG. 7-3, packet data is supported by the SprintNet packet data network through ISDN access. In Europe, the PTT exchange must be provided with packet access. The gateway to other packet data networks is X.75.

With the advent of the Sonet optical standard for interconnecting international networks through a standard fiber interface comes the prospect of networks and services operating at bandwidths in excess of N-ISDN. In addition, the CCITT and ANSI T-1 committees are aggressively pursuing fast packet switching technology for voice, data, and images using statistical asynchronous transfer mode (ATM) switch fabrics.

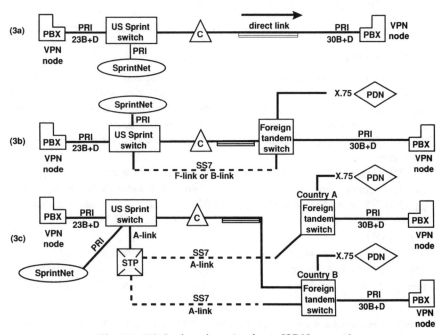

Fig. 7-3. US Sprint virtual private ISDN networks.

Frame-relaying through ISDN is the first major step beyond X.25 in the projected evolution of packet-mode ISDN services (X.31). The long-term objective is creation of fast packet ATM-switched B-ISDN. Clearly, ATM-type switching networks conflict with the traditional synchronized digital switch networks in basic concept. However, both ATM and current ISDN channels can be mapped within the Sonet payload, which readily supports both narrowband and B-ISDN. With the migration to ATM fast packet switching, the crucial area that will require considerable engineering design and cooperation is the interworking between the present signaling and switching networks and B-ISDN-type ATM networks. Undoubtedly, economics and technology will control the rate of Sonet, ATM, and B-ISDN introduction. Both N-ISDN and B-ISDN will coexist for a long time. Initial B-ISDN and ATM networks will provide high-bandwidth services as an overlay network with voice and lower bandwidth data services remaining on N-ISDN.

Industry experts suggest that switch architectures will evolve with a single common control complex and different switch fabrics with associated controllers. This switch architecture would allow for the coexistence of ATM, time division multiplex, and DCS switches.

Before services such as B-ISDN evolve, widespread deployment of global ISDN will have to become a reality. A primary criteria for that evolution is for multivendor ISDN equipment to internetwork across multiple ISDN networks in a multinational environment. One final criteria has little to do with technology: Carriers must see significant demand for data, image, and video services.[1]

Case study five: Networking LANs

LAN interconnect and extension: The untapped market for ISDN

Robert W. Warrick

FIGURE 7-5 depicts an architecture for remote LAN extension using ISDN circuit-switched services. In this figure, PCs in remote locations are equipped with ISDN Basic Rate Interface (internal or external ISDN adapters). The remote user connects to the LAN-based enterprise network as if directly attached to the LAN. The remote user has access to all the enterprise information and resources, as if locally connected.

LAN extension dial-up router products exist that will work with ISDN circuit switched networks and support multiple LAN enterprise network protocols, including IPX/SPX (e.g., Novell NetWare), TCP/IP (e.g., FIP), AppleTalk (e.g., Apple-Share), SPP/IPC (e.g., Banyan Vines), NETBEUI (e.g., LAN Manager), and OSI (e.g., 3COM).

LAN extension over slow serial dial-up connections has been made feasible and more attractive due to advances and standardization in protocol header compression technologies. For example, a standard exists (known as RFC 1144), which

---

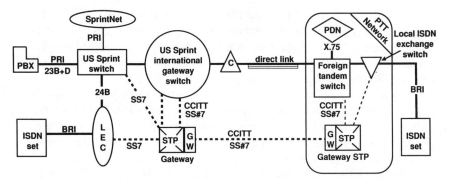

Fig. 7-4. US Sprint global public ISDN network.

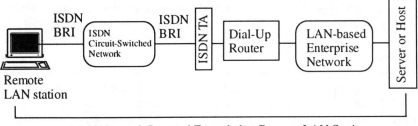

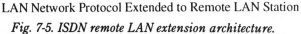

LAN Network Protocol Extended to Remote LAN Station

Fig. 7-5. ISDN remote LAN extension architecture.

compresses TCP/IP headers. Typically, this standard enables the overhead of a TCP/IP header to be reduced from 48 octets to 12 octets. The result is faster response time over the serial connection.

Examples of remote LAN extension products that can be used with ISDN circuit-switched networks include the Telebit NetBlazer and the ICC Remote LAN Node product, Hayes ISDN adapters for PCs, Macintosh and NeXT machines, the IBM ISDN Interface Coprocessor/2 for OS/2, Apple Computer ISDN NB Card for MAC's, Combinet LAN-ISDN products, and OSTs LAN Expand product line. In addition, more than a dozen vendors provide ISDN terminal adapters for PCs, Macintoshes, and minicomputers.

ISDN LAN extension

When appropriately priced and deployed by telcos and interexchange carriers, ISDN can be an attractive alternative to modems or dedicated private lines. When compared with dial-up modem connections, circuit-switched ISDN basic rate service offers better performance and full user-transparent access to corporate network resources.

Performance   Modems using the analog telephone switched network operate at speeds of 2.4 Kbps – 14.4 Kbps. LANs operate at speeds of 4 Mbps (Token

Ring), 10 Mbps (Ethernet), 16 Mbps (Token Ring), and 100 Mbps (FDDI). Even when used with compression modems and software protocol compression schemes, dial-up remote LAN access performance is bottlenecked by these comparatively low transmission speeds. With modems, much productive time is wasted waiting for information to be transferred.

In contrast, use of the two 64-Kbps channels that ISDN basic rate provides yields a combined bandwidth for LAN-access data applications of 128 Kbps. Although ISDN Basic Rate bandwidth doesn't approach LAN speeds, it represents a significant performance and productivity increase beyond what most remote modem users are familiar with.

Since the remote extended LAN user is limited by the speed of ISDN, remote users will use the ISDN LAN access to access data, but not to load applications across the network. To save time, users typically have the application software they need preloaded on their PC or laptop, and they use the remote extended LAN capability of their machine to access only the required information (not programs) at the main office location. In this way, the remote users avoid the time-consuming process of loading application programs from a LAN-resident server across the ISDN network.

User transparency and full access to enterprise network resources Traditionally, remote access to computing resources meant using a PC terminal emulation or communication package and communicating with hosts on a character basis using modems. In these scenarios, the PC connects to a port on a host and only has access to that host's resources. The PC doesn't have access to all resources on the network. Furthermore, if information transfer is required between the two machines, communications software that uses the same file transfer protocol would need to be available on both machines.

With remote LAN extension, the user interface doesn't change, and the user can readily use the LAN remotely without retraining. The user doesn't need to learn another communication package or another set of procedures for transferring information. Off-the-shelf work group and other LAN-based software can be used in remote ISDN circuit-switched LAN extension environments without modification.

Low-cost bandwidth on demand Circuit-switched ISDN used in a remote LAN extension environment is well-suited to meet the need for low-cost on-demand, periodic, but nondedicated access to LAN-based information or resources. For example, mobile employees (e.g., those on business trips) can have low-cost remote bandwidth-on-demand access to their corporate home-office information resources.

ISDN LAN extension markets

Remote LAN extension using ISDN could provide a competitive edge to businesses that have mobile workers or sites with single, isolated users needing access to corporate LAN resources and information. Likely markets include:

- Business travelers.
- Laptop PC owners.

- Hotel rooms.
- Conference centers.
- Field support personnel.
- Small branch business or sales offices.
- Construction sites.
- Telecommuters.

LAN Interconnect using ISDN (dial-up bridge/routers): ISDN positioning with other LAN interconnect technologies

Circuit-switched ISDN versus private line   In comparison with private-line, circuit-switched ISDN provides bandwidth on demand and usage-based costs rather than fixed costs. When used with LAN interconnect applications, ISDN Basic Rate provides an aggregate data rate of 128 Kbps, as opposed to the traditional 56 Kbps private line bandwidth.

Circuit-switched ISDN versus frame relay service   ISDN Basic Rate supports an aggregate LAN-interconnect-usable switched bandwidth of 128 Kbps that can be used together for circuit-switched data transfer. In North America and Japan, ISDN Primary Rate provides up to 1.536 Mbps switched bandwidth.

In North America, frame relay ranges from 56 Kbps to 1.536 Mbps using multiple PVCs (permanent virtual circuits). PVCs are analogous to leased lines. Frame relay can also be provided with SVCs (switched virtual circuits), however, at this writing, no one is providing frame relay SVC service.

Circuit-switched ISDN versus SMDS   Circuit-switched ISDN and SMDS have the following characteristics in common:

- Bandwidth-on-demand.
- Nondedicated switched connectivity between locations.
- Can be used for LAN interconnect.
- Supported by today's router products.

From a LAN interconnect perspective, the primary difference between circuit-switched ISDN and SMDS is the amount of bandwidth they switch. ISDN basic rate is two 64 Kbps (or 128 Kbps) channels. ISDN primary rate can switch up to 1.536 Mbps. In contrast, SMDS can switch between 1.17 Mbps to 34 Mbps. When competitively priced, relative to performance provided, circuit-switched ISDN should obtain a large share of the lucrative LAN interconnect market.

ISDN LAN interconnect architecture

Figure 7-6 depicts an ISDN and router-based LAN interconnect architecture. In this architecture, the dial-up router establishes ISDN circuit-switched connections (calls) based on the traffic demand. When the router receives a bridged or routed packet that's destined for the remote ISDN site, the router dials the ISDN phone number of the remote site. When the ISDN circuit-switched connection is established, any router-supported packet types can flow between the routers. Packet

Step 1: Packet with Enterprise Network
Address arrives at ISDN Bridge/Router

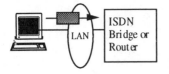

Step 2: ISDN Bridge/Router uses ISDN D-channel
to establish B-channel connection to remote site

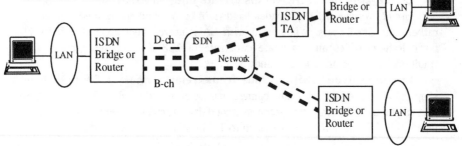

Step 3: Packet is sent to destination Bridge/Router

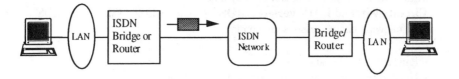

Step 4: When traffic idle, ISDN connection is released.

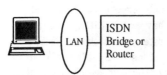

Fig. 7-6. ISDN LAN interconnect architecture.

type protocols typically supported by some router manufacturers over ISDN dial-up connections include TCP/IP, Novell IPX, AppleTalk, Banyan VINES, DECnet, OSI, IEEE 802.1d spanning tree algorithms and support for bridging nonroutable DEC protocols. When the router receives no packets for a configurable amount of time, the router disconnects the ISDN connection.

Some router manufacturers currently provide native (built-in) ISDN Basic Rate hardware and plan to have native ISDN Primary Rate hardware by 1993. LAN interconnect using both ISDN Basic Rate and ISDN Primary Rate was demonstrated at TRIP[2] '92. The introduction of router-native ISDN Primary Rate will allow up to 23 concurrent, on-demand circuit-switched connections to be established to up to 23 different locations using a single ISDN serial port on the router. This would be analogous to a Fractional or Nx 64 Kbps Frame Relay SVC (switched virtual circuit) support, if it existed. However, at this writing, no such Frame Relay SVC service currently exists.

As we've seen, router-native ISDN support increases the router's control over ISDN call establishment algorithms. However, LAN interconnection using ISDN can also be accomplished by bridge/routers that don't have native ISDN support. Bridge/router products exist today that support dial-up, on-demand connections between bridge/routers.

To establish the ISDN circuit-switched connection in these products, the router communicates with a DCE device, such as an ISDN TA (terminal adapter). This is depicted in FIG. 7-7. The protocol between the router and the ISDN TA typically conforms to the CCITT V.25bis Recommendation. V.25bis specifies dialing and call management procedures between DTE (e.g., routers) and DCE devices (dial and answer modems or ISDN TAs). In addition, some ISDN TA products also provide for the attachment of a standard analog RJ11 telephone equipment, so the ISDN connection can be used for both LAN interconnection and voice, fax, modem or answering machine, etc.

A variation of the above architecture is to attach an ISDN inverse/reverse multiplexer device to the router. As shown in FIG. 7-8, the ISDN inverse/reverse multiplexer connects to multiple ISDN lines. The dial-up router uses a single interface to the inverse/reverse multiplexer. The dial-up router dynamically manages the ISDN connection establishment to the remote router. In some products, the router can request the ISDN inverse/reverse multiplexer to supply enough connections for the specific amount of bandwidth needed.

Products that currently support all or a subset of these architectures include the Cisco Software Release 9.0 for the AGS+, the Cisco 3000 router, the DigiBoard IMAC Ethernet/ISDN LAN bridge products, the Gandalf Premier LAN-Line 5500 product line, and the Telebit NetBlazer product line. Some early '90s products provide ISDN Basic Rate LAN interconnect service for around $2,000 per site, plus the cost of an ISDN Basic Rate line.

ISDN LAN interconnect customer benefits

Usage-based costs rather than high monthly leased line charges
The customer only pays for the time that the wide-area-network link is actually

---

[2]TRIP '92: Transcontinental ISDN Project 1992, November 16–18, 1992. TRIP '92 was a three-pronged showcase of ISDN in the United States, Canada, Europe, and Asia consisting of user open houses, the opening of the National ISDN-1 Network in the United States and Canada, and a kick-off event. The initial National ISDN-1 network consisted of 22 interconnected switches. The open houses showcased 185 applications. 74 companies sponsored open houses at 150 locations. Nearly 70 ISDN CPE products that are presently available were demonstrated. At Telecom '91, more than 170 companies were identified as having ISDN products.

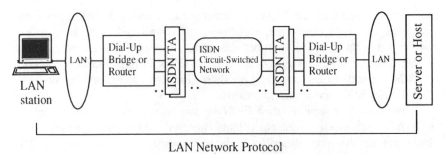

LAN Network Protocol

Fig. 7-7. ISDN LAN interconnect architecture using ISDN TAs.

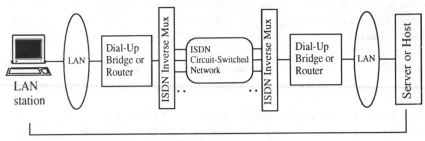

LAN Network Protocol

Fig. 7-8. ISDN LAN interconnect architecture using ISDN inverse/reverse multiplexers.

used. In comparison, some customer applications aren't a good match for use with other LAN interconnect services such as private line, Frame Relay, or X.25. If the transmission technology employed is not a·good match for the application, the customer might pay more than is necessary, relative to the amount of use of the service. For example, some customer locations have a limited, but periodic, need to communicate or share information. In such situations, the volume of traffic can't be sustained enough to warrant the cost of expensive leased line and other WAN link alternatives. In Japan, for example, NTT's INS-Net 64 ISDN service is more cost-effective than a monthly fee for a digital leased circuit for eight hours or less of use per day.

User transparency All users on the LAN can use the ISDN access to the remote sites without any change to the user interface. The user has no knowledge or involvement in the remote connection. The connection is completely transparent to the user. Once communication is established with the remote site, the user has access to all enterprise LAN-based resources and up-to-date information.

This is in contrast to traditional modem-oriented software that requires user involvement in protocol selection, etc. (e.g., XMODEM file transfer software). This is also in contrast to the nontransparent user-involvement with communication software designed to take over a remote PC and send keystrokes and screens over the communications link.

Fault-tolerance for dedicated leased lines or other WAN links   When used with other types of WAN links (e.g., private line or Frame Relay), the routers can be preconfigured to make backup ISDN circuit-switched calls to a remote site in the event of a failed primary WAN link to that site. The routers are also smart enough to monitor the failed primary WAN link. When reliable operation on the primary WAN link resumes, the router automatically disconnects the backup circuit-switched connection, and service is restored on the primary link.

Multiuser shared use of the ISDN connection(s)   Since all users in each location are on a LAN that can communicate with an ISDN-attached router, all users can share the ISDN connection to the remote site. There's no need for each user to have a direct ISDN or dial-up modem connection from their PC or workstation. With ISDN LAN interconnect, customer costs are lower, since multiple users share the ISDN connection(s).

Granted, the first user to communicate with the ISDN-connected remote site will experience delay due to the initial connection establishment procedures. However, if traffic activity to this location is maintained for a length of time, subsequent users sending traffic to this same destination will not experience this overhead delay, since the ISDN connection will be maintained within a user-defined period of time.

Dynamic bandwidth allocation   Traffic loads vary throughout the day and peak at different times. Dial-up router technology employs algorithms to dynamically establish (and disconnect) ISDN connections (B-channels) on an as-needed basis.

Faster response time   ISDN establishes circuits faster than dial-up modems. ISDN calls can be established within a few seconds. ISDN digital technology provides higher reliability than analog lines. Unreliable lines result in data protocol retransmission to correct errors, and retransmission takes time, causing users to wait.

Furthermore, bridge/router products exist that will support the combined bandwidth of both 64 Kbps ISDN B-channels between routers using the ISDN Basic Rate Interface, which yields an effective data path of 128 Kbps (thousand bits per second). When compared with today's use of 4800 bits-per-second (bps) or 9600 bps modems and analog phone lines, the performance advantage of ISDN is clear.

For example, some LAN interconnect ISDN products are known to transfer a 30 KB (kilobyte) file up to six times faster than remote LAN software with a V.32 modem and up to three times faster than conventional remote dial-up software using V.32bis with V.42bis compression. With some ISDN LAN interconnect products, the time required to start a 100 KB network server-resident application or to transfer a 100 KB file is 13 seconds, as compared to more than 90 seconds using remote LAN software with V.32bis and V.42bis compression. These factors' combined result is faster response time for the LAN user of ISDN services than the user of traditional dial-up analog technologies.

ISDN LAN interconnect markets

Within the universe of LAN interconnect technologies, ISDN enables on-demand LAN interconnect solutions to the following types of customer needs:

- Small office networks of users that need only an occasional access to other networks. These users are characterized by the need for either relatively infrequent, but periodic, access to remote information resources, or frequent access but low-volume data transfer (e.g., sending reports to other locations).
- Due to these factors, small offices can't justify the cost of dedicated lines, Frame Relay, SMDS, or other LAN interconnection between locations. The amount of information and resource sharing required between some locations simply can't justify the use of these higher-cost networks. Yet, when these locations need to communicate, the speed of dial-up analog lines is too slow for some users and applications.
- Examples of these types of network users include field support offices (access to problem resolution database and customer records), retail stores (inventory control and credit verification applications), insurance agency branch offices, small sales offices (point of sale applications), and bank branch offices (automatic teller machines, printers, and administrative network applications).
- Customers desiring backup in case of failure of leased lines or other LAN interconnect services.

Challenges to telcos and interexchange carriers

ISDN-ready LAN interconnect products are available today for immediate productivity gains wherever ISDN exists. The LAN interconnect market is clearly where growth in the telecommunications industry is occurring. The ISDN ball is clearly in the telco and interexchange carrier court. The telecommunications service providers need to step up to the challenge and attractively price, sell, invest, deploy, and support ISDN services needed by these market segments.

ISDN market demand and deployment relationship

Surveys of the mass market for ISDN have found that nearly half of residential and small business customers express a high or moderate likelihood of subscribing to ISDN. Seventy percent of small businesses with 4 to 20 lines gave a moderate to high rating of their likelihood to subscribe to ISDN. These survey results are in spite of the relatively low deployment of ISDN.

Ubiquity To enable remote LAN extension and LAN interconnect markets to blossom, ISDN needs to be ubiquitously deployed. As deployment increases, demand will accelerate and the value of ISDN will increase because connectivity with more people and LAN-resident information resources will be possible.

Consider the increase in demand we've seen for lines used for fax. If no one else has a fax machine, then I don't need one. If everyone has a fax machine, then I need one too. Analogously, if nobody else needs remote LAN access, then I don't need it either. If everyone else needs remote LAN access to stay competitive, then I need it too.

Standardization   To enable ubiquitous deployment between telcos and carriers, the move toward the National ISDN standard must accelerate.

ISDN market demand and pricing relationship

Today, the price of ISDN generally continues to be well beyond the customer's willingness to pay. From a customer perspective, the price of an ISDN line is greater than the price of an analog switched line, therefore customers can't justify the use of ISDN based on voice usage alone. However, as the previously discussed markets, applications, and product case studies tend to show, I believe customers can justify the price of ISDN strictly for data transfer in a LAN interconnect or LAN extension environment. Any additional revenues from voice or fax attachment to ISDN LAN interconnect adapters will be icing on the ISDN cake.

To accelerate market penetration and customer demand, ISDN needs to be attractively priced at cost in relation to the performance and connectivity flexibility of related LAN interconnect data network services. Also, since ISDN can be used for voice and fax traffic, pricing somewhat consistent with analog telephone service should be taken into account.

LAN customers will compare ISDN circuit-switched prices with other switched data services, including switched 56, switched T1, X.25 Switched Virtual Circuits, Fractional Frame Relay Switched Virtual Circuit service (when available), SMDS, ATM and other LAN interconnect services. These data customers will compare these data services based on the price per payload and bit per second. (*Payload* is the useful information transferred, excluding protocol overhead).

Sales incentives and LAN interconnect products and technology training

Sales compensation incentives for selling ISDN need to be offered to telco sales representatives. Sales representatives need to be retrained on ISDN with a focus on the LAN interconnect applications of ISDN.

LAN interconnect technical support proficiency

To effectively enter into the LAN interconnect marketplace with ISDN, telcos must retrain their existing technical support staff as well as infuse (hire) LAN interconnect experts from the outside. LAN interconnect technologies are perhaps one or more orders of magnitude more complex than what telcos are used to understanding. The sheer volume and alphabet soup of LAN interconnect technologies and troubleshooting methodologies that a person must become individually proficient in requires expertise that can't be gained in a short period of time. To effectively compete, telcos will most likely need to secure the services of many highly experienced LAN integration specialists.

Telcos shouldn't be lulled into thinking that by their past exposure to large

IBM SNA accounts that, without training, they understand and can effectively compete in the LAN interconnect world. There's a vast difference between SNA and LAN technologies.

Challenges to LAN work group application developers and integrators

Since ISDN and LANs assume different architectures (bandwidths), applications designed for LANs must be tested with ISDN to ensure compatibility. When selecting work group or other LAN-based software for use over ISDN, users should inquire whether it has been tested in an ISDN LAN extension or LAN interconnection environment.

Some early work-group applications were designed and tested only in local environments (where native LAN speeds are used: 10–16 million bits per second). These have been known to fail in enterprisewide environments (where slower WAN speeds are used: 64–1536 thousand bits per second). Some failures have been attributed to application timers for network server inquiries set to expire before responses to server inquiries have been received. The good news is that these types of failures can easily be fixed by LAN application developers, once detected. To detect these failures, however, LAN application developers will require access to ISDN test facilities.

Case study six: A future information network architecture

Jim Conlisk

Where do we go from here?

As we consider the possibilities of the global broadband network's evolution/revolution, here's an alternative perspective on the future network concerning the direction of ATM/STM hybrid technology. Many analyses have been performed within the context of Broadband ISDN. Here, a ubiquitous transport and switching solution is provided that's popularly referred to as Asynchronous Transfer Mode (ATM) to provide constant-bit-rate (CBR) and variable-bit-rate (VBR) services within a BISDN environment. The following analysis illustrates the need for a transition policy that expands ATM BISDN parameters to include STM capabilities in hybrid arrangements.

Some have noted that ATM is somewhat similar to present-day transport of packet data, which is disproportionately small in comparison to the present circuit-switched, digital (STM) network. Yet, packetlike technology is expected to bear the bulk of information payloads of the future. The transition from a present-day, circuit-switched network to a high-speed, packet-switched or hybrid network of the future will be a complex undertaking and will necessitate a change in the way we view the telephone network. As such, the dissimilarities between packet and circuit switch technology need to be understood with special consideration given to the effect on network evolution of assimilating a new technology (e.g., ATM, STM, frame relay) with an existing technology (i.e., STM).

The statistical nature of packet (VBR) versus circuit (CBR) traffic patterns affects the type, size, and number of fabric structures incorporated in switching systems and network elements. Traffic patterns, and especially traffic pattern trends, directly affect which interim and longer-term transport architecture should be selected to most efficiently meet changing customer needs.

In terms of traffic characteristics, CBR and VBR traffic are at opposite ends of the spectrum. One is continuous; the other is bursty. CBR traffic patterns, e.g., voice, is fairly easy to forecast, but VBR traffic, e.g., LANs, is fairly difficult to predict. In addition, bandwidth requirements must be considered to provide timely transmission throughput of delay sensitive services, e.g., video, high-resolution medical imaging, etc.

Network architectures designed to meet bursty, VBR traffic patterns might also be capable of providing a vehicle for circuit-switched traffic as an integrated transport solution. Alternatively, circuit-switched networks might be designed to provide a broadband vehicle for bursty data traffic such as Switched Multimegabit Data Services (SMDS). As such, the integration and convergency of packet-switched data networks (capable of transporting voice) and circuit-switched voice networks (capable of transporting data) might be considered as an alternative hybrid architecture for future consideration. As we've seen, network strategies concerning one such high-speed data transport, i.e., SMDS, and the evolution to Broadband-ISDN (BISDN) are being actively pursued within the standards bodies to converge on one common SONET/ATM transport solution.

Channel bandwidth and use of these high-speed data networks will be considerably different than the present-day voice network and might warrant special consideration. Subdividing traffic patterns into message duration and then bandwidth provides the capability to cross-match the best technology enabler. The following categories provides a starting point in such an endeavor:

- Short duration (e.g., CAD/CAM/CAE using LAN network).
- Medium duration (e.g., file transfer, FAX, graphics, video imaging).
- Medium-long duration (e.g., voice, switched DS1/DS3).
- Long duration (e.g., full-motion video, DS1 and DS3 private lines).

To provide an integrated network solution for both short-duration (bursty) and long-duration (nonbursty) message sets presents a transmission paradox. Low-delay, Synchronous Transfer Mode (STM), (e.g., circuit switch) networks are ideal for long-duration (delay-sensitive) voice and video services but are inefficient for the short-duration message sets associated with bursty LAN traffic. Conversely, the higher-delay ATM (packet switch) networks might provide transport for bursty LAN traffic but appears to be inefficient for the transport of delay-sensitive voice and/or video services.

Short and medium-duration VBR messages can be efficiently and effectively transported through virtual connections where fast-packet technology (ATM, SMDS, or frame relay) is deployed. Conversely, STM transmission of these short- and medium-duration message sets would require the inefficient use of dedicated, private line connections or, alternatively, the numerous build-up and tear-down of switched connections; this is clearly a suboptimal solution. In addition, services identified for short- and medium-duration messages aren't inordinately sensitive to the transmission path delays that are typically associated with ATM and/or frame relay transmission.

Medium-long and long-duration CBR messages can be effectively transported through physical or logical connections where circuit-switched technology, e.g., (STM) is deployed. Here, efficiency might be gained when STM switches are endowed with fast set-up/tear-down capabilities. Conversely, efficiency would be wasted on the ATM transport of medium-long and long-duration CBR message sets. In addition, services identified with medium-long and long-duration messages are generally sensitive to any increased transmission path delay that's common to ATM transmission, and ATM switches are significantly more complex than STM switches for any fixed CBR bandwidth.

To provide an integrated network solution for both short-duration (bursty) and long-duration (nonbursty) message sets presents a transmission paradox. Low-delay STM networks are ideal for long-duration (delay-sensitive) voice and video services but are inefficient for the short-duration message sets associated with bursty LAN traffic. Conversely, the higher-delay ATM and/or frame relay networks provide efficient transport for bursty LAN traffic but are inefficient (and technically inferior) for the transport of delay-sensitive voice and/or video services. Here, the transport of voice and/or video services via ATM requires:

1. Adaption, control, and storage complexity, which adds significant transmission delay.
2. Separate ATM switches for each traffic class, which appears cost prohibitive.
3. Mixtures of segregated STM and ATM switches.

A transport technology that provides encapsulation and transport of variable-length user packets would be ideal for LAN traffic, but the transmission path delay associated with packetization and queuing degrades the quality of delay-sensitive voice and/or video services. As a result, a new technology was sought that could integrate the best of both worlds, i.e., low-delay characteristics for the transport of voice/video services as well as provide transport for short, medium, and longer-length user data packets. Pure ATM was developed to provide variable-length packet transport but was compromised to short, fixed-length packets to provide for delay-sensitive voice traffic.

Ironically, ATM might prove to be the worst of both worlds, in which:

1. The low-delay characteristics aren't low enough for voice and video.
2. The short, fixed-length packets provide inefficient and inferior transport of data services characterized by variable-length user packets.

As a result, the widespread use of echo cancellation equipment will be required to mask echo problems on voice services, but additional echo cancellation management must be provided to "turn off" these devices when video and/or other services that require digital transparency are deployed. In addition, the complex, ATM Adaptation Layer (AAL) process of segmentation and reassembly (SAR), where user data packets are sliced-up, packaged with added destination/origination addressing and other overhead data, might promote network congestion and/or lost (dropped) cells. As additional ATM customers are added to the network, complex network traffic management and signaling should be expected to be required.

As a result, transition strategies might be desired that expand beyond BISDN/ATM. A transport/switching structure should provide very low transmission path delay for voice/video services and also provide encapsulation and transport of data services with minimal (if any) segmentation/reassembly or other intrusive manipulation techniques performed on user data packets.

The subsequent introduction of STM/frame-relay switching fabrics that employ horizontal hybrid technology[3] appear to provide cost effective and technically viable transport capabilities for comparable frame-relay transport, STM transport, and/or integrated multimedia applications. Here, an evolving and dynamic routing/bandwidth management system directs longer-duration CBR calls through an embedded STM fabric, where shorter duration VBR traffic is directed initially to a frame-relay permanent virtual circuit (PVC) node for transport.

The distinction between frame relay and cell relay is that frame relay operates with a variable-length frame (usually the same length as that generated by the LAN) and relays frames at level 2 of the OSI model (data link layer).

Frame relay technology uses layer 2, Link Access Procedure — D (LAPD), which is similar to Link Access Procedure; Balanced (LAPB), a subset of High-Level Data Link Control (HDLC) is used for X.25 links. Because many existing data products use HDLC/X.25, they can be upgraded to frame relay with little, if any, modification other than software.

CCITT, recommendation I.122, has targeted frame relay applications for < 2.048 Mbps[4] (CEPT) as follows:

1. Block interactive data applications for use with high-resolution graphics, e.g., high-resolution videotex and CAD/CAM. The main characteristics of these applications include low delays and throughputs of 500 Kbps to 2.048 Mbps.
2. File transfer applications targeted for large file transfers where transit delay is not crucial and throughput rates might extend from 16 Kbps to 2.048 Mbps.
3. Multiplexed low-bit-rate applications characterized by milliseconds of delay and throughput rates of 16K b/s to 2.048M b/s.

---

[3]Horizontal hybrid technology permits segregated transport and switching of STM and frame-relay based services. For example, STM-based services (e.g., voice and video) are switched via STM switching fabrics, and variable-bit-rate services (e.g., LAN) are switched via frame-relay. This might be contrasted to a vertical hybrid technology, e.g., BISDN, where all services are targeted for ATM switching and transport.

[4]For U.S. applications, frame relay technology is presently targeted at < 1.544 Mbps.

4. Character-interactive traffic (e.g., text editing) with characteristics that include short frames, low delays, and low throughput.

Current frame relay specifications provide for data transmission speeds of up to 1.544 Mbps, but contributions have been submitted to standards bodies for increasing frame relay speeds to DS3, albeit concern has been raised that increasing frame relay speeds could "stifle the interest in and deployment of SMDS."

Some of the various techniques to increase the efficiency of transport networks make use of adaptive differential pulse code modulation (ADPCM), packetized data and voice, and silence elimination by using a time assignment speech interpolation (TASI) solution.

Each of these bandwidth-compression techniques has an associated set of problems. TASI techniques typically cause speech clipping. Packetization of voice circuits causes additional fixed delay and potential speech clipping. In addition, connectionless routing via "virtual circuits" creates variable path delay effects that require fairly large far-end buffer storage (i.e., packets are transmitted sequentially from the near-end, but some packets might arrive at the far-end out of sequence; hence, a large buffer requirement is needed to sort and assemble the packets in the original order). High traffic conditions typically cause congestion that results in additional variable path delay. The answers to such delay and congestion problems often result in reconsideration of an original solution (e.g., single-fabric packet architecture with echo cancelers). However, certain services must not be intercepted by an echo canceler and must not have any other processing equipment inserted in a connection (e.g., digital pads, operator services, etc.). Four-wire digital loops at the originating and terminating end are used. The following are examples of these types of services:

1. Encrypted voice.
2. Digital data.
3. Transmission standards other than 64 Kbps u255 encoded North American Standard.

ATM has been advocated as a vehicle for the transmission of voice (without echo control) by use of partially filled cells. Here, voice signals encoded into digital, 125-microsecond samples are serially loaded into ATM cells. The ATM cell can accommodate 48 bytes, but to serially load 48 samples would result in an excessive transmission delay of 6 milliseconds one-way delay or 12 milliseconds round-trip delay. Rather, it has been recommended to partially fill the cell with 16 bytes.

As a result of the increased transmission path delay associated with ATM packetization, etc., coupled with a reduction of cell efficiency to 25 percent (from 48 bytes to 16 bytes), broadband transition strategies for delay sensitive, voice services should include alternatives to ubiquitous ATM transmission. Such an alternative, as found in the current network, uses STM transmission to provide a low-delay solution for CBR services, albeit not an efficient transport platform for VBR services. Alternatively, the use of a horizontal hybrid that continues to incorporate STM in addition to newly introduced ATM (or SMDS and frame delay) technology provides a transport platform for both CBR and VBR services.

In a hybrid environment it's expected that variable bit rate (VBR) services, such as bursty data services that are mostly delay insensitive, will be transported via the ATM component. Constant bit rate (CBR) services, such as delay sensitive voice, real-time video, and telemetry-types of data, will be transported via the STM component. There might be some limited access and transport capabilities for all services via ATM.

The subsequent introduction of frame-relay switched virtual circuit (SVC) capability and bandwidth evolution to the DS3 rate (or higher, e.g., SONET OC3c) would complement an evolving narrowband ISDN network with switched wideband data services at the DS1 (primary rate access) rate. Here, an extended Q.931 protocol (for frame-relay) assures ready accommodation by Q.931-ISDN and ready market acceptance, where CPE LAPD equipment might be easily upgraded via simple software upgrades.

Therefore, we can readily note that:

- Short-duration messages, as associated with LAN traffic, can be provided primarily with cell-relay technology, e.g., early availability SMDS at the DS1 and DS3 rates and subsequent transport via ATM. As an alternative, currently available frame-relay technology might be deployed for these short-duration message sets at the SD1 rate, with potential updates to the DS3 or SONET OC3 rate.
- Medium-duration messages, as associated with file transfers, can be provided primarily with frame-relay technology at the DS1 rate with potential updates to DS3 and/or SONET OC3. As an alternative, cell-relay technology could be deployed, e.g., SMDS initially and subsequently with ATM, albeit cell relay technology being more inefficient for these longer message sets.
- Medium-long duration messages, as associated with voice and switched DS1/DS3 services, can be provided primarily over switched STM transport via virtual circuits with fast setup/tear-down time. Alternatively, dedicated STM-based facilities could be provided, albeit less efficient.
- Long-duration messages, as associated with full-motion video and/or private lines, can be provided with dedicated STM transport. Alternatively, switched STM-based facilities could be provided, e.g., switched DS1/DS3.

In summary, an evolving transport/switching framework for both VBR and CBR services has been identified. Specifically, transition strategies have been presented as stepping stones to a future network capable of providing narrowband, wideband, and broadband CBR and/or VBR services. In this manner, the network could evolve over the '90s in the following phases:

- Phase I (1994 – 1995). STM/FRAME-RELAY/SMDS transport with static partitioning.

- Phase II (1996–1997). STM/FRAME-RELAY/SMDS transport with dynamic partitioning.
- Phase III (1998-1999 +). STM/ATM transport with dynamic partitioning.

What technology for what architecture? A more detailed look

Asynchronous Transfer Mode (ATM) has been proposed and accepted as the base platform from which to build future services. Here, narrowband, wideband, and broadband services are provided through vertical layering of the ATM Adaptation Layer (AAL). This vertical hybrid approach to network integration has promised to provide efficient and cost-effective evolution through single-fabric, cell-based switching and transport.

A more critical analysis might suggest that an ATM architecture strategy might not be cost-effective, efficient, or technically justifiable when compared to Synchronous Transfer Mode (STM) alternatives. As such, let's consider an alternative evolution strategy for narrowband, wideband, and broadband services based on SONET/STM alternatives.

The integration of services via cell-based technology has been presented as an efficient and cost-effective transport and switching technology. However, preliminary information suggests that cell-based technology might not be efficient might be cost effective only when:

1. Integration is applied to all services (i.e., voice, video, data).
2. Pushing traffic loads on available switching and transport facilities to the point of congestion, i.e., blocking/dropping cells.

Hence, we need to determine if:

1. The integration of all services is not feasible within the context of cell-based technology.
2. Efficiencies gained through maximizing traffic loading might subject networks to increased volatility, congestion, and potential shutdown of all traffic.
3. Insufficient traffic loading creates inefficiencies, requires a vastly overbuilt transport network, and doesn't appear to be cost justifiable.

In addition, we need to consider performance-related issues of congestion, throughput, efficiency, and transmission path delay as related to voice, video, and data services within the context of a cell-based architecture, as well as the consequences of vertical integration. It's possible that cell-based technology, implemented on a grand scale, might result in degraded network performance, where LAN-to-LAN interconnection and general data "throughput" might well decrease by orders of magnitude. Voice services could experience echo, hollow-sounding circuits, and/or speech clipping. Video services might experience blackouts and black lines as congestion storms rage throughout these newly established cell-based networks. Ironically, the more successful we are in implementing cell-based technology into the network, the faster we might be bringing about the potential for disaster, i.e., an apocalyptic network strategy. Alternatively, it does appear that horizontal integration provides a cost-effective and flexible architecture for both present and future capabilities via circuit-switching, similar to that employed within a N-ISDN architecture.

As a result, we need to establish an evolution strategy for narrowband (NB), wideband (WB), and broadband (BB) services through horizontal integration of NB/WB/BB circuit switching, where broadband cell switching (i.e., ATM) capability is provided on a parallel basis. Service profiles for voice, data, and video can then be distributed according to bandwidth requirements and use. These can evolve accordingly as increased bandwidth becomes available.

Narrowband voice networks are somewhat tolerant of error conditions but are very unforgiving of additional transmission path delay. Conversely, narrowband data networks have evolved to be tolerant of additional transmission path delay, but intolerant of bit error pollution.

Integration of these seemingly incongruent narrowband networks has been a continual challenge for the telecommunication network planner/manager. As a result, we've seen an increasing demand for the deployment of data-over-voice devices and newer Integrated Services Digital Network (ISDN) equipment. Other vendor arrangements that maximize available resources provide access to DS0-based DS1s (e.g., reverse/inverse multiplexers) and DS1s that integrate voice, data, and video via statistical multiplexing, thereby creating a hybrid private line (PL) DS1.

It's expected that narrowband network solutions will evolve to use available bandwidth resources. In addition, as wideband and broadband applications (e.g., high-definition television, computer aided design, computer aided manufacturing, etc.) are introduced, available bandwidth resources will be inadequate. As such, it has been suggested that new fabric, high-speed (i.e., ATM) solutions will be required.

These high-speed ATM networks are structured quite differently than conventional circuit-switched networks. Specifically, they contain header processing circuitry and buffer facilities. If congestion and blocking occurs within the high-speed switching network, cells are buffered and eventually sent with a delay when there are gaps in the multiplexed information flow (or if the delay is excessive, cells will be dropped).

Congestion and cell blocking/dropping should be expected to lead to degraded network performance, but the advantages of a single fabric ATM solution for the homogeneous transport of voice, data, and video services has been touted to outweigh these disadvantages. What has not been demonstrated is that a single fabric ATM solution (i.e., BISDN) presents a cost-effective or technically viable solution for the transport of continuous bit rate (CBR) voice and video services. As an example, considerable delay is introduced as 47 PCM speech samples are packetized into ATM cells, exceeding existing voice service delay requirements.

As a result, special techniques such as echo control devices might be required to "cancel" the effects of this delay for voice over ATM networks. The subsequent introduction of multiple echo cancellation devices might produce unwanted speech impairments, such as speech clipping and/or interruptions, to the normal rhythm of speech.

When viewing cell-based technology (e.g., ATM) for eventual ubiquitous deployment and as a replacement vehicle for the current circuit switching TDM network, we need to carefully consider:

- Transport efficiency comparisons of cell-based versus circuit switch TDM.
- Protocol efficiency comparisons of fixed-cell versus variable-length packet transport.
- Transport/protocol efficiency of "primitive" versus "tunneling" technology (i.e., vertical stacking of technologies).
- Analysis of voice, video, and data applications for cell-based technology and skeptical analysis of rationale for doing so.
- Analysis of congestion within a cell-based transport system in terms of technical and economic windows on the congestion curve.

Without providing an in-depth technical analysis of each of the preceding areas, I've garnered a synopsis of information to reveal several of the key attributes associated with each.

Transport efficiency comparison of cell-based versus circuit switch TDM   Protocol overhead and/or partially filled cells might contribute to inefficient transport when using cell-based technology. In addition, higher-efficiency ATM models for CBR-voice services might lead to costly administration and control systems and/or near ubiquitous deployment of echo cancellation equipment. Here, speech impairments such as speech clipping and the associated costs of the echo cancellation equipment should be carefully considered.

Several efficiency comparisons are provided in TABLE 7-5 to illustrate potential cell-based versus circuit-based technology approaches, e.g., ATM, SMDS, TDM.

Protocol efficiency of comparison of fixed-length cell (ATM/SMDS) versus variable-length packet (frame-relay) transport   Figures 7-9 and 7-10 compare cell-based SMDS technology with "primitive" frame-relay transport over TDM technology. A 20-byte packet transport reveals 3.5 percent efficiency for SMDS, versus 80 percent for frame-relay.

Transport/protocol efficiency of "primitive" versus "tunneling" technology (i.e., vertical stacking of technologies)   The vertical stacking of technologies, such as frame-relay over SMDS, implies "tunneling." Here, the primitive protocol is encapsulated for transport over the underlying carrier technology.

Several important detriments that usually occur are provided as follows:

- Transport efficiency suffers. For example, FIGS. 7-9 and 7-10 show that if frame relay were encapsulated for transport over SMDS, a 20-byte user

Table 7 – 5. Efficiency Comparisons

CBR Voice (w/o TASI) via circuit-switch TDM	≈	100%
ATM with full fill cells 47/53 (definitely requires echo cancellation)	≈	88%
ATM with partially filled cells 16/53 (probably requires echo cancellation)	≈	30%
ATM with composite filled cells (costly and complex administration and control) 47/53	≈	88%
CBR Video via circuit-switch TDM	≈	100%
CBR Video via ATM (47/53)	≈	88%
VBR Data (10 Byte sample) via TDM (FR)	≈	67%
VBR Data (10 Byte sample) via ATM AAL5	≈	20%

packet would now have a transport efficiency of 80 percent of 3.5 percent, i.e., 2.8 percent. Here, we've gained the worst of both technologies (for efficiency).

• Encapsulation ensures inaccessibility to useful "primitives." As a result, such primitive features as frame relay flow control and congestion control bits, e.g., FECN, BECN, and DE bits are inaccessible, and the benefits might be lost unless redundantly provided by the underlying carrier, e.g., SMDS.

Analysis of voice, video, and data applications for cell-based technology and skeptical analysis of rationale for doing so Voice. Partial filling introduces transport inefficiency and adds significant transmission path delay. Ironically, as networks are "upgraded" to conform to Regional Switched Digital Network (RDSN) plans (and as CPE is upgraded from 2-wire telsets to 4-wire telsets) customers might suffer degraded performance (i.e., hollow-sounding circuits, echo, and/or speech clipping).

Here, the signal level has been increased with the new RDSN, plan and if the far-end equipment (e.g., in an other RBOC or independent TELCO) has not been upgraded to 4-wire to the customer (this will be the condition for years), an increased echo signal will result. This is due to an echo path from the 2w/4w conversion equipment (hybid) presently installed at the far end.

This condition is further exasperated with any additional transmission path delay. ATM network upgrades provide this additional transmission path delay. Proponents of cell-based technology propose the use of echo cancellation (EC) equipment to negate this problem; however, further analysis is required for consideration of:

a. The increased network costs due to this additional equipment.
b. Speech clipping and other voice impairments due to multiple ECs beating against each other and/or other network/CPE simplex equipment, e.g., TASI, speaker-phones, etc.

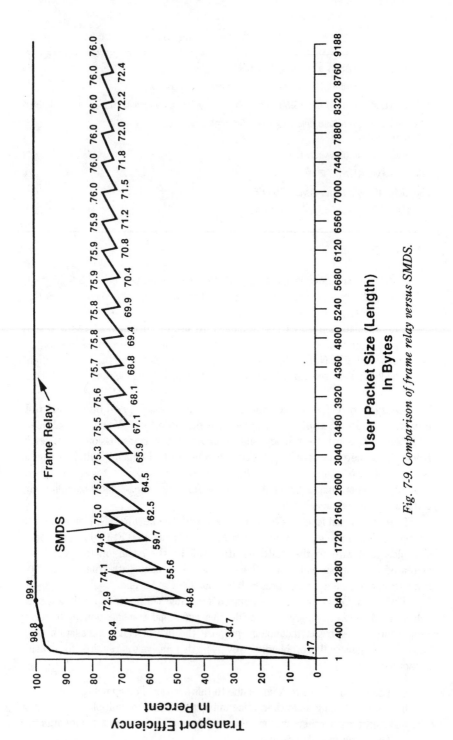

Fig. 7-9. Comparison of frame relay versus SMDS.

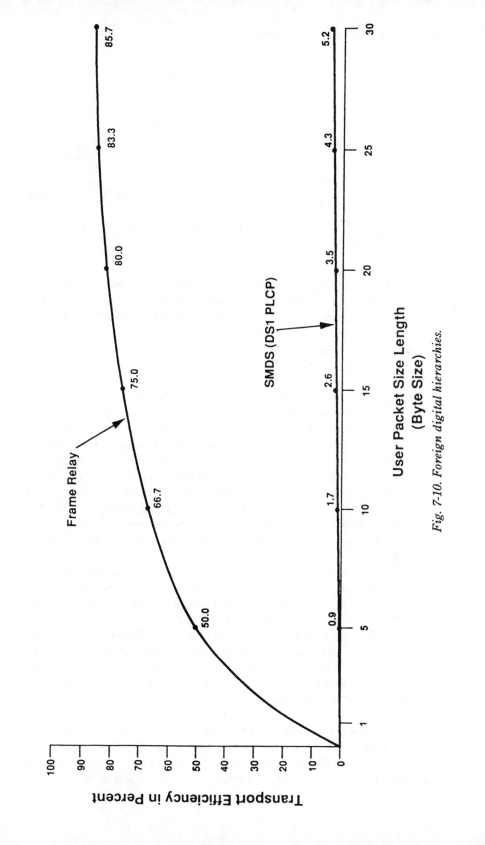

Fig. 7-10. Foreign digital hierarchies.

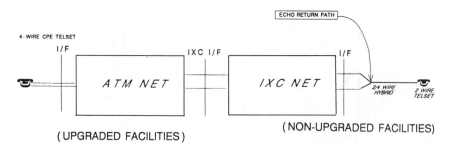

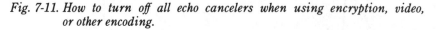

Fig. 7-11. How to turn off all echo cancelers when using encryption, video, or other encoding.

   c. The complex equipment and administration to assure that only one EC (or simplex equipment) is allowed on and others are turned off (CPE equipment adds additional complexity, i.e., how to gracefully "turn-off" a customer's speaker-phone from the network).

   d. How to turn off all echo cancellers when using encryption, video, or other than mu-law encoding. (See FIG. 7-11.)

- Video. As a continuous-bit-stream service, wideband and/or broadband isochronous video service might be provided most efficiently over CBR TDM transport. It appears inefficient to segment a continuous bit stream into many cells. Transport efficiency suffers as additional overhead is added, greater processing power is required at each node, latency increases, and transmission fixed path and variable-path delay increases. In addition, the potential for congestion becomes enormous when considering an aggressive video deployment strategy within a cell-based (e.g., ATM) network. As a CBR service, it appears that video might be best served via TDM. Here, fast circuit setup, e.g., dial-up DS1/DS3, could easily be used with DCS network elements.

- Data. Due to the bursty nature of data traffic, packet transport appears to provide more efficient transport than primitive TDM techniques. Prime consideration should be paid to which type of packet transport is most efficient and what technique should be employed.

     Fixed-cell transport, e.g., SMDS or ATM, is inherently inefficient due to protocols and excessive overhead, whereas variable-length user packets that are encapsulated in the primitive (e.g., frame-relay or IBM's PTM for gigabyte transport) provide efficient, simple, and low-cost data transport capability over TDM facilities.

Analysis of congestion on cell-based transport in terms of technical and economic windows on the congestion curve   Cell-based technologies present significant challenges in the area of network congestion. Typically, congestion within a packet network requires that the window of operation be maintained

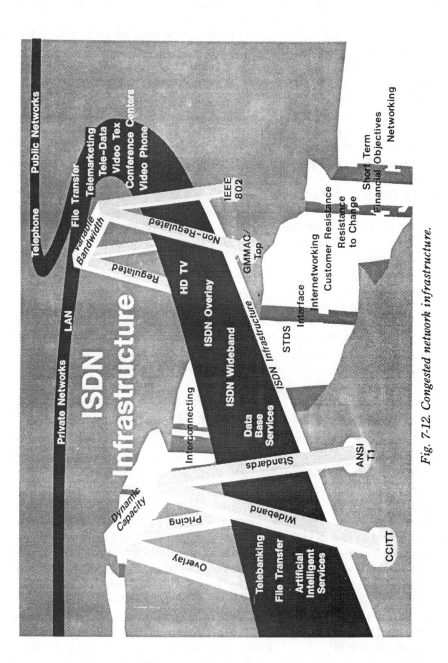

Fig. 7-12. Congested network infrastructure.

at a very low level (i.e., not cost effective) to assure adequate network operation. Figure 7-12 provides an indication of a perfect, desirable and congested network curves.

When cell-based technology is intended to be used for multimedia and/or integrated network operation, it might be expected that a congested network curve will prevail. Here, complex congestion control methods could be deployed to toggle-back the window of operation to prevent dropped cells but, unfortunately, this results in drastic inefficiencies. In addition, reactive control systems, such as these, aren't fast enough to prevent the damage incurred by congestion storms. Digital network speeds will be so fast in future SONET networks that reactive systems will be ineffective.

Herein lies the dichotomy! Enthusiasts of cell-based technology proclaim that integration works well, and they take advantage of statistics to maximize the use of cellsem.but perhaps it only works well on the low end of the congestion curve. For example, can a life-cost study prove it in this area of the curve? Enthusiasts of cell-based technology also say it's economical by taking advantage of statistically allocating cells for integrated services. They're now operating high on the congestion curve (pushing close to the peak) and "dropping a few" cells. One potential problem with this is that when we push the curve by loading it, say, with multiple video connections, cells begin to drop, and the results can be cataclysmic.

Dropping cells for uncompressed video might cause a few blank lines or blank screens if the synch bits are dropped. Compressed video is more quickly destroyed by dropping cells. In addition, it must be assumed that ATM integrated services include FDDI LAN interconnects. Here, 3000 to 4000-byte block transport is not uncommon. If one cell is dropped, the destination end initiates a NACK that's transmitted back to the originating end, where a retransmittal of the entire 4000-byte block is required. As a result, an already congested network is further congested to the point that all traffic might be halted.

Conclusion

ATM has been suggested as the singular, effective transport and switching technology for integrated voice, video, and data services. It's also proposed as the vehicle of choice to provide the high bandwidth capabilities anticipated in future networks. However, these views that SMDS and ATM provide high bandwidth capabilities is considered by some as somewhat misleading in that SMDS and ATM require high bandwidth but might provide drastically reduced "throughput." In addition, various technologies to provide flexibility and bandwidth evolution for TDM platforms are advancing on all fronts. Frame relay technology is currently provided via PVC at the TDM-DS1 rate, but announcements for evolution to TDM-DS3 and switching via SVC have been proclaimed (both might be provided via SONET/STM). In addition, ATM's underlying SONET architecture is a TDM platform that might provide for all STM rates, as well as the proposed ATM rates. Within SONET/STM, fast circuit setup and tear-down (e.g., switched DS1, DS3, OC-N) can provide a noncongestive transport facility for as long as a customer requires (without cell-based ATM technology). Here, SONET/STM provides more bandwidth available for more payload than SONET/ATM (due to the overhead requirements of SONET/ATM). As just illustrated, there are enough serious concerns to warrant caution in the singular implementation of cell-based technology.

Some corporations have announced SONET bandwidth evolution to OC-192 (9.6 GBps), and AT&T Bell Telephone Laboratories has made significant progress in the area of photonic switching. In addition, significant advances have been made in the area of dense wave division multiplexing (D-WDM), where multiple windows appear within one fiber optic strand, each carrying a full SONET rate, e.g., OC-192. One might well ask, "Why should resources be allocated to the further development of a complex and costly cell-based architecture that might be fraught with technical limitations, when multimegabyte/gigabit bandwidth might well be expected to become very cost effective, especially when endowed with extremely fast call setup/tear-down capabilities?"

It appears that the allocation of resources on architectures that are both forward (and backward) compatible might prove more cost effective and forward compatible. Transition strategies that use hybrid TDM architectures might consider the following suggestions for voice, video, data service:

- Video. Always place on TDM facilities—segregated into:
  a. Narrowband (Px64), e.g., PC video windowing.
  b. Wideband (FDS1, DS1) entertainment/teleconferencing.
  c. Broadband (NTSC/HDTV).
- Voice. Always place on TDM facilities. Maximize use of class 5/class 6/ vertical services.
- Data. Place on narrowband ISDN and frame relay. Encourage frame-relay evolution from PVC to SVC and frame-relay bandwidth evolution from DS1 to DS3. This should be accomplished through proactive participation in the "standards" bodies—ANSI, etc., as well as proactive involvement with vendors. Therefore, always provide primitives (i.e., frame-relay on TDM), and never engender encapsulation, i.e., tunneling, techniques.

Strategic network planners must expect customer and IXC demands for ATM and must be prepared to deploy this technology. More importantly, it's absolutely essential that network planners plan solutions with viable TDM technology to prevent potential congestion and crashes.

As such, recommendations should include provision for backward and forward compatible architectures, e.g., transport with dynamically partitioned hybrids for primitive data, as well as voice and video transwitching. We can also provide a sufficient number of broadband ATM switches per metro area. Always remember, however, that this is not the long-term goal; rather, it's essential to proactively push for photonic switching, SONET bandwidth evolution to OC-192, dense wave division multiplexing, and dynamic nxDS0 and nxDS1 TDM techniques for low-delay, bandwidth-on-demand capabilities.

Case study seven: information telecommunications

In the '80s, corporate networks could select low-speed dial, low-speed private line, and high-speed printed line services. High-speed dial service was not available. In the '90s, this deficiency is being addressed.

The ISDN data networking game took a serious turn in 1992 as the ISDN Executive Council for the Corporation for Open Systems International (COS) launched National ISDN-1 (NI-1) to resolve ISDN connectivity between different vendors' central office switches. This alleviates the proprietary pre-ubiquitous ISDN implementation problems, where CPE terminal equipment, working well with one vendor's network switch, required a different programmable ROM to work with another vendor's switch. Prior to 1991, the number of access lines equipped to deliver ISDN was only 200,000 or so. By the end of 1992, Bellcore estimated that ISDN was available to approximately 62 million lines. NI-1 addressed many of the analog needs for BRI, while PRI, at the local level, was addressed in NI-2 and NI-3 software releases. NI-1 is available by AT&T 5ESS Software Services 5E8, May 1992; Fujitsu Network Switching of American Fetex-150 Release G3, February 1992; Northern Telecom DMS-100, BCS 34, September 1992; Siemens Stromberg-Carlson EWSD, Rel 10, November 1992; and Ericsson AXE, Rel 6, March 1994.

While local exchange carriers (LECs) have pushed the deployment of BRI, interexchange carriers (IXCs) have opted for PRI. LEC-BRI is essential for the CPE, as well as Centrex offerings. PRX vendors use BRI on the line side and PRI on the trunk side to connect directly to IXCs.

Trip '92, coordinated by COS and Bellcore in November of 1992, achieved the "golden splice," denoting the entrance to the Information Age. Coast-to-coast ISDN communications were achieved, connecting 20 cities and providing numerous ISDN voice, data, image, text, and video demonstrations for education and medical imagery applications. The "golden splice" is similar to the origination of the beginning of the Industrial Age. When the coast-to-coast railroad track was finally completed, builders drove a "golden spike" connecting tracks from both the East and West coasts. So this "golden splice" similarly marks the linking of ISDNs coast-to-coast and the entrance into a new age — the Information Age.

The North American (N.A.) Users Forum, in Gaithersburg, Maryland, participated in identifying some of ISDN's most valuable applications as the following:

1. Videoconferencing.
2. Telecommuting.
3. ISDN telephone/ISDN workstation integration.
4. Multipoint screen sharing.
5. Customer service call handling.
6. ISDN access in geographically remote locations.
7. Image communications.
8. Automated number identification.
9. Multidocument image storage and retrieval.

10. Multimedia services.
11. Multiple ISDN telephones on a single BRI loop.
12. ISDN interface to cellular, mobile radio and satellite systems.

Several issues were noted, such as tariffing and provisioning of ISDN, where ISDN's service negotiation procedure involves hundreds of subscription parameters such as those for billing, location, and function. To reduce this, a special grouping of ISDN subscription parameters now enables a number of ISDN parameter groups and settings to be deployed.

CPE stimulus/functional protocols for working with the network to accomplish particular services is also a concern, as NI-1, 2, and 3 solutions are delivered. It's also important to ensure that compatibility with existing solutions is also resolved with national ISDN solutions. NI-1 relies extensively on network intelligence embodied in service protocols, which are also known as stimulus protocols. For example, to achieve call forwarding in NI-1, a user would dial an access code or hit a feature indicator. Here, the CPE would essentially sit on the sidelines as a passive entity.

However, more intelligent, functional protocols would let the CPE interact to a greater extent with the network. The CPE would then understand and use protocols different from stimulus protocols that enable it to functionally intermix with the network to achieve the designated task. These are known as *functional protocols.*

Achieving the whole host of new ISDN supplementary features that the "D" channel can deliver with intelligent CPE will require SS7 signaling fully implemented with ISDN. Here, calling line identification, call hold, selective call forwarding, voice-to-text types of features will require considerable support and interoperability as defined by Bellcore's "General Guidelines for ISDN Terminal Equipment on Basic Access Interfaces" document. This document needs to be further detailed throughout the '90s to resolve ambiguous areas, expand "D" channel features and services, and address terminal compatibility, data networking, CPE testing, power requirements, and maintenance of ISDN CPE. As NI-1 is available in '92, NI-2 in 1993, and NI-3 by mid decade, they'll continue to address consistency, connectivity, and cooperation issues and concerns, for ISDN is as yet "not too late for the data party."

Applications driving virtual data

Today, the most popular video application relying on these new switched digital services is national and international videophone and videoconferencing. Videoconferencing users typically rely on multiple 56 Kbps or 64 Kbps channel services, known as Nx56/64, or on 384 Kbps digital services.

Switched data services are also increasingly being used for:

- Replacement of private-line Dataphone Digital Service up to 56 Kbps with switched digital connections.
- Extension of high-speed data links to small, remote locations where leased lines have been uneconomical.

- The internetworking of geographically separate LAN traffic — on a demand basis — through the use of intelligent bridge/router/hub/node controllers.
- The addition of capacity to existing leased circuits on demand during traffic peaks or when unanticipated demand grows beyond leased circuit capacity.
- For redundancy, backup, and disaster recovery when DDS and private leased lines fail."

While waiting for ISDN, various providers such as AT&T, MCI, Sprint, Wiltel, and the RBOCs are deploying numerous data-handling "virtual" data networks, providing many private network services to encourage users to shift from direct leased lines to shared usage-based facilities. Here, 56/64 Kbps, nx 56/64 Kbps, and fractional T1-384K, and 786 Kbps offerings are available.

Several data transport services have developed as "rate adaption" techniques use V.110 or V.120 to enable different subrates to use ISDN BRI or 56K/64K b/s switched facilities. Single application "inverse multiplexers" are just the tip of the iceberg in the world of public data network services, previously occupied by channel banks and T1 backbone networks. Next, "continuous bundling" of 64 Kbps channels to the 384K, 1.5, and 2.08 rates compared favorably with the alternate reverse multiplexing techniques, enabling dynamic selection of multiple BRI channels to fulfill needed bandwidth requests. "Continuous bundling" takes only 2.5 seconds compared to reverse multiplexing's 30–45 seconds of setup. In this regard, working with the switched digital services application forum, bandwidth on demand interoperability groups (BONDING) has addressed inverse multiplexing interoperability issues. Also, numerous firms such as Ascend Communications, Digital Access Group, Newbridge Networks, TynLink and Axxess, telcos, and Prompters Communications Inc., are deploying their product solutions to inverse multiplexing.

ISDN's setup time, typically less than one second, compares favorably with traditional 10-second to 20-second dial-up connections. This reduction is significant enough to justify using ISDN over alternative dedicated T1 facilities, depending on traffic volumes.

Thus, AT&T's Software Defined Data Network (SDDN) offers Nx56/64 Kbps and switched 384 Kbps as part of their Switched Digital Services. MCI began offering switched data services in 1991 under its VNET virtual services umbrella. MCI's virtual data services family includes switched T1, DS-3, 56/64 Kbps, frame relay, and continuous 384 Kbps service. Sprint's Virtual Private Network provides VPN56, Switch 64, and 1.536 Mbps. (See the Global ISDN case study).

Both MCI's Digital Gateway Service and Sprint's Integrated T1 Access Partitioning let users rely on a single access line for private and switched transport. Similarly, PRI services will enable direct access to "B" channels within the 1.544 bit stream, as it completes with T1 leased-line offerings. These data speeds have taken a quantum leap in magnitude from the 2.4K, 9.6 Kbps top-of-the-line V.32 modems.

PRI is appealing in that, unlike T1, individual B channels in a PRI can be dynamically reassigned to different carriers on a call-by-call basis, so it's a highly flexible alternative to T1 for access to a diversity of carrier services such as switched 56 Kbps, WATS, and end-to-end ISDN B channel data calling such as voice data, Group 4 fax, or LAN interconnection.

As one analyst observed,

"Besides these data transport operational characteristics, the spectrum of ISDN BRI equipment 'repeats a cornucopia of capabilities' ranging from devices that contain video cameras and codices, which use one or more switched ISDN B channels for carrying full-motion video conferencing, to those confined to perform LAN gateways, such as remote Ethernet LAN bridges, which use the very fast call set up times of ISDN to dynamically establish a high-speed data telelink to forward data when requested and then just as rapidly drop the connection."

New switching systems

The role of CO switching is changing dramatically, as noted by Rendal and Pecorori:

"In 1878, American District Telephone Company of Chicago began telephone operations, having the first private telephone system in New Haven, Connecticut, which was created with 21 subscribers and a manual switchboard. In 1889, A. B. Strowger developed the step-by-step system that was installed in 1892 in LaPorte, Indiana. In 1900, the Rochester rotary system was introduced from Stromberg-Carlson. In 1915, the Panel System was introduced and installed by AT&T. In 1916, Bell adopted the Strowger Switch. Late in 1924, Bell Labs redesigned the crossbar. In 1930, L. M. Ericsson developed the ME 500 switch for small rural areas. In 1941, AT&T's No. 4 crossbar was deployed, and in 1948, No. 5 crossbar was provided in Philadelphia suburbs. In 1955, the EMC rotary switch system/crossbar switches were widely used by AT&T No. 1 and No. 5. In 1960, the first electronic wired Logic Switch by GTE, Automatic Electric for Autovon. In 1967, Stored Program Control switches were developed by Bell Labs. In 1976, Digital Switching No. 4 ESS and common channel signaling. 1977, Digital CLASS 5 switches by Northern Telecom, followed by, in 1978, GTE with Digital Remote Switch Units. In 1991, Broadband Switching by Fujitsu, and in the early 1990s, photonic switching prototypes by Bell Labs."

The role of CO switching is, however, finally changing:

- The line functions need to exhibit multimedia capability closer to the end user.
- Services are database managed and provided.
- Signaling creates intelligent communications.
- Support systems are service driven.
- Switching is on a per call, per channel, per facility basis with bandwidth defined in line units and billed in the central office.

However, capitalizing on this discontinuity is another matter . . .

As ISDN moves into the switched multirate arena, Jack Kelly noted the following:

"As enticing as new switched digital access might be, real excitement can be generated with devices that match multiple network choices in a single platform. These new network access servers must seamlessly integrate and access both dedicated and switched digital networks, since the objective is still to match the application with the best possible network service. What's required is an integrated platform of connection technologies that provide access to dedicated and switched digital networks with consistent user control, interchangeable interfaces, and each under a single network management system. This is the concept of Dedicated and Switched Digital Access.

DSDA can revolutionize network optimization because, for the first time, applications can truly be matched with the appropriate network services. In addition, newer switched digital servers can provide access to both dedicated digital networks and switched digital services over the same local access facility. In this way, local access charges are minimized. DSDA is particularly well-suited for combining dedicated and switched digital services via $N \times 56$ Kbps methods. DSDA will be the preferred method of LAN-to-LAN connection. A dedicated high-speed digital connection at 768 Kbps can meet many requirements of LAN-to-LAN traffic. During peak transmission periods, incremental bandwidth can easily be added and removed, as traffic patterns vary. When tariffs permit, similar flexibility can be applied to ISDN networks.

Intriguing possibilities emerge when inverse multiplexing is combined with T1, frame relay, and ISDN. Multiple switched 384 Kbps or switched 1.536 Mbps calls can be combined for efficient transport, and could present an alternative to switched multimegabit data service. Multiple T1 calls can be established to back up T3 backbone networks. Single access to private-line, frame relay, and switched digital networks is also possible.

The right combinations of technology solutions and lower network prices can now provide users with a continuing array of network alternatives. By combining the method of access to both dedicated and switched networks through standardized interfaces, the communications professional can match applications requirements with the best possible network alternative."

More sophisticated bandwidth on demand devices that support multiple applications are needed . . . So it goes.

We're moving rapidly from a traditional AT&T-based network to a global ISDN-based network with distributed switches closer to the customer, providing a whole host of new, exciting information services in the new global "information telecommunications" era.

8

Workshop
The information marketplace

Would that we could have provided ISDN networks, products, and services that might have been, could have been, should have been, would have been, but weren't . . . We would have a different marketplace than we have today . . .

During the three phases of ISDN, there will be many features and services provided to various users in the marketplace. We've seen how the C&C integration phase will move the formerly independent communication and computer services into more interdependent C&C offerings.

Hence, I've provided several studies here to enable you to establish your view of what services will be successfully established in each of the three phases, as we move from evolutionary transport data and video offerings overlaid on the voice network (called Overlay ISDN) to the more integrated private and public transport and application offerings that enable different types of computers to share databases in the C&C phase of ISDN. Here, traffic will build up from every market segment until fiber has been sufficiently deployed to foster cheap integrated services in the wideband/broadband ISDN phase of the Information Era.

Study one: the new users of integrated services

As we in the telecommunications arena become extensively involved in proposing, designing, and building new worldwide digital integrated services, networks, and products, it's important to constantly reassess what "user needs" must be met. The term *integrated service* means many things, depending on your perspective. This analysis addresses the issue from a "needs" basis. It attempts to step back and take a "big picture" view of evolving, new user requirements in terms of their transport technical attributes' impact on terminals, switches, networks, and services.

Today, many firms are planning products for the new Information Age. The timing appears to be the late '90s rather than the end of the '70s, now that the information-handling satellites and local networks are being implemented. Digital islands of fiber optics and digital switches are being inserted into the local plant, and the PTTs, BOCs and IDCs are placing special emphasis on new services in order to obtain more revenue. However, now is also the time to take a very careful review of the anticipated new users and identify them in terms of their immediate needs, their modes of operation, and their technical characteristics.

We went through this type of thinking in the '70s only to find that, for numerous reasons, new users didn't emerge in the quantities that were originally envisioned by the planners and developers. This, then, is a top-down planning look at the new users and their immediate and future integrated services needs in terms of transport requirements for network products.

It's time to redetermine who the new users really are and what they need. This analysis will use a different methodology than that of the blindfolded men in the child's fable, with, hopefully, better conclusions. (See FIG. 8-1.)

Fig. 8-1. Identify the new users' needs and requirements.

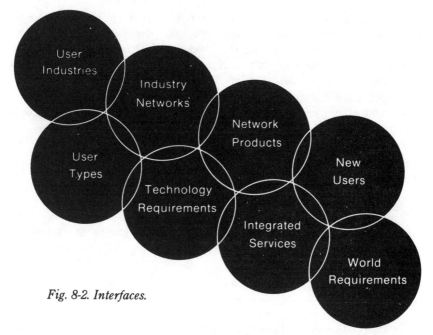

Fig. 8-2. Interfaces.

User industries' networks

A review of 18 major industries and groups provides an excellent basis for under-standing the new users. (See FIG. 8-2.) Each group can be analyzed in terms of its projected future telecommunication networks. They can be reviewed for information handling, transmission, and processing needs.

The following list is representative:

- Banks.
- Federal agencies.
- State government.
- Education.
- Entertainment.
- Insurance.
- Transportation.
- Small business.
- Investment firms.
- Manufacturing.
- News/magazine.
- Wholesale/retail stores.
- Information services.
- Law agencies.
- Health care.
- Home communications.
- Operations/utilities.
- Large business complexes.

As discussed in many trade articles, each of these groups will need, over the next ten years, new integrated voice, data, and video networks and services. Various firms within these groups will develop specialized information grids, as shown in FIG. 8-3. These will emerge in phases, as the company's user resistance decreases and usage expands.

In FIG. 8-3, combinations of local and remote computer banks are tied together over switched or leased facilities. The networks are composed of class-level switches, PBXs, concentrators, MUXs, local controllers, and intelligent terminals. In reviewing many of the specific networks for each major group's firms, it's interesting to see that each has a particular configuration that overlays on this type of general grid but emphasizes one or two special aspects more than others.

User mode

Further understanding is achieved by reviewing the network user's mode of operation, not only for voice features, but also in terms of total information flow.

Mode of operation — categories

- Interactive-inquiry/response (single or sequence) (I/R).
- Data collection — polling/sensing (DC).
- Data distribution networks (DD).
- Interactive — remote access/time sharing (RA/TS).
- Remote display/documentation (RD/D).
- Interactive — graphics (G).
- Transactions (T).
- Video conferencing (VC).
- Voice (V).

For example, the investments and securities information network's users would perform tasks using one or several modes of information transfer shown in TABLE 8-1. A similar analysis can be performed on each major group, using selected

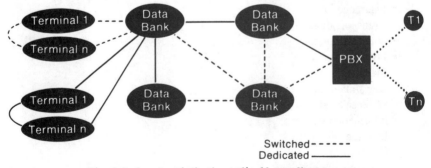

Fig. 8-3. A network that's applicable to all sectors.

Table 8 – 1. User Tasks and Modes of Operation

Tasks	Modes of operation
Inquiries	I/R
Buy/sell transactions	RD/D, T
Portfolio monitoring	I/R, RD/D, VC
Remote to central transactions	T
Central to stock exchange transactions	T
Central to remote billing	RD/D, T
Internal paperwork transactions	RD/D, T
Research survey monitoring	DC
Information to broker	DD

representative firms. The tasks for each of the groups can then be sorted by mode to obtain a cross-view of users from each industry. It will show, for example, all the industries and groups who might be performing inquiry response tasks, graphic type tasks, etc.

Technical requirements — attributes

Next, the mode of operation of the users can be translated into these kinds of telephony characteristics over an accepted range of values:

- Connect time.
- Holding time.
- Attempts.
- User facility location.
- User error rate tolerance.
- Terminal device speed.
- Encryption.

From this, various types of specific technical users are identified. They're obtained by making permutations of these requirements over a range of values. Not all permutations of users exist, at least in any reasonable quantity. The next step is to determine what user types will realistically be prevalent, if a cost-effective integrated services network is available to meet their needs.

For example, a user type who is in a broadband graphics category and has an extremely low holding time, generating an excessive number of attempts, and having an extremely sensitive error rate tolerance will possibly not be found in any group. On the other hand, an inquiry/response user type generating greater than normal POTS (plain old telephone service) traffic, with an average error rate tolerance over low- to medium-speed terminals will most likely be present in all groups.

Range of values

The range of values becomes an important issue in identifying the new users. The range can be related to traditional POTS values, in terms of equal to, less than, or greater than normal. Similarly, error rate tolerances, transmission speeds, etc., can be broken down into two or three broad ranges of values to enable a clear division among user types. (See TABLE 8-2.)

Table 8–2. Range of Values

Connect Time	(Normal POTS, instantaneous)
Holding Time	(Less than, normal, greater than POTS)
Attempts	(less than, normal, greater than POTS)
Error Rate Tolerance	(Low, med, high)
Terminal Speed	(Less than 2400-low, less than 9600-med, greater than 9600-high.)

User types

Each category has several distinctive types of users. These types are characterized by their attributes' range of values. Not all of the permutations exist. Hence, it's necessary to crosscheck each possible combination against the real world.

User type = f(user category (attribute (range)))

(User types are a function of user category, which is subdivided over a range of specific technical values . . . for particular attributes . . .)

An example of how we can analyze each category's user types is demonstrated by this representative process analysis for determining category 1 inquiry/response user types (I/R).

Definition

The inquiry/response data user makes a single inquiry or sequence of inquiries to determine the status of a remote file. As noted in the attribute values, the single inquiry will normally require fast connection and only hold for several seconds. The I/R user will, in general, operate on the 4 kHz network, switched (dial-up or packet) or private (for fast connects). The I/R call volume will be very large, as indicated by the large list of I/R users from each industry group. See TABLE 8-3.

Category 1 attributes

The attributes associated with this category were carefully investigated. Three main attributes were used to identify potential users (connect time, PBX/local exchange facility, and terminal device operation speed). This resulted in eight possible user types. As the applications for each were examined, some were eliminated as not existing in this category. The final user types for each category are described TABLE 8-7, which determined the realistic user types from the eight

Table 8–3. Category One Users — IR

Federal state info exchange	Manufacturing
Inventory control	Book distributors
Planning	News/mag info transfer
Marketing	Research staff operations
Purchasing	Entertainment
Legal	Theater setting
Logistics	Performance bookings
Field maintenance	Medium/business
Accounting	Wholesale-orders
Utility, oil, tele, power, gas	Food industry distribution
Distribution control	Drug business order/customer bill
Control (planned)	Inventory control for chain stores
Records	Hotel/motel reservations
Maintenance clusters	Auto rental chains
General message operations	Home communications
Air, rail, car transportation	Time sharing accounts management
Travel agencies inquiry	Shopping selections, remote
Customer control	University accounting
Operations control	Civil defense
Maintenance control	Red cross network
Logistics control	Political organization nets
Personnel control	Government services
Payroll/accounting	Health care
Hospital patient files	Insurance-hospital claims
Hospital med records	Hospital equip control
Hospital staff control	Dr-education (remote) files
Dr-consultation files	Remote test reports
Information services	Library files for inquiry
Lib-distrib info exchange	Library-to-home/bus terminal
Library-to-home	DP into services (statistics)
Education	University file-student statistics
Remote student grading	University library files
	Stock market inquiries

Table 8–4. Possible Permutations

Communication Facility	Transport Rate	Connection Time	
		Normal	Inst
Internal to User	Low	1	2
(PABX,PAX)	Med	3	4
External to User	Low	5	6
(Class Exchange)	Med	7	8

possible inquiry/response user types shown in TABLE 8-4. Three main attributes generate six distinct user types. These attributes are:

1. Connect time (normal POTS, instantaneous).
2. User facilities location (internal, external).
3. Terminal device operation speed
   (Low < 9600/Med < 64K/High > 64K).

Category 1 possible user types

The user types all have the following same general requirements (see TABLE 8-5).

Table 8–5. Possible User Types

Attribute	Single	Sequence
Connect Time	Instantaneous	Normal (N)
Holding Time	<N	N
Attempts	>N	>N
User Facilities Location	Internal(I)/External(E)	Internal(I)/External(E)
Connection Facility	P/SW	SW
Operation Mode (RT = real time)	RT	RT
Error Tolerance	Medium	Medium
Terminal Device Operation Speed (TDOS)	Low/Med	Low/Med

- Online.
- Medium error tolerance with retransmission.
- Attempts greater than POTS.
- Initially analog, later digital.
- Initially private and switched — later publicly switched.
- Holding time less than three minutes — normally less than one minute.

The TABLE 8-4 number refers to position in TABLE 8-6. Every chart has eight positions, one for each user type listed, showing the relationship between connect time, terminal speed, and error rate tolerance. TABLE 8-6 shows the user types and their network attributes for PABX users.

General conclusions

- If the switched networks are upgraded to handle requirements of the user types eight and four, then the large private distribution-type network can be switched and need not be on expensive private lines (point to point).
- Cost for this I/R type of call should be a function of call duration or amount of bits rather than a flat one-minute rate.

Table 8-6. User Types and Network Attributes

User type	Network attributes
1	PABXs with low speed input devices.
2	Economical concentrators replace the need for this user type's PABX requirements.
3	Normal PABX port if the line quality can transmit at less than 64K rate.
4	Internally hardwired to computer ports and can be captured by a PABX port, if the PABX can provide fast connections and medium speed trunks. This type will not be switched unless the PABX connect time is decreased and the switching network can pass up to 64K bits/sec at reasonable error rates.
5	Acoustic coupler type user on the Telco's present switched network. This user type will grow to be very large. This will effect processor capacity and offset traffic load projections for telephone offices. These users will go from voice data to data in the future, which will further effect switch capacities. They are currently getting a free ride on unlimited local "call pack" offerings and inward WATS facilities, where use of these facilities is much more than initially estimated.
6	A fast connect, low speed transmission, local exchange facility is unwarranted for this user type.
7	Requires up to the 64K rate of transmission available on the present trunks that are on the present exchanges.
8	Requires a fast exchange connection using medium speed trunks, presently is on the private point-to-point network. Hence, this user requires a fast non-blocking switch, but will not be switched unless the exchange connect time is decreased and the trunk/matrix switching transmission network can pass up to 64K bits/sec.

- Traffic patterns generated by these lines and trunks will be inconsistent with previously established voice traffic patterns.
- Volume of calls and transactions for the 1990s is the most difficult to predict. Gross statistics can be given for major groups. Projections are usually made by extending a trend, relating to another industry, or by curve fitting. Otherwise, the consumer demand curve must be determined, using an extensive list of specific products soon to be available to the consumer. Information transfer is a new industry that's not independent but has a definite cross-elasticity relationship to the computer industry, transmission medium, terminal market, and programming language advancement. So, the industry is too early to project by macro-econometric models. Some have chosen micro-economic techniques such as demand forecasting.
- Demand for past services has mostly been technology driven. Companies determined the products for the user. The user didn't initially demand them until they learned about them.
- Market-driven services can greatly increase usage. Computer usage breeds computer dependency, which breeds more computer usage. This increase in usage and sharing of costs brings down costs, which increases usage and

user demand. In addition, if hard copy can economically replace oral communication, many people such as doctors, druggists, police officers, etc., will switch from this type of oral conversations (voice data) to data conversations. This will decrease the volume of voice communications and further increase the number of data transactions.

The new users

As noted in TABLE 8-4, user types are simply possible permutations of users over a range of technical values for each mode of operation. They must be overlaid on each industry or group and be identified as a reasonable possibility. In this way, the many possibilities are reduced to only realistic types.

However, some of their requirements might be so extensive that the time frame for their actual existence might not be until the third or fourth phase of their industry's network evolution. Alternatively, they might exist today, but not in the near future.

This approach will enable extensive lists of new users to be identified for each industry. As the analysis progresses, the number of similar user types from each industry can be determined. However, these will not be numbers of potential customers for marketing to project sales, but merely profiles of users. For example, the number of banks in the United States that have remote tellers that perform inquiry/response functions of a particular type will not be quantified. However, the analysis will identify the number of realistic inquiry/response user types that are common in each industry. Their needs are met by a particular network, product, or service. (Later, more extensive marketing sampling and projection models can provide quantities for sales projections.) In other words, if you're a bank in New York, these are your transport "needs," but what's not identified is how many banks in New York will pay for meeting these needs in 1990, 1995, 2000.

In reviewing the new user types shown in TABLE 8-7, we might come to the following conclusions that affect the type and time frame of the evolution of the integrated services network phases:

- For PBX and local exchange type applications, many new user types would be satisfied with a fast-connect, medium-speed transaction system. The network and processors must handle a greater than normal volume of call attempts that have less than normal holding time duration.
- Extreme wideband users will be more economically handled on private lines until their number increases or until video conferencing on separate wideband switches over digital pipe networks are available to handle them.
- An error rate of one error in 10^7 would probably be acceptable for most data user types, with the exception of air traffic and long transaction computer-to-computer users.
- The 9600 bit rates or less will easily handle many of the new users during the first phase of their evolution into the information world.
- The 64K or multiples of it will handle many data users during the late '90s

Table 8-7. User Types

Attributes (range of values) User type/category	Attempts	Connect time	Holding time	Error tolerance	Data speed
Interactive/time share					
Type 1 (remote programming)	<N	N	>N	L	L/M
Interactive remote access					
Type 1 (remote batch processing)	N	N	>N	L	L/M
Interactive TS					
Type 2 (remote programming)	>N	F	<N	L	M/H
Interactive RA					
Type 2 (remove batch processing)	>N	F	<N	L	M/H
Remote display/doc'mt					
Type 1 (facsimile)	>N	N	N<N	M	L/M
Type 2 (printing)	<N	N	<N	M	M/H
Interactive graphics					
Type 1 (computer graphics)	<N	N	>N	M	M/H
Transactions					
Type 1 (bank network)	>N	F	<N	L	L/M
Type 2 (stock exchange network)	>N	F	<N	L	M/H
Type 3 (wide band users)	<N	F	>N	L	M/H
Voice inquiry					
Type 1 (reservations)	>N	N	N	M	—
Inquiry/response					
Type 1 (credit check)	>N	N	N	H	L/M
Type 2 (auto parts inv.)	>N	N	N	M	M/H
Type 3 (airline reservations)	>N	F	<N	M	M/H
Data collection					
Type 1 (retail inventory control)	>N	<N	H	L/M	
Type 2 (gov't status network)	>N	F	<N	L	M/H
Data distribution					
Type 1 (motel network)	>N	N	<N	H	L/M
Type 2 (police network)	>N	F	<N	H	L/M
Type 3 (medical network)	>N	N	<N	L	M/H
Type 4 (news network)	>N	F	<N	L	M/H

years of growth, until variable bandwidth on demand (channel or bit rate) is required.

- Inquiry/response user types will exist extensively in all major industries, as they generate single and multiple inquiries in various modes of voice, voice/ data, and data communications.
- Terminals will be switched through PABXs and local offices rather than

point to point. Industrial private networks will increasingly use more and more switched terminals to reach numerous local and remote data banks.

- Transactions, data collection, and data distribution with inquiry/response user types will greatly increase traffic on communication switches and facilities as retail stores go to the debit/smart card point of sales and "online" inventory controls.
- Due to excessive volume, transactions for some industries' users (such as banks) need not be circuit switched, but could be handled by packet switches or facilities that are controlled and selected by variable channel selectors or contention systems.
- Circuit-switched systems and packet-switched systems will continue to compete for a large number of similar user types, who are transparent to the medium except for response time, security, and block size. These three requirements will be crucial, as longer calls might favor circuit switching over fast packet switching.
- Traffic patterns generated by data users will be inconsistent with previously established voice traffic in terms of attempts, time of day traffic peaks, call duration, and area concentration.
- WATS and unlimited local calling will have to be seriously addressed to economically move data users to separate nonregulated integrated services networks.
- Protocol, connect time, error rate, grade of service, data tariffs, barred access, three attempt limit, polling, retry, code conversion, multiaddress calls, direct calls, short clear down and data collection transport services, as well as list processing, word processor reformatting, and file management are features that are greatly dependent on understanding these new user types and their technical requirements.

New users' impact

The new users of the networks and products will use the home communications centers and offices of the future, and, for the most part, less than 20 or so distinct user types can be realistically identified by performing a detailed top-down planning analysis. The following are recommendations on the types and time frame of integrated services that the suppliers of telecommunications products should include in their network products so that the providers of these services will be able to meet the needs of the new users.

This methodology could be applied to each individual business or home communications market area to identify which of the twenty user types will be most prevalent for an application. Such an analysis should consider the following points:

- Home computers that are unable to communicate with large external databases will have limited growth. The future trend will be towards interactive access to several types of external databases, i.e., obtaining information on stock exchanges, airline reservations, weather, initial retail transactions from the home, etc. These connections might require only low-speed facilities or a residential-type public data packet network.

- Before there will be widespread acceptance of office automation, users of the offices of the future must first see an extensive human-factors analysis to ease the human-machine interface problems.
- Governments might want to encourage tax incentives to subsidize the formation of large topical public databases that can be economically accessed and administered so that new users can access new information networks from more remote locations. This will encourage rural growth and help relieve demand for new, bigger roads to handle rush-hour traffic and encourage rural growth.
- Internal country requirements must be carefully identified in terms of what the new users will expect and how the initial information overlay networks can be economically provided to encourage growth. The overlay networks must be provided in phases over the next decade. Waiting for user demand to justify the overlay networks will not encourage sufficient growth on a cost-effective basis.
- Growth of usage will also be dependent on gateway switching exchanges to enable users to access multiple networks, both internal and external to a country. Standards must be identified and adopted before real growth can be expected.
- The business community will lead the residential use of databases and networks and will bear the initial cost for overlay network facilities. Hence, the next development step for future integrated services should be business communication centers that truly solve the problems of inventory, electronic mail, information access (reservations, stock market), etc., using easy human interfacing.

In summary, the home communications center and the business communications center (office of the future) that have been described in trade journals over the past fifteen years can indeed become a reality, as the overlay and broadband phases of the ISDN network are completed in the '90s . . .

Study two: The human element — a user's view

In the early '90s, Coy, Schwartz, and Hammonds made the following observations in a McGraw-Hill *Business Week* analysis . . .

Human beings are creatures of habit. We fundamentally want the machine to come to us rather than the other way around . . .

Where were you when the Information Age dawned? If you're like millions of American office workers, sometime during the 1980s you found a personal computer on your desk. When you finished figuring out how to use a spreadsheet and zip off a report without a secretary's help, you were expected to take the next big plunge: using your new computer to get in touch with the head office, or to tap into a database, or to send pitch letters to prospects via electronic mail. Maybe you never really got that far. However, it's likely that you became part of this revolution all the same — through that most familiar instrument, the telephone. Increasingly, the nation's 240 million phones are doubling as computer terminals. Rather than teach consumers — or office workers, for that matter — the arcane process of data communications, businesses are finding that it's far easier to get people to punch a few buttons on a Touch-Tone phone or to send and receive digitized audio messages.

Voice response equipment allows depositors to tap into a bank's mainframe computer from their Touch-Tone phones to find out when a check cleared or how many payments are left on a loan. The information is "read" to the caller by systems, which, instead of displaying the information on a screen, renders it as digitized speech. Then there are computerized voice services. One type, Audiotex, gives callers everything from stock prices to horoscopes. The industry might be a great deal larger, save for one small problem: Lots of people hate doing business with a machine, even if it's attached to the good old telephone. Who hasn't encountered a computerized receptionist that leads you through a twisted maze of options before you realize you're not going to reach the party you're trying to call? Or heard from a computerized direct-marketing machine that automatically dials your number and delivers a recorded pitch? One such system dialed every room at a hospital to deliver an audio ad for a liquor store. Despite the problems, voice processing is spreading. By uniting the simplicity and omnipresence of the telephone with the power of the computer, it enhances both. Communicating with machines by phone, you can find out when your CD will mature, order tulips, reserve an airline seat, broadcast a voice message to your sales force, or have your E-mail read to you in a robotic monotone. It's faster, cheaper, and more private than dealing with a person, and it can be done at 4 a.m. because machines never sleep.

While computers are involved in all these operations, they're so hidden in a well-designed system that even technophobes can cope. The ultimate in user-friendly computers — systems that recognize human speech so that people can talk directly to them — are beginning to move out of the lab. While phone-based information and transaction systems lack the technological pizzazz of online computer networks, voice processing is becoming an important tool for businesses that are struggling to find a cost-effective way of providing services. One firm noted how many people call it at one, two, three o'clock in the morning. In the past, those calls would have gone unanswered because the company couldn't afford to have specialists by the phone at all hours. However, voice processing isn't only — or even mainly — a way to save money. Primarily, it's a way to improve communications with employees, suppliers, and customers by eliminating wasteful routines such as telephone tag, where people spend hours trying to make contact. One firm's test sample found that 75 percent of the internal telephone calls didn't reach the intended party, and 60 percent didn't require conversation. Now, it uses voice systems for internal and external communications. Customers can get answers to routine queries on claims and coverage directly from its mainframes by calling an 800 number. That frees customer service representatives to tackle the complex questions. To speed up decision making, it encourages employees to leave messages in each other's voice mailboxes at all hours. One department head broadcast a voice memo into several mailboxes simultaneously on a Saturday morning and had 14 responses by 4:30 that afternoon. "We're finding that voice mail is a 24-hour, seven-day-a-week tool." Employees with voice mailboxes have upped their productivity 20 percent to 30 percent. "It has become part of our culture."

The latest twist on phone-based information systems is fax-back. Callers simply indicate what information they want—a sales brochure or map, say—by punching keys on their phones. Then they key in their fax numbers and, voila! the information appears. One magazine in Newport, RI uses a fax-back on a 900 toll number to help yacht buyers shop. Key in a code for the boat you like, and it will fax you the phone numbers of readers who own the model. The charge per call produces a modest profit, but more important, the service frees the staff from answering up to 300 inquiries a week.

It has taken nearly three decades for voice processing to get this far. AT&T laid the groundwork in the mid-1960s, when it began Touch-Tone phone service. Few customers knew it, but the beeps emitting from their new phones were really a kind of computer code—a different tone for each number from 0 through 9. Those same tones are now what make a telephone a computer terminal. The industry didn't take off until the 1980s, when microprocessors, inexpensive memory chips, digital signal processing chips, and large-capacity disk drives became readily available. These devices made it possible to build a voice processing system for a fraction of the cost of earlier models. Voice systems need powerful computers because just storing digitized recordings takes more than 200 times as much computer memory as storing the same words in text form.

While the technology has advanced, the need for it has expanded because the pool of skilled workers is getting tighter. The systems let operators, receptionists, clerks, and salespeople focus on human interactions instead of the drudge work. At the same time, rising postal rates and falling long-distance rates have made dealing by phone more attractive. Indeed, in 1990, approximately $196 billion worth of goods were sold by phone. Nearly all big telemarketers tie their phones to computers for efficiency.

Computers that can understand and respond to human speech have been science-fiction staples for decades. Not only is speaking to the computer easier and faster than typing, but it's also less error-prone. While versatile conversationalists, like the HAL computer in 2001: A Space Odyssey, have not yet arrived, recent advances make it practical to add much simpler forms of speech recognition to everyday tasks in offices, homes, hospitals, and factories. The dream of getting computers to process speech the way humans do has exasperated some of the world's best minds. Many researchers have concluded that it's not really imperative to create computers that can comprehend everything. "Let's have a machine that knows all about just one thing." If a computer is trained to understand, for instance, the vocabulary of booking an airline reservation or trading stocks, then the problem becomes far simpler.

Thanks to this new approach, the technology is finally living up to its promise. Speech-recognition programs, which a few years ago required massive mainframes, can now run on powerful but inexpensive desktop computers . . . Some savings will come from reducing fraud by storing a "voiceprint" of each calling-card customer. Since a voice is as unique as a fingerprint, phone cheats would be foiled. Alternatively . . . it will enable automating tasks such as providing directory assistance or allowing consumers to order merchandise directly by phone, or automating dictation—instantly converting a person's voice into computer text . . .

Voice recognition is also expected to boost overall phone use. Phone companies figure that consumers will soon be calling in orders to voice-recognition computers owned by direct marketers, rather than filling out mail-order forms. One firm now uses such a system for its thousands of dealers to place merchandise orders around the clock. While telephone applications might soon become the most pervasive form of speech recognition, the technology causing the most excitement involves converting speech to text. The holy grail is a system that will allow people to treat their PC like a human secretary, verbally telling it to take dictation and then printing copies of documents. However, large-vocabulary systems have their drawbacks.

Besides not being able to recognize continuous speech, they must be trained to "learn" the nuances of each speaker's voice. It often takes hours for a system to gather sufficient voice samples from each speaker. That's not acceptable in most over-the-phone tasks, which require "speaker independence." Fact is, not one of the dozen or so speech systems now available commercially can instantly understand large vocabularies of naturally paced speech from any person. New techniques promise to overcome such limitations. Linguistics programs, for example, can increase accuracy by anticipating where a noun or verb is likely to occur in a sentence. "Word spotting" makes small-vocabulary systems far more useful by filtering out irrelevant words or phrases. So if you reply, "Um, well, yes, thank you," to a question that requires a simple yes or no, the computer is able to disregard everything but the key word.

Researchers all over the world are still racing to make new breakthroughs. In Japan, for instance, almost every high-tech company is working feverishly. Hitachi Ltd. is experimenting with so-called neural network systems that simulate the learning abilities of the human brain. NEC Corp., meanwhile, is trying to combine voice recognition with machine translation. A 1991 prototype grasps words spoken in Japanese and renders them into computer-synthesized English.

Experts predict that systems with HAL-like capabilities will indeed arrive— but probably not before 2001. Until then, the struggle continues. "Machines should deal with humans on human terms, not on their own," noted Skrzypczak at Nynex. If that happens, when people complain of computer phobia, at least the computer will be able to listen . . .

The Information Appliance

George W. Welles III

Global communication technologies without good end-user interfaces are like automobiles without controls. No matter how powerful we make them, communication technologies can't advance without good human interfaces. One answer to the interface problem, the information appliance, will allow the user to easily and intuitively access whatever information he or she needs, no matter where that information is located. The appliance will then allow the user to process the information into new forms as a value added product. Such a device is key to improving office productivity and allowing the United States to become a major player in the information society.

What is an information appliance?

The word appliance is not threatening. The term is often associated with electric-powered consumer devices serving humans — often in a home setting. The term "information appliance" might have come from marketers who desired to create a nontechnical description for universal communication and information processing devices capable of easily acquiring and processing data. A number of office automation studies reveal that the level of office productivity has not significantly increased since World War II. A study in the early '90s by Nolan, Norton and Company, noted that the real costs of owning PCs are at least double or are perhaps closer to five times the investment in hardware, software, and support costs of each unit. Those hidden costs reflect poor human-machine interfaces and the fragmented functionality of information gathering and processing tools.

Unfortunately, the marriage of desktop communication and information technologies has not been as successful as "the experts" had hoped. True, faxes and LANs have changed the face of American business, but the fax has proven to be a paper band-aid for our failure to properly marry communications with good human interfaces.

George Guilder used the word "teleputer" to denote the amalgam of the telephone and computer. A subsequent view of Guilder's "teleputer" as a "desktop information appliance" fits the description of a device that would drastically improve the human-machine interface with information, computing, and communications resources. More advanced, wireless versions of such machines could move information appliances from the desktop to the hand, pocket, or even wrist. Input would switch from the traditional keyboard and mouse to a pen, or even the human voice.

In the late '80s, NEC trialed the 1ST 500 — an early version of the desktop information appliance. This prototypic PC-based device combined the capabilities of a DOS computer, telephone, color scanner, and video conferencing terminal. Running on Basic Rate ISDN, the units enabled users to see and talk with each other, as well as work collaboratively, dynamically changing documents.

By the mid '90s, times and technologies had changed. The power of modern desktop computers continued to explode. Price performance ratios improved rapidly. Internal gigabit storage capacities were becoming commonplace.

Imagery was presented in 24 or 32-bit color instead of 8-bit. Personal computing speeds surpassed those of the stand-alone minimainframes of the late '80s and early '90s.

Online databases were proliferating — though transport speeds of 2400 Kbps appeared excruciatingly slow to many users. Even 19,200 Kbps rates weren't acceptable for those running image-intensive applications. Users wanted economical gateways to existing high-speed networks like Internet or new national, broadband networks.

People wanted to use their computers to see, talk to, and collaborate with colleagues, no matter where on the planet their colleagues were located. They wanted to explore a multimedia world of color, sound, and information. Even more importantly, they needed to accomplish all of this in an easy, intuitive, economical way. They wanted the technologies to occupy little precious space in their world. Most of all, they needed the information appliance to be a "partner," not a frustrating impediment to accomplishing tasks.

What will the information appliance of future look like?

A look into the crystal ball (you might want to use an active matrix LCD or gas plasma display, or . . .) suggests that the information appliance of the future might present information on a 60-centimeter-by-90-centimeter (24-inch-by-30-inch) or larger backlit active matrix LCD screen, suspended on an adjustable arm out from a wall or office panel. With this configuration, the user can adjust the viewing angle to meet his or her needs. The 2000 × 3000 pixel screen will provide an image resolution similar to current 35mm photographic color negatives —much higher than most proposed U. S. digital high-definition television standards. On-board RISC-based imaging engines can ensure that the processing power is available to drive the display at real-time speeds. With such displays, rendering delays would be negligible.

Compression algorithms and chip sets will keep pace with the increased demand for full-motion imagery. While the digital high-definition video signal from built-in 300 plus channel optical cable television decoders will probably not initially use the 2000 × 3000 pixel screen to its fullest capabilities, the quality will be very good.

Image input to the system could come from a tiny, transparent, multisensor imaging chip embedded part way down the display screen surface. The chip would use multiple microscopic lenses, marrying the sensor outputs electronically to form a single, coherent, wide-angle, high-resolution, color image of the area around the display. The screen image would be barely impeded by the imaging chip. Special software could enable the on-site user, or a remote conferee, to control the angle of view by selecting the pixel array need to form a chosen angle.

In sync with the image, audio could be delivered by several small, but very efficient, audio transducers providing full binaural "surround" sound. The sophisticated "surround" audio system of proposed future systems could therefore be designed to produce the highest quality audio experience in the smallest possible space. This system could deliver clear spatial imaging over the entire workspace and would be engineered to provide as much privacy as possible using advanced noise cancellation techniques.

A separate CPU could be stored in a slide-out rack below the work surface, allowing easy access to add capability and reconfigure hardware rapidly. Built-in diagnostics should track even momentary glitches and warn the user of impending problems. Finally, to complete the picture, the almost unlimited storage capacity of photochromic memories or other new storage devices would provide support for even the most powerful applications of the late '90s and beyond . . .

Everything is changing, as numerous ways to store information are devised using flash EPROMS, Ferroelectric RAM (FRAM), and other gigabit solid-state technologies. Here, information that needs to be stored and moved in the "old-fashioned way" can be written to credit-card-sized solid-state cards. This information-dense "smart card" allows users to tuck large amounts of data into a wallet or purse with little fear of losing it. Even higher storage densities will be possible on gigabit 2.5-inch flopticals.™ The high-density storage on flopticals™ will be made possible by the development of blue lasers operating at room temperature.

Other display options likely to be available to users will include a set of infrared-triggered, virtual reality (VR), LCD miniscreens for viewing 3D VR imagery. The soft headband supporting the miniscreens would also support a pair of extended-frequency holographic audio transducers. When needed, a virtual reality glove could connect to the system, via a wireless link, to support VR applications. Similarly, full-body virtual reality suits might be available for special projects such as telepresence and advanced research and development projects. More advanced displays, using eyeglass-sized minilaser retina writers, will continue to evolve; however, concern remains over the long-term effects of writing holographic color images directly onto a human retina.

The ongoing issue of repetitive motion injuries will continue to push the need for voice recognition control of information appliances. Other nontraditional input devices, likely to become more common, include pressure-sensitive arm rests, knee paddles, and foot switches. Alpha wave brain control of computers might in time be declassified by the Air Force, allowing research to continue toward controlling machines by human thought!

Workspaces will be required to be designed for maximum ergonomic efficiency and safety. Lighting will need to be full spectrum, nonflickering, indirect, and user-adjustable to avoid eyestrain and other health issues. The information appliance will be designed to be used from almost any human position — standing, walking, running, lying down or perhaps even asleep!

What are the applications driving these technologies?

For an answer to that question, let's look at how you might work in the future. As you step into your company-provided home workspace, you turn up and adjust your desktop information appliance. It's 1998. You don't have a traditional office at work. Your company does maintain a number of small distributed work centers scattered around the world. Some days you book a company workspace to confer face-to-face with colleagues, meet with customers, or use technologies that remain too expensive to install in your home. One room in the company work center, a break area with a life-sized wall display, allows similar break areas, kilometers away from yours, to become part of your virtual space. You can hold a conversation with a friend, as if you were taking a coffee break together.

At the start of a work period, after turning up the display, engaging in a sophisticated security procedure, and entering your work needs into the system, you can begin accessing information that has been flowing into your home workspace on a continuous basis. First, you might choose to view your video mail messages from colleagues around the world or delete a video mail ad from an overly aggressive supplier. If the supplier's behavior annoys you, you might enter the offender's network address and instruct the computer to deny access in the future.

In checking your on-screen mirror image, you might notice that the room behind you is not as tidy as you'd like. By using an advanced form of graphic background fill, and a scene from your library of background images, you can present a more pleasing, electronic image to your colleagues. Once satisfied with what you see, you can begin comfortably returning video calls to colleagues in London, Los Angeles, Fiji, or wherever they're located in this globally linked society.

Meanwhile, the computer system's offline broadcast monitoring software takes note of an upcoming CNN news story of interest to you. The system functions by doing key-word/key-word-string searches in the background, using closed captioning as a text source. A message appears on your screen asking if you want the information displayed, recorded, or ignored. You might choose to watch the news story on a window displayed on your screen, while conferencing with a colleague on a second window, and working collaboratively on an image for an upcoming ad campaign on a third larger window.

Let's pretend that the advertising image of a Scottish castle that you and your co-worker are creating doesn't seem quite right. Perhaps the graphic information you need in order to make the illustration more accurate and powerful can't be easily found. So, your co-worker volunteers to don a virtual reality headset and glove to research the information. Entering Cyberspace, she "flies" into one of several virtual reality online library gateways. Access time in the virtual reality library is expensive and can add up quickly, but both of you are adept at maximizing the VR technology to find information. The bill for her online time will go directly to her corporate account to be automatically rebilled with a suitable mark up—to the client.

Meanwhile, you decide it's a pleasant spring day in the Southern Hemisphere, and you step outside onto your white sand beach. While you stand on the beach mulling over the illustration, in the Northern Hemisphere, your colleague continues her "flight" through the Cyberspace of the virtual library in her quest for information. If you and she had more time, you might have chosen to send an electronic software surrogate called a *knowbot* to locate the information.

As you enjoy the sun and warm breezes, you can remain in contact with the outside world via a wireless wrist screen and audio communicator—linked to the host desktop information appliance inside your home. The desktop unit is doing the majority of its communication via an advanced version of basic rate ISDN running on existing copper wires.

Broadcast video for your system is down-linked from direct broadcast satellites (DBS) to a small, flat-array VSAT receiving plate on the north side of the house. Fiber optics haven't made it to the islands where you live yet, making advanced ISDN data circuits running on existing copper crucial to information delivery. In cities and industrial areas, digital high-definition video is delivered by fiber optic to the home.

Meanwhile, your colleague finds the needed imagery of Dunvegan Castle in the online image library of an obscure Scottish museum on the Isle of Skye. The accuracy questions are resolved and a copy of a seventeenth century woodcut is downloaded. Billing for one-time use rights to the image is again handled electronically and debited from your corporate account.

Mission accomplished, you're called back via your wrist communicator. Taking a last look at the turquoise sea, with a sigh you step back inside your workspace. Though you often collaborate on projects with your co-worker, you've actually met, in person, only once a year at work-team meetings. She lives thousands of kilometers away.

As you work, you can also use your information appliance display to monitor remote video cameras allowing you to keep an eye on your son in his crib and your daughter playing on the beach.

When you aren't logged on as working (and your work day is spread out to meet your personal needs and the needs and time zones of those with whom you work) you might use other personal information appliances to order groceries or view entertainment and educational programs. Many of the programs are interactive, allowing you to create your own custom programming. When watching a play or a concert, you can remotely choose your desired camera angle.

Though much can be accomplished from your home, you can also book space at the work center when you feel the need to be away with colleagues. You, like many of your peers, need to spend some time each month in face-to-face social interaction with co-workers. As noted, several times a year, your entire work group from around the world gathers at a "business resort" to combine business and recreation as well as to renew acquaintances without going through the "silicon window." Since you work for an enlightened company, spouses are included to make them feel part of the universally distributed corporate family of the Information Millennium.

Much of this future technology will be possible by the year 2000, as it was derived from its forerunners of the early '90s. Our success in marrying the capabilities of future information appliances to human needs will be key to making this Information Age a reality. We must answer the challenge of this vision of the future.

So it might be . . .
So it will be!

Study three: The trials and tribulations of videophone

Peter K. Heldman

In 1968, AT&T Bell Laboratories introduced the first picturephone at the world expo. Unfortunately, consumer and technology issues of cost, quality, and availability contributed to its demise. Since that first attempt at videophone, new technology has made revolutionary improvements in the price and performance of the videophones that can be offered today, thus making the twenty-five-year-old dream of a ubiquitous videophone offering a technical possibility.

In the early '90s there were numerous videophone trials. In one extensive trial among suppliers, providers, and users in particular, the latest video technology was tested using a group of twenty-six users across a five-state area. The user test took form in two major parts—one at 45 Mbps, the other at 384 Kbps, as well as specialized lab tests at other commonly used rates.

From these activities, several key conclusions were drawn, covering: bandwidth and network requirements, delay and audio quality issues, terminal ergonomics, ambient lighting challenges, features on the features, and support requirements, as noted by the following observations and conclusions.

Bandwidth and network requirements

Video services offer perhaps the best example of the price/performance trade-off of bandwidth. Broadcast television today provides a natural benchmark for users when evaluating a video solution, presenting a known and accepted level of video and audio quality. Current codecs, operating at various bandwidths, offer a range of quality that falls both above and below that provided by television today. *Future Telecommunications* categorizes videophone into three levels: I, II, and III, each corresponding to the narrowband, wideband, and broadband networks needed to support them.

However, what level is required to provide adequate quality? The trial results concluded that Level III videophone service at 45 Mbps was overwhelmingly accepted, as it provided a high-quality service that proved to be an effective tool in the participant's busy lives. However, at 384 Kbps, issues of latency and synchronization, stemming from the delay introduced by the codec's processing of the video signals, severely inhibited the system's effectiveness and utility. Subsequent lab tests indicated that Level II, wideband videophone at 1.5 Mbps, seemed to be the minimum bandwidth at which high-quality videophone could be best universally achieved with existing codec technology.

However, given the high price of bandwidth and the limited ubiquity that results, users today face many of the same obstacles that their forebears confronted in 1968. As a result, adequate quality tends to be relative to the often compromising balance of price and performance that satisfy a customer's needs and expectations. Customers today must try to find acceptable quality service at an acceptable price from the right selection of codecs and bandwidth. Although in recent years, codec manufacturers have dramatically improved the quality that they can provide at lower and lower bandwidths, this balance of price and performance might not yet exist for many users. This indicates a great need for an ubiquitous, next-generation public digital data network at narrowband, wideband, and broadband rates.

Delay and audio quality issues

It's evident that real-time video puts stringent delay requirements on the network end to end. Several main sources of delay were found, including: speakerphone clipping, codec processing, network transmission, and switching devices.

Traditional half-duplex speakerphones introduce annoying delay, as the audio gain devices toggle back and forth between conferees. This delay is pronounced in video conferencing, when the viewer sees a person's lips move without the corresponding sound. Full-duplex speakerphones address this problem, but other nettlesome forms of delay remain.

The codec's processing delay slows delivery of the video signal, but the audio signal remains uncompressed. Thus undelayed, it arrives ahead of the corresponding video. The greater the compression, the greater the delay, so that at lower rates from 56 Kbps to 384 Kbps, this synchronization problem can become quite pronounced. Buffering the audio can introduce sufficient delay to synchronize its delivery with the video signal. However, there still remains a significant delay end-to-end that results, to a great extent, from codec processing. There are also delays from network transmission and switching devices, but to a far lesser degree. This latency in the signal dramatically impacts the nature and quality of communications at lower rates (below 1.5M). With highly compression video signals, this is a fundamental issue that's neither easy nor inexpensive to solve.

Terminal ergonomics

Today's sophisticated ISDN terminals provide an excellent, user-friendly interface allowing conferees to easily establish two-party or multiparty audio and/or video calls. This user-friendly interface was praised by trial participants and emphasized the need to provide users a friendly, easy-to-learn interface.

Perhaps the most significant ergonomic issue identified in the demonstration was the eye-to-eye capability. To provide a high-quality videophone service, the camera and monitor must be arranged in a way that allows eye contact.

Telecommunications Management Planning first noted this as an essential attribute and requirement for any high-quality videophone system. From the viewer's perspective, eye contact is lost when the camera and monitor are separated by an angle greater than 13 degrees. (See FIG. 8-4.) One solution—used in the trial—was to optically fold the image of conferees into a highly sensitive camera mounted below the monitor. The result allowed eye contact among conferees rather than the profile views of individuals, which results from traditional camera/monitor combinations. (See FIG. 8-5.) Emerging flat-screen technology will further reduce the size of the terminals required to achieve this eye-to-eye contact. The impact of eye-to-eye contact was verified in the trial results, with nearly unanimous user feedback on the necessity of this feature. Clearly, eye to eye is a key attribute of any quality videophone solution.

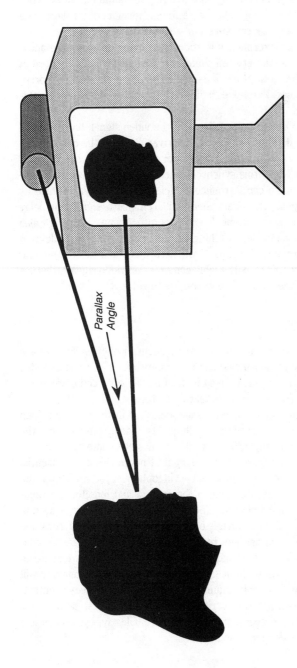

Fig. 8-4. Angle for eye contact.

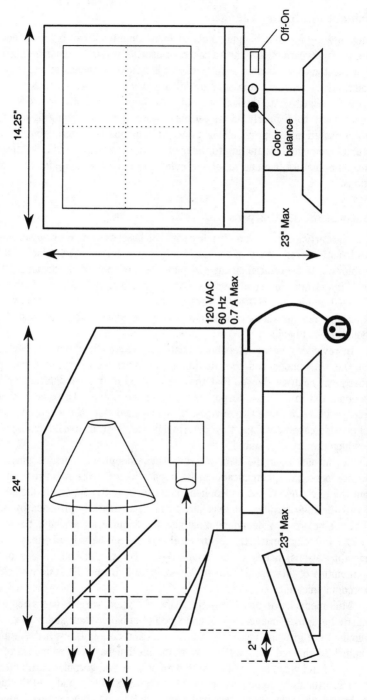

Fig. 8-5. Setup for allowing eye contact among conferees.

Ambient lighting challenges

Compensating for the changing ambient light conditions, which vary depending on time of day, weather, and the variation of user locations, remains a difficult issue. Sophisticated cameras must sense ambient light and compensate for changing light conditions. A less-desirable solution is to provide users the means to make the necessary adjustments themselves, but it becomes unrealistic, in the long run, to expect users to regularly adjust terminals to adapt to changing light conditions. Another solution is to provide bright, face lighting on the conferee, but this solution is cumbersome and distracting to the user. The technology to address these issues remains immature, expensive, and in many cases, cumbersome for desktop applications.

Features on the features

Once the participants became familiar with the basic system, they began requesting additional features. Many of the CLASS family of features were included in their list, along with secretarial pickup and some form of easy-to-use document-handling capability. Group three and four fax, document cameras, scanners of all types, and PC-based multimedia platforms were all considered. This raised some very interesting and key questions concerning where the videophone ends and the multimedia terminal begins.

In reviewing initial videophone trial requirement definitions, it became clear that the videophone and the multimedia terminal were very different devices. Subsequent analysis showed that they've evolved from very different origins and are dedicated to different purposes. Although there might be some similarities in the capabilities of these two devices, their origins dictate the way they administer and provide capabilities and thus determines the different market and applications for which they're best suited.

So, in assessing the two, we see that: videophone's unique purpose is to enhance personal communications. Its applications for the mass market evolved from the telephone. Thus, videophone must be easy to use, and it should meet or exceed the high quality and reliability standards currently provided by our voice telephone network. Videophone must also be ubiquitously available to the market at large. In today's market, one size rarely fits all. So the videophone, as with most new applications, needs to be tailored to meet the specific needs of various communities of interest. However, Videophone I, II, and III still must be able to intercommunicate.

Multimedia has evolved from the PC/workstation world as users begin seeking animated graphics, images, audio, and video to enhance their ability to convey and assimilate the growing volume of information and data in the world. A multimedia terminal is achieved using a PC or workstation that has been enhanced to support both audio and video applications with data, image, and graphics capabilities.

Unfortunately, some proponents of multimedia have abandoned the high-quality, broadband videophone terminal requirements, as they pursue a multimedia platform. Some have even recommended removing the eye to eye feature and relegating the video to a small window on the much larger monitor screen, with the remainder of the space dedicated to the document-handling capability that was originally ancillary to the videophone. They also proposed that the ISDN telephone user interface be dropped in favor of a multistep menu-driven PC-based solution.

Many users who were asked to evaluate the alternatives chose to separate the high-quality, noncomplex videophone from a multimedia PC-based alternative, although they did acknowledge the merit of a multimedia solution for other users with different application needs. Thus, both multimedia and videophone are different solutions addressing different market needs for which, it appears, there will be great demand, if this trial is indicative of user needs and preferences.

Support requirements

Given the public telephone industry's long history of providing high-quality voice telephone service, support requirements is an area of great interest as we focus on meeting advanced communication market needs with new, sophisticated telecommunications networking solutions. The strong service record of the past was ensured by the slow, deliberate, and controlled introduction of selected new technology into the public network. Today, providers — both public and private — face a blithering array of new technologies and applications that require special training and expertise for successful delivery. No longer can the network service providers declare that their interest and involvement stops at some invisible line drawn between the user and network provider. As one participant once noted when reflecting on the complexities of offering videophone, "It has become clear that expertise to support video communications is at a premium . . . in most cases, network personnel have very little desire to work with the video equipment because it's considered to be CPE. If we've learned anything from these trial activities, it's that video systems are quite complex and require a technical support staff with additional (if not unique) degrees of expertise." New, more intense focus must be placed on user applications and their networking requirements. All who provide services for these activities must accept responsibility not only for the performance of their unique piece, but also its interaction with all other elements of the solution!

Conclusion

Videophone offers great potential for enhancing personal communications, reducing the need to travel, and broadening our freedoms — to live and work where we choose. Videophone could indeed be the killer application, driving the deployment of a truly ubiquitous public information network at the narrowband, wideband, and broadband rates, which, once deployed, could support a host of new data and video services and applications to meet changing market needs.

9

A final footnote
The last word

"Actions speak louder than words..."

Time for ISDN

Ten years after the introduction of ISDN to the world community, ISDN standards and interface chip technologies are now finally, and firmly, in place. As noted in my *Future Telecommunications* book, the data-handling needs of 17 major industries, from banking to real estate, have been carefully assessed to clearly show the needs and opportunities for future ISDN-based narrowband, wideband, and broadband networks and services. During this turbulent period, the RBOCs and the other providers have had ample time to test customer market response to potential dataphone and videophone offerings, noting both the pros and cons, especially with regard to the need for ubiquitous availability and economical prices to attract and facilitate mass-market services. In the computer arena, it's now quite apparent that the major computer firms need to transport information from their remote customers over friendly, "switched" data transfer facilities to their large mainframes, as well as between the rising proliferation of powerful PCs/workstations distributed throughout the customer's community of interest. (See FIG. 9-1.)

As the 1990s give way to the new Information Century, it will become more and more apparent that numerous global financial and political benefits can be obtained from locally and nationally deploying new ISDN data-handling technologies; these will offer the ability to quickly launch new data services to many of the new users within the major industries as they require more and more data transport. Similarly, the excellent "Visions of the Future" by Tom Bystrzycki, Dr. John Mayo, and IBM's "Information Networking" architect note the tremendous technical advances that will be forthcoming in the integrated computer and communications arena. With this in mind, now is indeed the time to act, to aggressively pursue a public data network using narrowband ISDN technologies over current copper-based facilities. However, to do this, the RBOCs and independent public data network providers need to drop the price to $16–$35 a month on a tiered, usage-based price structure. Supporting their offering, these providers need to

Fig. 9-1. ISDN network, products, and services.

launch massive advertising campaigns to teach customers how to use the ubiquitous, switched public data networks. RBOCs also need to train and encourage (financially reward) their marketing staffs to sell data transport services to the residential, small business, large business, and educational markets. The telecommunications industry needs to offer not only circuit switching and packet switching at the higher 64 Kbps/128 Kbps rates, but it also needs to introduce service nodes, where multiple ISPs and ESPs can enable enhanced and advanced data-handling services. Finally, and most importantly, RBOCs need to introduce a dataphone directory. It's essential to have a directory available that data users can easily access so they know whom to call for a given data-handling service or to determine the location and address of some remote terminal. Many ISPs and ESPs are picking up on this massive financial opportunity, as some of the large database suppliers are setting their sights on providing their "electronic version" of this data users directory for future dataphone networks.

In addition, as noted in previous works, we need to seriously consider offering a broadband ISDN-based interactive videophone network service in high-resolution, high-definition form. (Videophone can occur: in the flickering narrowband 64 Kbps, compressed, problematic, voice-synchronized wideband in 1.5 Mbps, and high-quality, full-featured broadband 40–50 Mbps forms.)

Unfortunately, or fortunately, depending on your vantage point, prior to the turbulent times after divestiture, both AT&T and IBM stood as giants in their respective communications and computer fields, controlling when, where, and how new technologies would be deployed. However, during these past ten years (post divestiture), we've seen their kingdoms shrink and shrink again as new competition, using new technologies, enter every facet (and crack) of the expanding information (voice, data, and video) marketplace. To address this forthcoming highly competitive and changing global information game, *Future Telecommunications* and *Global Telecommunications* explicitly note the need for several new, parallel dataphone and videophone networks to help offset the decreasing revenues from basic telephone service, as more and more competitors enter the local marketplace. To be successful, full public-provider participation is required in all aspects of the information arena. The absence of these parallel public data and video networks (provided in their fully supported, advertised, directorized versions) will open extensive opportunities for highly competitive alternative providers, but will foster an unnecessary continuation of the complexities of internetworking autonomous private networks. Hence, it's time to develop these new national public dataphone and videophone ISDN-based networks. The time to act is now, not only within our major cities, but also in our key county seats. Initial data services should be tied to the national narrowband ISDN 1, 2, and 3 offerings, encouraging new families of sophisticated CPE terminals, computers, printers, image systems, etc., etc. Then, the wideband/broadband videophone offerings should follow once standards are in place. (Note: Considerable effort should be spent in the standards arena to ensure that it doesn't take ten years to achieve the desired broadband ISDN standards.)

However, even by the mid '90s, many people remained confused in the deployment of ISDN. It's essential that they begin to realize that ISDN is only an interface that enables the network service offerings to be accessed. We need to visualize this access as an entrance to three forms of switched public networks — narrowband, wideband, and broadband — where the narrowband version contains three functional networks in circuit and packet mode form. This narrowband offering can be easily handled by the digital upgrade of outside plant and switches, enabling extensive revenue growth from existing facilities.

We need to view the full offering and not a piecemeal version. We need to offer parallel networks to our telephone network. This first overlay network is one especially designed to handle ubiquitously low- to medium-speed data at 64K/128K rates. This narrowband version will meet 80 percent of existing business application needs, especially for small business and residential applications; it will also provide remote access to large business and education entities. For 20-some years, this narrowband version has been called a switched public data network, as provided by our European and military (465-L) counterparts. This network has numerous data-handling networking features and provides an incentive to shift from dial-up modems to a truly "data-supporting," switched transport entity. (Many people didn't understand the reason for going digital. As voice is converted to digital numbers, these numbers fit nicely with data numbers in digital bit streams. Hence, the purpose of going from analog to digital was to provide high-quality, low-error-rate, high-speed digital transport and switching that foster the movement of both voice and data. In this manner, IDN — Integrated Digital Networks — were established in the late '70s, while ISDN — Integrated Services Digital Networks — of the '80s and '90s add the data-handling capabilities on a publicly switched basis. Thus, IDN becomes ISDN.)

Hence, we need to launch a full program to achieve the parallel narrowband data network. We should visualize it as a "dataphone" network, similar to our telephone network with similar dataphone deployment opportunities and strategies. Next, we need to deploy a wideband version for the private networking applications, as noted by IBM's "Blueprint for the Future," but on a publicly switched basis for massive private-to-public-to-private "information networking" that enables "computer networking" speeds up to 45 megabits. Then we need to establish a publicly switched ubiquitous videophone offering using the tremendous technical possibilities offered by the next generation of fiber-based switches, noted by John Mayo's vision of the future. However, to get started in these endeavors, we need to begin with narrowband ISDN first. Here's a ten-point program that will enable us to achieve a narrowband ISDN-based, public switched data network:

Public switched data network: ISDN 10-point plan of action

1. Establish ISDN in every major city and rural county seat by the end of 1994 (target).
2. Deploy ISDN by:
   - Condition outside plant — remove bridge taps and loading coils.

- Change out 1As in the metro area and ensure that the "B" channel packet switching 64K/128K is part of the new digital switch, handling a 20 percent traffic mix.
- Establish a"D" channel to SS7 signaling protocols so CPE can "talk" to the network for new stimulus/functional data-handling features.
- Participate in national ISDN 1, 2 and 3 offerings.
- Connect to the national public data network, working with the IXCs and RBOCs and interfacing to local VANs (Telenet, Timenet, etc.).
- Establish gateways with (or to) global data networking VANs.
- Address addressing. This is key to a switched public data network. ISDN addressing standards offer a new 15-digit dataphone number for this network for local, national, and international usage. We need to adopt these standards and provide a dataphone directory, similar to a telephone directory, with lucrative advertisement, etc., etc., so all terminals, workstations, etc., have an identifiable address (which can also be kept unlisted for closed user groups, with appropriate protection mechanisms).
- Establish seminars and workshops between LECs and CPE vendors to obtain parallel 64K/128K terminal offerings for both circuit and packet modes, as well as the 9.6K packet "D" channel.

4. Change mass-market ISDN pricing to clearly reflect the three public switched data network offerings:
   - $16 per month, with $25 initial hookup for "D" channel packet data.
   - $20 per month with $25 initial hookup for "B" channel circuit data (64 Kbps).
   - $25 per month for "B" channel packet data (64 Kbps).
   - 128 Kbps inverse multiplexing option for an additional $25 per month circuit or packet.
   - A-D at a tiered local usage price, with a $10 per month usage increments fee.

5. Change LEC marketing incentive programs to promote (encourage) the large userships' shift to the public data network, with financial rewards to marketers if large groups of customers are achieved on the public data network. (Note: Provide education programs to marketers and packaged offerings to be easily marketed.)

6. Establish a massive advertisement campaign to teach users what a switched public data network is and how it's different from dial-up voice grade modem on the existing network. Also show the array of applications that can be best served by a shift in mode of operation by using the public switched data network.

7. Work with large switch suppliers (AT&T, Northern Telecom, Siemens, Ericcson) and LECs to obtain the 30 or so data-handling features that the international CCITT arena has agreed should be part of a public switched data networking offering.

8. Overlay specialized infoswitches, such as IBM's protocol internetworking

service node, on top of the public switched data network. (Note: There are numerous infoswitches that can be owned by residential customers and small businesses in customized packages and general packages for their user groups.

9. Organize a public switched data network support group within residential, small business, and network customers to advise marketing and network personnel on how to deploy the three public switched data networks, as well as how to achieve the enhanced overlay options and infoswitches.

10. Spend 500 million or so (LECs) for local distribution plant narrowband ISDN upgrade during these next two years (internal numbers to service major cities) and use the profits over the '90s to finance fiber-based wideband and broadband offerings. (See FIG. 9-2.)

Those points will help achieve the narrowband ISDN public data network for "dataphone." There should be a similar 10-point program to achieve the wideband information switched network for "infophone," as well as a 10 point program for a switched broadband information network for "videophone." These subsequent possibilities are based on moving from narrowband ISDN to wideband ISDN to broadband ISDN. Here, there's need to establish the correct ONA interfaces and

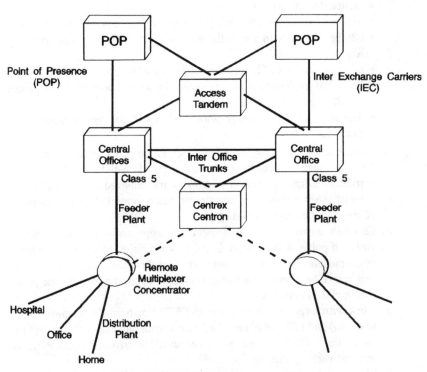

Fig. 9-2. The telephone company today.

ISDN standards for these offerings to ensure success in the marketplace. Thus, we've moved from "telephone" to "dataphone" to "infophone" to "videophone," in parallel with some RBOC's "cablephone" endeavors. The time is now for the dataphone offerings. It's a window of great, great, great opportunity and immediate financial success at minimum risk and minimum cost, if launched appropriately, as noted in the 10 point program. If any step is missing, the offering will most likely not be successful, as adequately demonstrated by past endeavors.

ISDN pricing

A few thoughts on ISDN pricing. As noted earlier, when Henry Ford was asked about pricing his new car, "Do you want to make a lot of money from a few high-priced sales?" "No," he answered, "I want to make a lot of money by charging a reasonable price so I have many customers to buy my cars."

We need to think this way in pricing ISDN for the mass market, especially residential and small business. First, a look at past history. By not deploying ISDN, or having limited ISDN deployment by using "brite card" ISDN extenders, there's a "built in" overhead (and/or distance) cost to the first customers, who actually want/wanted ISDN. It's clearly apparent to all that this nonubiquitous physical ISDN deployment overhead factor added an additional cost to areas where ISDN was actually deployed, so that prices are $60–$70 or so per month, with high initial installation fees. This is quite discouraging to the customer, especially if providers are trying to encourage people to move from a dial-up, low-speed, cheap, error- prone, voice-rate analog modem type of operation that customers have lived with for so many years. The industry needs to first get the customers "hooked" on the new medium-speed (high-speed to them) 64/128 Kbps low-error-rate network. To do so, the end user needs to see a bill at the end of the month for normal, nominal usage at $20 or so per month, definitely less than $30.

On the other hand, customers will pay for services that they find helpful in doing their job faster and easier. To provide enhanced or improved service over the dial-up modem, RBOCs need to establish a family of transfer services that they deliver for free to customers using services costing $20 or so per month. Thus, data users will want to use the network for fast, effective, error-free, addressable, traceable, etc., data transport. Then, we should have packages of additional features in $10 increments that provide further enhanced value such as code conversions, audit trails, barred access, network retries, etc., etc., services. We need a tiered usage pricing structure that also has a price differential for shared-packet over full circuit offerings. As noted, additional money will be received on the dataphone directory, gateway services, protocol networking interfaces, encryption, and database accesses. Finally, packaged offerings for large user blocks, as well as shared packages for small users, will provide further value added revenues similar to voice centrex offerings. In addition, third-party offerings overlaid via private and public infoswitches and service nodes will again offer more and more revenues as their usage increases and increases again.

It's essential that the pricing of this new public data network service (not called ISDN, but based on narrowband ISDN) encourages usage and growth. It shouldn't be confused with wideband and broadband variable bandwidth offerings, which will, over time, become more and more a commodity. In time, "videophone" (broadband) and "infophone" (wideband) networks should have similar pricing strategies. Improper pricing and availability for ISDN drove the dissatisfied customers—who couldn't handle the $3,000-per-year narrowband ISDN costs— to limited, specialized alternatives, thereby achieving minimum revenue return to the telcos.

In trialing narrowband ISDN deployment possibilities, 200 or so possible test customers were initially reduced to 100, and then only 50 were qualified for the offering. This 150 reduction in acceptable customer loops was attributed to excessive use of loading coils, bridge taps, attenuation (perhaps water in the cable), and the lack of an available second pair, resulting in only a 25 percent offering possibility. Some have used these problems as the reasons for not deploying ISDN. Other studies have noted a five-to-one cost of plant to switch in order to achieve a functional data network. However, as outside plant is cleaned up, these numbers will reduce and reduce again for follow-on customers who request new data-handling services. Providers should, therefore, not be dismayed by initial negative figures. We need to realize that as we go forward with cleaning up existing facilities, we're simply preparing them for an entirely new revenue stream. As Milton Freeman said,"There's no such thing as a free lunch," but a data network on top of our voice network is the closest thing to it—requiring minimum investment and generating potentially high returns. (See FIG. 9-3.)

Unfortunately, public providers (RBOCs and independents) don't have an overall plan of action. Many traditional voice service marketers believe ISDN is a pricing threat to existing offerings. They fight among themselves, where narrowband ISDN is simply not promoted. Primary rate ISDN is considered a threat to T1; digital cross-connect dial-up T1 is a threat to fractional T1; fractional T1 is a threat to T3; frame relay/SMDS is a threat to leased line; etc., etc., with different product managers fighting among themselves to land the customer, never telling the customer of alternative offerings, especially not ISDN. This conflict has been noted over the years by seasoned marketing personnel, who were amazed (dismayed) at how mistreated the customers have been as fragmented marketers hawk their new but segmented family of switched/nonswitched transport offerings. There should be a series of packages that bring the customer an array of switched narrowband, wideband, and broadband public data/information offerings. Point-to-point transport should be offered only as a final resort, after the switched network sale is lost. In past cases, this form of marketing, having uncoordinated, unruly in-fighting between product managers or market units, resulting in external take-it-or-leave-it tactics, has simply driven many of the largest and best customers to consider establishing their own private enterprise networks, using alternative providers' wireless transport (satellites, microwave) or to consider dark fiber. Hence, unless the full deployment of parallel, switched, full-featured networks are offered as a complete family of services, we're simply "robbing Peter to pay Paul."

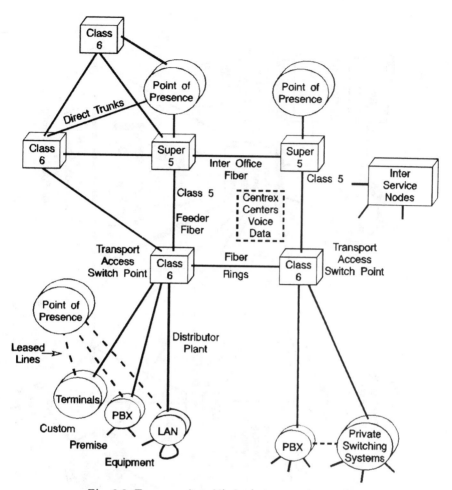

Fig. 9-3. Tomorrow's public basic transport company.

Conclusion

Thus, to be successful, the telecommunications industry's public providers need to consider the full picture, from pricing to support, to ensure that their future publicly switched interactive dataphone and videophone networks are successful. (See FIG. 9-4.) If these public networks are appropriately and timely established, then private networking overlays by multiple telecommunications providers will flourish and ensure new sustained growth in the computer industry, not only for large business, but also for small business and residential. If history is to be our guide, military networks dedicated to the movement of data (such as 465-L) have shown extensive growth and use, once customers became accustomed and dependent on ubiquitous, rapid data transport mechanisms. In this regard, Japan has seen

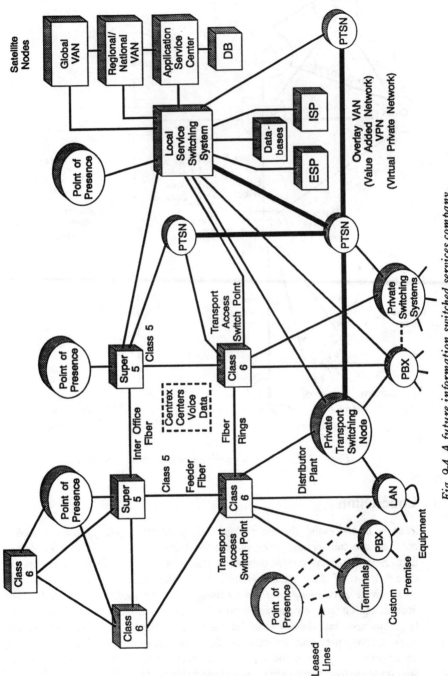

Fig. 9-4. A future information switched services company.

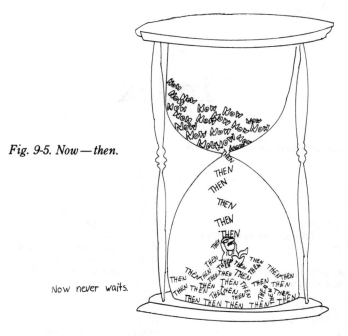

Fig. 9-5. Now—then.

Now never waits.

a tremendous growth in data transport, once ISDN became nationally available. It's now evident that various independents and RBOCs are seriously considering the deployment of ISDN. Each is looking at the other to see who will act first and to what extent. Some appear to indeed be serious. ISDN will require a serious commitment, very serious, if we're to be successful! Is it not time to be serious? Is it not time, to act—now? Now never waits! (See FIG. 9-5.)

Now is the time!
The time is now!

Index